TOWN AND SQUARE

TOWN AND SQUARE

FROM THE AGORA TO THE VILLAGE GREEN

BY PAUL ZUCKER

COLUMBIA UNIVERSITY PRESS, NEW YORK & LONDON

First printing 1959
Second printing 1966

LIBRARY OF CONGRESS CATALOG CARD NUMBER: 59-11183
PRINTED IN THE UNITED STATES OF AMERICA

To the memory of Talbot Hamlin

PREFACE

HERETOFORE there have been many excellent books about the various aspects of city planning, past and present, but they have been written essentially from the viewpoint of the architect, of the man who imagines and thinks primarily in terms of the three-dimensional mass, of *volume*. *Space* as a three-dimensional void has been considered rather as a by-product, although more and more attention has been given to this matter during the last decades. This book takes as its starting point a concept different from the usual position. It tries to develop the history and aesthetics of the artistically shaped *void*, which finds its most outspoken and characteristic form in the square, in the plaza, the focal point in the organization of the town.

Although a comprehensive survey is aimed at, completeness is of course unobtainable. The problem is to combine broadness of scope with contextural depth. Actually such a comprehensive evaluation should be undertaken only when detailed research in all individual locations and epochs has been carried through and clarified. However, since progress in research goes on indefinitely and future scholars may find source material yet unknown, the author believes that the basic aesthetic categories must first be established and succinctly defined; later, detailed special studies may follow.

Some paragraphs in this book concern areas outside the development of Western civilization. In dealing with this material the author has been fully aware of his limited knowledge in these fields, but, on the other hand, he felt the necessity of touching on these areas in order to round out the complete picture. However, as Lao-tse said, "Those who justify themselves do not convince."

An author is expected to express his gratitude to all those who have contributed to whatever extent through their advice, especially in a work of this kind which covers such a broad field and which needed so much time for completion. In return for all this generous help, kindness, and friendship there is woefully little that one can give. There is no way to reciprocate, and the assurance of deepest gratitude must alone suffice.

To the American Institute of Architects, New York Chapter, I am most indebted for granting me the Arnold W. Brunner Scholarship Award for research and completion of the manuscript. And I am especially grateful to my friend and colleague Professor Carl Feiss, Washington, D.C., who was kind enough to complete the story with the chapter on the public square in the United States. I benefited very much indeed from the counsel and special information of many friends and colleagues, particularly Professor Turpin C. Bannister, University of Florida; Professor Peter H. Blankenhagen, University of Chicago; the late Dr. Emil Kaufmann; Pál Kelemen, Norfolk, Conn.; Professor George A. Kubler, Yale University; Clay Lancaster, New York; Professor J. Marshall Miller, Columbia University; Dr. Gerd Muehsam, Cooper Union Art Library; Dr. Ernest Nash, Rome; Professor Erwin Walter Palm, Santo Domingo; Dr. Adolf Placzek, Avery Library, Columbia University; Elizabeth Roth, New York Public Library; Professor Homer A. Thompson, Institute for Advanced Study, Princeton, N.J.; Professor Christopher Tunnard, Yale University; Professor James Grote Van Derpool, Avery Library, Columbia University. I should also like to express my deep appreciation of the tireless care that the staff of Columbia University Press has given to the complex details of preparation, with special thanks to Henry H. Wiggins, William F. Bernhardt, and Eugenia Porter for services above the call of duty. Last but not least I should like to express my appreciation of the understanding help of Dr. Lotte Pulvermacher-Egers and my admiration for the unending patience with which she endured all manner of difficulties in collecting the vast material.

New York
Fall 1959

PAUL ZUCKER

CONTENTS

PLATES

Following page 118

FIGURES

TOWN AND SQUARE

The fact is that architecture is a more difficult and intellectual art than music. Music—that's just a faculty you're born with, as you might be born with a snub nose. But the sense of plastic beauty—though that's, of course, also an inborn faculty—is something that has to be developed and intellectually ripened. It's an affair of the mind; experience and thought have to draw it out.

ALDOUS HUXLEY, *Antic Hay*

I · THE SQUARE IN SPACE AND TIME

ST. PETER'S Square in Rome, St. Mark's Square in Venice, and the Place Vendôme in Paris are as generally known and admired as are Leonardo da Vinci's *Mona Lisa,* Michelangelo's *Moses,* and Rembrandt's *Night Watch.* These squares are undoubtedly as much "art" as any painting, sculpture, or individual work of architecture. The unique relationship between the open area of the square, the surrounding buildings, and the sky above creates a genuine emotional experience comparable to the impact of any other work of art. It is only of secondary importance for this effect whether and to what extent in each instance specific functional demands are fulfilled. Obvious as this statement may be, in our age of overrationalization this fact must be emphasized. During the last decades city planners have been primarily concerned with such problems as the use of land, the improvement of traffic and general communication, zoning, the relationship between residential and industrial areas, etc. These considerations have somewhat overshadowed the fundamental importance of the square as a basic factor in town planning, as the very heart of the city. Only now does interest turn toward this central formative element, "which makes the community a community and not merely an aggregate of individuals."

This physical and psychological function of the square does not depend on size or scale. The village green in a small New England town, the central square of a residential quarter within a larger city, the monumental plaza of a metropolis—all serve the same purpose. They create a gathering place for the people, humanizing them by mutual contact, providing them with a shelter against the haphazard traffic, and freeing them from the tension of rushing through the web of streets.

The square represents actually a psychological parking place within the civic landscape. If one visualizes the streets as rivers, channeling the stream of human communication—which means much more than mere technical "traffic"—then the square represents a natural or artificial lake. The square dictates the flux of life not only within its own confines but also through the adjacent streets for which it forms a quasi estuary. This accent in space may make itself felt some blocks in advance—an experience shared by everyone who has ever driven a car into an unfamiliar town.

This psychological function of the square is as true for the present and future as it has been for the past. As a matter of fact, the city planner of the past faced the same kind of problems as does the city planner of today: either the building of an entirely new settlement or—much more frequently—the reorganization of individual quarters within existing towns. Whether the curve of a street corner must be planned for the stoppage of a noble coach drawn by eight horses or for a line of Fords, bumper to bumper; whether an open area has to be shaped for royal spectacles or for political rallies, does not make any difference in principle. Such functional considerations have influenced width, length, and depth of streets and squares, their directions and their connections, then and now equally, so that one can say that planning in space today is hardly more functionalistic than it was in earlier centuries. The needs and demands of the past may have been fewer and less complex, but they were as basic for the determination of the final shape as they are now. Thus our analysis of typical examples of the past need not remain a mere historical discussion, but should also stimulate some thoughts for town planning of today. While technical and socioeconomic conditions have changed completely since the Industrial Revolution, this should not deter us from applying lessons from the past to conditions and needs of the present. This does not mean, however, that the most impressive and convincing achievements of earlier centuries should simply be copied—a mistake to which nineteenth-century architects unfortunately succumbed only too often.

There exist today in towns and cities "squares" marked as such on maps which actually are no more than plain voids, empty areas within the web of streets. They differ from other areas of the town by the mere fact that they are bare of any structures. Artistically relevant squares, however, are more than mere voids; they represent organized space, and a history of the square actually means a history of space as the subject matter of artistic creation. For the consideration of the square as a work of art it is not even important whether the confines of this "space" are real and tangible or whether they are partially imagined, if only the planner is able to guide and force our imagination in one distinct direction.

The term "space" has been used and misused so often and in so many contexts that it seems to have lost its intrinsic meaning. Therefore it may be helpful to define it anew in relation to city planning in order to give it freshness and usefulness. Here, "space," designating generally a three-dimensional expansion of any kind, is used more specifically. It means a structural organization as a frame for human activities and is based on very definite factors: on the relation between the forms of the surrounding buildings; on their uniformity or their variety; on their absolute dimensions and their relative proportions in comparison with width and length of the open area; on the angle of the entering streets; and, finally, on the location of monuments, fountains, or other three-dimensional accents. In other words, specific visual and kinesthetic relations will decide whether a square is a hole or a whole.

Exactly as towns in their totality either have grown naturally from villages, trading posts, military camps, castles, and monasteries, or were built following a preconceived design, so the individual square within a town either might have developed gradually out of certain existing conditions or might have been planned. Conditions which furthered the natural growth of a square were manifold: the intersection of important thoroughfares within the town; the open space at the approach of a bridge or in front of the west façade of a church, etc. In some instances, such sites became the nucleus for an artistically meaningful square of distinct three-dimensional form. However, most frequently a village green or an old market square expanded gradually into a definite spatial pattern through the successive erection of buildings around it. Such a development, typical for so many squares in Hellenistic and late medieval towns of Central Europe, needed, of course, centuries until the harmonious present-day appearance evolved.

In contrast to these organically grown squares, the planned square always appears as clearly defined as any individual piece of architecture. In some instances, generations of anonymous builders may have anticipated the underlying basic design in area and form before its actual realization; more often, individual artists have conceived the final scheme.

Planned squares, clearly recognizable as such, appeared in ancient Greece and her colonies from the fifth century B.C. on. They resulted indirectly from the gridiron scheme which then was introduced into Greece and Asia Minor by Hippodamus, although archaeological research has not yet definitely proved his personal part in these creations. In Hellenistic times, the majority of squares were planned. Here again, documentary evidence for the activities of individual architects is lacking. The same holds true for the most grandiose organization of squares in antiquity, the Imperial Fora in Rome. After the decline of ancient civilization with its Hellenistic and Roman creations, planned squares appeared again in the French and English bastides and the foundations by the Teutonic Knights in eastern Germany. In the early Renaissance, from the time of Leone Battista Alberti and Leonardo da Vinci onward, architects, in drawings and theoretical treatises, competed as fervently in the planning of whole towns and of individual squares as they did in creating churches, palaces, villas, and gardens. Later this architectural interest in the design and execution of squares reached its climax during the seventeenth and eighteenth centuries, the era to which posterity owes the majority of world-famous squares, especially in Italy and France.

The abundance of squares in Italy and France may be explained by a combination of climatic conditions and temperamental attitudes characteristic of the Romance peoples of Southern and Western Europe. These conditions led to a form of public life—and life in public—which made street and square the natural locale for community activities and representation. Not by chance then, Rome and Paris are the cities which we associate primarily with the idea of the perfect public square, and it is therefore logical that in an analysis of generic types so many Roman and Parisian squares should be discussed.

However, almost identical climatic conditions in Spain and Greece, in the same Mediterranean area, have brought forth since ancient times neither a considerable number of squares nor any individual square comparable to the great creations in Rome and Paris. The reason for the lack of consciously shaped squares in Spain may be sought in the fact that even at the apex of Spain's political and economic power, in the sixteenth and seventeenth centuries, her specific societal structure and the psychological attitude of her population were not equally favorable for the development of a public life. And England, even during such a great era as the Elizabethan age, did not create any monumental solutions in town planning; nor did Holland in the seventeenth century, in a period of great commercial expansion and magnificent artistic activities. In these two countries it is the northern climate and the strong emphasis on domestic life that mostly prevented any desire for public spatial expression.

Being part of the living organism of a city with its changing socioeconomic and technical conditions, a square is never completed. In contrast to a painting or a sculpture, there is no last stroke of the brush or any final mark of the chisel. A painting or sculpture, once completed, never changes in itself but preserves its original appearance from the time of its creation except for the patina of age. Elements of the square, however, such as the surrounding structures, individual monuments, fountains, etc., are subjected to the flux of time; some may vanish, destroyed or razed, others may be replaced and new ones added. Thus the original form of squares and streets may undergo fundamental changes, as the juxtaposition of old engravings and paintings with modern photographs of the same square and streets often shows. While at one time a square may have been primarily an accumulation of important individual buildings, the same square in another century may have developed into a comprehensive spatial form.

Frequently future spatial potentialities of a square were already latent in its initial stage. However, the basic spatial concept of a square is not always so strong that it prevails through centuries. Its appearance may change for two reasons: physically, through the erection of new buildings and the alteration or destruction of old ones, through a modification of the building line, etc.; psychologically, through the different way in which each generation experiences and reacts to given proportions and distances, and through the new approach by which it interprets spatial relations. It is this combination of objective and subjective factors which makes the same square appear different to each generation. The large variety of impressions received from an identical reality is evidenced by descriptions in travel diaries. The Piazzetta in Venice or the Piazza del Popolo in Rome have stimulated the visual imaginations of travelers in the seventeenth, eighteenth, and nineteenth centuries in such different ways that it is sometimes hard to recognize the identity of the same locality. After all, our reaction toward nature presents a similar phenomenon: the same landscape is perceived quite differently by a painter of the seventeenth century and by an artist of the nineteenth century.

To mention another transformation of visual impression, closer to our days: in the nineteenth century, squares were no longer regarded as three-dimensional units. With the rise of classicism the awareness of the third dimension had vanished. Nor was it by chance that Impressionism, the ultimate fulfillment of the naturalistic development in painting since the Renaissance, never aimed at any conscious articulation of space—which was to be rediscovered by Cézanne and the twentieth-century Cubists. This lack of interest in space became even more obvious in nineteenth-century sculpture, architecture, and city planning. Squares simply provided opportunities for planting bushes and flowers, for placing statues and comfort stations without any spatial ties—briefly, they represented a vain attempt to transplant the charm of a miniature English park into the heart of the city.

With the twentieth century, as a consequence of new beginnings in architecture, the awareness of spatial relations and of the possibilities of their architectural expression returned. The increased kinesthetic sensitivity for three-dimensional forms, which leads from Thorwaldsen to Maillol, from Thomas Jefferson to Frank Lloyd Wright, distinguishes also the judgment of a Camillo Sitte from that of Raymond Unwin or Pierre Lavedan in their evaluation of famous squares and streets of the past. Shakespeare's *Hamlet* and Bach's fugues have been reinterpreted with each generation, as have Leonardo da Vinci's *Last Supper* and Michelangelo's Medici Chapel. Likewise the great creations of town planning of the past must be studied anew in our time. Such reevaluation will stimulate and help, consciously or unconsciously, the creative work of our own generation.

THE ARCHETYPES

Space is perceived by the visualization of its limits and by kinesthetic experience, i.e., by the sensation of our movements. In the state of "visual tension," kinesthetic sensation and visual perception fuse most intensely—and the conscious enjoyment of townscapes as artistic experience produces just this visual tension. People in their movements are influenced and directed by three-dimensional confines and by the structural lines of such confines; in other words, the general tension becomes a specifically "directed" dynamic tension. If these confines are architectural structures, their volumes and their scale exert pressure and resistance and stimulate and direct our reaction to the space around us.

For the square, then, three space-confining elements exist: the row of surrounding structures, the expansion of the floor, and the imaginary sphere of the sky above. The forms of these three space-shaping elements—architectural frame, floor, and ceiling—are, of course, most decisively defined by the two-dimensional layout of the square.

These three factors which produce the final three-dimensional effect may vary in themselves: the surrounding structures may be of uniform height, proportion, and design, or they may differ; they may be more or less coherent. The floor, an equally important factor for the appearance of the square, may be homogeneous in expansion and texture (pavement), or it may be articulated by slopes, steps, different levels, etc. Its surface pattern may unify or isolate the framing vertical structures. The sky, the "ceiling" of the square, although distant, offers a visual boundary which in spite of its purely imaginary character confines aesthetically the space of the square just as definitely as do the surrounding houses or the pavement. The subjective impression of a definite height of the sky is caused by the interplay of the height of the surrounding buildings and of the expansion (width and length) of the floor. It is strongly influenced by the contours of eaves and gables, chimneys and towers. Generally the height above a closed square is imagined as three to four times the height of the tallest building on the square. It seems to be higher above squares which are dominated by one prominent building, whereas over wide-open squares, such as the Place de la Concorde in Paris, the visual distance of the sky is only vaguely perceived.

The correlation of these principal elements that confine a square is based on the focal point of all architecture and city planning: the constant awareness of the *human scale*. As long as the size of the human body and the range of human vision are not recognized as the basic principles, any rules about absolute proportions, about design and composition of forms and motifs, about symmetrical and asymmetrical organization, etc., are meaningless. Experiments have proved that the human eye without moving perceives an expanse of a little more than 60° in horizontal direction. In vertical direction, the expanse depends, of course, on the degree to which the eye opens. An angle of 27° is most favorable for the perception of an individual work of architecture, and the beholder moves instinctively to a distance which allows this angle. However, in order to fuse various architectural units with their surroundings into a total impression, which effect is the genuine task of all city planning, the eye can employ an angle of 18° only.

The appearance of each individual square represents a blend of intrinsic lasting factors (topographical, climatic, national) and of changing influences (stylistic, period-born), i.e., of static and dynamic forces. Although squares of certain types prevail in certain periods, general space-volume relations are independent of particular historical forms. There exist definite basic types of squares which appear again and again. They show common characteristics in their spatial form, although the artistic expressions cannot be pressed into dogmatic categories. The specific function of a square, for instance, as a market square, as a traffic center, or as a parvis, *never* produces *automatically* a definite spatial form. Each particular function may be expressed in many different shapes.

Hence it is necessary to separate the various functions from the basic spatial concepts. On the one hand, many market squares may develop later on into monumental civic centers; on the other hand, grand, eloquently decorative plazas may sometimes be transformed amidst a changed neighborhood into mere recreational squares. Such developments prove that the archetypes are structural, that they are spatially, and not functionally, defined. These archetypes—not at all theoretical abstractions—become alive and real as soon as one visualizes typical examples. They may be classified as follows:

1. the CLOSED SQUARE: space self-contained
2. the DOMINATED SQUARE: space directed
3. the NUCLEAR SQUARE: space formed around a center
4. GROUPED SQUARES: space units combined
5. the AMORPHOUS SQUARE: space unlimited

This classification differs principally from the concepts of Camillo Sitte, Josef Gantner, Pierre Lavedan, and Sir Patrick Abercrombie; of course, it does not imply that any square represents only one *pure* type. Very often an individual square bears the characteristics of two of these types: it depends on the point of view, for instance, whether St. Mark's Square in Venice is regarded primarily as a closed square or as one element of the grouped squares of Piazza and Piazzetta; or whether New York City's Rockefeller Center is a closed square or a dominated square.

Moreover, it is quite obvious that even within one and the same category a variety of architectural expressions exists: the Forum of Trajan in ancient Rome was a closed square, as is the Place Royale in Brussels; but differences in function and sociological meaning in each instance created spatial units entirely different from each other. Likewise, the church-dominated medieval parvis, such as the original one of Notre Dame in Paris (now remodeled), differs widely in meaning and appearance from the baroque St. Peter's Square in Rome. And yet in both instances the dominating volume of a church structure directs the space.

Thus the above-outlined scheme of principal and basic categories should be taken rather as a starting point for aesthetic and historical analysis than as a rigid and dogmatic system.

THE CLOSED SQUARE. As the child imagines in its fantasy each mountain in the archform of a rising cone, looking like Fujiyama, so the average man thinks of a square primarily in the shape of the "closed" square (Pl. 1A). Such a square would be visualized as a complete enclosure interrupted only by the streets leading into it. In terms of town planning, the closed square represents the purest and most immediate expression of man's fight against being lost in a gelatinous world, in a disorderly mass of urban dwellings. Certainly the perfect realization of this form, in its Platonic purity so to speak, as, for instance, in the Place des Vosges in Paris (Pl. 1B), will be encountered infrequently. This type, without being bound to specific periods or definite architectural styles, appears in its most perfect form in the Hellenistic and Roman eras and then again in the seventeenth and eighteenth centuries.

The primary element in the appearance of any closed square is its layout, be it a quadrangle, rectangle, circle, or any other regular geometrical form. Equally important is the repetition of identical houses or house types, facing the enclosed area, either with their broad fronts or with their gables. Such uniformity need not imply monotony, even when only one single type of structure is repeated all around the square. Mostly, however, a rhythmical alternation of two or more types is employed, the richer architectural accents concentrated on the corners or on the central parts of each side, or framing the streets running into the square.

The spatial impression of the square depends furthermore on differences in scale of the individual units, on the contrasts of higher and lower structures, on their relationships to the width and breadth of the horizontal area, on the location of monuments, fountains, etc., and finally on variations in architectural decoration. Within this organization, the spatial balance of the square will always be achieved by the equation of horizontal and vertical forces. Each façade fulfills a dual function: on the one hand, it is part of an individual structure; on the other hand, it forms part of a common urban spatial order.

Differences in stylistic forms are of secondary importance. The single architectural elements may change. In antiquity, from the Hellenistic agora to the Imperial Fora in Rome, continuity and context of the framing structures were achieved by the *porticus* (colonnade), the rhythmical repetition of the vertical direction through columns. This was the main factor that tied the space together, as, for instance, on the agora in Priene (Fig. 1). Later, no

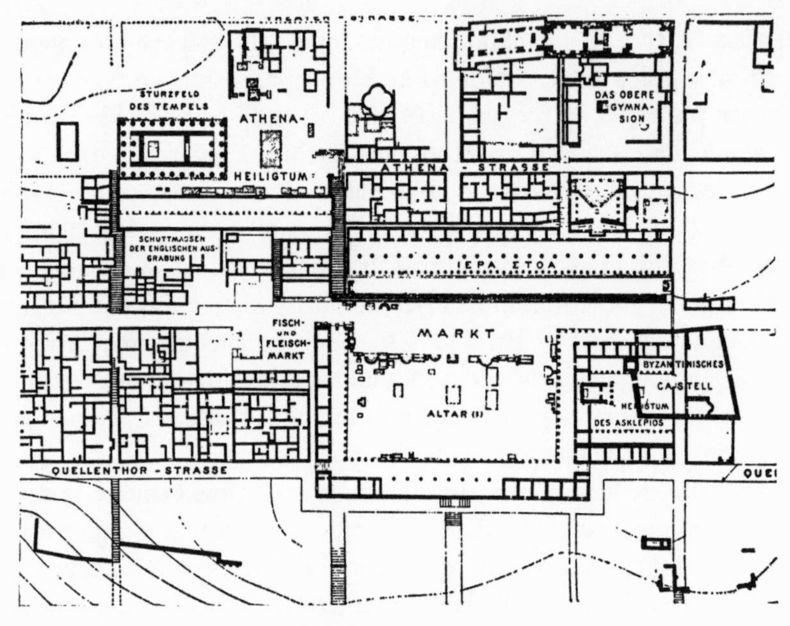

FIG. 1. PRIENE. PLAN OF THE AGORA
From Wiegand and Schrader, *Priene*

longer columns, but another architectural element served to bind the framing elements of the square: from the end of the Middle Ages through the seventeenth and eighteenth centuries, arched arcades connected the surrounding houses, as in the Place des Vosges in Paris. Sometimes the arcades of a closed square are continued into the adjacent streets, as, for instance, in Turin and Bologna in Italy, or in Madrid, Spain. This architectural element of the arcade is anticipated as an ornamental motif in the sculptural organization of Roman sarcophagi, in the arrangement of figures at the portals of early medieval churches, etc.

Yet, not every spatial enclosure, surrounded on all sides and thus creating a tightly knit architectural entity, can be considered as a closed square. The dimensions of the cloisters of a medieval monastery, such as Monreale or the Certosa in Pavia, Italy, or of an English collegiate square as in Oxford, or of the inner courtyard within a complex monumental structure, such as the Palace of the Doges in Venice or the l'Hôpital de Dieu in Beaune, may be almost identical with the dimensions of a smaller Hellenistic agora or of a medieval arcaded town square. Nonetheless, those enclosures are not "squares" from the viewpoint of town planning. They represent rather an element of a comprehensive architectural organization and differ from the square in their sociological function by not serving public life and traffic.

THE DOMINATED SQUARE. The dominated square is characterized by one individual structure or a group of buildings toward which the open space is directed and to which all other surrounding structures are related. This dominating building may be a church—the medieval parvis represents the most obvious example of the dominated square—or any other monumental structure, a palace, a town hall, an architecturally developed fountain, a theater, a railway station. In any case, such a commanding volume directs the spatial relations of the open area. Expressed in terms of stage design, all perspectives lead toward a backdrop. Usually the direction of a main street which opens into the square establishes the axis toward the dominant building (e.g., Versailles). The perspective of the surrounding buildings and the suction of the dominant structure create the spatial tension of the square, compelling the spectator to move toward and to look at the focal architecture. Thus the dominant square produces a dynamic directive of motion, whereas the closed square by careful proportioning creates a static equilibrium.

The most distinct relationship between the dominating building and the square exists in the parvis, originally the enclosed vacant area before a church. The original medieval parvis of Notre Dame Cathedral in Paris is a good example of this relationship (Pl. 2).

Although the Renaissance and baroque squares before churches occasionally are given the name "parvis," their spatial shape has an entirely different meaning. The aesthetic effect of the medieval parvis is characterized by its limited perspective, with the church façade functioning merely as a two-dimensional wall. The later squares, however, are planned in such large dimensions that because of the greater distance the whole church building can be perceived in three dimensions. The cupola over the main body of the Renaissance and baroque churches becomes the center of attraction, and with it the development into depth becomes important, creating a spatial counterpoint (e.g., St. Peter's, Rome; Dôme des Invalides, Paris). Hence, the lateral houses, colonnades, or arcades represent merely framing elements for the dominating structure and a stage effect is achieved. Whereas the medieval parvis as space element is *subordinated* to the church, anticipating the spatial directions of its interior, the Renaissance and baroque "parvis" creates a *coordinated* void in contrast to the controlling architecture. The same relation exists later on when the dominant building is no longer ecclesiastic but secular —a palace (Versailles), a theater (Place de l'Odéon, Paris), a railway station, or any other type of monumental architecture.

There is, however, a definite distinction between a dominated square in front of a palace and the court of honor of the palace. The latter is most intimately connected with all other architectural elements of the palace and is spatially a part of it. The square before the court of honor, however, is public and emphasizes the contrast to the architectural mass of the palace. Hence, here the usual sequence develops as follows: the street leading to the public square opposite the palace; the expanse of the public square proper; the more intimate court of honor; and finally the vestibule within the palace —the whole a gradual decrescendo in space (e.g., Versailles).

The preponderant structure need not necessarily be voluminous. Very often it is merely a gate or an arch which may dominate a whole square, independent of its actual size. In such a case the imaginary continuation of the main thoroughfare toward the gate creates the main axis of the space between. All buildings surrounding such a square are subordinated to the street-gate axis, independently of their individual prominence (e.g., Piazza del Popolo, Rome; Pariser Platz, Berlin [Pl. 3A]). It was not before the Renaissance that the architectural form of a gate became monumentalized and could develop into the main accent of an area. For in medieval times, gates were more or less but articulated openings in the enclosing city walls and therefore could not visually dominate the square inside of those passageways.

A fountain may also dominate a square if it constitutes an entire front in combination with architecture, sculpture, and water. Then the falling waters compete with vertical elements of the architecture in commanding our attention, especially in Mediterranean countries where the display of water in varied forms assumes such a decisive part in the townscape, e.g., Fontana di Trevi, Rome (Pl. 3B).

It seems natural that a vertical structure like a church, a gate, or a fountain should direct the space of a square. Sometimes, however, even the adjacent horizontals of a bridge may have the same organizing quality. The direction of the main thoroughfare leading to a square is continued by the roadway of the bridge and vice versa. A firm axis is established along which the limited width of the street, the expansion of the square, and then again the relative narrowness of the bridge shape an alternating rhythm of space. Such a spatial sequence increases the visual effect by subordinating the square to a continuous axis. After the monumental solutions of antiquity (Pons Mulvius, before Moles Hadriani [the tomb of Hadrian], Rome), the motif was taken up again in the great axial organizations of the seventeenth and eighteenth centuries (e.g., the bridge and square before the Rue Royale, Orléans; the bridge and entrance before the Rue Nationale, Tours; Andreas Schlüter's project for the bridge and square before the Royal Palace, Berlin; the bridge over the Po River and Piazza Vittorio Veneto, Turin [Pl. 4A]).

Paradoxical as it may sound, the dominating element may also be *a void*, allowing a vista toward a mountain range in the distance (Maria Theresienstrasse, Innsbruck). It may also be a broad river (Praça do Comércio, Lisbon; Contant's eighteenth-century project for the Quai Malaquet, Paris) or the open sea or a lagoon (Piazzetta, Venice). The view toward a distant landscape or the surface of bordering water dominates the direction of the square as if the opening into such an indefinite expansion were an actual structure. Seen from the water, in reversed direction, such a square appears as a closed area, resembling a stage set with its three walls. The same type of square is repeated in the innumerable enchanting small Italian towns around the north Italian lakes and along both Mediterranean coasts through the whole peninsula down to Sicily. The fourth wall of the stage has been substituted by the edge of river, lake, or sea, and nature and architecture melt into unforgettable vistas of unique spatial intimacy. These so-called marinas must be clearly distinguished from even the broadest quays and boardwalks whose directions parallel the shoreline or bank, without development into depth (e.g., Quai aux Herbes, Ghent; Quai du Montblanc, Geneva).

THE NUCLEAR SQUARE. The self-contained space of the *closed square*, shaped by the continuity of the surrounding buildings, is easily perceived. The space conception of the *dominated square*, although different in kind, is equally clear. It is directed through the visual magnetism of the governing structure or the dominant vista. More complex, although no less real, is the aesthetic sensation of what we would call a *nuclear square.*

The spatial shape of the nuclear square is of a definite order, although not so tightly knit as in both aforementioned instances—an entity, even without the frame of a continuous row of buildings or without the domination of a frontal structure. As long as there is a nucleus, a strong vertical accent—a monument, a fountain, an obelisk—powerful enough to charge the space around with a tension that keeps the whole together, the impression of a square will be evoked. As the pyramid in the vast expanse of the desert creates an aesthetically impervious space around it, with invisible walls and the sky as dome above, so the monument, the obelisk, or the fountain, or even an individual building, will tie the heterogeneous elements of the periphery into one visual unit. This spatial oneness is not endangered by any irregularity of the general layout or by the haphazard position, size, or shape of the adjacent buildings. Since the visual effect of the central monument, fountain, etc., is naturally limited, the dimensions of such a nuclear square are consequently restricted. If the expansion of the square in relation to the size of the focal volume becomes too large, the square loses its unity.

The not too numerous examples of nuclear squares are confined to certain historical periods. The most typical nuclear squares belong to the Renaissance, exactly as the most outspoken closed squares originated in Hellenistic and Roman times and again in the seventeenth and eighteenth centuries in France, and as the most evident dominated squares appeared in the late Middle Ages and then again in baroque times. The Piazza di SS. Giovanni e Paolo with Verrocchio's Colleoni monument in Venice (Pl. 37) and the Piazza del Santo in Padua with Donatello's equestrian figure of the Gattamelata show the artistic impact of the nuclear square most cogently.

However, it would be a mistake to believe that each fountain, each obelisk, or each monument within a square can become a space-shaping nucleus of three-dimensional orientation: the column on the Place Vendôme in Paris; the obelisk on St. Peter's Square in Rome; the monument to King Stanislas Leszczynski on the Place Stanislas in Nancy—they do not create a nuclear square but merely contribute to the impression of an otherwise closed, dominated, or combined square.

GROUPED SQUARES. The visual impact of a group of squares may be compared with the effect of a cycle of murals. In both instances, each unit, the indi-

A: A CHILD'S IMAGE OF A SQUARE

DRAWING BY A NINE-YEAR-OLD GIRL

From Hans Friedrich Geist, "Paul Klee und die Welt des Kindes," *Werk* (June, 1950)

B: PARIS. PLACE ROYALE (PLACE DES VOSGES)

COPPER ENGRAVING

From Martin Zeiller, *Topographia Galliae* . . .

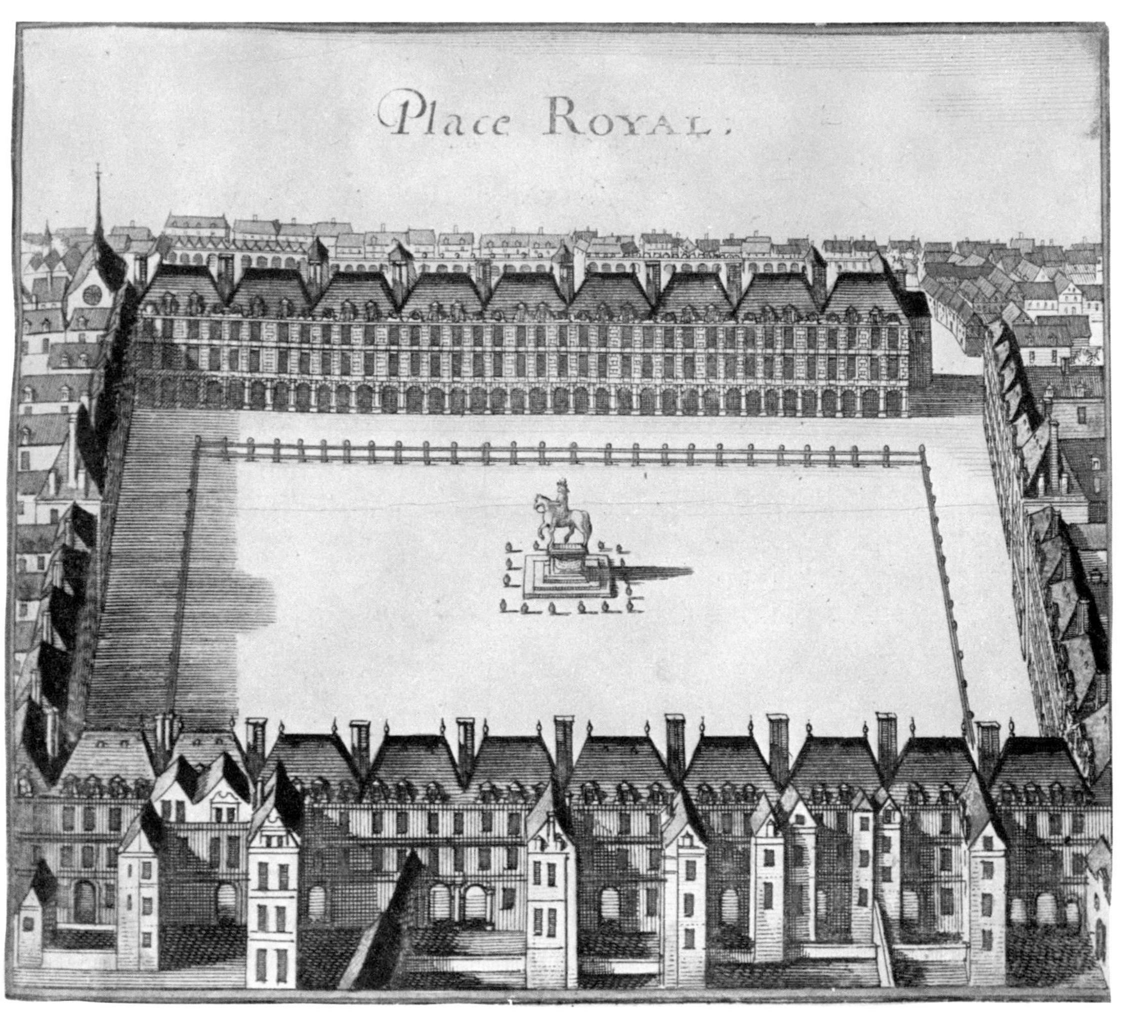

PARIS. NOTRE DAME CATHEDRAL AND PARVIS

ABOVE: BEFORE ITS REMODELING
IN THE NINETEENTH CENTURY
COPPER ENGRAVING
From Martin Zeiller, *Topographia Galliae . . .*

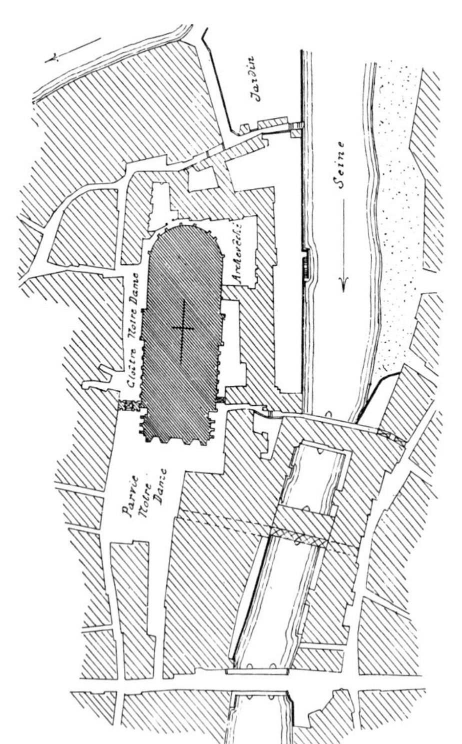

LEFT: PLAN OF THE FORMER STATE
From Brinckmann, *Platz und Monument*

A: BERLIN. PARISER PLATZ

Photo Landesbildstelle Berlin

B: ROME. FONTANA DI TREVI. ETCHING BY GIOVANNI BATTISTA PIRANESI

Courtesy Metropolitan Museum of Art

A: TURIN. PIAZZA VITTORIO VENETO

Photo Edizione S.A.C.A.T., Turin

B: LÜNEBURG. JOHANNISKIRCHE AND THE SAND

Photo Hans Boy-Schmidt; courtesy German Tourist Information Office, New York

vidual square and the single fresco, represents an entity per se, aesthetically self-sufficient and yet part of a comprehensive higher order—"individuation and unity." An analogy on a more limited scale would be the relationship of successive rooms inside a baroque palace: the first room preparing for the second, the second for the third, etc., each room meaningful as a link in a chain, beyond its own architectural significance. Similarly, individual squares may be fused organically and aesthetically into one comprehensive whole.

Such combinations exist in various forms, of which four occur most frequently:

A sequence of squares, different in size and form, develops in only one direction, thus establishing a straight axis, e.g., the Imperial Fora in Rome, or the sequence of squares in Nancy.

Or, in a non-axial organization, a smaller square opens with one of its sides upon a larger square, so that the individual axes of each square meet in a right angle, e.g., the Piazza and Piazzetta in Venice.

Or, a group of three or more squares of different shapes and proportions surround one dominant building, as in Salzburg, around the Cathedral, or in Bologna, around the Palazzo Podestà.

Or, finally, squares are related to each other without any direct physical connection. In other words, two individual squares fall into a coherent pattern although they are separated from each other by blocks of houses, thoroughfares, etc. These indirect spatial ties may differ in kind: in medieval times they are most likely irregular and the strongest connecting link, as, for instance, the mass of a church steeple, dominates both squares, e.g., in Lüneburg, the Johanniskirche and the Sand (Pl. 4B); or short streets between both squares may function as passageways, e.g., in Verona, Piazza d'Erbe and Piazza dei Signori. However, the most subtle relations are created in the planned organizations of the eighteenth century, e.g., Rheims, the project for the Place Royale; Rennes, Place Louis XV and Place Louis le Grand; Copenhagen, Amalienborg and Frederikskirke.

In whichever way individual squares may be connected, the aesthetic effect of the whole depends on the mental registration of successive images of changing spatial relations. It is irrelevant whether this connection is direct or indirect. There are so many architectural means by which to achieve dynamic crescendos in the transition from one square to another—arcades, the position of monuments, change in scale of the adjacent buildings, etc.—that the town planner is as free to mold the empty space of a group of squares as the sculptor is to mold the volume of a group of figures. Perspective potentialities and relative proportions are the decisive visual factors in reference to a system of grouped squares. Here the contrast of larger monumental buildings and smaller adjacent houses, of higher and lower eaves, of the location of monuments and fountains, of separating or connecting arcades and triumphal arches may increase or decrease the actual dimensions. The possibilities of illusionistic deception as to distance and expansion may come close to the effects of stage settings.

THE AMORPHOUS SQUARE. It may seem odd to include the amorphous square in this discussion since by its very definition—amorphous, i.e., formless, unorganized, having no specific shape—it does not represent any aesthetic qualities or artistic possibilities. However, if it shares at least some elements with the previously analyzed types of squares, it may appear at the first glance to be like one of them.

New York's Washington Square is laid out as a regular rectangle, framed by houses on all sides—and yet it is not a "closed" square. For its dimensions are so large, the proportions of many of its surrounding structures are so heterogeneous, so irregular, even contradictory, and the location and size of the small triumphal arch are so dissimilar to all the other given factors, that a unified impression cannot result. Disproportion in scale destroys all aesthetic possibilities.

Another factor spoils any aesthetic effect of Trafalgar Square in London: it could have developed into a "nuclear" square had not the tremendous façade of the National Gallery in contrast to the small adjacent blocks of houses and the irregular directions of the streets leading to the "Square" counteracted the effect of the Nelson Column as a space-creating element. But as it is, the column does not become a center of spatial relationships, a kernel of tension.

Correspondingly, the Place de l'Opéra in Paris could not become a "dominated" square in spite of the monumental façade of the imposing opera house. The width of the Boulevard des Capucines running through it off-center and the presence of small structures like the entrance to the Metro, etc., scattered all over its area ruin any spatial effect.

Not by chance did the three aforementioned examples originate in the nineteenth century, in an era which had almost no feeling for three-dimensional qualities. However, these examples are at least "squares" from the surveyor's viewpoint, although without any artistic impact. But other metropolitan traffic centers, such as New York's Times Square, are "squares" in name only; they are actually mere crossroads or *carrefours*.

Another type of amorphous square resulted from a typical misconception of the nineteenth century. The various eclectic revivals of that century tried to isolate, and in this way to emphasize the visual importance of, a church, a court of justice, a theater, etc., by surrounding it with a free area. However, a mere void as such does not create any specific three-dimensional impression. If in the Middle Ages the cathedral of a town, a monumental building which by its very mass and height dominated decisively all other structures, was surrounded by open areas and an irregular network of streets, it meant that the isolation of the building created the possibility of an overall vista for the spectator, and the volume of the edifice could be perceived in relation to the human scale. But then the awareness of the human scale was helped by small structures closely clustered around the cathedral. Most of these structures were removed during the nineteenth century's attempts at "stylistic purification." However, in the process, genuine external space was not shaped (e.g., the remodeling of the space around the Freiburg and Ulm cathedrals).

The amorphous squares of the past, although they neither unified nor confined the surrounding empty space, at least emphasized the volume. The nineteenth century, however, merely turned the void around a building into a tray or platter, on which the particular structure was presented.

PARADOXES OF HISTORY

As was said before, the visual appearance of squares, in contrast to that of a painting, a sculpture, or even of an isolated individual work of architecture, cannot be understood or enjoyed as an expression of a single historical epoch. The square as a living organism changes continuously with varying socioeconomic conditions and altered technological possibilities. Morphological differences of successive stylistic epochs are of minor importance. They mold the form of the surrounding buildings rather than the intrinsic shape of the square proper. And yet the historical approach will clarify certain inner connections between seemingly heterogeneous solutions in the pattern of a town which could not be grasped by a mere aesthetic analysis. It will confirm the obvious fact that certain epochs brought forth, or at least preferred, certain types of squares. But it will also become evident that paradoxically such preferred types sometimes wandered, that they were taken over by epochs and countries where material conditions, sociological structure, and even functional needs were entirely different, sometimes contradictory. Thus the post-Hippodamic regular closed agora reappears after many centuries in the French bastides of the thirteenth century and somewhat later in the foundations of the Teutonic Knights in Germany. The axial organization of the Roman Imperial Fora is repeated more than one and a half millennia later in the sequence of squares in eighteenth-century Nancy. Certainly the political, economic, and spiritual realities had changed meanwhile as much as topographical and climatic situations differed. And yet the spatial structures are almost identical, although architectural details vary stylistically.

As the art forms of the Homeric epos, of the symphony, and of the altar-triptych gradually have become autonomous, existing per se as definite structural patterns, no longer time-bound, no longer specific but general, so have the three-dimensional archetypes of squares. The original motivation and the reasons for the development of each form are forgotten, are perhaps no longer existent, but the achetypes remain as prime elements in the history of human society, of village, town, and city.

II · TOWN AND SQUARE IN ANTIQUITY

TOWNS WITHOUT SQUARES

IT MAY seem strange to start a study on the appearance and the meaning of squares with some modest notes about distant countries and ancient civilizations in which the square did not represent an essential element of the town. However, this approach seems helpful in order to define exactly what a square is and what it is not, and how relatively late in history social conditions and aesthetic urges came to shape this specific spatial form within the urban community.

Only after 500 B.C. did genuine squares develop in Greece. City planning as such, conscious collective and integrated action beyond the mere construction of individual houses, existed already in India and Egypt in the third millennium B.C., but never the impulse to shape a void within the town into a three-dimensional area which we call a "square." This may be explained sociologically: only within a civilization where the anonymous human being had become a "citizen," where democracy had unfolded to some extent, could the gathering place become important enough to take on a specific shape. This sociological development was paralleled by an aesthetic phenomenon: only when a full consciousness of space evolved and at least a certain sensitive perception of spatial expansion began to spread—one may compare the essentially frontal sculpture of Egypt and Mesopotamia with the roundness of Greek classical sculpture—only then could the void before, around, and within a structure become more than a mere counterpart to articulated volume.

Which of these two motifs, the sociological or the aesthetic, is more important may be left to the philosophy of the individual historian. To one who believes in the primacy of ideas, there seems no doubt that the growing concept of man in relation to his environment and the awareness of the human scale gave a stronger impetus to the shaping of space within the town than the merely socio-functional need for a gathering place. One may even play with the idea that both trends are not simply coincidental but go back to one last cause: the sanction of reason as the guiding principle of human life, which Greece contributed to the history of man.

INDIA. The earliest planned towns appear in ancient Indian civilization, but nothing resembling a square-like area has been found. The gridiron scheme, with its individual blocks of houses or *insulae* arranged in the form of a checkerboard, was known in India as early as the beginning of the third millennium, as excavations and literary documents prove, thus refuting the oft-repeated statement that it was the settlements of Alexander the Great which brought this idea to the East. In India, as in Egypt, Asia Minor, Hippodamic Greece, and later on in Rome and Central American civilizations, the appearance of the gridiron may be explained by mankind's generic urge for order and regularity in contrast to the chaotic growth of nature. The gridiron system developed from the practice of orientation, that is, the placing of a structure in correspondence to the points of the compass. Orientation, first applied to the town as a whole, was later on extended to the street layout, which in turn gradually led to the gridiron system. The desire to establish a connection between man-made structures and celestial powers, which orientation accomplished, is elemental and universal. Any attempt, therefore, at tracing the origin of the gridiron system to only one region of the inhabited world and to seek its diffusion from there is historically wrong.

The excavations at the site of the Indian town of Mohenjo-Daro (Fig. 2) show clearly that the concept of an organized city existed as early as 2500 B.C. as the spatial expression of a competent, businesslike civilization, severely practical. All parts there were designed to function within the whole. The slightly inaccurate gridiron covers about a square mile of ground and all streets, about thirty-three feet wide and unpaved, run from east to west and north to south. The considerations which created this comprehensive, no longer merely individual scheme were probably dictated by ritual laws as well as by the direction of the prevailing winds. A sewerage system and drainage with clay pipes existed, the houses were built of burnt bricks, had bathrooms, etc. The town lasted until about 1600 B.C. In spite of this technologically highly developed system, squares in the sense in which they appear in Western civilization seemingly did not exist. The few open spaces must be considered rather as courts in connection with individual houses and temples.

Later Indian civilizations which flourished after the town-building culture of the Indus Valley with its towns like Mohenjo-Daro and Harappa developed

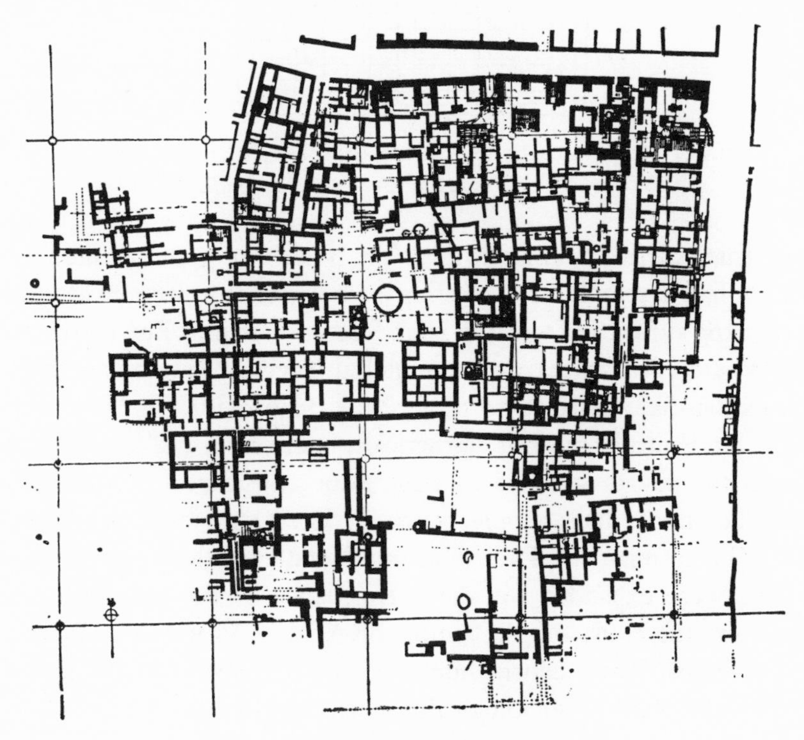

FIG. 2. MOHENJO-DARO. PLAN

various forms of layouts. However, none of them provided for squares. In these later Indo-Aryan civilizations a "town" meant just a village enlarged and vice versa, and no basic differences between them are evident. Villages and towns either grew naturally or were founded and fortified for military purposes. They housed between 400 and 10,000 people. Various types of villages with characteristic patterns such as "Chaturmukha" (Fig. 3), "Nanyavarta," etc., were established. Most of these regular patterns show gates, either in the center or at the corners of the four sides. Generally these schemes, whether they were grid-like (Chaturmukha), or circular with radial avenues (Kharvata), or of any other variation, were very close to those sacred

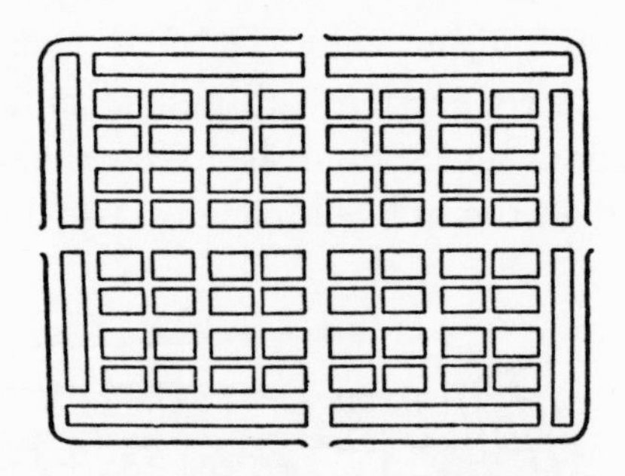

FIG. 3. THE VILLAGE IN INDIA; CHATURMUKHA PATTERN
From Dutt, *Town Planning in Ancient India*

diagrams which carried a symbolic meaning. If laid out on the gridiron scheme, the villages had a temple or a meeting hall at the intersection of the main streets, not too different from the later Roman castrum. But there were no squares. Where open spaces are encountered in villages or towns, they were planted, garden-like, destined to offer shade, to provide for "free and pure breezing," hygienically but not aesthetically motivated.

Nor can the courts attached to temples be considered as squares within a town. The tremendous temple courts of later Dravidian dynasties, such as those of Tiruvannamalai, Baillr, Purudkul, and even the great temple court of Madura, were expanded for the performance of the elaborate religious ritual, as were the courts of the temple of Angkor Wat in the Khmer Empire of Cambodia. These courts, however, always remained part of the temple district and neither sociologically nor spatially can be considered as squares.

MESOPOTAMIA. It is not exactly known whether the successive Mesopotamian civilizations from Sumer in the third millennium, with its numerous cities (Lagash, e.g., with 20,000 inhabitants), to the second Babylonian Empire in the sixth century B.C. took over the gridiron idea from India via Persia. As was said before, the mere fact of orientation led more or less automatically to the development of the gridiron scheme in different places. At any rate, the city of Babylon, with 80,000 inhabitants under Nebuchadnezzar around 600 B.C., had a gridiron pattern. Certainly it was not carried through everywhere, however, and Herodotus' enthusiastic description of straight streets doubtless referred only to certain quarters of the city. Another example of a strict gridiron scheme is offered by Dur-Sharrukin, founded by King Sargon in the eighth century B.C. These examples of the grid scheme probably occurred in founded towns only, since there were towns like Assur whose streets simply followed topographical conditions. In such towns the free spaces between the individual palaces and houses represent courtyards and are not public squares. The existence of circular Hittite cities is absolutely hypothetical.[1]

Gridiron or not, there were no "squares" in Mesopotamian towns. Not squares, but temples and palaces and—above all—the great axes of streets for sacred processions were the dominant factors in Mesopotamian towns which defined their shape. The great open spaces extending in front of temples and palaces were part of these establishments, shapeless in themselves, courts for jurisdiction or sites for religious ceremonies, as was, for instance, the great area before the Ishtar Gate in Babylon. Whether in connection with a gate, an altar, or a palace, these wide areas were neither geometrically nor architecturally regularized. The same is true of the great markets outside the town. As everywhere in the East, it was outside the walls (*extra muros*) that people met and bargained, as is so often mentioned in the Scriptures. The only functional demand for any Mesopotamian town was the long straight road for processions; there were no public squares comparable to agora and forum for people who lived as subjugated masses. Probably these processional streets later stimulated the layout of the great axes in Hellenistic towns of the East and in Africa.

EGYPT. Because of their basic political, sociological, and economic conditions, the towns of Egypt, like those of Mesopotamia and India, were entirely different from the Greek *polis*. Temples and palaces were the most important elements of the Egyptian town, but were isolated and without reference to any kind of overall pattern. Whether they developed from accumulations of clustered primitive huts, interspersed occasionally with more pretentious houses, or as special royal foundations, carefully oriented and planned under consideration of the inundation of the Nile River, Egyptian towns were irregular in their layout. Relatively few are preserved and excavated com-

[1] The theoretical reconstruction of the circular Hittite towns Zendjirli, Kadesh, and Karkemisch in, e.g., Robert Koldewey and Otto Puchstein, *Ausgrabungen in Sendschirli: Mitteilungen aus den Staatlichen Sammlungen*, Felix von Luschan, *Ausgrabungen in Sendschirli*, and Pierre Lavedan, *Histoire de l'Urbanisme* (2 vols., Paris, 1926, 1941), is based on insufficient evidence. Nevertheless, this concept is taken over by many later historians of town planning, most recently by Christopher Tunnard, *The City of Man* (New York, 1953). However, Josef Gantner, *Grundformen der europäischen Stadt* (Vienna, 1928), correctly rejects the theory entirely.

pletely. They are lesser known in their totality than individual temples, palaces, pyramids, and tombs. A few well-researched towns, however, prove that the gridiron scheme was employed in Egypt, probably some centuries later than in Mohenjo-Daro in India.

Kahun (Fig. 4) was destined as a settlement for laborers working on the Sostris pyramid, built after 2500 B.C. Within a very regular grid, a wall separated the larger blocks of the richer quarters from those of the laborers on the pyramid of King Usertesen, for whom the settlement was originally

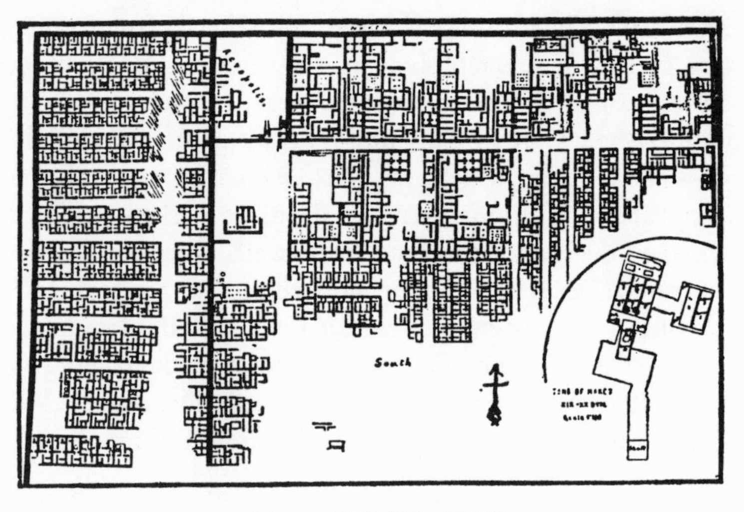

FIG. 4. KAHUN. PLAN
From Petrie, *Illahun, Kahun and Gurob*

projected. The streets were relatively broad, up to twenty feet, but no squares were marked. An open space existed at the end of the main traffic lane, but it was architecturally not defined.

About 1,200 years later, around 1370 B.C., Pharaoh Akhnaton built along the Nile River his new metropolis Tel-el-Amarna following the principle of the grid. Although the streets ran at right angles, the individual houses were neither regularly grouped nor were the blocks equally divided. Some large houses stood isolated. In one quarter, however, complete uniformity proves exact town planning. This quarter represented a perfect quadrangle and was divided by streets which ran at equal intervals from north to south, connected by crossroads at either end. A certain amount of space was left free at the entrance to the workers' quarter, in this instance within the walls, but here also without any organic connection with the overall scheme and not at all a "square."

The large courtyards or sequences of courts within Egyptian palaces or temple districts often had the measurements of a public square. But although these areas were architecturally framed, symmetrical, and organized in axial sequence, not shapeless as in Mesopotamia, they are not genuine squares because they did not function as such. Whether in reference to Deir-el-Bahri (Fig. 5), the temple of Queen Hatshepsut, constructed around 1480 B.C.,

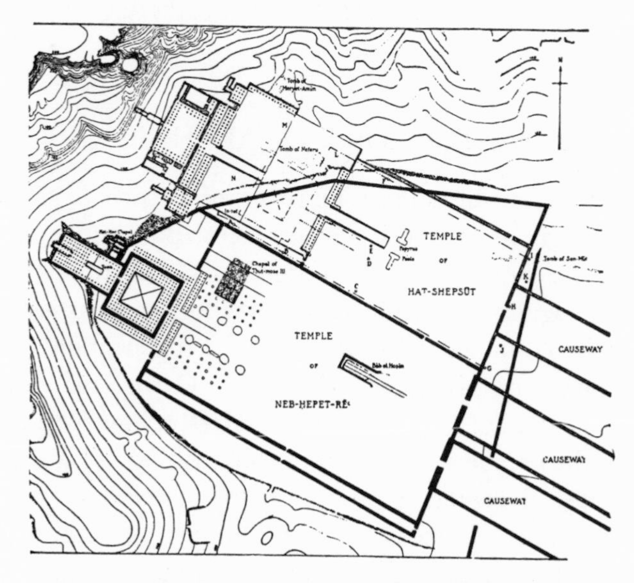

FIG. 5. THE TEMPLES AT DEIR-EL-BAHRI. PLAN
From Winlock, *Excavations at Deir el Bahri, 1911–1931*

or to the great temple complexes of Karnak, erected under Rameses II and Rameses III, around 1250 to 1180 B.C. or to the still later Ptolemaic temple of Edfu, built from the third to the second century B.C., the aesthetically decisive element is not the individual spatial unit of the courts themselves, but the succession of courts following each other. Like the alleys of sphinxes, this sequence of courts, framed by strictly symmetrical architecture, mostly colonnades, leads toward the entrance of the respective temple or palace. It is the axis as such which dictates the movement. The individual courts as rhythmically organized units are mere way stations, either on the same level throughout or terraced and connected by ramps. No deviations into other directions seemed to be allowed, time for a pause did not exist, only the continuous drive and dynamic force of the axis proper, its propellent trend, channeled toward the final goal of the procession. And therefore these courtyards cannot be seen as individual space units per se, as genuine squares.

As was noted above, the Indian, Mesopotamian, and Egyptian civilizations did not provide the political, governmental, social, and—most important—psychological conditions which would create the need for gathering places. We must wait for the unfolding of the Greek concept of life, with its new relation between individual and state, before a gathering place for people, a real square, could develop.

ACROPOLIS AND AGORA IN ARCHAIC GREECE

Great myths always attribute the foundation of a town to the unique deed of courage and wisdom of one legendary hero. But reality does not quite correspond to these stories since the origins of Greek towns can be traced back to different beginnings. Neolithic settlements in the earliest era of Greek civilization developed under the protection of a fortification (an acropolis), as in the beginnings of Mycenae and Tiryns. Or age-old sanctuaries like Delphi became the core of later settlements. Mostly, however, the new town developed from the combination of previously existing villages and became a political and physical center, a process called *synoikism* (synoecism). As related by Thucydides, Theseus founded the city of Athens in this way, centralizing the various local administrations and the economic forces of the region—a symbolic glorification, of course, of an achievement which happened only gradually. Similarly, Marathon was a combination of four villages and so was Eleusis. In the sixth century B.C., the city of Tegea was formed out of nine villages and Mantinea out of five; and still later Olynthus, Thebes, and others originated in similar fashion.

Finally, planned colonization created cities of irregular or regular patterns. Such towns in Greece proper which stemmed from Cretan colonial settlements were as irregular as were Knossos and Palaikastro on Crete itself. There was usually one broad main street and certainly no clearly defined square. There may have been streets with continuous rows of porticoes, e.g., in Gurnia and Hagia Triada, which to a certain degree substituted for what later would become public squares. They certainly did not evoke any spatial feeling, but were merely formed as a functional architectural element, protection against sun and rain. The spatially expressive courtyards of Cretan palaces, on the other hand, were not "public," but parts of an individual palace architecture, without any connection with the organization of the town as a whole.

If a Greek town had grown out of the fusion of earlier separate villages, the former sacred area of one of them became the focal point of the new organism. The structure of the new community as a whole remained unchanged, which, of course, means irregular. An agora in the later sense did not exist yet. It would develop from the need for a political and commercial center for all the inhabitants together.

At any rate, whether of neolithic, or of Cretan-Helladic, or of synoikistic origin, the early Greek town had an irregular layout, and either topographical conditions or the location of already existing individual houses defined the direction of the streets. Parallel rows of houses forming more or less regular blocks and straight streets, comparable to Indian and Egyptian towns almost two thousand years earlier, did not appear before the fifth century B.C., and a regularly organized agora even later.

The chaotic web of streets in Athens, still in existence deep into Roman times, and many similar layouts prove that this irregular pattern was general throughout Greece. From at least the seventh century B.C. on, an acropolis existed in connection with each larger settlement as well as a void of irregular shape which later would become the agora. These two distinct elements were characteristic of Greek towns as long as Greek civilization prevailed and shaped the life of the inhabitants. Only in late Hellenistic times did the importance of the acropolis begin to pale.

THE ACROPOLIS. The acropolis, the nucleus of early Greek towns, developed generally from a fortified place of refuge. The possibilities of an easy defense were decisive for its establishment. So it became gradually the seat of the dominant power and eventually a sacred area, where temples, monuments, and altars were located, as were in earlier times the palaces of the kings. The acropolis was walled, but never became part of the fortification of the settlement which stretched beneath it. Once the whole town had become walled, the acropolis gradually lost its importance for defense. During the earlier archaic centuries it also served as a gathering place, a function which it lost to the agora with the increasing growth of the town proper.

On the acropolis, temples and statues were located according to topographical conditions of the hill. Often the respect for the tradition of previous sanctuaries or temples, sometimes dating back to prehistoric times, determined the site of later structures. But notwithstanding the representative character of the acropolis and the importance of its sacred area, no kind of space-creating relationship between the individual buildings can be observed. From the beginning to the very end of Greek civilization we find at the acropolis the same lack of an organized overall plan that is evident at the great sanctuaries, such as Eleusis, Olympia, and Delphi.

Without any doubt, the glorious temples, statues, and other monuments of an acropolis prove that the early Greeks, long before classical and Hellenistic times, had tried consciously to beautify and decorate their sacred areas. But quite obviously they did not aim at any kind of spatial unification and integration.

Space as such was neither felt aesthetically nor formed artistically from archaic Greek times through the sixth century B.C. The technique of spatial definition on a scale commensurate with human needs was not yet developed by the Greeks. It was volume, the mass of a structure or sculpture, that was of interest to the artist. Hence the acropolis represented but an accumulation of irregularly dispersed shaped volumes, each existing in its own right without being tied together into a spatial unit. Generally the desire for shaping space developed only very slowly after 500 B.C., steadily increasing in Hellenistic times until its culmination in Roman architecture and town planning, when it became the aesthetically decisive factor. But even then this spatial development referred only to the agora and never to the acropolis.

This lack of the desire for spatial integration expresses itself also in the approach to the propylaea of an acropolis. Even if the latter was located on a relatively low elevation, the road uphill was never axially directed as in Egypt but wound up gradually in serpentines. Not only did this make the defense against the onmarching enemy easier, but it was also motivated aesthetically. It seems that a succession of oblique views of each individual temple and monument was desired, where each step forward opened a new and different aspect —without, however, aiming at a genuine three-dimensional impression.

In order to find some kind of system for the layout of the archaic acropolis, K. A. Doxiadis, a Greek archaeologist, by comparative studies of ancient Greek acropolises and city centers, tried to prove that the individual buildings were arranged corresponding to the laws of perspective and the capacity of the human eye and its angle of vision. Through the varying orientation of all structures, through their angles toward each other, and through their partial dependence on the site of existing structures, an apparent continuity of the overall outline would originate. However, even if this holds true (Doxiadis is rather liberal in his interpretation of excavated foundations), the continuity of successive visual impressions would certainly not create any simultaneous awareness of volume and still less any feeling of space. At the most, a kind of two-dimensional stage perspective would have resulted. The Greeks looked at individual buildings as they looked at sculpture, with a highly developed feeling for the volume of each single structure. A perspective connection of these individual structures through foreshortening, overlapping, etc., may have been consciously perceived, but those sensations are not identical with the awareness of space. The development of Greek vase painting, with the late and only very gradual introduction of perspective, may be considered a parallel proof of the lack of interest in space relations by the archaic Greek.

Some Greek acropolises can be reconstructed in their preclassical layout by thorough excavation and archaeological research. Out of the great number of preclassical examples only a few may be mentioned here: Athens, Corinth, Selinus, and Thera. All of them prove that space on the ancient acropolis had never been organized and that the general interest was concentrated on the perfection of form and design of the individual volume, be it a building or a sculpture. Although the various acropolises originated centuries apart—from the neolithic to the archaic period—it is quite evident that never before Hellenistic times had any kind of specific "system" directed their layout; that no overall plan had existed; and that in each instance only topographical conditions and the traditional places of earlier sanctuaries had led to the choice of sites for the later structures. Later developments and additions through centuries could never have allowed adherence to any hypothetical previous plans.

The development of the acropolis of Athens (Fig. 6) from the time when it was a pre-Hellenic sanctuary onward is so well researched and so widely known that repetition seems superfluous. One glance at the map of the acropolis even in Periclean times proves the volume-consciousness and space-blindness of its builders, which resulted practically in visual isolation of the respective structures. It explains also the complete lack of any axial references.

The tremendous differences in level within the sacred area contributed further to its irregularity, and only in the last Hellenistic centuries were attempts made—mostly unsuccessfully—to overcome them to a certain degree.

The same characteristic irregularity is encountered at Acrocorinthus and at the original, archaic acropolis of Selinus, prior to its destruction by the Carthaginians in 409 B.C. (see p. 39). The acropolis of Thera is of special importance. This city was a new Doric foundation of the ninth century B.C.

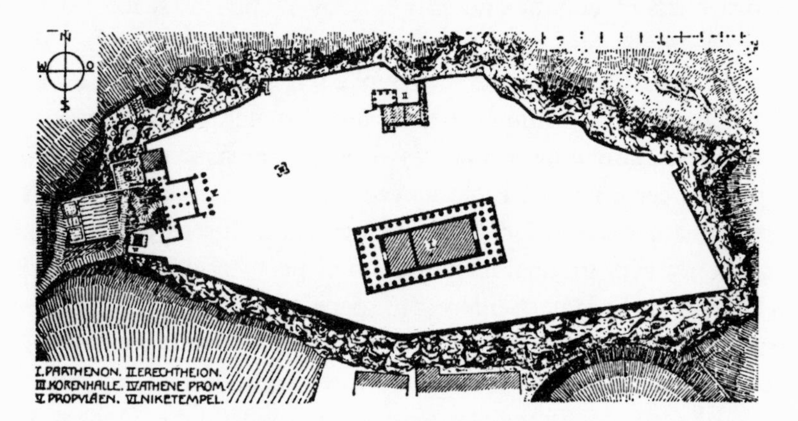

FIG. 6. ATHENS. PLAN OF THE ACROPOLIS, FIFTH CENTURY B.C.
From Sitte, *The Art of Building Cities*

after some earlier Phoenician settlements at the same site had perished. No regular scheme is recognizable. The situation is extraordinary in so far as the acropolis—named here "the agora of the Gods"—was, because of topographical conditions, on the same level as the real agora at the utmost end of the town, both connected by a level street.

THE AGORA. It is only in Thera that the archaic agora can be reconstructed with any certainty. Here the agora proper consisted merely of a broadening of the main street, as in many of the village greens of New England settlements. This agora is one of the few where the original layout was not changed by the later erection of a stoa, since the importance of this archaic city decreased very rapidly after the seventh century B.C. Actually, in this special instance, acropolis and agora may be considered as more or less monumental enlargements of a general thoroughfare.

In most instances, the archaic agora underwent so many alterations and changed so much through later Hellenistic and Roman additions that little can be said about its appearance in the archaic centuries. We know, for instance, that in Athens the agora during the Bronze Age served as a burial ground; later on this area was covered by private houses which from the beginning of the sixth century B.C. were supplanted gradually by public buildings such as the first *bouleuterion.*

There exists a decisive difference between agora and acropolis. While generally the alterations and additions on the acropolis grew fewer and fewer after the fifth century B.C. out of respect for sacred tradition, the agora changed continuously in most intimate contact with the political and economic life of the citizens. So its ancient structures were more often razed or remodeled. Therefore the reconstruction of the earlier archaic layers of the agora is always more difficult than that of an acropolis.

It is the agora that makes the town a *polis.* As originated by the Greeks, the *polis* introduced an entirely new element into the civilization of the West and the Near East. This new element, represented by the agora, new from the sociological as well as from the architectural viewpoint, was based on the potentialities of a gradually growing democracy and may be *contrasted* with the principle of the axis. The latter, whether in Mesopotamia or in Egypt or during the last Roman centuries, always represents the architecturally crystallized form of a dictatorial concept of society.

Usually the agora, as the focal point of the town, was located in the center if topographical conditions allowed it; in harbor cities as close to the port as possible, as, for instance, in Delos and later in Rhodes and in Alexandria. In some towns of the early period, the agora has been found near the gate. In the beginning, as described by Homer, the agora was primarily the place for political gatherings and legislative assemblies. It changed gradually into a center for marketing and eventually became solely commercial, whereas the political function of the agora was taken over by representative meetings in the sacred area of the acropolis. What was left of governmental, administrative, and judicial activities in connection with the agora now was attended to in closed special buildings.

Origin and gradual change in function of the agora do not suffice to explain the change of its shape. Here as always it is *impossible to deduce the form of a work of art solely from social and economic conditions,* as is so often attempted nowadays. In painting, sculpture, and even in architecture, purpose-bound as it may be, the dependence of the artistic concept on the social structure at the time of its origin may help to explain functionally its *raison d'être*, but never its morphological development.

During the archaic period, from the end of the eighth century down to the beginning of the fifth century B.C., the layout of the agora was as irregular as that of the whole town and, as mentioned above, it was mainly defined by topographical conditions. The area, mostly as open as possible, was visually in immediate contact with the streets that ran into it and fitted into existing road systems. Nowhere is a definite space concept recognizable and still less any overall three-dimensional structure. Even if an archaic or an early classical agora seems to be almost closed, the enclosing elements do not refer to each other. They are discontinuous, interrupted by incoming streets and therefore cannot create any real spatial configuration.

Thus, the individual temple can only be perceived in open space, without reference to anything else, and is meant to be comprehended as isolated volume, as a self-contained three-dimensional unit. Again: space was never formed before Hellenistic times. No wonder then that modest shacks stood in the immediate vicinity of public buildings. These consisted usually of a *bouleuterion*, as meeting room for the city council; a *prytaneum*, a private chamber for the chief officials of the magistrate, where official hospitality was extended to distinguished citizens and visitors; and later one or more stoas (porticoes). Foundations of some smaller government buildings have also been found occasionally and—besides individual altars—sometimes one or a few small temples in the center.

Thanks to the research of the American School of Classical Studies we know most about the archaic agora of Athens, but other archaic agoras, such as those of Olynthus, Corinth, Delos, and Elis, can also be reconstructed rather completely.

The archaic agora in Athens, extending originally not more than six acres, developed gradually in the late seventh century, its area being already inhabited at the end of the third millennium, in neolithic times. The public buildings whose remnants are today excavated date back not farther than to the fifth century B.C., mostly to the third century B.C. through the second century A.D., in other words, to Hellenistic and Roman times. But they are located on sites where certain structures had already existed in archaic times, for example, the *metroon* on the *bouleuterion* of the sixth century B.C. and the stoa of the king (*stoa basileios*) on a site dating from the end of the fifth century. Important in this context is the fact that all these older structures were not coordinated, neither as to direction nor as to any other kind of mutual architectural reference. The most decisive factor preventing coordination was the direction of the Panathenaean Way, which cut diagonally through the area while the other existing roads bypassed tangentially. Not before the second century B.C. was the agora framed by the Stoa of Attalus, one more proof that nothing was less in the mind of archaic and classical Athens than the creation of a regularized, closed or half-closed square, and that there were no continuous formal boundaries of the area.

HIPPODAMIC AND HELLENISTIC TOWNS AND THEIR AGORAS

The decisive step toward regularity was taken roughly around 500 B.C. Whether Hippodamus of Miletus had actually invented the new "Hippodamic" system or had only established its theoretical principle and introduced it into Continental Greece no longer presents a relevant archaeological problem. Allegedly he had laid out the plans for Piraeus (before 446 B.C.), for Thurii (around 445 B.C.), and for Rhodes (408 B.C.). The last is highly improbable since by then he would have reached an age unusual even for city planners. In Piraeus certainly, and probably in Thurii, he organized only some quarters and not the whole town. Thus one may suppose that Hippodamus' main activities lay between 470 and 430 B.C., when he probably died. At any rate, the plans for Miletus (see p. 38) were executed between 475 and 470 B.C.[2] Research considers Hippodamus rather a kind of half-legendary Homer of city planning who at a period of expanding Greek trade and crystallizing political power merely introduced into Greece a concept developed from earlier Oriental examples in Ionic settlements of Asia Minor. There the *economic advantages of a regular distribution* of building lots may have contributed to a preference for organized planning in the process of orderly colonization, and the town plan became more and more the result of collaborative effort. The Ionians, who counted among their great philosophers and

[2] According to M. Erdmann, *Zur Kunde der hellenistischen Städtegründungen* (Strasbourg, 1879), and "Hippodamos von Milet und die symmetrische Städtebaukunst der Griechen," *Philologus: Zeitschrift für das klassische Altertum*, Bd. 42 (Göttingen, 1884). In agreement with Erdmann are Josef Gantner, *Grundformen der europäischen Stadt* (Vienna, 1928), Pierre Lavedan, *Histoire de l'Urbanisme* (2 vols., Paris, 1926, 1941), and Armin von Gerkan, *Griechische Städteanlagen* (Berlin, 1924). On the other hand, Jean Hulot and Gustave Fougères, in *Sélinonte* (Paris, 1910) attribute Rhodes to Hippodamus and give his death date as around 400 B.C.

mathematicians Thales, Anaximander, and Pythagoras, were accustomed to thinking in rational mathematical terms.

Even Greek colonies of the seventh century B.C., like Marseilles, where the site of the ancient Phoenician-Greek agora remained the site of the later Roman forum and even of the medieval market square, and colonies of the sixth century B.C., like Naples and Paestum, already showed a rather regular layout in spite of the early dates of their foundations.

However, Greek theoreticians from Aristotle in his *Politics* onward and even later Roman writers have always connected the gridiron scheme with the name of Hippodamus, with the *νεώτερος καὶ ἱπποδαμεῖος τρόπος*, the new and Hippodamic system. Aristotle contrasts this system distinctly with the *αρχαιότερος τρόπος*, the earlier procedure of building without plan or organizing system as it had existed in archaic towns. He and Plato, in his *Republic*, discuss the "ideal city" only in rather general terms. This is all the more astonishing since after all Aristotle was the first philosopher to deal with aesthetic problems in general. And yet he never discusses city planning from an aesthetic point of view. Similarly, Hippocrates—more correctly called Deinocrates—a contemporary of Alexander the Great who participated in the planning of Alexandria, thinks primarily in practical hygienic terms and bases his theoretical demands for the well-planned town on them. Both Aristotle and Plato stress the importance of the agora, however. Aristotle especially emphasizes the functional difference between the commercial and the sacred agora, almost identifying the latter with the acropolis.

Actually it is not Plato and Aristotle, the philosophers, but a man living definitely in the realm of reality, Pausanias, from whom we learn most about the ancient Greek town. Pausanias, the Greek traveler and geographer of the second century A.D., gives very exact descriptions in his work, *Description of Greece*, a kind of ancient Baedecker. And although he saw the towns he described in the second century A.D., there was still so much left from earlier centuries that we are able to cull most valuable data for the preceding centuries from his observations, published between A.D. 160 and 180.

Pausanias, exactly as Aristotle centuries before him, emphasizes repeatedly the difference between the older agoras and the post-Hippodamic or Hellenistic ones, which are supposed to have been regular, surrounded by colonnades, etc. And he is also fully conscious of the differences between Hellenistic and Roman principles, as evident, for instance, in his description of Elis.

Now what is meant by ἱπποδαμεῖος τρόπος? It is the gridiron scheme, well known to us, of straight parallel streets crossing other straight parallel streets at an angle of 90 degrees. Out of this basic idea develops a general tendency for spatial classification and regularity, even a certain symmetry as it manifests itself in Hellenistic planning. Only now, during and after Hippodamic times, the idea of overall integration as expressing the corporate whole of the town becomes typical for Mediterranean towns. The orientation of the whole scheme may depend on topographical factors, on the direction of prevailing winds, on the tracks of already existing through traffic, or on religious traditions, as, e.g., axes of important earlier temples. However, no sacred ritual laws existed for the foundation of new settlements, as was the case later on in Roman times.

Certainly a specific psychological attitude contributed also to this development. The pre-Socratic concept of man as the measure of everything expresses a general feeling which—at least subconsciously—became basic in classical times and which in the field of town planning led to new concepts.[3] The idea of an organized city, where all parts were designed to function within the whole, developed beyond merely individual and topographical considerations.

So much about the gridiron as the basic organizational scheme for a town. Still more clearly than in the street scheme the aesthetic effect of this new concept becomes evident in the most important individual element of ancient town planning, the space of the agora.

THE AGORA. It is necessary first to realize the size of Greek towns in Hippodamic and post-Hippodamic times in order to understand their inner structure. Athens, for instance, then had a population of about 200,000 inhabitants including the slaves; some other Greek towns, between 30,000 and 40,000. In all these cities not one but many agoras developed. Besides the traditional agora where public buildings and public functions continued to prevail, there were individual agoras where specific goods were sold, e.g., the pottery market, the fish market, the meat market, etc. Markets for perishable and nonperishable goods were separated.

Around the main agora the government of the town often leased shops

[3] See F. Tritsch, "Die Stadtbildung des Altertums und die griechische Polis," *Klio*, Vol. XXII, 1928. In contrast to this author, we believe that the change from pre-Hippodamic irregularity to the Hippodamic system was not purely morphological but was also philosophically and psychologically motivated.

and stalls to merchants and craftsmen who in turn brought a relatively high income to the administration. In connection with the levy of these rents, some prices of goods sold there were controlled. As more and more space was taken over by business, the political function of the agora decreased and retreated into specific buildings like the *bouleuterion* or individual stoas which were no longer under the open sky. Eventually stoas and halls were erected exclusively for marketing purposes and for exchange, often presenting just a glorified façade for rows of modest shops behind a magnificent portico.

The location of the main agora in Hippodamic and Hellenistic towns was principally the same as in archaic times: in the heart of the town, and in harbor towns as close to the harbor as possible. Its size varied from two rectangular city blocks in Priene, to six in Magnesia (Fig. 7), and sixteen in Miletus.

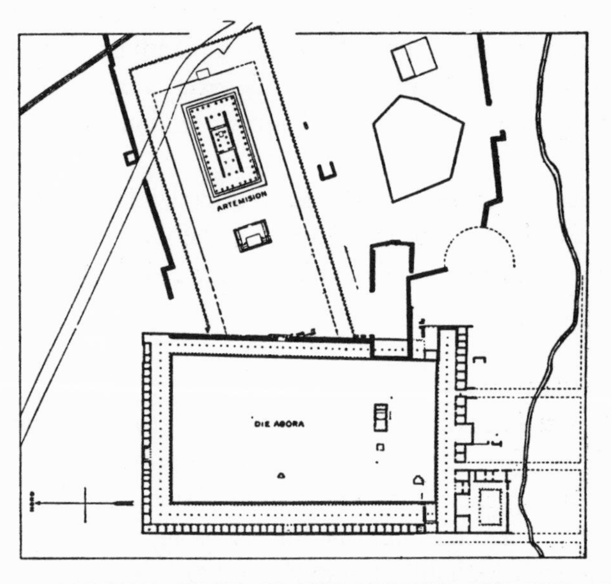

FIG. 7. MAGNESIA. PLAN OF THE TEMPLE AND THE AGORA
From Humann and Kohte, *Magnesia am Maeander*

Before analyzing the relation between the agora and its adjacent streets, a brief remark about the streets themselves: on the average they were about five to six yards wide, the main street being from twelve to about eighteen yards broad. They were usually well drained, but became paved only in Hellenistic times.

From the very end of the fifth century on, the late classical and Hellenistic agora developed a typical shape, although it would be a mistake to suppose that the completely closed rectangular space now became the common ideal of all Greek town schemes.[4] However, the tendency toward strict and regular confines became more and more evident and the space, in contrast to earlier times, was conceived as a distinct configuration, a *Gestalt*. The single structures surrounding it were architecturally subordinated to the idea of the enclosed space as a whole. To compare, however, the Hellenistic agora with an enlarged peristyle would be as misleading as to compare an arcaded medieval square with a cloister. The peristyle represents a complete enclosure and is by its very nature secluded, while the agora in Hellenistic times is never completely enclosed and resembles rather a horseshoe.

Yet public buildings adjacent to the agora were frequently built as peristyles. The agoras of Ephesus and the lower agora in Pergamum, which are at least three-quarters closed, are very late and without any doubt already influenced by Roman concepts. During the last pre-Christian centuries, altars, shrines, statues, and small temples were erected in increasing numbers, e.g., in Magnesia. Thus the functional distinction between agora and acropolis was in this way partially abolished. Individual temples were mostly framed by colonnades or porticoes. Similar colonnades closed also the courtyards of temples adjacent to the agora, in this way unifying the whole area, e.g., the north market in Miletus, and in Priene. These porticoes were lower than the temples they surrounded, so that they accentuated the architecture of the buildings and dramatized their appearance. Hence they represented structurally a transition from the individual architecture of the temple to the free and open space of the agora. Porticoes, the steps leading to them, and paved terraces became more and more integral parts of later Hellenistic agoras; they articulated space and established proportion and scale as the columns, architraves, and pediments accentuated the volume of an individual structure. "The stoa defines the total space which is divided into the volume of the temple, that of the open area, and that of the stoa itself." The stoa proper was not at all sacred but became the place for marketing and bargaining, as mentioned earlier.

Not only temples but also secular structures adjacent to the agora were decorated by porticoes, built before or into them. The totality of all these

[4] Joseph A. Wymer, *Die Marktplatzanlagen der Griechen und Römer* (Munich, 1916), is mistaken in this respect and is refuted by Armin von Gerkan, *Griechische Städteanlagen* (Berlin, 1924).

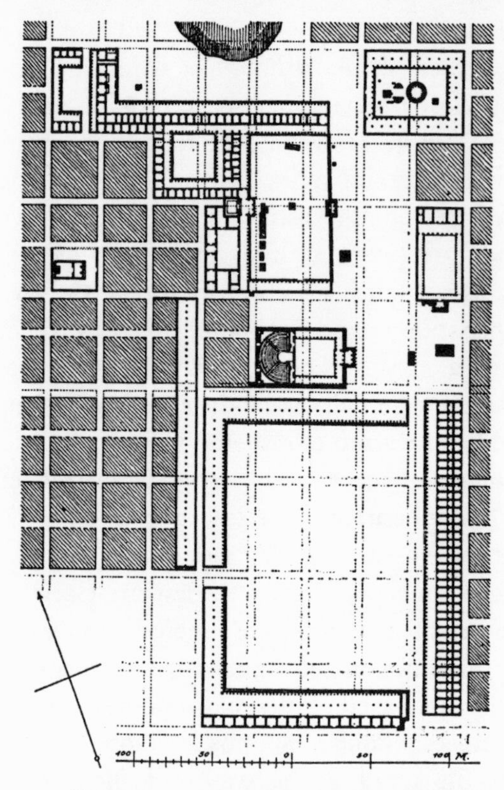

FIG. 8. MILETUS. PLAN OF THE MARKET
From Gerkan, *Griechische Städteanlagen*

porticoes created the monumental expression of the agoras' public character, especially from the third century B.C. on. Visually they helped to set off the agora from the adjacent tangential streets.

After the death of Alexander the Great, Asia Minor became more characteristic for the new trend in city planning than Greece proper. Priene (Fig. 1), e.g., offers an excellent example of the spatial tendencies of the controlled design of this period, although the slope of the site demanded certain specific considerations. It was newly founded or rather resettled around 350 B.C. The agora is centrally located, the main street in this instance cutting through it. The *prytaneum* and other public buildings are set back from the square on its north side. On the other sides of the agora, shops are located, all unified by porticoes. West of the square are small separate food markets. The monumental temples of Athena and Zeus, the latter also surrounded by colonnades, are not visible from the agora, although close to it.

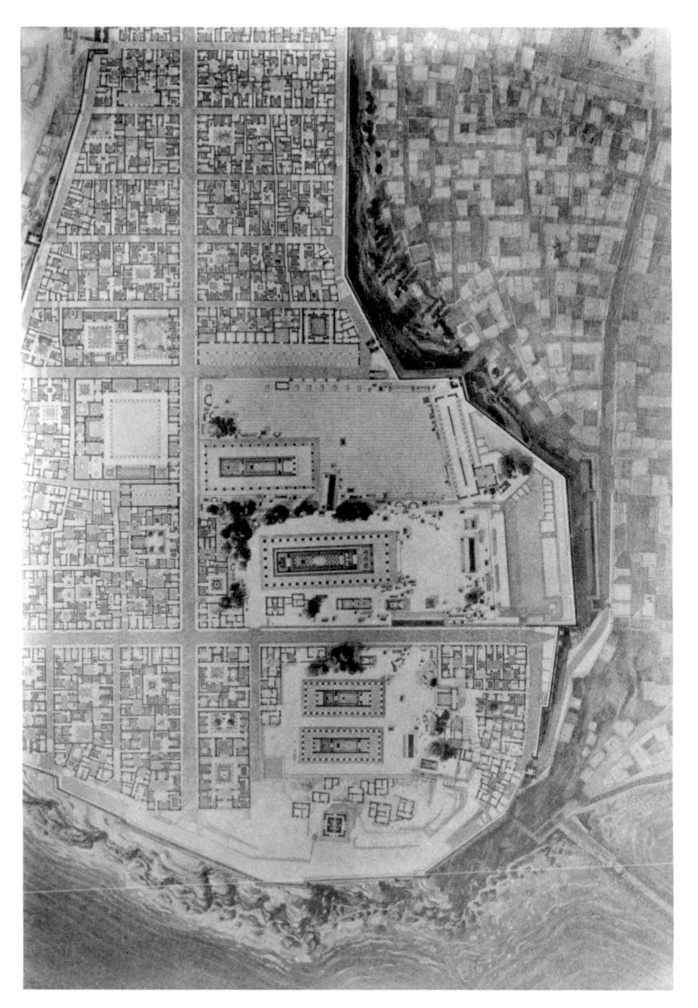

A: SELINUS. PLAN

From Hulot and Fougères, *Sélinonte*

B: TURIN. ROMAN SCHEME AS PRESERVED AFTER THE RENAISSANCE

Courtesy New York Public Library

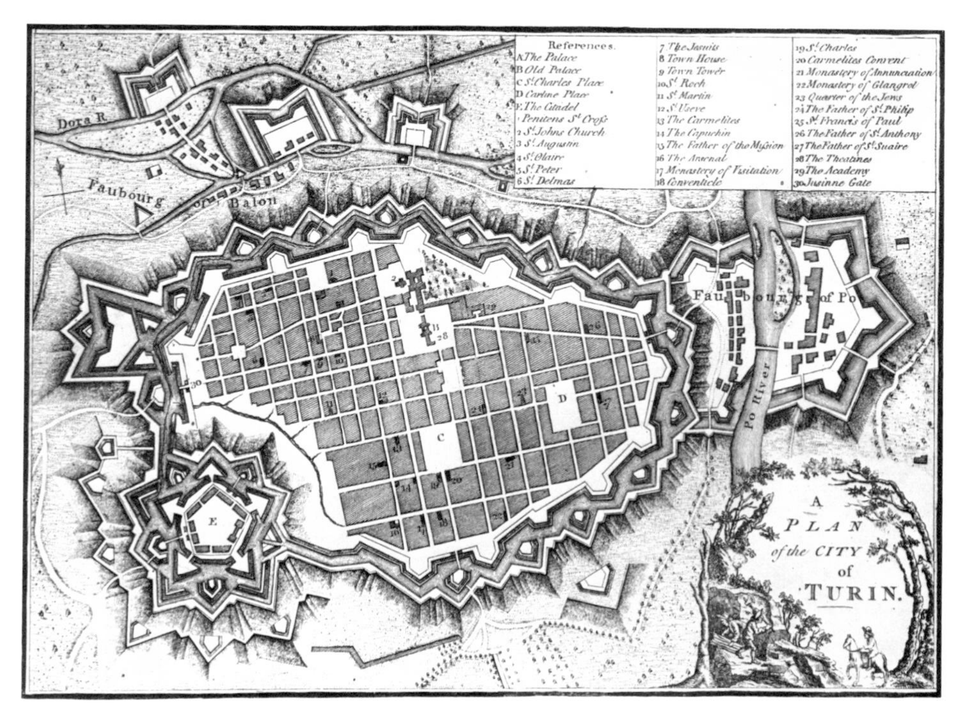

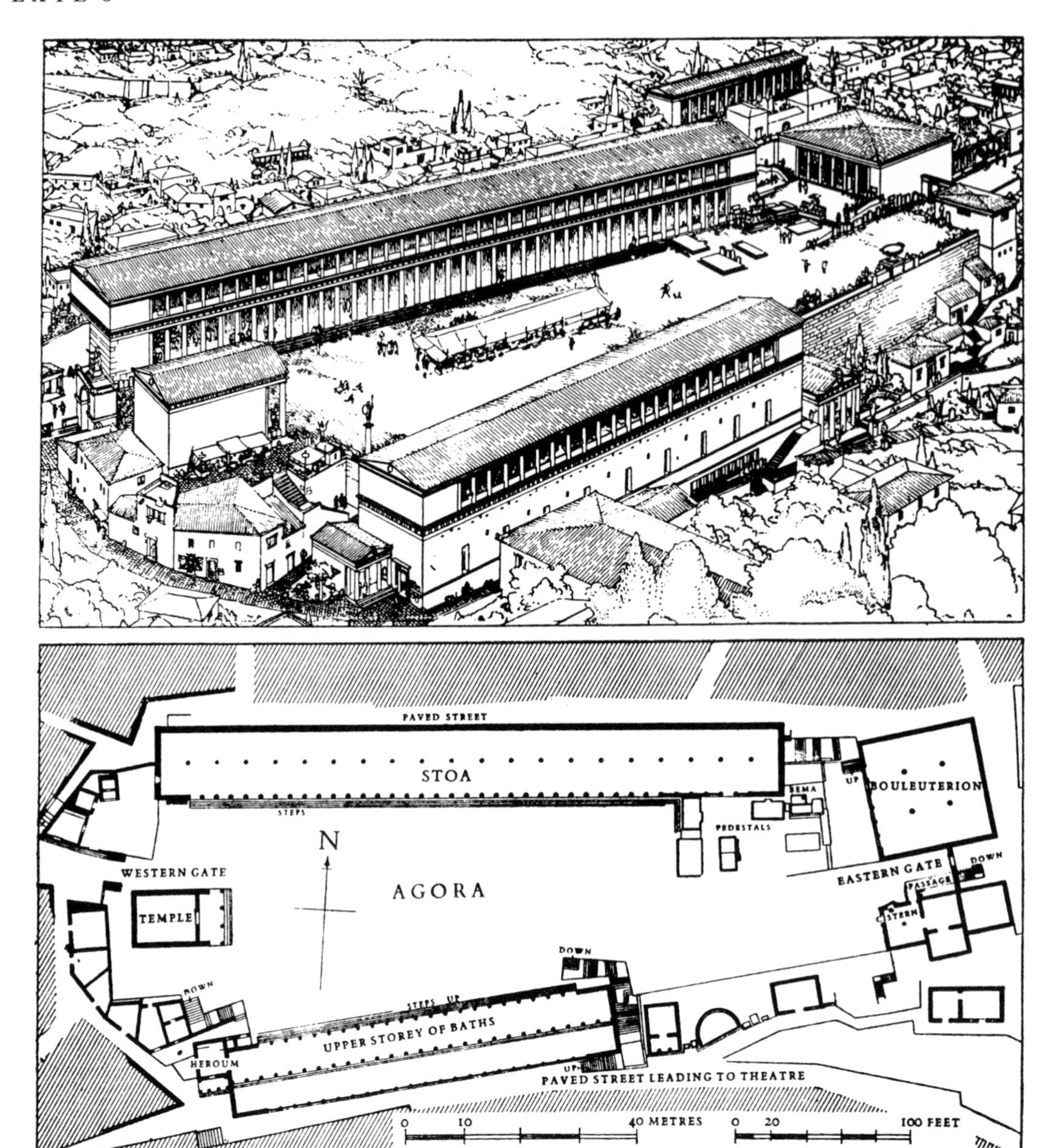

ASSOS. THE AGORA. PLAN AND RECONSTRUCTION

From Bacon, *Investigations at Assos*

ROME. FORUM ROMANUM. RECONSTRUCTION

ROME. FORUM ROMANUM. ETCHING BY GIUSEPPE VASI, 1765
Courtesy Metropolitan Museum of Art, Whittelsey Fund, 1951

POMPEII

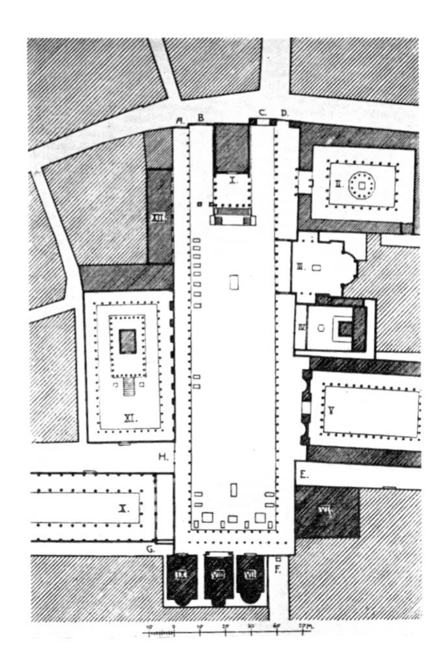

FORUM. PLAN

From Sitte,
The Art of Building Cities

FORUM, WITH THE TEMPLE OF JUPITER

RECONSTRUCTION

From Weichardt, *Pompeji vor der Zerstörung*

TIMGAD

PLAN

From Gerkan, *Griechische Städteanlagen*

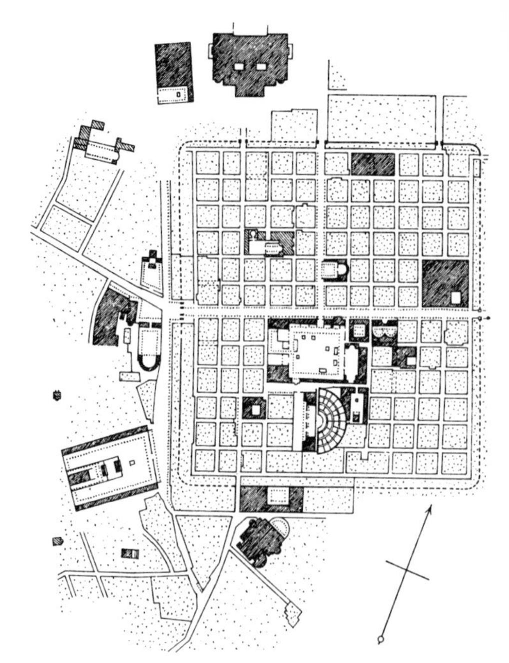

BELOW: GENERAL VIEW FROM THE THEATER

Photo Compagnie des Arts Photomécaniques

BOTTOM: DECUMANUS MAXIMUS AND ARCH OF TRAJAN

Photo Compagnie des Arts Photomécaniques

ROME. FORUM TRAIANI. RECONSTRUCTION *ca.* 1725

ENGRAVING BY J. A. DELSENBACH

ROME. FORUM TRAIANI

From Duperac, *I Vestigi dell' Antichità di Roma;* courtesy Metropolitan Museum of Art, Dick Fund, 1936

At the north market in Miletus (Fig. 8), where the temple was also surrounded by porticoes, the straight side of the horseshoe was closed by a wall with a central entrance. In this way a kind of closed court originated, an exception which somewhat anticipated later Roman fora, although not stressing an axis.

Selinus (Pl. 5A), whose whole layout shows a certain similarity to Miletus, was rebuilt in 408 B.C., immediately after its first destruction, allegedly by Hermocrates, who adhered quite obviously to the Hippodamic scheme. The temple area was integrated with the gridiron of the town and the location of the older temples must have been changed in order to correspond to the strictly axial layout which somewhat anticipated later Roman developments.

In Kos, the temple of Asclepius was approached over terraces by three successive axially located stairways—comparable to Egyptian schemes (e.g., Deir-el-Bahri) and also to late Roman organizations. The sequence here bespeaks the late Hellenistic tendency to frame the temple by homogeneous architectural elements, whereas in earlier times it was isolated. But the two wings of the colonnades are still of unequal length and are not exactly parallel; in other words, they are more autonomous than in later Roman layouts. The layout of Kos in its totality represents a square as much as the later Spanish Steps in Rome (see p. 155). While not exactly an agora, Kos is mentioned in this context since it represents a characteristic development in spatial feeling.

In Assos (Pl. 6) the agora, located on a leveled slope, was surrounded by porticoes in the form of a trapezoid. The north side was occupied by a hall of two colonnaded stories, each with two naves, which in this instance were not used for shops. The public bath opposite had also a portico in its upper story. Both sides together framed the view toward the relatively small temple on the narrower west side. The whole plan is not strictly axially organized because of topographical reasons, but the desire for the impression of a closed square, rhythmically directed toward the temple, shows a certain similarity to later Roman examples.

The two-storied stoa of the Hellenistic agora in Corinth (Fig. 9), begun in the first half of the fourth century B.C., was extraordinarily large with its Doric portico of seventy-one columns and thirty-three taverns on the first floor. It underwent only little change through the following centuries. After its partial destruction in Roman times, Caesar ordered the rebuilding of the stoa, which eventually was destroyed in A.D. 267. Throughout the centuries

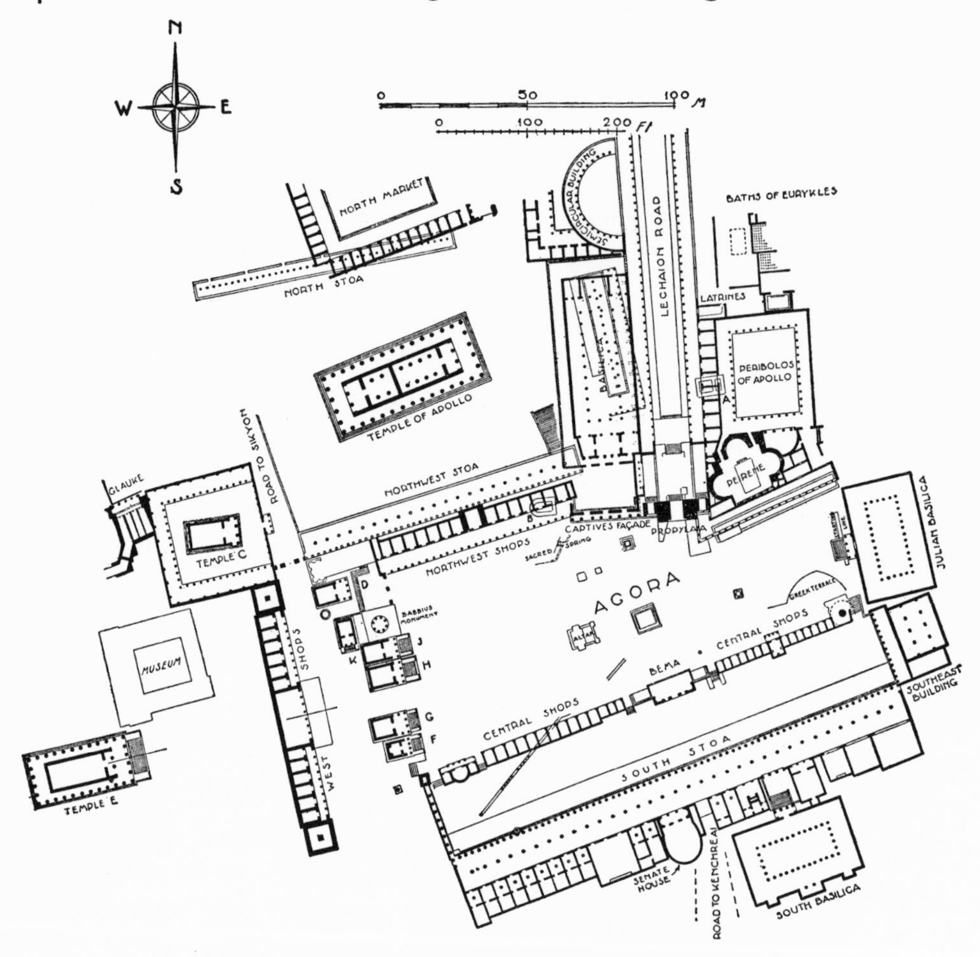

FIG. 9. CORINTH. PLAN OF THE CENTRAL AREA
Courtesy American School of Classical Studies at Athens

the stoa was essential in enclosing the area of the agora and in setting it off from the residential parts of Corinth, although the connecting road to the harbor cut through it.

Sometimes the incoming streets were distinctly separated from the agora by gates or by the continuation of the porticoes which framed the agora. These porticoes were by no means confined to the agora proper. At the end of the fourth century B.C., the main streets of Miletus, Ephesus, and Antioch, for instance, were also framed by porticoes, probably lit at night just as the colonnaded streets of Bologna and Turin in Italy or the Rue de Rivoli in Paris are today. These *viae tectae* became quite general later on, especially in the Roman East.

In most post-Hippodamic and Hellenistic towns in Greece and Asia Minor, and in other Greek colonies around the Mediterranean of which Priene, Miletus, Magnesia, and Cnidus are the most typical, stoa, porticoes, and tangential location of the streets can be reconstructed. The basic scheme of the gridiron and integrated agora, "closely knit into the fabric of the city," remained relatively constant, with only small changes and variations until the influence of Roman colonization made itself felt and led to a new form of spatial organization.

Occasionally topographical conditions led to the construction of steps in order to overcome differences in level, and in this way the open area was subdivided.

Some few individual agoras, however, developed quite differently, dependent on the number of archaic structures still extant in Hellenistic times. These structures remained unchanged out of respect for tradition, or they were removed and rebuilt at a new location; sometimes they were razed and their remnants used as building materials for new edifices or—still worse——for fortifications.

As one example of such a development, the most famous, the agora of Athens (Fig. 10), may be discussed here. More than two centuries had elapsed before the Periclean agora was changed essentially. When the Metroon was rebuilt in Hellenistic times, this new construction had more architectural than spatial importance. For the direction of the main public buildings below the Hephaestian hill, namely the fifth-century Tholos, Metroon, Bouleuterion, and Stoa of Zeus, remained unchanged, nor could the Panathenaean Way be shifted from its oblique direction. Around the middle of the second century B.C., the so-called Middle Stoa was erected, subdividing the whole agora into the larger principal public square and the smaller commercial one. This regularizing development was continued by the erection of the Stoa of Attalus (*ca.* 150 B.C.), rectangular to the Middle Stoa, with twenty-one shops on each of its two floors. Individual monuments were interspersed in the free space and probably trees were planted in order to conceal discrepancies in direction stemming from earlier structures. It was this scheme into which the later Roman additions like the Odeion (see p. 52) were fitted

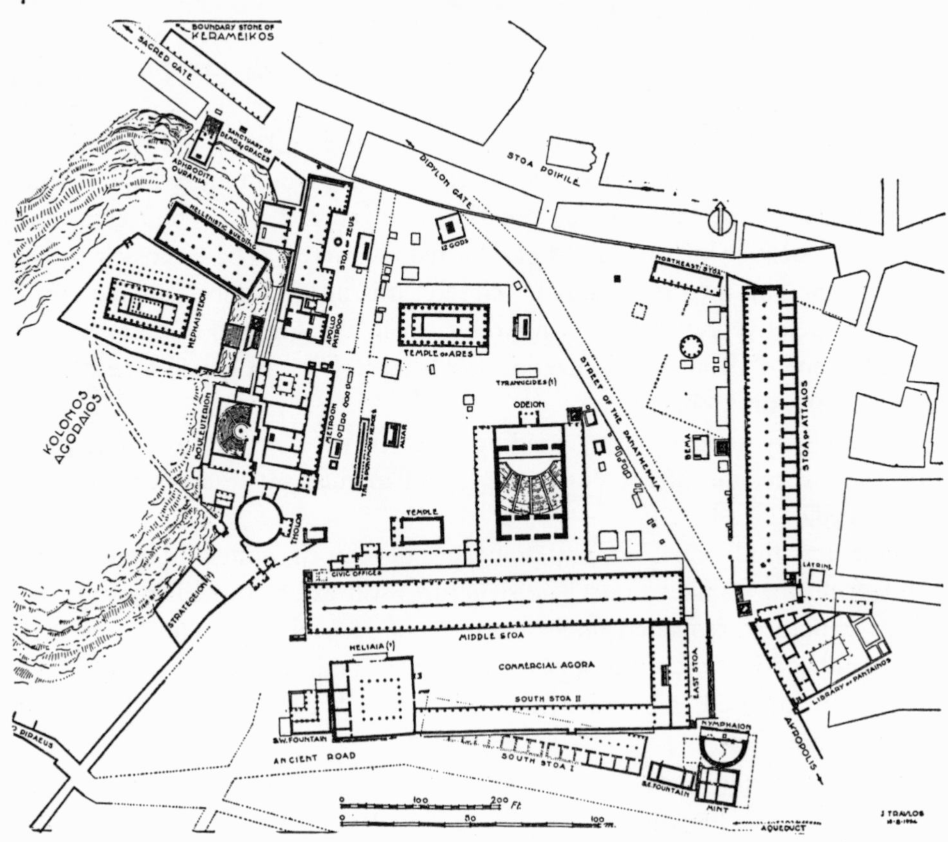

FIG. 10. ATHENS. PLAN OF THE ANCIENT AGORA
Drawing by J. Travlos; courtesy American School of Classical Studies at Athens

in the attempt at a still more closed appearance of the area. However, even so the agora could never become a regular square in the Hellenistic sense and still less so in the Roman concept. The direction of the Panathenaean Way and of the line of buildings from the Tholos to the Stoa of Zeus would have destroyed all attempts at axial integration, as would have the other streets traversing the agora. The tremendous differences in level made the task of regularization still more difficult.

The agora on the hill of the acropolis of Pergamum (Fig. 11) is not typical for a Hellenistic town. The original plan of the acropolis as a whole was quite irregular, although it was founded rather late by Attalid kings, at the end of the fourth and in the third century B.C. Its scheme, from the then prevailing Hellenistic viewpoint extremely irrational, was actually dictated by its location on steep and irregular slopes. The idea of a basic radial pattern, allegedly stemming from Hippodamus, is preposterous since such a theoretical scheme certainly never existed. However, within the fanlike organization of the whole specific spatial units were geometrized—somewhat less in the lower

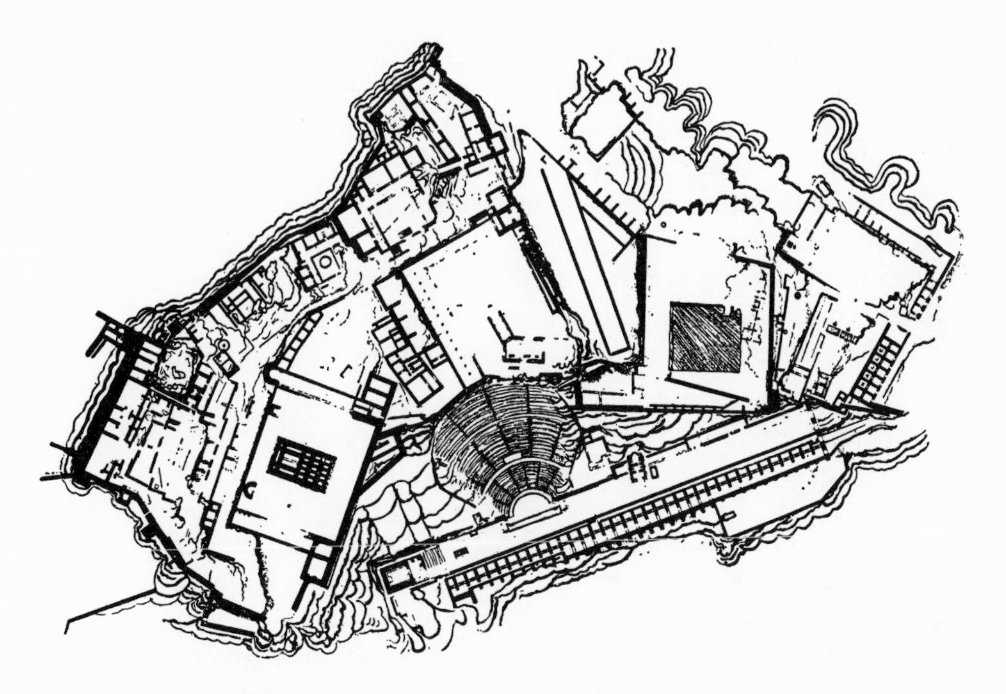

FIG. 11. PERGAMUM. PLAN OF THE ACROPOLIS, AGORA, AND THEATER
From Conze, *Die Ergebnisse der Ausgrabungen zu Pergamon*

town, in the residential quarters; somewhat more so on the acropolis. This partial regularization within an irregular overall plan expresses clearly the real tendencies of the period toward regularity—so far as it was possible to realize them under the given topographical circumstances. In the second century B.C., Attalus I and King Eumenes tried to eliminate some irregularities and to balance the overall picture. The squares were organized in angular connection so far as topographically possible. Terraces in front of the temple of Athena Nikephoras, the grandiose Pergamum Altar, and other structures were newly erected for this purpose. Almost all earlier temples were now surrounded by colonnades, like the Zeus Altar itself. The location of the wide terrace before the theater with the small temple of Dionysus, elevated by many steps, proves, as numerous other architectural devices do, that not only specific spatial effects were considered in this second-century scheme of the acropolis but that also the *bella vista*, the landscape background, was viewed as an essential element of the aesthetic effect. Short axes—converging because of topographical reasons—are recognizable, and quite obviously the spectator should comprehend large groups of buildings and the squares in between as a whole. What a contrast between such an essentially spatial impression, even if not based on complete regularity, and the sculptural effects of individual, isolated structures on the Athenian acropolis! While in the lower city of Pergamum the single smaller agoras were not yet quite regular, the groups of squares on the acropolis appear now as definite spatial units, individually as well as in combination. The overall organization, in spite of all later geometrizing regularizations and enlargements, seems to have grown out of the landscape, in no way artificial, without any spatial tensions.

THE HIPPODAMIC AND HELLENISTIC CONCEPTS OF EXTERNAL SPACE

Now, finally, in Hellenistic times, the agora had become an almost unified structure. Public buildings, temples around the agora, and occasionally a temple on it are no longer spatially isolated but are anchored in some system of mutual reference, as are the stoas and porticoes, each structure thus becoming part of a whole. And this development from archaic irregularity to Hellenistic order means simultaneously the change from open space to an almost completely closed spatial unit. Planned location, related proportions, and the repetitive rhythm of the porticoes had brought about this amalgamation.

The shape of the free open space, the form of the three-dimensional void, was, however, not yet felt as absolute form but rather as a by-product. Even in Hellenistic times the Greeks had no immediate interest in space form as such. Their interest in group design beyond the individual structure was concentrated on the relation of masses to each other, i.e., in volume. Structure, architecturally clearly defined in three dimensions, had not yet found an aesthetic counterpoint in the articulation of space. Space proper simply did not exist aesthetically. The intrinsic problem of Greek city planning was rather the fusion of abstract (geometrically controlled) volumes with whatever were the given local conditions. The creation of space, consciously handled and molded as such by three-dimensional design as the primary and decisive task of the planner, was achieved by the Romans, in architecture and in city planning alike. To the Greeks, space meant only a medium to define and set off the shaped volume—sculpture as well as the individual architectural structure. Even late Hellenism still thought and created in tectonic-plastic terms.

ROMAN TOWNS AND THEIR FORA

Throughout the nineteenth century, Roman art was generally widely underrated; measured by standards of the Greeks, it was considered essentially a deterioration or a meager copy. This concept led to the slogan of the "artistic" Greeks and the "practical," rational Romans. Meanwhile, this gross injustice has been remedied, and it is acknowledged today that in architecture as well as in sculpture the Romans created entirely new and original artistic values, although taking over the artistic vocabulary of the Greeks. In Roman sculpture, there are the sepulchral figures and naturalistic portrait busts to which no counterparts exist in Greek art; in architecture, the basilica, the triumphal arch, the public bath, etc., possible only through the introduction of arch, vault, and dome. This development may be traced partially to the survival of Terramara and Etruscan elements or it may be based on a general tendency toward functional expression.

However, these two explanations do not suffice for an understanding of the decisive new element which the Romans—and they alone—contributed to the development of architecture and city planning: the feeling for the shape of the void space, for its artistic meaning, and for its modification by specific proportions and by a superhuman scale. The Greeks on their part were unique in their feeling for tactile organic forms, in their sense for the proportions of volume and for the relative scale in reference to the human figure. And this basic distinction between Greece and Rome manifests itself in the difference between Greek post-Hippodamic and Roman city planning, evident especially where the greatest possibility of spatial expression is given: in the center of the town, in the forum, or in the sequence of fora.

The characteristic forms of agora and forum differ much more than the *overall layouts* of Greek post-Hippodamic and Roman towns, which at least share the gridiron scheme.

HISTORICAL ROOTS. The historical roots of the typical Roman forum probably go back to three successive sources: to the settlements of the Terramara civilization, to Etruscan towns, and to the military camp, the Roman castrum. The

FIG. 12. ROMAN CASTRUM. PLAN

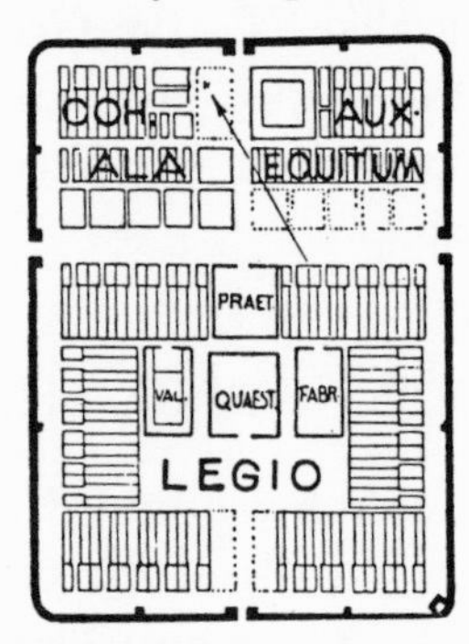

Terramara civilization in northern Italy stems from the Neolithic and Bronze Ages. The remainders of its villages exist today in the form of rather regular mounds; they may also have been lake dwellings (*Pfahldörfer*). The Terramare di Castellazzo shows a typical gridiron layout of five smaller streets in one direction and seven larger streets crossing at an angle of 90°, obviously anticipating the Roman castrum in which the crossing of the two main roads comes close to the later crossing of *cardo* and *decumanus*. The whole was encircled by moat and wall, and, very important for the later development, there was also a free area in the center, probably encircled by another moat and wall, destined for sacrifices for some unknown rites. Thus this space represents in its form the nucleus of the later Roman forum, while in its meaning it would correspond—though on a more primitive level—rather to the sacred Helladic acropolis.

The later Etruscan civilization shows a similar four-part gridiron scheme. Whether it had derived from the much earlier Terramara settlements is still an open question. At any rate, the Etruscans, from the eighth to the end of the fourth century B.C., preferred high hills and the crests of mountains as locations for their towns. Religious laws dictated the inner structure as well as the nowadays sometimes questioned regularity of the periphery of their settlements, founded under observation of sacred rites. Marzobotto, for instance, already in the sixth century B.C. anticipated in its layout what in the Roman castrum would become the two axes, *cardo* and *decumanus*, and also, at their crossing point, a small quadrangular area.

Functionally the layout of the castrum (Fig. 12) was regulated by the military needs of conquering armies. From provisional camps the scheme was taken over for the so-called *castra stativa*, which with their permanent fortifications were erected along the expanding frontiers. And it was from these that the newly founded Roman towns developed, besides those which grew out of previous villages. Polybius, the Greek historian of the second century B.C., and Hyginus Gromaticus, a Latin geographer, surveyor, and agriculturist of the early second century A.D., describe exactly the standard layout of the castrum town and its foundation (inauguration, limitation, orientation, and consecration).

Whether the measurements and proportions of the castrum were based on certain mathematical relations and the use of sacred numbers, as Pliny the Elder in the first century A.D. mystically hints at, is still an archaeological problem. At any rate, the sacramental laws were considered of utmost importance for the future of the castrum or the newly founded community. As in Etruscan settlements, *decumanus maximus* and *cardo maximus* were the basic streets. Secondary streets ran into them at an angle of 90°, creating *insulae* or blocks of different proportions. Again we encounter free space, the *templum* at the intersection of the *via principalis* (*cardo maximus*) and *decumanus maximus*, and here is where the *principia*, the main buildings for military administration, were located. The periphery was regular, almost always rectangular, fortified by entrance gates, and was established, as mentioned before, under observation of elaborate religious ceremonies.

THE ROMAN TOWN. From the very beginning the Roman town in its layout followed clearly and exclusively the castrum scheme, which differed from the Hippodamic by the above-mentioned traits. This is all the more strange because Roman expansion began with the end of the sixth century B.C., and the time interval between this period and the Greek colonization in Italy, employing the Hippodamic scheme, was not too long. But from the very beginning the difference in planning was marked.

Although the rectangular crossing of two main streets is also encountered in many Greek Hippodamic towns, their layouts nevertheless differ decisively from the Roman-Etruscan scheme. The main characteristics by which the Roman town is distinguished from the Greek post-Hippodamic gridiron scheme, and which continue throughout Roman history from Republican times to the Imperial foundations, are:

1. the axes *cardo* and *decumanus;*
2. emphasis on the void area at the intersection;
3. axial location of main buildings and square proper in contrast to the lateral location in the Hellenistic town;
4. mostly, though not always, a quadrangular periphery of the settlement, clearly set off from the surrounding landscape, contrary to the transition from town to the landscape as usual in Greece.

In many towns of Roman origin, inside and outside of Italy, the original layout of town and forum is recognizable without any excavations. The buildings may have been changed but not the plan. Of all the ancient Italian towns still important today, Turin probably shows the Roman layout most clearly. It already existed as a settlement in the third century B.C. and was fortified before 218 B.C.; in A.D. 27 it became a veterans' colony. These mere dates show the close relation between the town plan and the Roman castrum out of which it developed. And this scheme with its *cardo* and *decumanus* did not change till the sixteenth century and is still evident today (see pp. 159–60). It was only when Turin became the capital of the dukedom of Savoy that the citadel was laid out and new quarters with their own independent gridiron scheme were added (Pl. 5B). After Turin, probably the towns of Piacenza, Aosta, and Verona reveal layouts in which the Roman scheme is still most clearly recognizable.

The enormous power, strength, and vitality of the Roman Empire were mirrored equally in its military system, in its centralized administration and government, in the *Corpus Romanum*, and in the numberless foundations of towns everywhere. Not only France, England, Germany, Switzerland, and Austria, but also Spain, Portugal, and the Balkan countries are studded with Roman foundations, identifiable as such because their layouts are still preserved in one form or another or because of excavations. An enumeration of Roman foundations through Europe, in Asia Minor, and along the North African shores would mean almost an index of the most important places of Western civilization today. Some examples will be discussed in connection with medieval settlements based on Roman foundations (see p. 67). Actually there existed so many of these Roman settlements that from about the seventh century A.D. to the end of the twelfth century hardly any new towns were founded in Europe, but only some of the more or less dilapidated Roman foundations were partially restored.

THE FORUM. These few general remarks about Terramara and Etruscan settlements, about the castrum, and about their influence on the Roman town as a whole were necessary in order to understand the development of its nucleus, the forum.

The Forum Romanum (Pls. 7–8), of course, is as little typical for the majority of Roman fora as is the agora of Athens for the Greek agora. Its foundation goes back to the earliest time of the Republic, when the original swamp between the Capitoline, the Esquiline, and the Palatine hills was drained. Legend places the dates of some of its buildings very early. The depression between the hills had been a burial place before the seventh century B.C.; then it was built over by dwellings till the beginning of the sixth century B.C. when seemingly the first public buildings were erected. It is known that the temples of Saturn and Castor stem from the fifth century B.C. and that the *curia*, the *comitium*, the *carcer Mamertinus*, the first *rostrum*, and many wooden shops existed from the very beginning. The forum then served both public and commercial purposes, and the sacred temples were surrounded by taverns and simple market stands. This combination of functions was gradually changed and the forum became more and more public domain. Now the people no longer gathered on the *comitium* for political meetings but on the forum proper, which with its many structures still was completely irregular, owing to its gradual growth through preceding centuries.

Only in the second century B.C. were basilicas erected (Basilica Porcia, 184 B.C.; Basilica Aurelia, 179 B.C., both later restored by Augustus). The great change from the earlier irregularity, however, came about in the first century B.C. through the erection of the Basilica Julia, begun by Caesar, and through his second *rostrum*. Although the complete axiality and the closed form of the newly built Roman fora of the first century B.C. and later centuries were never achieved at the Forum Romanum, at least some axial relations between the old and the new *rostrum* and the Templum Divi Julii were established (Fig. 13). The almost parallel location of the two great basilicas lent to the forum an appearance which corresponded more closely to the spatial order of Imperial Rome. The old shops and taverns stayed in existence, but were pushed into the background by the porticoes which accompanied the front of the Basilica Aemilia and lay behind the Basilica Julia.

The Forum Romanum had become the sacred area of Rome, comparable in function and in representative appearance to Greek acropolises, to late Hellenistic agoras, and to the new Roman fora of this period. It was definitely distinguished from specialized commercial fora in Rome like the *forum bovarium*, *forum vinarium*, *forum piscatorium*, etc.

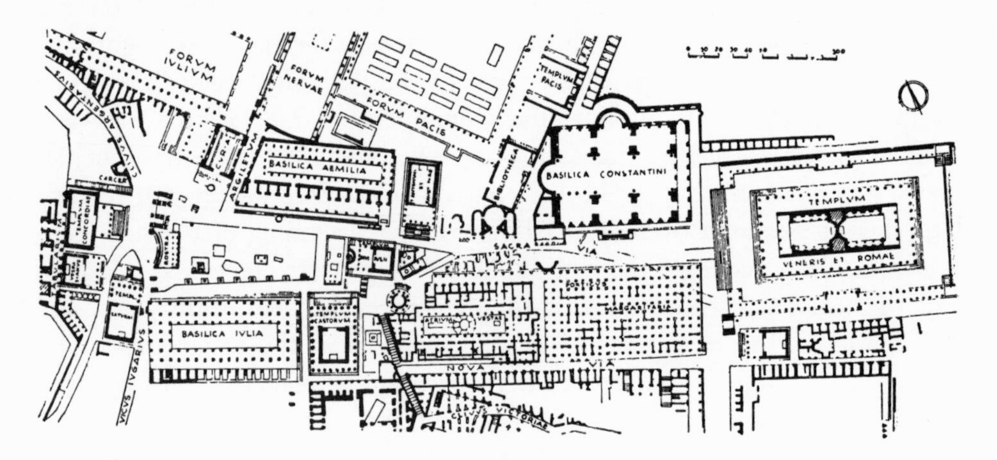

FIG. 13. ROME. FORUM ROMANUM. PLAN

More typical than the Forum Romanum is the forum in Pompeii as it has been excavated after its destruction in A.D. 79 (Pl. 9). Almost equally as old, it had already been developed in the sixth century B.C.—from what was originally a long extended area in Etruscan times. But when under Sulla Pompeii became a settlement for his veterans, around 80 B.C., the layout of the forum was regularized. Older temples and new ones alike, as well as adjacent markets, basilicas, and other buildings, were separated from the free area through two-storied porticoes which surrounded the forum on three sides and concealed the individual structures. The temple of Jupiter dominated the whole space, which was closed against all vehicular traffic. The colonnades also covered the few entrances to the streets. Thus the forum proper was reserved only for public representation. The whole organization became a completely closed square, axial, dominated by the temple, and kept together by porticoes—a perfect solution of a Roman forum.

As typical as Pompeii is for the first centuries B.C. and A.D., so Ostia is for the period from the first to the fourth century A.D. From the viewpoint of town planning, the excavations there are still more interesting than those of Pompeii. Already founded in the seventh century B.C., Ostia, as Rome's harbor and in Imperial times especially as its storehouse for grain, increased continually in importance. Quite obviously there was no need for a sequence of Imperial Fora as in Rome, no desire for the glorification of the state or of the respective emperors—after all, it was just a provincial town of about 70,000 inhabitants and not the metropolis. Thus, when the town was partially built anew at the end of the first century A.D. and from then on into the fourth century, all squares were destined predominantly for practical purposes. The levels of the successive stages vary; the last is five feet above that of the Republican old town. The backbone of the town was, as everywhere, the old *decumanus*. The fora were dispersed over the whole town and were connected by rather broad streets; they were situated before individual temples, or had temples erected on them. All of the fora were rectangular, and they were mostly surrounded by porticoes. The most interesting forum is purely commercial. It is the so-called *piazza dei corporazione*, around which are located the agencies of various shipping lines, export and import houses, indicated by beautiful mosaics with ship designs, symbols of Africa, etc., on the pavement. The layout is probably typical for the splendor of public squares in the great commercial centers all over the Roman Empire, when the worldly business of intercontinental traffic and commerce competed with the glorification of the gods in importance for the town. The true public forum located at the intersection of *cardo* and *decumanus* was dominated by the Templum Vulcani. Opposite the Capitol lay the large Templum Romae and Augusti, on the other sides were a portico and a basilica—all elements in strict axial organization around the square. Smaller courtyards, surrounded by shops, supplemented the main squares.

It is characteristic of Roman cities that with the decline of the Empire the feeling for strict regularity and the desire for the architectural limitation of a closed square also declined. For instance, in Byzantium (Constantinople) the Forum Constantini, built in the fourth century A.D., was no longer barred to vehicular traffic, as had been the large fora of earlier centuries. The main street here cut straight through the forum, as did probably other streets also, and in its center the statue of Constantine was erected. In spite of its surrounding two-storied porticoes, the Byzantine forum no longer represented an isolated space, firmly shaped—what had been the ideal of the previous Roman centuries.

The Romans' attempts to regularize earlier Greek agoras and to change them according to their own taste provide an extremely interesting chapter in the history of agora and forum. Thus we must turn back again to the archaic and Hellenistic agora in Athens (see pp. 32, 41), which had already undergone so many changes. After the attempt at an almost regular Hellenistic scheme in the second century B.C., the Romans, from Caesar on, continued the system by locating all new structures correspondingly. Two of these structures stand out as decisive in this respect, although they are somewhat incongruous: the Temple of Ares and the Odeion. The first was actually a building of the fifth century B.C., removed from its original location on the agora and rebuilt around A.D. 100 with its long sides almost exactly parallel to the Middle Stoa, which was the basic structure in the organization of the new scheme. The Odeion, on the other hand, built by Agrippa, the son-in-law of Augustus, at the end of the first century A.D. and altered in the second century A.D., was placed just halfway between the Stoa of Attalus and the Metroon, in strict axiality in reference to the Middle and South Stoas. And yet the impression of a Roman closed square was not achieved. The Odeion was much too large in proportion to existing buildings and monuments, and actually filled the small open space which had still remained on the agora; however, it could not become the "dominating" structure of the square because there were too many others.

The so-called Roman agora in Athens, a new foundation of the first century A.D., shows what the Romans were able to achieve when they were free on virgin soil. A rectangular area is surrounded on all sides by an Ionic portico with shops on one side. The center, the open space, lies two steps lower than the portico proper. If anywhere at all, one may speak here of a peristyle-like square with a large gate in the central axis of the west side—closed like the squares in Ostia and the Pompeian forum—an ideal realization of the Roman concept of space.

On a smaller scale, Delos is another example of the intrusion of Roman ideas into Greece. Originally one of the holiest shrines of Apollo, the sanctuary eventually became a free port under Athenian government and with it a center of commerce. The archaic sanctuary is, of course, completely irregular, the individual temples in their orientation entirely independent from each other. Even the later Hellenistic stoas, one of them built by Philip V of Macedonia around 200 B.C., and a Roman quarter of the third century B.C. at the slope of the theater hill are without any spatial context in their location and without any tectonic ties.

The later Roman sections of Delos contrast decisively with this environment. The Roman agora, the so-called agora of the Italians, connected with the sacred area in the north, was a bazaar-like square built by a corporation of Roman merchants in 97 B.C. Amounting almost to an interior court, this square was rectangular in shape and had shops and magazines on two sides; its center probably contained a small temple of Venus and Apollo. With the addition of this square a completely new motif invaded the Greek town: the closed, rectangular, typical Roman forum with Doric porticoes on the sides, and shops, workshops, etc., behind them. In contrast to other Roman fora, there was in Delos no regular street system into which the forum could have been integrated. In this environment the Roman agora represents a completely alien body. Nowhere else is the contrast between Greek concepts and the Roman desire for a shaped spatial order more apparent.

In larger towns, as, for instance, in Rome proper, smaller market squares supplemented the central one and a definite specialization developed between the *fora civilia* (civic centers) or *fora iudicaria*, which functionally corresponded somewhat to the Greek acropolis, and the *fora venalia* (markets), such as the *forum bovarium* for meat, the *forum piscatorium* for fish, and the *forum olitorium* or vegetable market.

SPECIFIC ARCHITECTURAL ELEMENTS OF THE FORUM. In the preceding pages there has been frequent mention of basilicas, porticoes, and the relation between streets and fora. Perhaps some specific remarks about these architectural elements would not be out of place here.

The structural type of the *basilica* was definitely Roman. Its origin still remains one of the great archaeological problems of today. The basilica served as administrative building, as court of justice, and as market hall; its aisles sometimes also served as a public promenade. In Imperial times its axis was parallel to the main direction of the open space of the forum. Generally, the relation of the basilica to the forum corresponded to that of the Hellenistic temple and its courtyard to the agora. This relation made the basilica almost more important as an element of town planning than as an independent piece of architecture.

Porticoes were not only an essential architectural element of the basilica but were also erected in Roman towns in their own right. Without any doubt, their use was stimulated by Hellenistic Ionian architecture. In Rome they were attached to the aforementioned basilicas or other public buildings or were at least part of them. In their totality, they served to tie together heterogeneous edifices and to carry through an axial composition. They formalized previous irregularities and usually covered the entrances of the streets which led to the forum. The uninterrupted continuation of these porticoes concealed the transition from street to square. Since in later times the *forum iudicarium* served essentially as a place of public representation and was no longer meant as a public promenade, easy access from street to forum was not necessary and was often sacrificed for the sake of monumental unity, e.g., in Pompeii. While in post-Hippodamic and Hellenistic towns the streets ran tangentially to the agora, the Roman *decumanus* cut into the center of the forum. Both *cardo* and *decumanus*, from about the second century B.C., were architecturally developed as main axes which led to prominent buildings. Their ends were often emphasized by monumental gates as parts of the porticoes.

Also, porticoes often stretched into the main streets, and in these instances streets and fora represented elements of one integrated plan. Porticoes with Ionic or Corinthian columns along the streets (*viae porticatae* or *viae tectae*) played a greater part in Roman towns than in earlier Hellenistic layouts.

In Republican times the streets were usually about 6 yards wide; later they broadened until, in Imperial times, they had an average width of 15 to 25 yards for the main streets and 4 to 7 yards for secondary streets (e.g., in Pompeii, main streets are mostly 10 yards wide, the side streets 5 yards). But all these measurements were variable, so that, for instance, Hyginus Gromaticus gives smaller sizes. During the last centuries of the Empire, street porticoes were especially magnificent in the Eastern provinces and in Africa, in towns such as Alexandria, Carthage, Antioch, Damascus, Gerasa, Seleucia, and particularly in Palmyra and Timgad. In Gerasa, an old settlement which had become a Roman town in 64 B.C., the crossing of *cardo* and *decumanus* was developed into a circular plaza with four monumental piers surrounded by curved façades. In Palmyra (Fig. 14), founded in A.D. 116, the main street, 3,500 feet long, was 69 feet wide. The open road of 37 feet was framed by porticoes, each 16 feet wide, supported by 454 columns, 31 feet high, with an entablature of 7 feet. In Timgad (Pl. 10), a Roman settlement built by Trajan around 100 B.C. for veterans, with a very regular forum taking up 4 blocks, the porticoes framed only the individual blocks and were

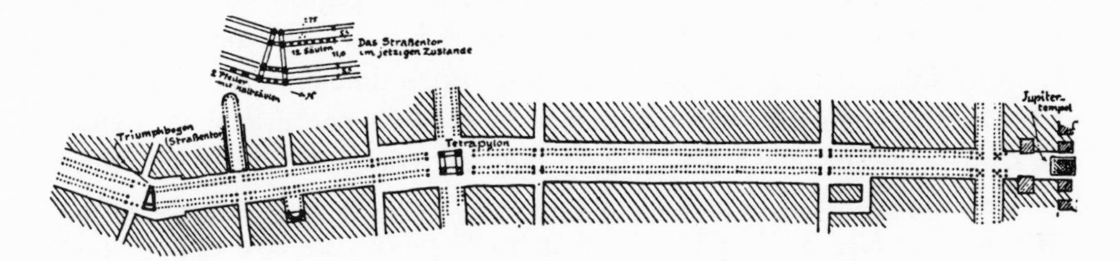

FIG. 14. PALMYRA. PLAN OF THE MAIN STREET
After Cassas, *Voyage pittoresque de la Syrie, de la Phénicie . . .*

not continuous but were interrupted by crossing secondary streets. Behind the porticoes were shops and the entrances to apartments, similar to those still so clearly visible in the streets of Ostia, a well as those in later times in Bologna, Turin, Bolzano, and other places. The blocks or *insulae* were rectangular, three stories high. Already in Republican times their size, about 110 x 480 feet, was based on the ancient Roman agricultural measure, the *jugerum*.

IMPERIAL FORA. In towns where many fora existed—and that applies to the majority of the larger cities during the last centuries of the Roman Empire—the connection and combination of the individual fora depended, of course, a great deal on specific topographical conditions and on the interval between the growth of the original forum and the development of the later ones. To mention some examples: in Delos, the ancient agora and the Roman agora ("agora of the Italians") were not connected at all. In Athens, the ancient agora and the much later Roman agora were connected by a passageway with a monumental arch; in Petra, two fora lay side by side.

The Roman ideal of the Imperial centuries, however, was always the axial connection, and its most grandiose realization was the Imperial Fora where the spatial and special unity of each square is absolutely preserved, but at the same time each individual forum becomes a link of an axial sequence.

There, on the Imperial Fora, such spatial impressions were achieved as corresponded to the aesthetic needs of the Romans of Imperial times, of the period in which Roman art actually came into its own. In spite of all attempts during the first century B.C. to straighten out and to regularize the irregular appearance of the Forum Romanum through the erection of the Basilica Aemilia, the Basilica Julia, and the Templum Divi Augusti with their porticoes, too many older sacred buildings and shrines still remained to effect the spatial integration of the whole. From Caesar's time on, the combination of Hellenistic architectural forms and strict axial Roman discipline resulted in a spatial concept which was *entirely different* from even the most regular late Hellenistic squares. The sequence of symmetrically closed space units is *Italic and not Greek.*[5] If this statement needs proof, the two most regular Hellenistic squares need only be recalled: the agoras of Miletus and Kos (see pp. 38–39). In Kos, the colonnaded wings are of different lengths, while the Roman Imperial Fora are strictly symmetrical as to direction and expansion of the framing porticoes. In Miletus, the horseshoe embraces only the sanctuary, and the temple does not dominate the square in the same way as do the temples in the Roman Imperial Fora.

The first of the Roman Imperial Fora (Fig. 15), the Forum Caesaris, was begun by Caesar who, besides his other qualities and merits, had the vision of a genuine city planner. It was completed under Augustus. Its construction was originally caused by the lack of space on the Forum Romanum proper. It was connected with the area behind Caesar's *curia*, itself in loose connection with the Forum Romanum. Double colonnades with taverns surrounded it. The temple of Venus Genetrix, consecrated in 46 B.C., was located at the rim of its rectangle, its walls exactly parallel to the colonnades. Additional shops which accompanied the temple on its left side were added by Trajan. The Forum Caesaris with its rigid axial symmetry became the starting point for the whole development, since the Imperial Fora dovetailed into each other.

The second Imperial Forum was built by Augustus at an angle of 90° to the Forum Caesaris and likewise was surrounded by colonnades. On its small northeastern side the large temple of Mars Ultor was erected. The position of this temple and of the temple of Venus Genetrix on the Forum Caesaris

[5] E. Gjerstad, *Die Ursprungsgeschichte der roemischen Kaiserfora* (Opuscula Archaeologica 3, 1944), believes that the Hellenistic towns and their Oriental precursors are the decisive influence on the Augustan and post-Augustan fora.

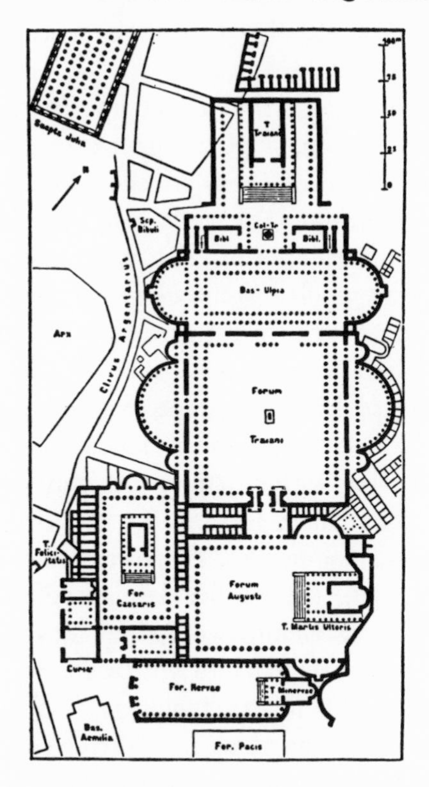

FIG. 15. ROME. IMPERIAL FORA. PLAN

From Borrmann, *Geschichte der Baukunst*

in relation to the open void of their respective squares is noteworthy. However, the squares do not yet represent "dominated" squares in the sense that some parvises in the Middle Ages do. Nor, on the other hand, are the structures protruding into the square, or subordinated to it. Two large apsides (*exedrae*) broaden the area around the temple but cannot be perceived from the forum proper, since they are located behind the colonnades.

Parallel to the Forum Augusti lies the Forum Nervae or Forum Transitorium, begun by Domitian and completed by Nerva, with the temple of Minerva on one of its small sides. It actually represents not much more than a glorified colonnaded street as developed so magnificently in the Eastern Roman provinces from the first century on. Its byname, Forum Transitorium, defines exactly its function as a connecting link between the Forum Augusti and the Templum (later Forum) Pacis or Forum Vespasiani, preserving an earlier thoroughfare. Consequently the Forum Nervae with its small width is not framed by colonnades but merely by rows of attached columns with entablatures. It would be misleading to interpret any spatial meaning into this area.

The adjacent Forum Vespasiani, originally the Templum Pacis, built simultaneously with the Forum Transitorium, appears again as a genuine square, surrounded by colonnades, one side of them attached to the wall which it shares with the Forum Transitorium. The very small temple, the Templum Pacis proper, is hidden by the colonnades and its volume in no way affects the spatial impression of the whole. Archaeologists may decide whether the free area was actually planted as a formal garden.

The last of the five Imperial Fora, the Forum Traiani (A.D. 111–14) (Pls. 11–12), built allegedly by Apollodorus of Damascus, represents the definite triumph of the Roman spatial concept based on absolute axiality and symmetry. It consists of an enormous free area with an equestrian statue of the emperor in its center, surrounded by colonnades. It is enlarged by two symmetrically located *exedrae* behind these colonnades. Opposite the slightly curved entrance from the Forum Augusti, the Basilica Ulpia confines the space in a corresponding scale, with five aisles and two apsides. Beyond the basilica, the main axis of the forum is continued into an *exedra* with the column of Trajan, framed on both sides by library buildings from whose upper stories the reliefs of the column could be viewed. In direct continuation of the axis starting from the Forum Augusti, Emperor Hadrian later erected the Templum Divi Traiani as the terminus of these integrated squares. The whole area is *one* spatial unit, open in the forum and covered in the Basilica Ulpia, and is planned for successive visual perception.

It is true that the dovetailing of all these spatial units can be completely conceived only in the two-dimensional ground plan, as is the case with the utopian patterns of ideal cities devised by the theoreticians of the Renaissance (see p. 100). But no ground plan can convey the spatial cogency of the whole complex of the Imperial Fora. The absolute dimensions take on such superhuman scale that space becomes almost something palpable. The successive vistas in actual three-dimensionality must be conquered by walking around, the same way as the interior space of the great public baths or the interior rooms of the palace of Diocletian in Spalato may be experienced.

But all this does not mean that the open space of the forum is subordinated to the covered space of the basilica as a kind of gigantic parvis. On the contrary—a comparison of the mere dimensions proves that the open space of the Forum Traiani in connection with the open area of the Forum Augusti is the dominating motif. Only in this way can the purpose of all of these successive tremendous expanses be grasped.

The architecture of the individual structures surrounding the fora, seen from the outside, is much too heterogeneous in volume and proportion to be considered as an element of a higher, "super-foral" architectural order, and to be appreciated as a whole, as volume. The horizontal motif of the porticoes connects the individual units inside. These porticoes have the sole function of framing and regularizing the void—they are not part of any independent volume-architecture. The spatial unification of the squares is increased through this common motif of the porticoes. The symmetry of each individual layout in reference to one common axis was the second most important factor in increasing spatial unification, and last but not least was the seclusion of the regular, architecturally framed space from the web of the neighboring streets. The external appearance of these fora from the streets outside was architecturally neglected and considered unessential. For topographical reasons all the fora could hardly be perceived together, a further symptom that now the closed space and not the volume of any architectural structure was the main objective of artistic creation. In spite of the intimate inner integration of all the squares, there occurs nevertheless one change in the aesthetic approach from Caesar to Trajan: in the Forum Caesaris the temple still represents the main motif whereas in the Forum Traiani—about 150 years later—the buildings, the Basilica Ulpia and later the temple of Trajan, are merely parts of the architectural frame of the open space.

It is astonishing that Vitruvius, who after all wrote at the time of the construction of the Imperial Fora, was hardly conscious of the contemporaneous artistic evolution which they demonstrated. Obviously the rational mentality of the Romans allowed a most explicit elaboration of actual facts, measurements, and data, but was not interested in the development of any purely aesthetic theories. When Vitruvius in the same chapter deals with fora and with public buildings, it proves that he considers both equally as architectural archetypes. In his books IV and V, he gives some details about the fora proper. Their size should be always in relation to the size of the population. As an ideal proportion of the sides he suggests 3 to 2. The center should remain free, and the *curia* and other municipal buildings should be immediately adjacent, the prison close to them. For Vitruvius the location of the forum within the town was obviously a matter of course, only for harbor towns he recommends a site near the port. All his other suggestions for city planning merely concern matters of hygiene, climate, the direction of prevailing winds, and certain general functional needs.

THE ROMAN CONCEPT OF EXTERNAL SPACE

Contrary to Greece, the general layout of Roman towns and the form of their civic centers are inseparably integrated—an analogy to the centralized system of the state and the concept of strict order which pervaded Roman communal life in general. Since the pattern of the whole town was axial, even to some degree symmetrical, the center was emphasized as the controlling factor in the creation of the visual appearance of a town. And if already in Hellenistic times a certain feeling for space developed, only in Rome did it crystallize into the very definite concept of the square as a spatial unit within distinct borders. The intersection of the main streets at the center became the prime element of planning through the consciously aesthetic treatment of space. Consequently, this central area was much less interspersed with statues, altars, and shrines than it had been on the Greek agora. However, there were exceptions to this rule, of which the best known is the Forum Romanum itself with its sacred architectural relics.

In summary, the ground plan of a forum was in principle rectangular, but was occasionally adapted to local conditions, dependent in each instance on the importance of already existing buildings. Oval and circular layouts as in Gerasa and Antinoe (Antinoöpolis), founded in Egypt in A.D. 132 by Hadrian in memory of Antinous, are great exceptions.

The distinction between temple fora, basilica fora, and peristyle fora with regular porticoes on all four sides is self-explanatory and depends on the type of structure which contributes most decisively to the visual appearance of the forum. But in each instance the final artistic goal is the same: to create a clearly defined shape of the void, i.e., space. If Oswald Spengler believes that "swaggering in spatial dimensions is always a symptom of decadent civilizations," he misunderstands completely the meaning of this change in emphasis from volume to space. It is impossible to speak of "swaggering" when one of the most important characteristics of Roman architecture and city planning was the limitation of space, which per se, of course, is limitless. The limitation of space is absolutely necessary in order to give aesthetic substance to it—and the Romans were fully aware of that. They achieved this limitation in a twofold manner: space was closed by surrounding vertical planes, the combination of porticoes and edifices. It was opened by the introduction of the axis. These axes created perspectives which extended through the rhythmical sequences of colonnades, carried through toward a monumental stop. Triumphal arches occasionally served merely as a kind of break of this visual movement into depth.

The Greeks had no feeling for such channeling of vistas. They were interested in unlimited views with the landscape as background, as, for instance, at the acropolis of Pergamum and in most Greek amphitheaters.

But in Roman layouts, even when the axis traverses a forum, there will always be a final visual stop beyond the open square in the form of a monumental building. And it is this continuous alternation between expansion and confinement which makes the spectactor conscious of space as such, be it the closed space of the Maxentius Basilica and of the Thermae of Caracalla, or the open space of the Imperial Fora. The foremost means to realize the ever-increasing Roman urge for three-dimensional monumentality are the arch, the vault, and the dome for the interior; for the outer space it is the rhythmically articulated enclosure. Both architectural archetypes, basilica and closed square, represent the eternal Roman contribution to European architecture and city planning for the succeeding two thousand years and probably even farther into the future.

This new Roman concept of space, prior to its final triumph in Imperial times static, self-contained, and superhuman, becomes dimly recognizable already in the second century B.C. Together with the basic idea of axiality and symmetry, it distinguishes the Roman fora as *original* and different from the archaic and classical Greek agora and even from the groping attempts of the late Hellenistic period, just as the Roman basilica differs from a Greek temple. As much as the Romans may have borrowed individual architectural Greek forms and the whole principle of the Greek tectonic system, the difference in spatial approach cannot be overemphasized. Greek forms, although employed by the Romans, became merely decorative motifs and lost much of their meaning as basic architectural elements. And in this respect there exists no gradual transition from late Hellenism to Rome. Thus, e.g., the Pantheon is certainly not a tectonic structure built for the sake of its three-dimensional form and the shape of its exterior, but rather for the space it encloses. The combination of a Greek temple front with the original massive cylinder proves the relative lack of interest in exterior appearance. In contrast to the Pantheon, the shape of the Greek temple is based on the mass of its architectural elements and on the tectonic system which integrates these elements. For the Greeks space was only the means to envelop buildings and sculptures alike—to set them off and to establish the necessary aesthetic distance.

But the Roman fora create space consciously and immediately. The façades of their surrounding structures are a secondary feature, representing essentially the separating shell between the exterior space of the forum and the interior space of the individual structures.

As was said before, the difference between Hellenistic and Roman squares, based on the different attitude of the two civilizations toward space, cannot be considered as merely a gradual increase of the feeling for space. Rather it reflects the eventual breakthrough from the second century B.C. on of a very ancient general Mediterranean tendency—the conception of space as the basic objective of building activity, documented from the end of prehistoric times on by caves, tombs, and finally even temples in Malta, Cyprus, Sardinia, and also in Egypt. The same ancient awareness of space is evident in prehistoric drawings in the caves of Les Eyzies, Lascaux, and others in the Dordogne in France, or in Altamira in Spain. Design and arrangement on the walls, ceilings, and on isolated boulders prove the high sensitiveness of late prehistoric man for values of space and volume—a perception much more keen and acute than ours, although neglecting the basic principles of "orderly" tectonic design and, of course, of linear perspective.

The Roman urge to shape space proper may represent a resurgence of this very ancient space-forming Mediterranean tendency, even if Hellenistic forms were so widely employed. Actually, it meant a new beginning in contrast to the earlier Greek concept—at the same time age-old—equally evident in architecture and city planning and, above all, in the shape of the square.

III · THE MEDIEVAL TOWN AND SQUARE

DURING the Middle Ages, understood here as being the period from the ninth to the fifteenth century—in other words, from the beginning of the Romanesque to the end of the Gothic style—the concept of a town was so entirely different from the Greek idea of a *polis* or the Roman concept of an *urbs* that the problem of town and square must be approached from new angles, both sociologically and visually. Except for the bastides in France and England and the foundations of the Teutonic Knights, the organization of a town as a *whole* was neither understood nor desired by the builders of the Middle Ages. Even in those medieval towns which were of Roman origin, any changes or additions were interpolated without reference to the ancient general plan.

There was only one city which was imagined as an entity with a symbolical meaning—the "Heavenly Jerusalem," depicted in innumerable mosaics, murals, tapestries, and manuscripts, from late Byzantine times through the Middle Ages (Pl. 13). In very early Christian mosaics, like those from Santa Maria Maggiore and SS. Pudenziana in Rome from the fifth century, the depiction of the Heavenly Jerusalem deviates from the glorified Jerusalem of the Apocalypse in so far as it is reduced to a simple round wall without any characterization of buildings within. The same type is still encountered in the ninth century in the mosaics of S. Prassede; it is somewhat more elaborate in the image of S. Cecilia, where the walls are fortified by towers above which some gables and monumental columns are visible. This imaginative concept is further modified in murals and illuminated manuscripts during the subsequent centuries until finally Hans Holbein's well-known woodcut shows the Prophet Ezekiel's vision of the Heavenly Jerusalem: a central-domed building on a square in the center of the town forms the nucleus of its quadrangular layout. This visualization proves the influence of the contemporary Italian projects for ideal cities on European artists everywhere (see p. 101). Thus in Holbein's woodcut of Ezekiel's vision the traditional medieval plan of the earthly Jerusalem is combined with the new concept of an ideal town as it developed through the fifteenth and sixteenth centuries. The shape of the square around the Dome of the Rock is also based on contemporary ideal plans. Actually, the area before the Dome of the Rock (ambiguously called the Omar Mosque also) in no way represents a shaped square but merely an irregular open space, as is the case before so many later mosques.

The earthly Jerusalem itself was mostly represented as being subdivided into four sections with the Temple of Solomon in its center. Such depictions of the earthly Jerusalem were repeated and varied up to the beginning of the Renaissance (Pl. 14). They certainly have no documentary value but were merely symbolic. Certain biblical localities such as the Mount of Olives and the Temple of Solomon were portrayed in naturalistic likeness within the otherwise imaginary delineation. For instance, an erroneous belief of the Middle Ages and the early Renaissance identified the existing Dome of the Rock, a seventh-century structure, with the ancient Temple of Solomon. Nor was this Temple of Solomon distinguished from the later temple of the time of Herod.

In contrast to these imaginative concepts of the heavenly and the earthly Jerusalem, however, the actual medieval town was an irregular and haphazard affair. If one strolls through medieval towns still extant essentially in their original form, like Cahors in France or Dinkelsbühl in Germany—in contrast to such overrestored tourist attractions as Carcassonne in France and Rothenburg in Germany—one wonders how many people succeeded in surviving during that period, for behind each corner a murderer could have lain in wait. The winding streets and alleys (*ruelles* and *Gaesschen*) were so crooked, with sharp corners and angles often blocked by isolated houses and shacks, that visual surprises were continually the rule in contrast to the open vistas of earlier centuries.

The earlier medieval towns, the result of centuries of growth, are characterized not only by the irregularity of their streets but also by the extreme narrowness of the streets and squares without any expansion in width. The need for space in the open (external space) was hardly felt—if at all, only in reference to a dominating building, like a church with its so-called parvis in front. Mostly, however, the churches were erected as isolated structures, without any planned relation to the surrounding town. Small shacks and little houses were often attached to them, providing the best natural means of contrasting the human scale of daily life with the towering mass of the edifice erected *ad majorem dei gloriam.* In Strasbourg, Freiburg im Breisgau, and Ulm, for instance, the houses around the cathedrals left just distance enough to admire the magnificent sculptural decor of the west portals and of the entrances to the transepts. There has never been a parvis in front of these three cathedrals. The lateral square of the Cathedral of Strasbourg was created only during the eighteenth century in connection with the building of the Episcopal Palace (Pl. 15A). Similarly, in Freiburg im Breisgau (Fig. 16) the Münsterstrasse leads directly toward the west façade of the cathedral,

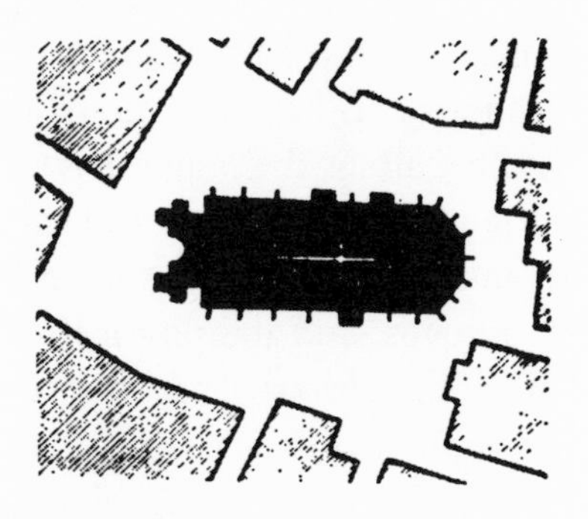

FIG. 16. FREIBURG IM BREISGAU. CATHEDRAL SQUARE. PLAN
From Sitte, *The Art of Building Cities*

which originally was surrounded by a walled churchyard. The divergence between the diagonal position of the cathedral and the direction of the neighboring streets results from the strict orientation of the sacred building toward the east. At any rate, at the time of its erection the church was imagined as a completely isolated mass. The voids around it have no spatial meaning beyond the original purpose of isolation. The small lateral market place was opened in 1514 only after the abolishment of the churchyard. In Ulm, a churchyard had surrounded the cathedral as an isolated structure. The nineteenth-century restoration, however, without any feeling for truly medieval concepts, has completely destroyed the original impression. The edifice today looks as if it is served on a platter—a consequence of the radical razing of all adjacent houses.

The lack of space awareness as exemplified by the location of these three cathedrals refers only to space in the open, to external space. It contrasts peculiarly with the outspoken feeling for space as shaped *inside* the large cathedrals, the development of which is clearly mirrored in the evolution of vaulting from the Romanesque to the Gothic style.

Not by chance do the above-mentioned examples refer to German towns. For obvious historical reasons, the most characteristic developments of the medieval town and its square took place in Germany. The thinly populated country with much fewer remainders of Roman town planning than Italy and France brought forth a much wider variety of new urban forms than those countries. Thus, German examples in the Middle Ages will outnumber by far those from other European countries, exactly as Italy comes to the fore in the Renaissance and France during the seventeenth and eighteenth centuries.

Only very slowly toward the end of the twelfth century did trade and traffic overcome the geographical parochialism of the European countries, and with this development erudition and scholarship began to flourish also outside the Church. Towns in Italy and France, along the Rhine River, and in the Netherlands gained in importance in the general economic and spiritual development. The growth of the guilds and the increasing financial independence, municipal home rule, new tax systems, and the physical expansion of the town into *faubourgs* outside its fortifications made the town a definite concept in the imagination of the people as distinct from the open country. More and more people began moving into the town, which now became the town of the "burgher," no longer that of monk and knight. Whereas around 1200 only 250 towns existed in the Holy Roman Empire west of the Elbe River and only about 10 east of it, around 1400 there were already 1,500 towns in the west and the same number in the east. By 1500, 15 cities had a population of over 10,000. The majority of the towns in the west, developed primarily from older settlements, were irregular for the most part, while in the east the majority of the new towns, as colonial foundations of the Teutonic Knights, were regularly planned. Only a very few grew from earlier clusters of villages.

THE ORIGINS OF MEDIEVAL TOWNS

The morphological development of the medieval square can be understood only after a clarification of the different origins of medieval towns in their totality. While Italy was still crowded with towns of Roman origin, France and Germany witnessed new urban developments from about the tenth century on. For obvious historical reasons fewer examples of larger early medieval settlements can be found in England, hardly any in Spain and Greece, and very few in Scandinavia.

Medieval towns essentially developed from four different beginnings:

1. from existing Roman cities, preserving the old plan in the scheme of their reconstructed streets;
2. around existing castles, monasteries, or independent church structures, their local immunity areas becoming the nucleus of later expansion;
3. out of favorably located trading posts at a crossroad, or at a ford across a river, or at a harbor or bay, etc.;
4. as newly founded and organized communities.

In general, those towns based on Roman foundations or which were newly planned developed into regular shapes (see 1 and 4 above), while the others mostly kept their irregular shape (see 2 and 3 above). Quite naturally the form of their squares mirrored the same basic differences, and therefore a discussion of these various origins must precede that of the different types of squares.

1. TOWNS OF ROMAN ORIGIN. With the "decline and fall of the Roman Empire" the original Roman towns became too large for their decreased population and their smaller trade and traffic limited to provincial contacts. As was mentioned above, hardly any new towns were founded in Europe prior to the end of the twelfth century. Large parts of the still surviving ancient towns dilapidated, other parts were filled with makeshift structures, and only very seldom was a completely new building erected within the existing Roman scheme and ancient remainders. Such towns which had lain dormant or at least half-dormant for about six centuries are too numerous in Europe to be listed here. Some of them show the Roman gridiron without any change (e.g., in Italy: Turin, Piacenza, Aosta, Vicenza, etc.; in France: Autun, Nîmes, Besançon, Nantes, Dijon, etc.; in Germany: Regensburg, Treves, Mainz, Speyer, etc.; in England: Carvent, Silchester [Fig. 17], Colchester, Winchester, etc.). There are other towns where the Roman plan has been changed more radically by medieval alterations. But even in these instances it is possible to recognize the old scheme at least partially (e.g., Florence, Orléans, Strasbourg, Cologne, Ulm). The same holds true even for

Paris, which developed so rapidly—in the thirteenth century it already had 100,000 inhabitants—that the Roman scheme became almost completely submerged.

However, in all these towns with the more or less well-preserved Roman layout of streets and fortifications, the erstwhile forum or the center of the castrum is obliterated or no longer recognizable. Medieval churches, new

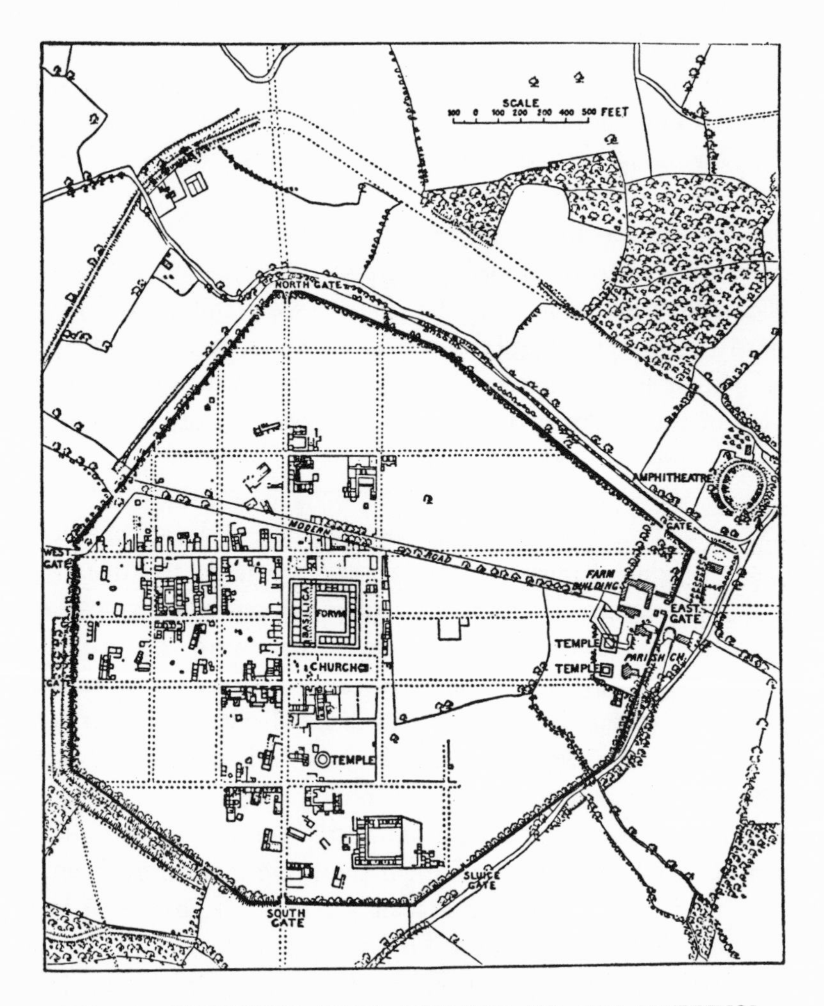

FIG. 17. SILCHESTER. PLAN, SHOWING ALL THE BUILDINGS EXCAVATED DOWN TO OCTOBER, 1897

From *Archaeologia or Miscellaneous Tracts . . .* ; courtesy New York Public Library street markets, all kinds of changed local conditions have destroyed the outline and often even the location of the ancient square, for whose original function the medieval town had no longer any use. Sometimes whole new blocks were erected over the formerly open area of the ancient forum and frequently individual buildings were squeezed into its space, as, e.g., in Aosta, Dijon, and Nantes. Thus the influence of the Roman origin may be evident in the town as a whole, but does not show in the form of the later medieval square.

2. EXPANSION AROUND AN EXISTING ECCLESIASTICAL OR SECULAR NUCLEUS. During Carolingian and Ottonian times (*ca.* 800–1000), urban settlements in France, Germany, the Low Countries, and England developed very slowly and without a preconceived plan. Many of these early medieval towns in France and Germany were founded originally as episcopal sees, and *civitas*, the community of urban dwellers, became almost identical with "diocese." The *Pax Dei* (Peace of God) and the sacrosanct right of refuge on church territory induced many people to settle down under the protection of an episcopal see. The town then grew around the physical nucleus of power, the complex of a monastery or the individual structure of a church, comparable to the development of the Greek town in its relation to an earlier acropolis. Examples of such a development are, for instance, Moissac, St. Dié, and St. Denis in France; St. Gall in Switzerland; Soest, Meissen, and Magdeburg in Germany. The irregular market square on secular soil outside the monastery contrasted distinctly with the rectangular or quadrangular shape of the cloisters inside. With the expansion of the town, the monastery often became part of the whole, as, for instance, in St. Gall, but even then it dominated the inner organism of the community (Pl. 15B). In towns which had developed in connection with a previously existing, more or less isolated cathedral, the market square generally extended laterally to the cathedral, or was even isolated from it; but at any rate it was outside the so-called local immunity area, as, e.g., in Lübeck (Fig. 18).

In this way one of the most typical features of medieval cities originated, a feature which became of the greatest aesthetic importance for the town as a whole: the parallel existence of two separate squares. One of them was located before the church as a parvis or was otherwise adjacent to it, the other a certain distance away, as market square. From the latter only the higher parts of the church structure with its towers and steeples would be visible (e.g., Lübeck, Stralsund, Stendal, Augsburg [Pl. 15c]). In some instances, the market square developed through a broadening of the main street, especially when the settlement, side by side with the episcopal center, became more independent. Mostly such squares completely lacked any

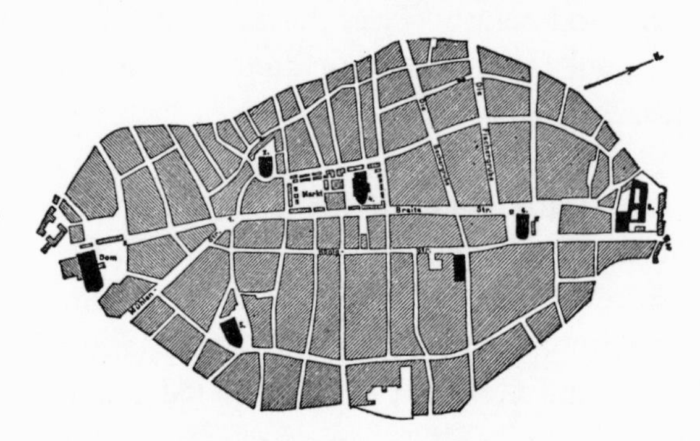

FIG. 18. LÜBECK. PLAN
From Meurer, *Der mittelalterliche Stadtgrundriss im nördlichen Deutschland*

spatial unity or three-dimensional form. They made good this irregularity by the contrast between the modest dimensions of the burghers' houses and the size of the cathedral or church: human scale against divine scale, a palpable symbol of the medieval set of values. Quite naturally these episcopal towns were very much furthered by their ecclesiastical rulers who helped them by privileges for their markets, by tax reductions, and by the distribution of free lots—all in order to aggrandize the power of the episcopal see.

In competition with the clergy, the Franconian kings from about 1000 onward extended similar privileges to towns which sprang up under the protection of an already existing castle (e.g., Bamberg, Aix-la-Chapelle, Frankfurt am Main). In such instances, a certain independence from local rulers and landowning lords was granted besides other privileges, and often special local laws became *Stadtrecht* (town laws), a kind of judicial charter for the expanding town.

3. EXPANSION FROM TRADING POSTS, ETC. Similar grants were given to secular settlements which had expanded around small trading centers. Existing fortifications of the market were strengthened, and sometimes even the construction of new fortifications was undertaken. This trend increased especially during the twelfth and early thirteenth centuries. The great

ruling houses of Central Europe sponsored such developments, e.g., the Dukes of Zähringen, who devoted much of their energy to the urbanization of Germany. They not only furthered existing communities but also founded new trading centers, such as Freiburg im Breisgau, Straubing, Rottweil, Wasserburg am Inn, and Friedberg in Hesse. As in Heidelberg, Miltenberg am Main, and other earlier communities, the main traffic arteries automatically became marketing centers in the shape of a broadened street.

The greatest political and commercial advantages, however, were enjoyed by the towns of the German Hanseatic League. Located mainly along the coast of the North Sea and the Baltic Sea, they had tremendous possibilities as planned harbor towns (e.g., Danzig, Elbing, Stralsund, Lübeck, and Hamburg; the last two maintained their independence for more than 800 years). It was this economic and political independence which made the Hanseatic League, with offices from Paris and London to Nizhni Novgorod, a historically unique international commercial federation, based entirely on urban rights and freedoms granted to these German towns in the twelfth and thirteenth centuries.

4. PLANNED CITIES IN FRANCE AND EASTERN GERMANY. Today one is inclined to associate the medieval town with "queer and picturesque Romanticism." But certain types of planned and therefore regular towns are as truly medieval as the irregular ones. From the end of the twelfth century through the first half of the fourteenth century a great number of towns were newly founded in addition to those remodeled from dilapidated ancient Roman cities. During these centuries, Europe overcame the worst tribulations of the earlier Middle Ages. Commerce and traffic began to flourish and the political situation, although not yet balanced, was at least so far stabilized that one could discern between friend and foe. The Church, at the apex of its power, tolerated worldly endeavors, from secular painting and poetry to philosophical studies and the formation of communities not founded under its auspices.

The intensification of the spiritual and material life through these centuries is reflected equally in the great cathedrals of Central Europe and in the newly founded towns. While the very few new foundations of the tenth and eleventh centuries were laid out merely for economic reasons, political, military, and missionary intentions were the basic motives for the rise of later towns.

France and Germany east of the Elbe River were the main regions of newly founded communities, aside from a few examples in England. The first glance at the layouts of such *bastides* and *villes neuves* in France and of the eastern German fortress towns of the Teutonic Knights shows the fallacy of the nationalistically inspired theory that French town schemes, influenced by Roman concepts, were always rigid and schematic, while German towns, inspired by Teutonic Romanticism, were always individualistic and less regular. Both have so many traits in common that they represent *one definite type*.

Actually the striking difference between earlier medieval communities on the one hand and *villes neuves*, bastides, and eastern German fortress towns on the other hand is based on the contrast between the strict schematism of the gridiron system and planned squares common to all of the latter, and the irregularity of the former.

The gridiron layout of bastides and *villes neuves* with one but mostly with two squares is almost identical. Aigues-Mortes (Fig. 19), founded by Louis the Saint in 1240, and Monpazier (Pl. 16A), founded by Edward I of England in 1284, are probably the most distinct prototypes. A still earlier example is Breteuil, founded in 1060. Since the bastides were meant as buffer towns

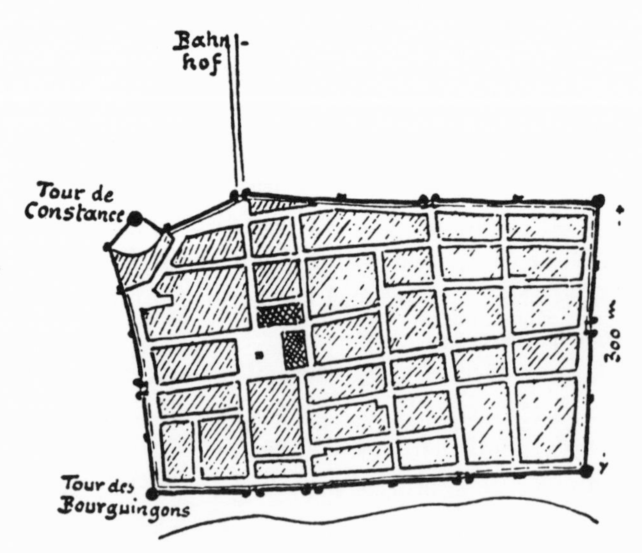

FIG. 19. AIGUES-MORTES. PLAN

From Stübben, "Vom französischen Städtebau," *Städtebauliche Vorträge* against feuding lords and invading armies, they were mostly located on the crest of a hill and their periphery was fortified. Louis the Saint and Alphonse of Poitiers, and also English kings like their nephew Edward I, who was then still in possession of a great part of France, founded numerous bastides —the English alone more than twenty, among them, besides Monpazier, Libourne and Monsegur.

Some bastides were founded in Wales, especially for military purposes, by the same Edward I, among them Carnarvon in 1280–1300 and others along the Menai and Conway rivers. They show the same gridiron scheme as in France, although on a smaller scale. Usually a castle is connected with the fortification of the town. While these bastides in Wales are as regular as their French counterparts, the very few foundations of this epoch in England proper do not show the same regularity in layout, e.g., Winchelsea. These English towns were populated by farm workers of the region who received certain limited privileges from the founder.

The *villes neuves* in France were not fortified except for the church in their center, which served as protection for the population and was usually under the auspices of one of the mendicant orders. One of the best examples is Carcassonne, whose *ville neuve* is located at the foot of an earlier strongly fortified hill-town of entirely different character.

The scheme of the French bastides can be encountered again in East Prussia and Silesia in Germany. For the sake of Christianity and Germanization the Teutonic Knights, stimulated by the Crusades, undertook during the thirteenth and fourteenth centuries a tremendous colonizing program among the Slavic people, from Pomerania and East Prussia to Poland and Bohemia. For this purpose they founded such new cities as Thorn, Marienburg, Elbing, etc. The Knights tried to expel the Slavic population whom they had first called in and to replace them by Germans. Their missionary work was very much helped by the Cistercians, an order which had been one of the main pioneers of the Gothic style since the time of its founder, Bernard of Clairvaux. In eastern Germany, they adapted the Gothic style to bricks (Brick Gothic) since brick and not natural stone, as in western Germany and France, was the building material at their disposal. The native Slavic population before them had mostly employed a primitive kind of timber work.

To evaluate the revolutionary character of these new settlements one should not forget that before the Knights had begun their building activities in northeast Germany, Bohemia, and Poland, the few earlier founded towns of these regions were of a very different type. The original native settlement had the form of the Slavic *Rundling*, a circular or oval combination of houses around an open center. The arrangement of the houses repeated the position of covered wagons shoved together for defensive purposes (*Wagenburg*). As time went on, houses had replaced the wagons. Behind the houses whose gables were directed toward the center, gardens and fields radiated toward the periphery of the settlement. Quite obviously there cannot be any sharper contrast in principal layout than between these old Slavic villages and the newly founded towns.

The layout of these eastern towns so far outside the orbit of earlier European civilization represents a further proof that founded cities always adhered to the gridiron scheme through all centuries and in all regions, with the exception of a very few rather artificial, intellectually conceived Renaissance creations (see p. 101). The small differences between the Egyptian Kahun (around 2500 B.C.), the Indian Mohenjo-Daro (third millennium B.C.), the post-Hippodamic Ionic colonies (after 500 B.C.), the Roman castrum town (after 300 B.C.), the bastides and eastern German colonial towns (around 1300), the seventeenth- and eighteenth-century foundations of the absolute rulers, from France to Russia, and finally the North American colonial foundations—these minor differences are irrelevant for the historian of ideas. Mere functionalism cannot explain this phenomenon of similarity. There must exist an inner urge for order which prefers the mathematical certainties of rectangularity.

In the concept of Thomas Aquinas this earthly world mirrors the heavenly order of the other world and represents a living organism, composed of independent elements. One might assume that the attempt to organize the plan of the town and of its individual parts, like square and streets, is subconsciously based on similar feelings.

THE MORPHOLOGY OF THE MEDIEVAL SQUARE

The preceding analysis of the various origins of medieval towns may help one to understand the variety of structural shape and visual appearance of medieval market places and church squares alike. As to origin, it is obvious that a regular closed square could develop only in Roman foundations which represented the heritage of the spatial feeling of Roman antiquity or in the new foundations of the thirteenth and fourteenth centuries. In those medieval towns which were neither derived from Roman foundations nor newly planned, the market place was bound to be as irregular as the town of which it was a part.

It is evidently difficult to give exact dates as to when individual squares developed the form in which they present themselves today. In the course of centuries too many changes have occurred as to area and framing structures. Furnishings such as fountains and monuments have been erected, structures have been added, razed, or altered, and other changes have been made that make it sometimes hard to decide whether a specific square is essentially medieval or of the Renaissance.

Nonetheless it is possible to distinguish clearly definable types of medieval squares in the various European countries. Sometimes these types succeed each other chronologically; often they exist simultaneously and their form depends more on locale than on the period of origin. Except for specific solutions in Italy and in the north, these are the principal types:

1. the market square as a broadening of the main thoroughfare
   a) as developed in the original previous settlements;
   b) planned as such in new foundations;
2. the market square as a lateral expansion of the main thoroughfare;
3. the square at the town gate;
4. the square as the center of the town
   a) as developed in the original previous settlements;
   b) planned as such in new foundations;
5. the parvis;
6. grouped squares.

1. THE STREET AS A MARKET SQUARE. In towns which have evolved naturally from former villages, trading posts, etc., the main thoroughfare automatically becomes the market square, since traffic is the vital element in the growth of the town (Fig. 20). Public and private commercial life are not yet separated. Most markets of this type, originally rather small, developed in Germany, Austria, and Switzerland. Since the country around was relatively thinly populated, not much space was needed for the market, as, e.g., in the main market street in Bernburg (northern Germany) or Münster in Westphalia. Centuries of razing and filling in were needed before a broad street of some

regularity developed out of primitive street markets. If sometimes a town hall or church was erected within this broadened area, it was built parallel, or at right angles, to the traffic line. In either way the respective building accentuated the spatial character of the broadened part of the street. On a larger scale, the broadened streets in Innsbruck (the Tyrol) and Augsburg

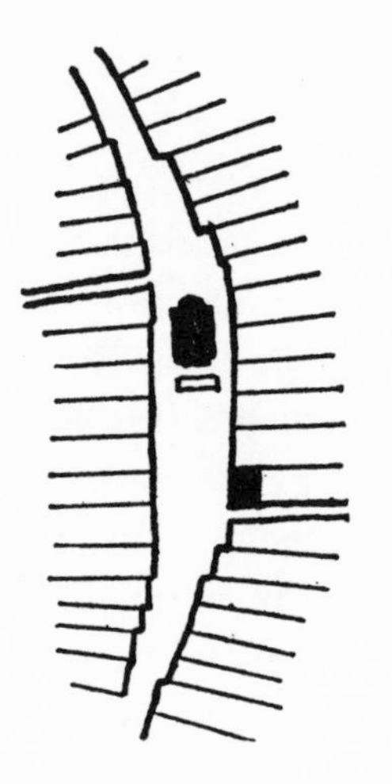

FIG. 20. A TYPICAL MEDIEVAL SQUARE AS ORIGINATED FROM A BROADENED STREET
From Meurer, *Der mittelalterliche Stadtgrundriss im nördlichen Deutschland*

(Bavaria) show how a street may create a three-dimensional impression without losing the character of a thoroughfare in a distinct direction. In Innsbruck, the St. Ann's Column is located amidst the broadened part of Maria Theresienstrasse and becomes the point of spatial reference for this section. The grandiose Alpine mountain range, serving as a backdrop, visually closes the vista from the square and makes it a spatial unit (Pl. 16B). In Augsburg, the broadened part of the lower Maximilianstrasse is separated from the continuation of the street in both directions through the Augustus Fountain (by Hubert Geraerd, 1594) and the Mercury Fountain (by Adriaen de Vries, 1599) respectively. The position of these fountains intensifies the spatial character of this section, which is helped furthermore through the curvation of the street. In both towns, fountains and monuments were not added until the Renaissance, but the streets had been broadened already during the late Middle Ages. So the spatial impression of today derives from a medieval concept.

In comparison to these examples from Austria and southern Germany, the Sand in the Hanseatic town of Lüneburg (Pl. 4B) in northern Germany offers another solution of a main traffic artery broadened in late medieval times for market purposes. Here, however, the gables of the Gothic and early Renaissance houses on both sides are directed toward the street. This sequence of gables emphasizes the verticalism of the framing structures. Therefore the spatial effect of this broadened area appears more fenced in and less compactly closed than in the street-squares of Innsbruck and Augsburg. Only the heavy mass of the early Romanesque Johanniskirche, located behind the curve of the continuing street, closes the area visually.

The idea of the market streets was so generally accepted that even in newly founded cities of the twelfth and thirteenth centuries very broad streets were considered sufficient for market needs and no special market square was provided. A typical example is Berne, Switzerland, founded in 1191, one of the many towns established by the Zähringen family. Here again, as in the broadened streets of Augsburg and Innsbruck, the spatial impression of the parallel arcaded streets with their regular and equal lots is increased by the many beautiful fountains, erected mainly during the sixteenth century (Pl. 17). The spatial impression is quite naturally stronger in these founded late medieval towns since it is helped by almost identical façades of simultaneously erected houses with similar fenestration, equal height, and mostly with arcades.

2. THE MARKET SQUARE AS A LATERAL EXPANSION. When vehicular and pedestrian through-traffic increased and began to interfere with the activities of the market and its minor local traffic, lateral expansions of the main thoroughfare were developed by razing impeding buildings. In this way the expanded market proper was protected against the free-flowing traffic but was nonetheless connected with it. Now real space was formed and framed continuously on three sides. The fact that the fourth side of this lateral expansion was at the same time part of the main thoroughfare did not diminish the impression of spatial unity; in some instances it even enhanced it, e.g., the Marienplatz in Munich (Pl. 18A). Since a market square gained in importance with such an expansion, the town hall or a church was often erected there, either on one of the sides or occasionally amidst the free area, but never in the line of traffic. These buildings further increased the spatial effect of the expansion; and one could actually speak of a square. Such a location of the market square, tangential to the main thoroughfare, can be

encountered in Minden in Westphalia, Braunschweig (the Hagen Market), Heilbronn am Neckar, etc.

Sometimes a larger town developed more than one such expansion from thoroughfares. In these instances, the markets were specialized as to function—the horse market, the fish market, the pottery market, etc.—exactly as in Greek and Roman towns.

In some instances, the main thoroughfare was split into two almost parallel streets and both developed lateral expansions, as, e.g., in Reutlingen (Fig. 21). Some of these stretched so far that the free area connected both streets.

FIG. 21. REUTLINGEN. PLAN

From Klaiber, *Die Grundrissbildung der deutschen Stadt im Mittelalter*

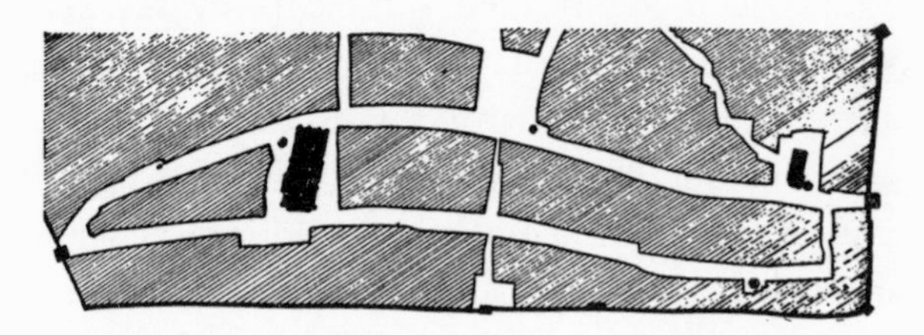

An interesting variant of the square as lateral expansion is proffered by an eastern German settlement which represents a surprising exception from the centralized market square otherwise so typical for that region: in Stallupönen (now Nesterov), two squares are successively laid out on opposite sides of the main street, both as regular rectangles (Pl. 18B).

3. THE SQUARE AT THE TOWN GATE. Squares before a gate inside the town walls were mostly of triangular shape. From these squares two or three streets radiated. The mass of the protective tower above or beside the gate dominated the free area, which sometimes functioned as a market for incoming rural products, sometimes only as a traffic hub. Although in function still a market square, such a small area, whence the incoming traffic was channeled into various diverging streets, never produced a real spatial impression but merely appealed through the picturesque view it provided toward the gate and tower, as, e.g., in Dinkelsbühl, Nördlingen, Rothenburg, and Landsberg am Lech (Pl. 19A). Occasionally, similar triangular squares developed also within the town where a broad street bifurcated, as in Quedlinburg, Miltenberg, Maursmünster, Stein am Rhein, etc. At the point of bifurcation a town hall was sometimes erected, creating a strong perspective accent for the small square.

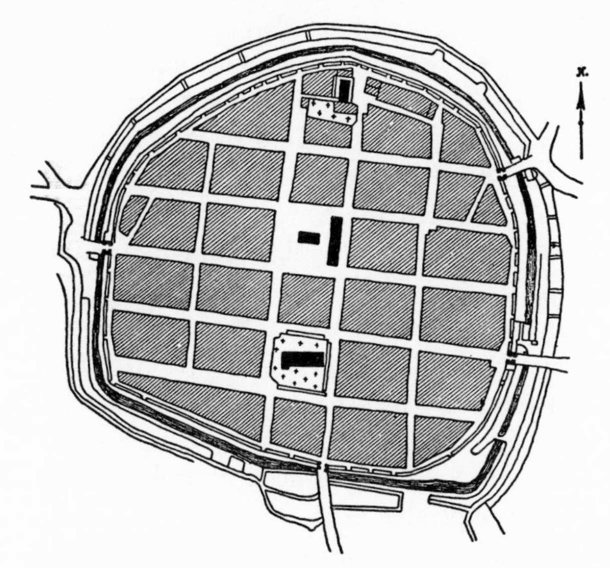

FIG. 22. NEUBRANDENBURG. PLAN

From Meurer, *Der mittelalterliche Stadtgrundriss im nördlichen Deutschland*

4. THE SQUARE AS THE CENTER OF THE TOWN. The centrally located square as the hub of a street system is logical in planned communities. Although characteristic for later Renaissance and baroque projects (see p. 101), it appears already during the thirteenth and fourteenth centuries in the founded and planned bastides and *villes neuves*, and in the settlements of the Teutonic Knights. The gridiron scheme of these towns allowed for clearly defined areas for the market square and—in some instances—for a second square for the church. These squares were regular void areas within the grid pattern. The bordering houses were mostly tied together by arcades, eaves, and roofs of the same height, which in their totality created the typical closed square, as, e.g., in Monpazier. If two squares existed, they were not directly connected but remained individual spatial units. However, bastides and *villes neuves* on the one hand and the contemporaneous eastern German foundations on the other hand differed in one respect: in France, the two squares were located rather haphazardly within the whole scheme of the town, whereas in eastern Germany the market place became the dominating element and the center of the whole grid, as, e.g., in Neubrandenburg (Fig. 22). In these planned central squares in eastern Germany, town hall and parish church were usually located either on the same side of the square or on opposite sides; in some instances, one or both of these structures also occupied part of the free central area of the square, especially in Silesia (Breslau) and

Bohemia. In those towns, the market squares were rather large, out of proportion to the size of the town, but they served also as cattle markets and for country fairs, as, e.g., in Hammerstein (Pl. 19B). The importance of the market square was so great that the adjacent lots were directed toward it, especially if the town hall was erected in the center. If a separate church square existed, it was generally subordinated in size and emphasis to the market square; the church roof and steeple were visible from the market square mostly as a kind of backdrop.

Whereas in these East German foundations the central location of the market square may be derived from the form of the earlier Slavic *Rundling*, a similar location in other parts of Germany may be traced back to the so-called German *Angerdorf*. Such an *Angerdorf* consisted of irregularly dispersed houses with their gables turned toward an open central area, the commonly owned *Anger*, somewhat comparable to the New England village green. When such a village grew into a town, this organization was kept, but the original *Anger* was partially built over and was subdivided into various quarters through crossing streets. A smaller central area was then still left as a market place. Outside Germany, this type is often encountered also in Flanders and northern France.

5. THE PARVIS. The medieval parvis, the square before the church building, is structurally different from the medieval market square in so far as the parvis is dominated exclusively by one building, being almost part of the structure, since all individual architectural elements of the square refer to the dominant edifice (see the section on the dominated square, p. 11). The parvis may be considered functionally as an expansion of the Early Christian, Byzantine, and Romanesque narthex, the entrance hall of the church, originally destined for the neophytes who were not yet admitted to the interior. It was on the parvis that the faithful gathered before and after the service; here they listened to occasional outdoor sermons, and here processions passed. Here, in front of the west portals of the church, mystery plays were performed from the twelfth century on. Here people from out-of-town left their horses, and soon stalls of various kinds were set up. Nonetheless, the parvis was never intended to compete with the market square. Although generally more regular than the contemporaneous market square, the parvis in the Middle Ages seldom showed a geometrically pure form such as de-

veloped later in Renaissance and baroque times, when some of the most glorious were created—such as St. Mark's Square in Venice, St. Peter's Square in Rome, or the Cathedral Square in Salzburg. In these later examples the square was executed in the stylistic forms and proportions of its own period, of course, but it was still basically a parvis.

Quite naturally the parvis was mostly closed—on three sides by houses, on the fourth side by the dominating west façade of the church. The sculptural details of the west portals were calculated for the near view, and it was the parvis which provided the opportunity for it (see Pl. 2).

Not all medieval churches were connected with a parvis. Very many were located on a free area, developed from the surrounding churchyard (e.g., SS. Giovanni e Paolo in Venice; Il Santo in Padua; Freiburg Cathedral), or were situated literally amidst the town (e.g., Strasbourg Cathedral) with little shacks encroaching so closely that the church was completely enclosed by them.

In England, a definite form of parvis did not develop; rather the largest void was often located parallel to the long axis of the cathedral, mostly without distinct spatial boundaries. Typical of this irregularity is the Cathedral Green of Wells (Pl. 20). There architecture and voids are in no way integrated and the squares in the immediate vicinity of the cathedral (built in the third quarter of the twelfth century and the first half of the thirteenth century) are not physically connected with each other. Yet the close before the west front creates the necessary distance for the enjoyment of the architectural and sculptural beauty of the church.

6. GROUPED SQUARES. The separation of the market square from the church square, be it by a parvis or just a surrounding free area, often led to the development of grouped squares, especially characteristic of many German towns. The separation often resulted from the necessity to locate the market square outside the area of "local immunity," to distinguish between the realms of this world and the other world. A consequence of this separation is the visual preponderance of church and steeple over the market square, even if both are not immediately connected. If the church proper is surrounded by houses quite close to it which by their lesser height emphasize the gigantic proportions of the house of God, they create a kind of frame for it, without cubic value of their own. Church and framing houses to-

gether, seen from the humdrum of the market square, impress the spectator as one domineering staggered mass, as, for instance, in two Hanseatic towns in northern Germany, Stralsund and Rostock (Fig. 23).

FIG. 23. ROSTOCK. MARKET SQUARE AND CATHEDRAL SQUARE. PLAN

From Stübben, *Der Städtebau*

The same elements—the church with its own square, town hall, and market square—create an entirely different situation in Braunschweig (Fig. 24). The Altstädter Markt here represents an almost completely closed square. The neighboring Martinskirche does not appear as an isolated unit, but becomes part of the sides surrounding the market square, since the architectural elements of the east side of the church and of the arcaded town hall are almost identical. Thus both are most intimately tied to each other and become a decorative backdrop for the square.

In the Hanseatic town of Bremen, one of the oldest bishoprics in Germany —it was founded by Charlemagne in 787—and her oldest seaport, the kernel of the medieval town was the area of "local immunity," originally walled.

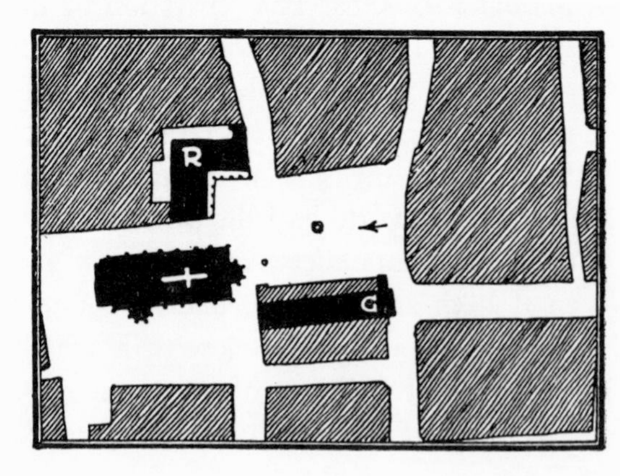

FIG. 24. BRAUNSCHWEIG. ALTSTÄDTER MARKT. PLAN

From Wolf, *Die schöne deutsche Stadt*

The town, however, developed its layout independently of this area. Thus the unique array of important historical buildings—town hall, cathedral, Schütting, Ratsapotheke, Liebfrauenkirche—appears as an accumulation of isolated showpieces of medieval architecture. The squares which stretch before and around them (the market place with its famous Roland statue, erected in 1404; the Domhof [the area of local immunity], at the north side of the cathedral; the small parvis before the cathedral, etc.) in no way serve as visual links among these single architectural volumes. The individual open spaces are not confined by definite boundaries but are entirely irregular and therefore cannot be perceived as parts of a comprehensive visual order (Pl. 21A).

The solution of the Hauptmarkt before the Frauenkirche in Nuremberg is quite different (Fig. 25). Here we can actually speak of a "solution" since the market place was planned and laid out after the Jewish ghetto in the

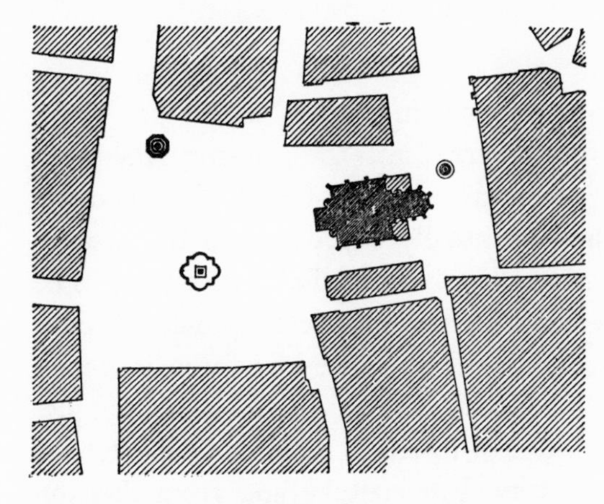

FIG. 25. NUREMBERG. HAUPTMARKT. PLAN
From Brinckmann, *Platz und Monument*

same area had been burned down at the end of the fourteenth century. The adjacent Frauenkirche, like the church in Braunschweig, is merely a part of one side of the square. The two famous fountains on the square abolish any spatial correlation between the church building and the free area since they become visual centers themselves. Their location characterizes most obviously the different spatial concepts of the Middle Ages and the Renaissance: the Schöne Brunnen (1385–96) is located in reference to the corner of one of the framing buildings, repeating the vertical outline of the structure; the Neptuns Brunnen of 1660, in typical Renaissance manner, is placed in the center of the free area, marking an attempt at architectural balance, without specific reference to any surrounding building. The square behind the apse of the church with the Gänsemännchen fountain of the mid-sixteenth century appears as an independent spatial unit in spite of its connection with the Hauptmarkt by two broader streets. In this instance, the squares are only physically, not visually, combined.

Nördlingen in southern Germany offers another different aspect of grouped squares (Pl. 21B). The town was rebuilt at the beginning of the thirteenth century, and expanded gradually in irregular concentric rings around the nucleus of church and town hall. Both these buildings stand as isolated volumes on their respective squares, connected by an area too broad to be called a street, too narrow to be called a square. The small voids around the town hall may actually be compared to those adjacent to the Nikolaikirche in Stralsund: the volume of the building proper outweighs the free area so strongly that the individual strips around it do not fuse into a spatial unit.

In France, medieval grouped squares are infrequent except for those originating from the interpolation of free areas into the gridiron scheme of bastides. Best known and most representative are the Petite Place and the Grande Place in Arras (Pl. 22). They are usually called typical Renaissance squares, although their original structures date back to the Middle Ages. The layout of the squares, both almost rectangular and completely closed, reminds one of the scheme of Monpazier (see p. 72). The Petite Place was originally destined as the market place. Its late Gothic town hall, built by Jacques Caron, stands isolated, as in eastern German towns. The Grande Place, part of a monastery, was secularized in the twelfth century and from then on functioned as a representative civic center. A small street connects both areas. The houses with their gables toward the street were originally individual units as in the not too distant Flemish towns of Brussels, Antwerp, etc. But from the middle of the seventeenth century special building laws required conformity: identity of materials, of height and number of stories, and even of the form of the gables; decoration was limited to the variation of a few ornamental motifs. In this way complete unity is achieved, and it is further emphasized by a continuous row of arcades, begun in the Middle Ages, which ties together all sides of each square. This identity of architectural elements in their rhythmical repetition is decisive for the impression of both squares in Arras.

As with the squares in Arras, so the grouped squares of the Flemish town of Bruges, the Grande Place and the Place du Bourg, also date back to the Middle Ages. Located amidst an irregular web of medieval streets and connected by a small street, both squares present an appearance of medieval irregularity in spite of the Renaissance forms into which most of the original thirteenth- and fourteenth-century framing structures were later remodeled. The distinction between civic and commercial functions is most clearly expressed by the spatial separation of the two squares.

As similar to the squares of Arras and Bruges as the neighboring Flemish squares of Antwerp, Brussels (see p. 129), Louvain, Ghent, Courtrai, and Veurne may appear, they must be considered real Renaissance squares. Although of medieval origin, they underwent, during the Renaissance, decisive spatial modifications. These alterations influenced their appearance so strongly that the medieval origin of these squares is merely of historical interest; the harmonious unification which is so characteristic of Renaissance squares prevails.

SOME SPECIFIC MEDIEVAL SOLUTIONS

THE ENGLISH COLLEGIATE SQUARES. Related to other medieval grouped squares are the collegiate squares of English towns. These squares, although often physically connected with each other, cannot, however, be labeled as "grouped squares." Closed off from public traffic, destined only for pedestrians, they cannot even be considered as genuine squares, functionally or sociologically. Their beautiful lawns surrounded by various buildings may be compared with the interior court of medieval town halls or palazzi or with the cloisters of a monastery, out of which many collegiate squares actually grew. But the expanse of the open area is mostly so large in relation to the dimensions of the surrounding buildings that the latter cannot be perceived merely as a frame for the void; rather they are architecturally independent structures in their own right. Thus a total spatial impression can never be evoked. In other words, the collegiate square resembles a highly organized English village green, surrounded by heterogeneous buildings, rather than a public square. In Oxford and Cambridge (Pl. 23A and B), for instance, the various collegiate squares, separated from each other but connected by small passageways, impress the spectator by their grass-covered expanses in contrast to the network of narrow streets around them. But the variety of dimensions and architectural forms of the individual chapels, halls, dormitories, etc., does not allow for a continuous and uninterrupted sequence of visual impressions, as do medieval cloisters and eighteenth-century residential squares. Those eighteenth-century London squares (see p. 200) show basically the same layout as the collegiate squares, but in the latter the continuity of the architectural frame in combination with an identical ground plan actually creates the impression of closed space.

SOME CHARACTERISTIC SOLUTIONS IN ITALY. In the Middle Ages, as in other times, the feeling for space in the south of Europe was different from that in the north. Therefore Italian medieval squares differ from those found elsewhere, and we encounter entirely individual spatial shapes.

The Piazza del Duomo in Pisa (Pl. 24A) certainly cannot be considered a square of any definite spatial form. With its Cathedral (1063–92), Baptistery (1153–1278), Campanile (1174), and the adjacent Campo Santo (1278–83), the area, shapeless in itself, is merely cleared for this accumulation of individual structures without any common spatial enclosure. Actually, from the city planner's viewpoint, the physical space around the three buildings represents nothing more than a chaotic void. The interesting successive views of these buildings from different angles in no way substitute for a comprehensive spatial experience. The grouping represents rather a kind of religious and civic center comparable to an ancient acropolis.

But the ancient Mediterranean space-consciousness reappears after about 1200 in a few original creations. During the last medieval centuries a general tendency became apparent to straighten out and to regularize, so far as possible, the crooked winding streets and irregular squares of the earlier Middle Ages—even before the actual beginning of the Renaissance.

The purely medieval Piazza del Campo in Siena (Pl. 24B), one of the best preserved squares in Italy, praised by Dante, offers an excellent example of that subconscious survival of Latin space-consciousness in Italy: the large half-circle of the square is closed by the building line of the four-storied Palazzo Pubblico (1288–1309), the extremely high Torre del Mangia (1338–49) which adds a strong vertical accent, and the Cappella di Piazza (1352–

THE HEAVENLY JERUSALEM. BY FRANZ HOGENBERG

From Braun and Hogenberg, *Civitates Orbis Terrarum*

THE EARTHLY JERUSALEM. COPPER ENGRAVING BY DONATO BERTELLI, 1578

Courtesy New York Public Library

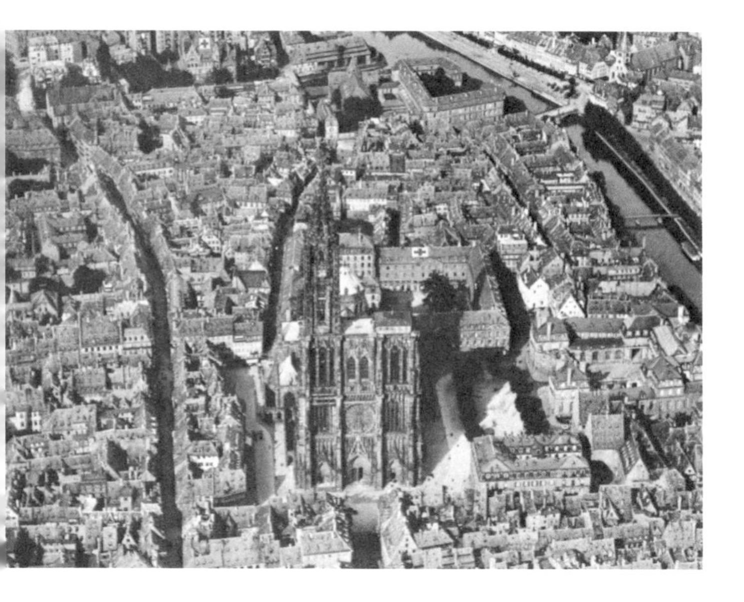

A: STRASBOURG. AERIAL VIEW OF THE CATHEDRAL AND ITS SURROUNDINGS

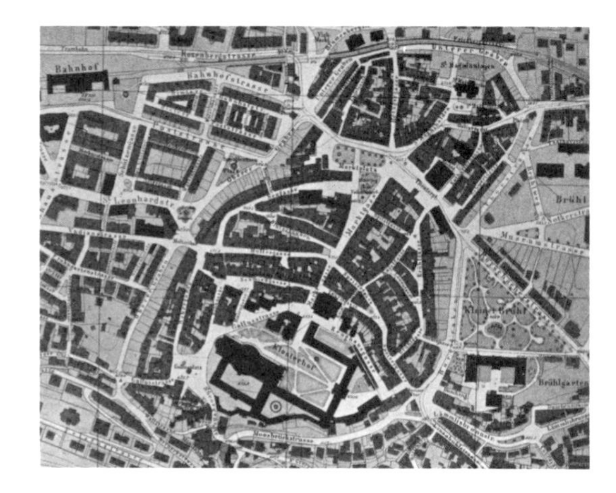

B: ST. GALL. PLAN OF 1907

From Gantner, *Grundformen der europäischen Stadt*

C: AUGSBURG. MAXIMILIANSTRASSE WITH THE HERCULES FOUNTAIN AND ST. ULRICH'S CHURCH

Photo E. Oerter; courtesy German Tourist Information Office, New York

A: MONPAZIER

AERIAL VIEW AND PLAN

Photo Ray Delvert

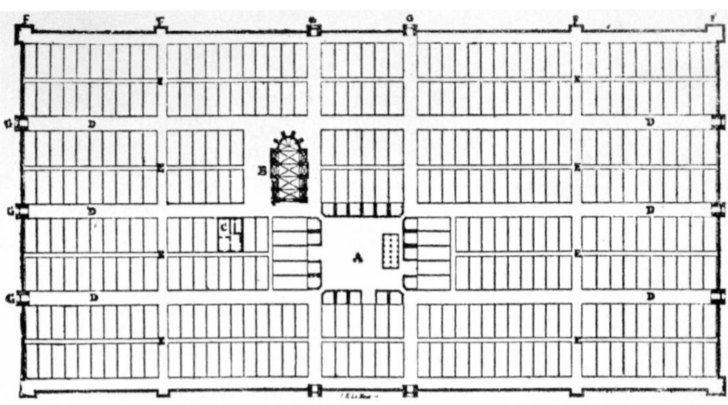

B: INNSBRUCK

MARIA THERESIENSTRASSE

Photo Tiroler Kunstverlag Chizzali, Innsbruck

AERIAL VIEW

Photo Astra Aero A.G., Zurich

BERNE

KRAMGASSE WITH ZÄHRINGEN FOUNTAIN

Photo A. Boss & Co., Schönbühl

A: MUNICH

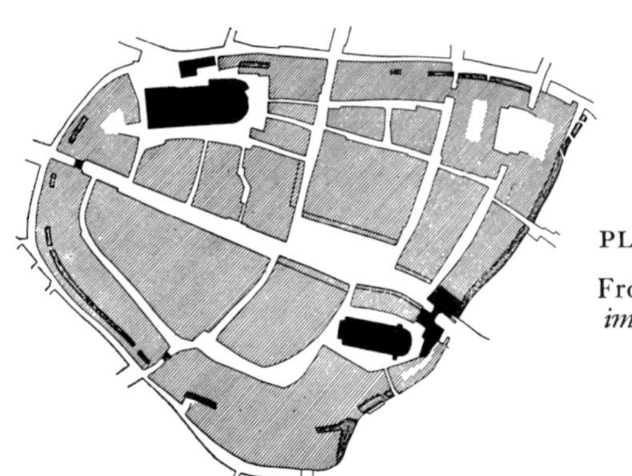

PLAN

From Meurer, *Der mittelalterliche Stadtgrundriss im nördlichen Deutschland*

MARIENPLATZ. ENGRAVING BY M. WENING, 1701

B: STALLUPÖNEN, EAST PRUSSIA [NOW NESTEROV, SOVIET RUSSIA] Photo Junkers Luftbild

A: LANDSBERG AM LECH. SQUARE WITH SCHMALZTURM

Photo Dr. Harald Busch; courtesy German Tourist Information Office, New York

B: HAMMERSTEIN, EAST PRUSSIA [NOW CZARNE, POLAND] Photo Junkers Luftbild

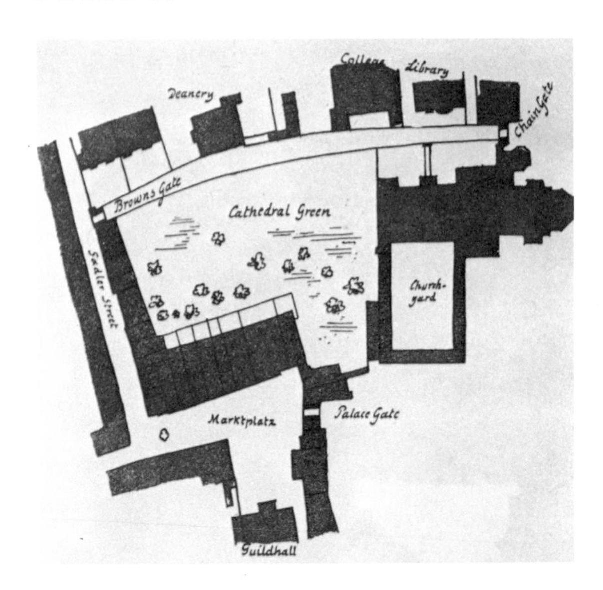

WELLS. CATHEDRAL SQUARES. PLAN AND VIEW

Photo Aero Pictorial, Ltd.; courtesy British Information Services, New York

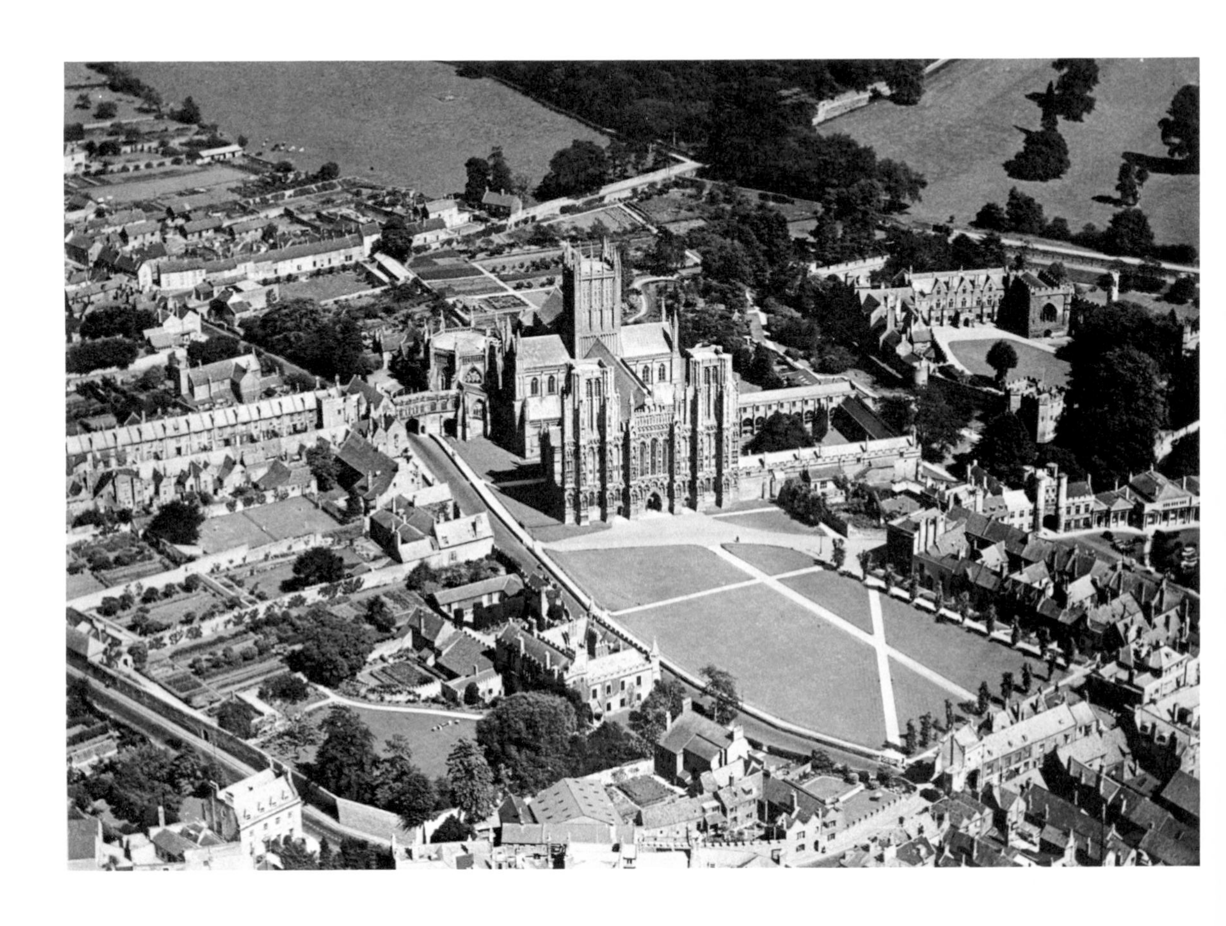

A: BREMEN. MARKET SQUARE WITH CATHEDRAL, TOWN HALL, AND ROLAND STATUE

Photo Saebens, Worpswede; courtesy
German Tourist Information Office, New York

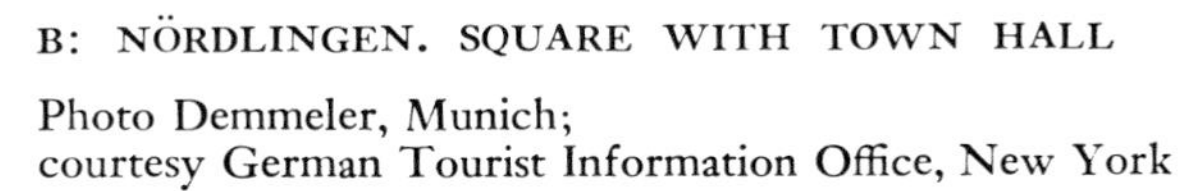

B: NÖRDLINGEN. SQUARE WITH TOWN HALL

Photo Demmeler, Munich;
courtesy German Tourist Information Office, New York

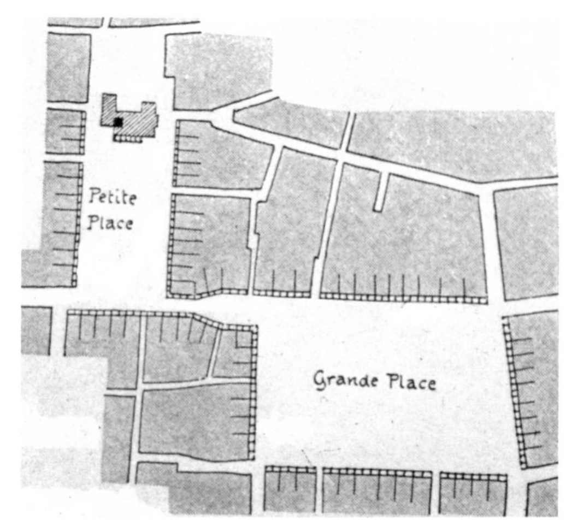

ARRAS

ABOVE:

GRANDE PLACE AND PETITE PLACE. PLAN

From Stübben, "Vom französischen Städtebau," *Städtebauliche Vorträge*

LEFT: PETITE PLACE

Courtesy French Embassy,
Press and Information Division, New York

PETITE PLACE. DRAWING FROM 1778

Courtesy French Embassy, Press and Information Division, New York

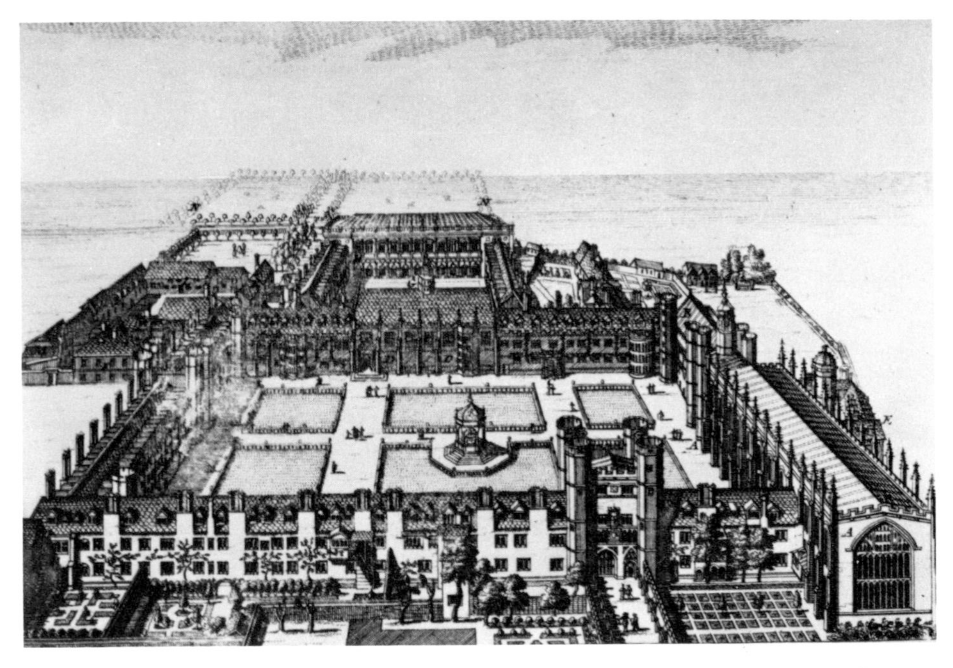

A: CAMBRIDGE UNIVERSITY, TRINITY COLLEGE From Loggia, *Cantabrigia Illustrata*

B: OXFORD UNIVERSITY. AERIAL VIEW Courtesy British Information Services, New York

PLATE 24

A: PISA. PIAZZA DEL DUOMO

PLAN From Sitte, *The Art of Building Cities*

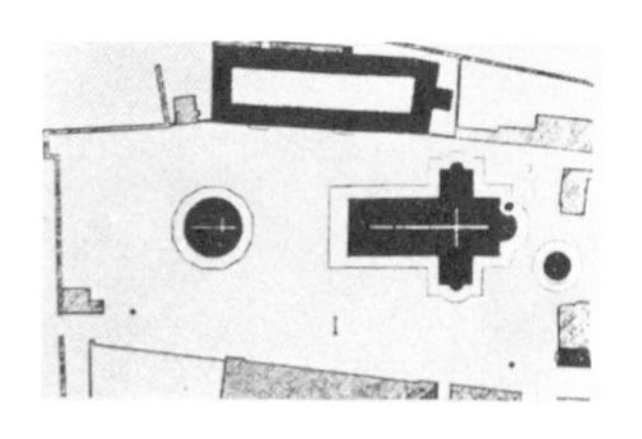

AERIAL VIEW

From Braunfels, *Mittelalterliche Stadtbaukunst in der Toscana*

B: SIENA. PIAZZA DEL CAMPO. AERIAL VIEW

Photo Edizione Ditta Stefano Venturini, Siena

PIAZZA SORDELLO. BATTLE BETWEEN THE GONZAGA AND BUONACOLZI, 1494
PAINTING BY DOMENICO MORONE
Photo Angeli, Terni

MANTUA

PIAZZA SORDELLO AND CATHEDRAL
Photo Edizione F.M.M.

VERONA

A: PIAZZA D'ERBE AND PIAZZA DEI SIGNORI

AERIAL VIEW

Photo Italian State Tourist Office, New York

PLAN From Sitte, *The Art of Building Cities*

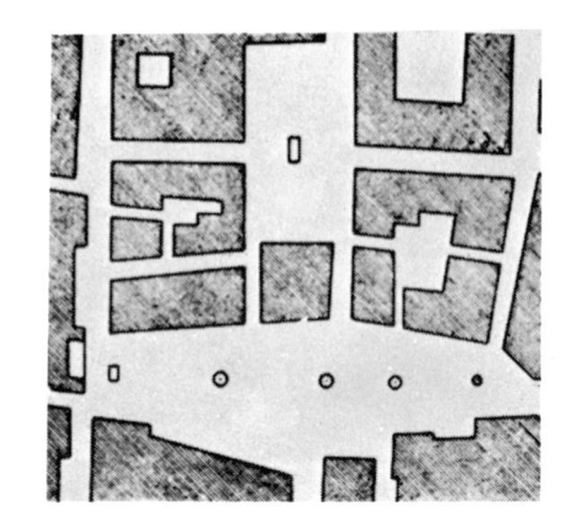

B: PIAZZA DEI SIGNORI Photo Gianni Ferrari, Verona

A: SAN GIMIGNANO

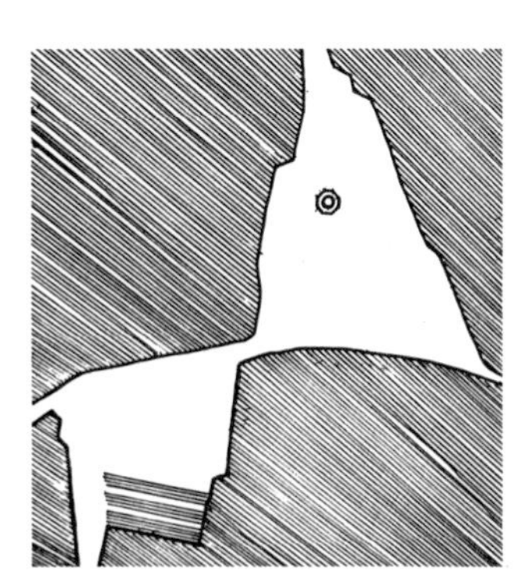

PIAZZA DELLA CISTERNA
Photo Cesare Capello, Milan

PIAZZA DEL DUOMO AND
PIAZZA DELLA CISTERNA. PLAN
After Smith, *Italy Builds*

B: BERGAMO. PIAZZA VECCHIA

A: MICHELSTADT. TOWN HALL WITH FOUNTAIN Photo Karl Peters Kunstverlag, Fürth

B: ASCHAFFENBURG. SQUARE BEFORE THE STIFTSKIRCHE
Photo Hartz, Hamburg; courtesy German Tourist Information Office, New York

76). With the whole square sloping gradually toward the center like an amphitheater, surrounded by medieval palaces of equal height—some of them still extant in their original form—the space opens like a shell. This impression is strongly helped by the radii marked in the fifteenth-century pavement. Jacopo della Quercia's Fonte Gaja (1409–10), which spouts water from a previously installed pipeline, is kept very low in order not to destroy the continuity of space.

The regularizing tendency in the late centuries of the Middle Ages may appear as a mere theory of a modern analyzing mind. It can be proved, however, that the administration of the medieval city of Siena was fully aware that the architectural frame for communal festivities such as the *Palio*, the medieval annual pageant still staged today, should fit the splendor of the occasion. Thus one of the earliest building laws in existence (a statute from 1262) provided regulations for the surrounding houses. And in the fourteenth century, when the total population of Siena was about 12,500, the citizens were asked to shape their windows in accordance with those of the Palazzo Pubblico. From then on the form of the square has been felt as perfect. During the Renaissance Vasari even planned to have colonnades underline the confining half-circle, and a drawing by Perruzzi suggesting arcades around the square is still preserved in the Museo del Duomo in Siena.

The Piazza Sordello in Mantua is exceptional among medieval squares because of its size (Pl. 25). It is surrounded by imposing Gothic palaces of the thirteenth and fourteenth centuries, the arcaded mass of the Palazzo Ducale (called La Reggia, begun in 1302), and the Duomo (begun in 1393, with a later baroque façade). From the time of its origin until today the large uninterrupted rectangular area has remained unchanged. Its dimensions are all the more striking since it terminates a sequence of four smaller squares, all tangential to the main street. Whereas the three other squares serve as typical market squares, the Piazza Sordello was intended as the representative center of the town.

The Piazza d'Erbe in Verona (Pl. 26A) may be compared with the Piazza Sordello in Mantua: it too is related to another square, the Piazza dei Signori, although not directly connected with it physically. Grown from the original Roman Forum, it owes its present shape to the Middle Ages. The south-north direction is strongly emphasized through three individual structures: the pillory (Capitello), the Market Fountain (1368), and a column crowned by the Venetian lion (1523). The square is irregular, bulging on both long sides, but the longitudinal axis, leading toward the Palazzo Maffei (1668) and the towering Torre del Gardello, is so prevalent that these irregularities exercise no visual influence. Although the street leading to the piazza continues at the opposite small side, self-contained space is yet created. This typical southern European medieval piazza contrasts sharply with northern market places; for instance, in Augsburg (see p. 76), where a street expansion never appears as space in itself but merely as a broadening of the thoroughfare.

The neighboring Piazza dei Signori (Pl. 26B) is separated from the Piazza d'Erbe by one block. Two small streets connect both squares; the one square serves as market place, the other as official administrative center. The Piazza dei Signori is surrounded by the medieval Palazzo della Raggione (1193), the Capitanio (thirteenth century), the Prefettura (thirteenth century), and the Renaissance Loggia del Consignio (1486). Archways over the streets leading to the piazza bind the framing structures even closer together so that a completely unified spatial impression is achieved.

The same basic constellation, the integration of two squares, which was so frequent in medieval Germany, exists in Italy also in San Gimignano (Pl. 27A). The fascinating charm of this unique hill town, which even in the mid-sixteenth century had only about 2,000 inhabitants, stems equally from the untouched medievalism of its menacing towers, palaces, houses, and churches and from the spatial forms of its two squares. The Piazza della Cisterna and the Piazza del Duomo are connected with each other by a very small passageway. Since the longest side of the triangular larger square faces the passageway, the pedestrian feels pushed toward it. This narrow link opens a vista into the second square, which, if isolated would appear merely as a parvis to the church of the Collegiata, the Duomo. However, in spite of the almost closed character of each individual square, their inner connection becomes visually and spatially evident.

Another type of medieval Italian square is based on the opposite principle: not the outline of the square is aesthetically decisive, but a monument or structure around which the square, or rather a combination of squares, extends. Yet the relationship between structure and free space around it does not create a "nuclear" square, since the individual space units are neither distinct nor organized. The medieval Piazza dei Signori in Vicenza (Fig. 26), for instance, preserved elements of the Roman origin of the town plan and represented in itself therefore a rather geometric form. But it became disorganized in medieval times. Actually there are three squares, all arranged around the medieval Palazzo della Raggione (thirteenth century) which later, after its remodeling by Palladio (in 1549) became so famous as the Basilica Palladiana; but none of the small squares appears as shaped space. Even the Torre del' Orologio, dating from 1174, and two Venetian columns do not give any spatial orientation. The squares merely set off the mass of the basilica from the surrounding blocks of houses.

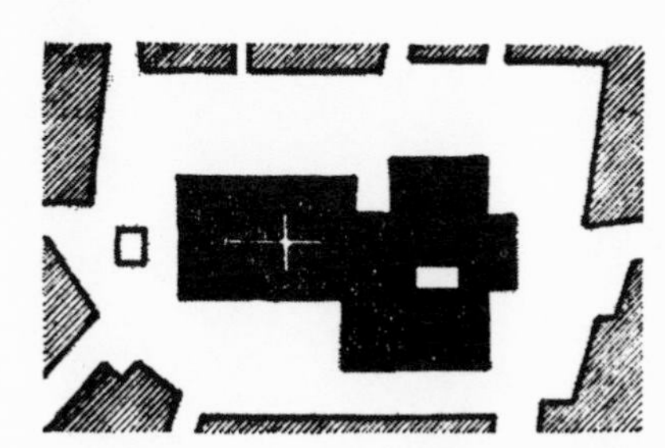

FIG. 26. VICENZA. PIAZZA DEI SIGNORI AT THE BASILICA OF PALLADIO. PLAN
From Sitte, *The Art of Building Cities*

Similarly in Padua, the Piazza dei Frutti and the Piazza delle Erbe merely surround the Palazzo della Raggione (1172–1219) without any intrinsic spatial meaning of their own. Nor, in Modena, are the Piazza delle Legna, the Piazza Grande and the Piazza Torre around the Duomo (built in 1099) organized spatial units but mere clearings for the mass of the medieval cathedral and the Torre Ghirlandina (*ca.* 1100).

The same lack of any meaningful spatial relation exists in Bologna among the three squares around the central mass of the Palazzo del Podestà: Piazza del Nettuno, Piazza Maggiore, and Piazza di Re Enzo (Fig. 27) (see also p. 116). Giovanni da Bologna's later attempt to organize the relationship between the area of the Piazza del Nettuno and of the Piazza Maggiore by the location of his fountain could not remedy the basic medieval incoherence. This incoherence, however, refers only to the shape of the *space.* As soon as we reverse our approach and concentrate on the *volume* of the Palazzo del Podestà, the individual space fragments immediately come to life as devices for articulating and molding the complex composite architecture of the palace.

Fragments of space as the means to intensify and heighten the mass of a dominant structure function also in Orvieto. There the cathedral (begun

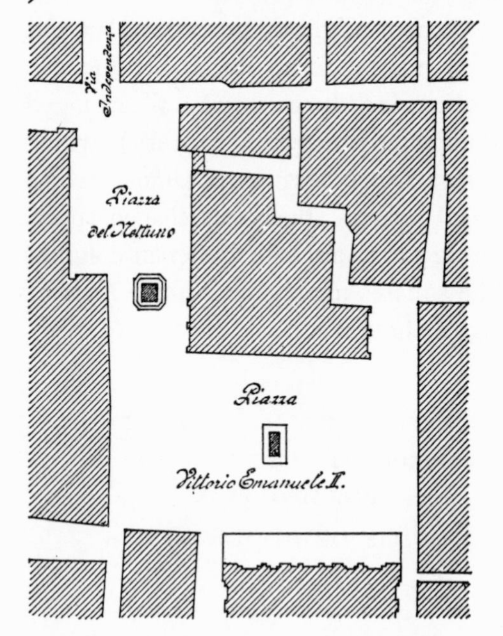

FIG. 27. BOLOGNA. PIAZZA DEL NETTUNO AND PIAZZA MAGGIORE. PLAN

From Brinckmann, *Platz und Monument*

around 1285) is surrounded by small irregular open areas into which the streets run. These small strips have no meaningful shapes of their own, but together they create a kind of negative frame around the building. Small houses opposite the cathedral on three sides emphasize the difference between human and superhuman scale. Rare in Italy, this contrasting relationship between a towering cathedral and its modest secular surroundings is more frequently encountered amidst the narrow network of streets in medieval France and Germany.

The Piazza Vecchia in Bergamo (Pl. 27B), one of the most picturesque squares in northern Italy, appears as an isolated closed square. Actually it is one of a group of squares around the Palazzo della Raggione, but the latter's wide-open arcaded hall does not visually connect the adjoining Piazza del Duomo with the Piazza Vecchia.

Equally charming in its irregularity appears the triangular square before the Romanesque cathedral of Spoleto, located in the upper part of the town. Narrow streets, one actually more a staircase than a street, interrupt the frame of medieval public buildings and houses. The whole piazza functions merely as a receptacle for the townspeople moving through the angular streets toward the church. In other words, the small plaza, actually a parvis, has no spatial shape in its own right but serves rather as an anteroom to the church.

SPECIFIC ARCHITECTURAL ELEMENTS OF MEDIEVAL SQUARES. It is the relationship between individual structures and the space around them rather than the expansion of space as such which distinguishes basically the appearance of medieval squares in the north from those in Italy. During the Middle Ages, specific additive architectural elements—fountains, small monuments, arcades, stairs, etc.—which enhance the effect of the square are of greater importance in the north for the total impression of the square than in the south. Only later, during the Renaissance in Italy, would the interrelation between the square and its furnishings lead to further decorative embellishments of what were originally medieval squares (see p. 115).

These additional props may unify or separate, dramatize or equalize, the visual appearance of individual and combined squares, but they very seldom create a definitely shaped space by themselves. A decisive factor is, of course, the location of adjacent buildings such as town halls, palaces, and churches.

Fountains play only a minor part on northern medieval squares in contrast to their role in Italy during the Renaissance and baroque centuries. Their location in Romanesque and Gothic times is merely accidental or dependent on topographical considerations, since the concept of symmetrical organization in town planning did not yet exist. Fountains, erected as religious or secular mementos, may create poetic corners or lively centers for the exchange of women's gossip but they are never more than a decoration of the square, without much influence on its three-dimensional shape. Their mass is usually much too small compared with the volume of a neighboring church or town hall, or surrounding houses. Thus their small vertical forms parallel the verticalism of buildings nearby, often repeating the vertical edge of a corner in the background (Pl. 28A).

Steps and staircases serve primarily as access to individual buildings, especially to churches, (e.g., St. Severin's in Erfurt; Maria am Gestade in Vienna; St. Michael's in Schwäbisch Hall; the Stiftskirche in Aschaffenburg [Pl. 28B]), or they are intended to overcome natural topographical conditions of the area. At the same time, however, they may become decisive for the final appearance of a square. By dramatizing the otherwise evenly horizontal floor of the square, they intensify its three-dimensional qualities and add to the movement in depth. Thus they become impressive architectural elements of its whole organization (e.g., the Plönlein in Rothenburg; Wimpfen am Berg).

Arcades meant for the medieval square what porticoes meant for the Hellenistic agora and fora to the Imperial era. Where they exist they appear as the only unifying element of the medieval square. They connect the otherwise unconnected architectural elements, they tie the discrepant structures, they create at least one common scale for the otherwise different individual proportions of all adjacent buildings. This effect was achieved in spite of the fact that arcades in the Middle Ages were still bound to the individual houses, had a different diameter for the single arch, and were of different depth (mostly one vault, seldom two vaults deep, as, e.g., in Montauban [see Pl. 63]). Their function originally was, of course, to protect against the sun in the south, and against the rain in the north. Besides, they offered an opportunity for displaying and selling all kinds of wares and goods.

The motif of the arcade originated in the south. Arcaded houses, stemming from the last centuries of the Roman Empire, have been excavated in Rome and especially in Ostia; they were then obviously exceptions to the traditional system of porticoes.

The term *porticus* means for the archaeologist either a porch supported by columns built before or into a house as part of it, or an independent structure resting on columns with only one solid back wall. During the last Roman centuries, these porticoes were no longer constructed with a horizontal architrave, but their columns were connected with each other by semicircular arches—"arcades."

These arcades later spread from Italy in two directions: westward to France (from Monpazier to Arras), to Switzerland (Solothurn, Zurich, Berne), and only rarely to western Germany (Münster in Westphalia, etc.); eastward via the southern Tyrol (Riva, Bolzano) through the Inn River valley (Innsbruck, Wasserburg am Inn) to Bavaria and farther east to Silesia (Hirschberg, Görlitz), Bohemia, and Poland (Cracow). Eventually the motif was taken up in some of the eastern German foundations whence it was introduced by Silesian settlers. This migration proves again that specific architectural forms have an independent life beyond geographical and national boundaries, independent of their original functional motivation.

SOME REMARKS ABOUT THE EAST. Italian and German, French and English towns of the Middle Ages, as much as they may differ from each other, share so many characteristics because of historical reasons that the basic solutions of three-dimensional problems can be compared. General conditions and psychological attitudes of West and East, however, differ so fundamentally that quite naturally they also create entirely different spatial concepts. Correspondingly, squares of the Near and Far East can be related to those of Europe even less than Oriental art to Western art generally. While in painting and sculpture at least some very few European influences may be traced in Asia (e.g., Gandhāra art), there is nothing which would connect the Eastern concept of a town square with Western ideas. Thus some brief remarks are added merely to clarify the basic distinctions.

In the *Near East,* the huge market places of Oriental towns were always located outside the town, before the gates, and were connected neither functionally nor architecturally with the bazaar streets which served the local retail trade inside the town. Around these market places no structural space-defining architecture existed, and the void areas were confined only by fences and similar makeshift markings. Even the open space before the Omar Mosque, located on the site of the old Temple of Solomon in Jerusalem, cannot be perceived as a square because it refers only to the mosque proper; the adjacent structures are without any inner connection with it.

The rectangular open areas within the complex of a mosque or madrasa, from Cairo and Constantinople to Baghdad, can be compared with cloisters or inner courtyards of medieval castles rather than with squares in Europe. Any seeming similarity to European closed squares is misleading since they resemble each other only in their two-dimensional projection but not so far as the third dimension is concerned. In the Orient, the width and length of the void are usually so large that the surrounding one- or two-storied arcades with their shops represent merely a decorative frame around a wide expanse, but never a spatial configuration.

One of the very rare instances in the East where a spatial organization of a free area produces effects somewhat similar to those of late Hellenistic agoras or Imperial Roman fora is the seventeenth-century Maidan-i-Shah in Isfahan (Fig. 28). Its very large expanse is surrounded by two-storied arcades and is accentuated by a monumental entrance gate, Aali-Kapu, to the

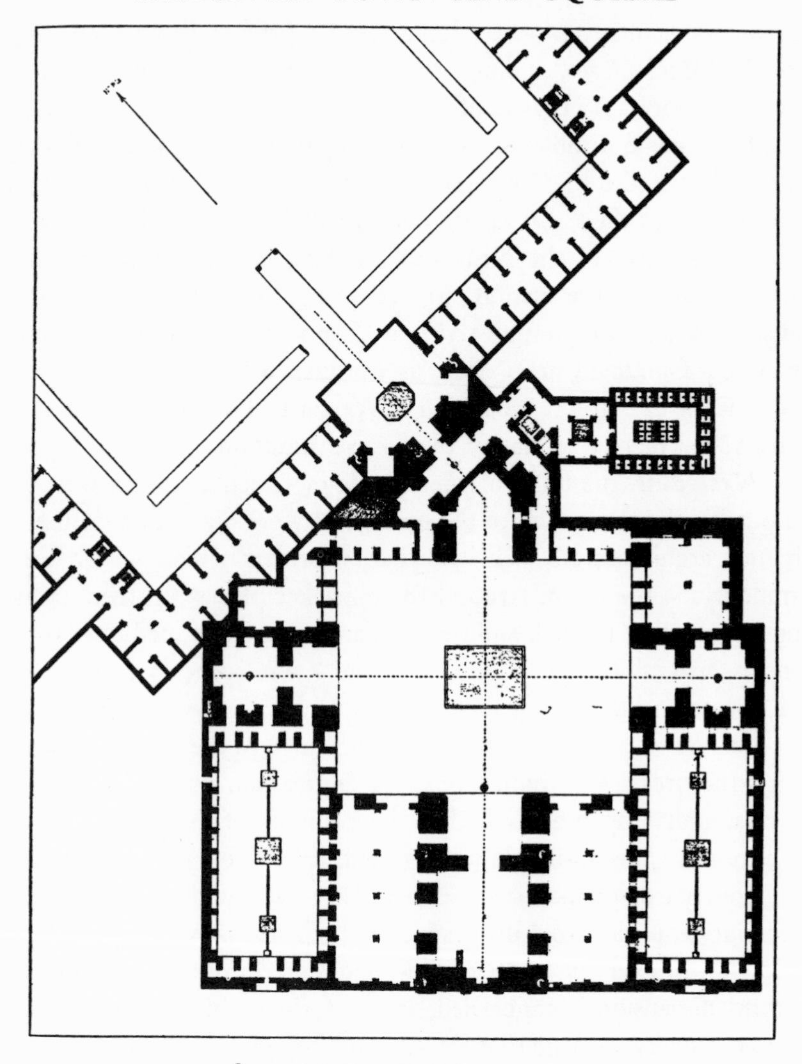

FIG. 28. ISFAHAN. MAIDAN-I-SHAH. PLAN

royal gardens. The whole complex is under an oblique angle connected with and dominated by the main mosque of the town.

Lao-tse once said that "the true reality of a room is not its walls but the emptiness they contain." This concept of the essentiality of the void is reflected in the interior of Chinese and Japanese houses, but certainly not in the squares of *Far Eastern* towns.

Many cities in China, in their beginnings mere irregular accumulations of haphazardly located individual houses, took on the gridiron plan. Some planned cities, such as Ch'ang-an and Loyang, go back even to the Han Period (202 B.C.–A.D. 220).[1] But this gridiron scheme was seldom carried through consistently. It had been stimulated by philosophical rather than by rational reasons: the layout of the town should mirror the organization of the world, orderly, systematic, regular. Since Peiping was considered the center of the universe, this idea was most obviously realized there; but similar examples may be found in many other Chinese towns, e.g., Shensi. The strict organization of Peiping, as rebuilt under Kublai Khan at the end of the thirteenth century, was based on an axis leading from the main temple to the "Forbidden City," the Imperial Palace, and on a symmetrical subdivision into various quarters. Yet the squares of the city never became integrated into this overall plan.

Japan had taken over the gridiron plan from China very early. For instance, in the new capital, Heian Kyo (Kyoto), founded in the eighth century, the focal point was the imperial residence; blocks were regular and public buildings lined the streets, but never in connection with squares. The axial organization was emphasized as strongly as possible, and gates and accompanying buildings were subordinated to it, although without direct architectural reference to each other. Often a hall structure on one side of the street corresponded to a pagoda on the other side, etc. In Japan the focal point of the axis was generally a temple, whereas in China it was mostly a palace.

A favorite topic of Eastern paintings is expansive houses—seats of the nobility—connected with each other by open pergolas of wooden construction and located amidst carefully defined areas. These "courtyards," usually confined by buildings on three sides, open on the fourth side toward a landscaped garden. They thus create picturesque views but never show a feeling for organized space.

The layout of these country estates in the East, as well as the plans of Eastern towns, proves that the freedom of design and the intended aesthetic effect of seeming casualness excluded any emphasis on a fixed structural system and with it any possible comparison with concepts of European city planning and the development of squares.

[1] I am very grateful to Professor L. Carrington Goodrich, of Columbia University, for this information.

THE MEDIEVAL CONCEPT OF EXTERNAL SPACE

The peculiar beauty of medieval squares results essentially from picturesque combinations of individual buildings, often contrasting sharply in height, width, and material. Private houses and public edifices alike represented independent architectural units. Sometimes they were erected in one uninterrupted building line, forming a continuous three-dimensional frame around the square; more often they receded and protruded irregularly, thus creating a broken boundary of the space between them.

A total visual sensation and still less an overall spatial effect are seldom achieved; the aesthetic significance is based on a sequence of successive individual impressions.[2] In other words, not structural relations, but painterly values, are decisive for the medieval square, especially the play of light and shadow on heterogeneous architectural forms. This absence of overall structural relations does not allow for any possible unity of space and therefore no unified three-dimensional shape could result; no feeling for exterior space could develop. This seeming inability to conceive of space under the open sky as something to be shaped contrasts completely with the gift of medieval man for shaping interior space. The history of medieval architecture actually could be written in terms of the development of interior, vaulted space: the evolution of the vault from the Romanesque to the Gothic period means the substitution of the earlier finite space units, strung along the axes of the Romanesque church, by indefinite spatial areas within the definite structural pattern of the Gothic bays. This change finds its parallel in medieval painting: from the flat two-dimensional golden background of Romanesque and early Gothic paintings to the beginning illusion of three-dimensional depth in High Gothic paintings.

Such a parallelism, however, does not exist between the interior space of the church on the one hand and the exterior space of the medieval square on the other. The latter does not show any characteristic change from the Romanesque to the Gothic period but appears merely "medieval," independent of whether it originally stemmed from the tenth or from the thir-

[2] The statement by Wolfgang Braunfels, in *Mittelalterliche Stadtbaukunst in der Toscana* (Berlin, 1953), that "the unifying effect and the subordination to a totality was more important to the Middle Ages than the beauty of an individual building" seems highly doubtful if applied to other regions outside Tuscany.

teenth century. Medieval squares owe their beauty to the growth through centuries, each epoch adding its specific architectural values, but never to the intent of conscious planning.

This idea of conscious planning for the town as a whole or for a specific square was completely alien to medieval man except in the thirteenth-century foundations in France and in eastern Germany. For medieval man, the town was merely a place to live in, more easily defensible than an isolated house in the open country. Only at the end of the Middle Ages did the town become the symbol of any political or social idea. Before, man had hardly considered himself as an individual, still less as a citizen of a specific town, but rather as a member of a specific parish or guild and as the subject of a feudal lord. Thus quite naturally the populace, not yet sharing in a general feeling for the community as such, did not see the need for public centers such as squares which would refer to the town as a whole beyond the limits of an individual parish. Cathedral and town hall sufficed as "civic centers."

Only after the mid-thirteenth century did a very vague feeling for space develop. The new attitude became evident in some town statutes and building laws, such as local laws in Florence and Siena and the German *Stadtrechtbuch* from 1347. These laws are symptomatic of a new concept of regularity and herewith indirectly of a slowly and gradually increasing space consciousness.

Actually the realization of these new ideas was very limited: in Germany as well as in Italy some streets were broadened and straightened where topographical conditions were favorable. But it is only the individual street and very rarely a small parvis or an unimportant little market square that shows this gradually increasing, still subconscious tendency for more regularity, since this trend did not yet crystallize in conscious overall planning.

Other symptoms prove the same underlying feeling: in Florence and some other Italian cities the municipal administrations recommended pavements for streets and squares yet unpaved. And, most characteristically, these suggestions were motivated not only by practical considerations but also by the desire for "more beauty." As the Renaissance concept of interior space is anticipated partially in the *Hallenkirche* (hall church) of the still Gothic fourteenth century, so the idea of Renaissance squares is already hinted at in these small endeavors of the late Gothic period. While, however, in architecture a clearly defined new type of building was actually created in the

Hallenkirche, in urban art the lack of overall planning, still evident in the late Middle Ages, confined the expression of a change in spatial feeling to small symptoms only. Thus, as in all other stylistic developments, no sudden changes take place, but gradual transitions prepare the way for the spatial concepts of the coming epoch.

IV · THE RENAISSANCE TOWN AND SQUARE

THE MAIN difference between the development of the town in medieval and Renaissance times is that in the Renaissance one can truly speak of "city planning." Towns as such, along with their inhabitants, become gradually more important with regard to the individual political units of the whole country. Theoretical thinking and aesthetic consideration begin influencing the creation of individual parts and of the town as a whole. Compared with the impact of this entirely new general approach, the appearance of stylistically new and thoroughly different architectural forms and even the basic change of proportions are of secondary importance. Now, structural clarity replaces the charms of picturesque combinations. At the same time, the astonishing contrast between the concept of interior space and open space which had prevailed during the last medieval centuries vanishes. From the fifteenth century on, architectural design, aesthetic theory, and the principles of city planning are directed by identical ideas, foremost among them the desire for discipline and order in contrast to the relative irregularity and dispersion of Gothic space.

With Leone Battista Alberti's treatises, written in 1449, conscious city planning begins. But the feeling for and the insight into the artistic possibilities of molding open space developed only gradually. This period of evolution has been considered by some historians as a specific stylistic period, the *Zwischenrenaissance* (intermediate Renaissance), comprising the last Gothic century and the first decades of the Renaissance, a period of evolution somewhat comparable to the development in painting from Giotto to Masaccio. The latter's historical position would be represented in city planning by Brunelleschi with his suggestions for the environment of Santo Spirito in

Florence, even before public interest in specific problems of urban beautification was documented.

BASIC ITALIAN THEORIES AND UTOPIAS

The bibliography of contemporaneous works dealing with theories of city planning in the Renaissance would make a small volume in itself. This tremendous interest in the aesthetic ideas of a relatively limited period—only two hundred years—and in a relatively limited field proves the inseparable connection between theory and practice during that period. Renaissance theoreticians and Renaissance artists believed firmly that human life could be entirely rationalized by philosophical and logical schemes, and they embodied this belief in their plans for human habitation. It must therefore be emphasized that rational ideas primarily, and only secondarily a new spatial concept, were decisive for city planning ideas of the Renaissance.

Gradually this rationalizing tendency and the growing feeling for spatial relationship crystallized in specific patterns of town layouts—mostly in centralized systems. The integration of structure and function, the increasing consciousness of spatial relations which was to dominate architectural design from the very beginning of the Renaissance through the tradition of the École des Beaux Arts, became also the basis of town planning. Plans for the surroundings of individual structures or for whole new quarters of a town were designed as "composition."

Although in their plans the Renaissance theoreticians liked to invoke the authority of Vitruvius, in spite of the fact that in his *libri* actually no exact data on city planning can be found, their suggestions were based much less on the traditions of antiquity than they themselves believed. Vitruvius presented no concrete schemes of exemplary planning. Any suggestions scattered throughout his treatises refer to entirely heterogeneous problems. An examination of the arrangement of subjects in the 1511, 1513, 1522, 1523, and 1543 editions of his work will demonstrate that the respective editor-publishers had no special interest in his ideas on city planning as such. Actually, those solutions which were executed during Vitruvius' lifetime, such as the fora of Imperial Rome or Rome's colonial cities in Asia Minor and elsewhere, neither illustrate nor clarify his ideas (see p. 58).

Despite their reference to the authority of the past, the Renaissance artists were actually original in their planning concepts. They shared with antiquity only a general preference for absolute measurements and regularity. Neither Hippodamus' theories for the development of Greek cities, nor Plato's utopian Atlantis, nor Aristotle's ideas in the *Politics*, nor Vitruvius' vague hints had any direct influence on the Renaissance. Nor did the work of Vegetius, a military writer of the fourth century A.D. who merely compiled ideas of older military writers, and who became immensely popular and was often quoted. (First editions of his work appeared in Utrecht in 1473, in Cologne in 1476, in Paris in 1478, and in Rome in 1478.) Actually his writings were of influence on city planning only indirectly through his discussions of defense works and fortification.

Contact with antiquity had been maintained, not by the planned towns of the Renaissance, but rather by those medieval towns which had been erected on genuine Roman foundations, or by the new foundations of the period which followed the old castrum scheme.

The first theoretician of city planning in the Renaissance was Leone Battista Alberti. In his work, published posthumously, the new ideas, however, are not quite clearly developed. He discusses the ideal topographical location of the town, its relation to the landscape, the principles of its organization, and the entire complex of economic and traffic conditions in their bearing upon the plan. However, since problems of fortification are not yet as important to him as to later writers, his ideas are in some respect more modern than the thoughts of those theoreticians who wrote one or two generations after him. Alberti gives exact proportions for the square and the height of its surrounding houses which, by the way, have never been observed in reality.

Whereas the central domed building suggested by Alberti as the chief monumental structure of a town soon became the basic idea of Renaissance architecture (e.g., Bramante's Tempietto in the courtyard of San Pietro in Montorio, Rome, built in 1503), his concept of a centralized square with radiating streets remained the crystallization of theoretical thought and was not realized until more than one and a half centuries later. At the time of its origin Alberti's town project meant but a two-dimensional pattern and was not yet felt as the basic new concept of Renaissance city planning. The first actually delineated Renaissance project, in Antonio Filarete's treatise, written between 1460 and 1464 but published only posthumously, relied partially on Alberti's ideas. Filarete's project, like Alberti's theoretical discussion, is obviously stimulated by Plato's vague description of his Utopia. Filarete's ideal town, called Sforzinda, is laid out as a regular octagon with eight streets radiating from a central square. In the center of this square of Sforzinda an isolated tower is erected, creating a nuclear square; the main buildings of this ideal town, cathedral and ducal palace, are simply parts of the square's periphery. This general scheme is of decisive importance for many future plans, from Palma Nuova and Granmichele in Italy to Washington, D.C., and Le Corbusier's *Ville Radieuse*. It actually became the *idée fixe* of most utopian projects.

Francesco di Giorgio Martini in his treatise uses the octagon for both the central square and the peripheral bounds of his projected city. This consistency proves how strongly at this time all the units of a town plan are subordinated elements of a greater spatial order. In contrast to his predecessors Martini designs his radial streets impinging on the sides of the polygon rather than upon its angles, for better protection against the weather—an arrangement reminiscent of Vitruvius' comments on the same problem. Actually Giorgio Martini's interest in city planning was not confined to these utopian projects. In his many paintings for *cassone* and even in his designs for intarsia work he plays continuously with town planning ideas and especially with the articulation of squares. In this he was not alone. Numerous contemporary designers of intarsia work showed their interest also in the depiction of urban views and especially of squares.

The determining factor in Giorgio Martini's town planning projects is clearly the relationship between the peripheral fortified polygon or circle and the central square, which he compares with the navel of the human body. However, this relationship seems still to be based on the idea of a two-dimensional pattern rather than on three-dimensional space concepts.

A slight variation of Filarete's and Giorgio Martini's projects may be recognized in a drawing from about 1500 which is attributed to Fra Giocondo (Pl. 29A). The periphery of the town as well as of the central square is circular. In the center of square and town a central domed building is erected, almost completely identical with Perugino's and Raphael's background structures in their paintings of the *Betrothal of the Virgin* (1501 and 1504 respectively) and the earlier *cassone* paintings by Luciano da Laurana *ca.* 1475 (Pl. 29B and C). Incidentally, the same Fra Giocondo designed a project for a business center in Venice which, as related by Vasari, included quadrangular closed squares.

Not all of the Renaissance theoreticians were interested in spatial relationships. In Leonardo da Vinci's ideal city no special consideration is given to the problem of the square and its spatial appearance. And it is astonishing that the same Sebastiano Serlio who in his stage design for the Tragic Scene employs a piazza as a perspective showpiece is obviously not interested in the square as a spatial creation (Pl. 30). Nor does Andrea Palladio discuss the square from an aesthetic viewpoint. Fully understanding the sociological importance of the square, he emphasizes merely its rational *commodità* (functional fitness). And yet it was Palladio who in his architecture was the first to succeed in transferring the two-dimensional relationship of a façade to the whole of a complex three-dimensional structure.

It was Pietro Cataneo who developed a large number of new town plans in varied detail, all of them based on the regular polygon (Fig. 29). Although he was not directly connected with the world of great architectural speculations of the Vitruvian Academy, a line of tradition is established by the fact that he was a pupil of Baldassare Perruzzi who himself, influenced by Francesco di Giorgio Martini, had designed some projects for ideal cities. Cataneo's plans include a special citadel for the ruler or tyrant of the city, repeating in miniature the scheme of the town proper. Cataneo plays with variations of a given two-dimensional scheme obviously for pattern's sake. Nevertheless, it seems that by this time the real spatial meaning of the centralizing tendency was actually felt. Too many buildings had already been erected whose elements were organized according to this concept. Fifty years later one of Cataneo's suggestions was realized in the original foundation of Mannheim, Germany (see pp. 207–8).

Generally, Cataneo's treatise presented an inexhaustible stimulation for the next two centuries, and was often plainly plagiarized. His basic suggestions are contained in the first volume of his work, published in 1554. There he criticizes the cities of antiquity because they "have sprung up without rational uniform plans, that means by mere chance"—a reproach, as we know today, not quite justified, at least not in reference to Hellenistic towns. "The essential squares lie outside of the periphery, as, for instance in ancient Rome, the Campus Martium." He, Cataneo, would create instead an organization, consciously planned, based on the forms of regular polygons. However, he admits that these ideal forms of the regular polygon can be carried through only on a plane where no topographical obstacles disturb the regular development.

In many respects, Bartolomeo Ammanati, writing around 1560, follows the ideas of Cataneo, as do Girolamo Maggi and Francesco di Marchi in their later treatises.

The last important theoretical project of an Italian writer is Vasari il Giovane's *Città ideale* (Fig. 30), showing again a quadrangular central square with a central building and eight radiating streets in combination with gridiron systems. Smaller squares are formed where radiating and straight streets meet, as executed almost a century later in Granmichele (see p. 108).

The "city" from the sixteenth century on became more and more a symbol of a definite social and governmental order. Thus it is not astonishing that a great number of "utopias" were developed in which theological, philosophical, and sociological concepts were combined with practical suggestions. Authors always mention some architectural and city planning details, from Thomas More to Tommaso Campanella with his astrological references and J. V. Andreae with his peculiar mixture of Christian symbolism and Platonic thoughts. When Campanella and Andreae discuss their ideal schemes of human society, they describe their utopian cities, respectively the *civitas solis* and Christianopolis, as completely centralized embodiments of their ideological and philosophical systems. Obviously the theorems of the Renaissance city planners were so generally known in the scholarly world that, even when entirely different problems were dealt with, this concept of a utopian city was the type closest to the imagination of the learned man of that period.

REALIZATIONS IN SPACE IN ITALY

The theoretical concepts discussed above are first encountered in reality in the architecture of gardens and parks of the early sixteenth century. Landscaping, which deals with the flexible material of lawns, bushes, and trees, anticipated to a certain degree the execution of the original ideas of Alberti and Filarete as they were first to be realized in three-dimensional form in Palma Nuova (see p. 107). During the Middle Ages the concept of regularly defined open space—completely unknown then in town planning—prevailed

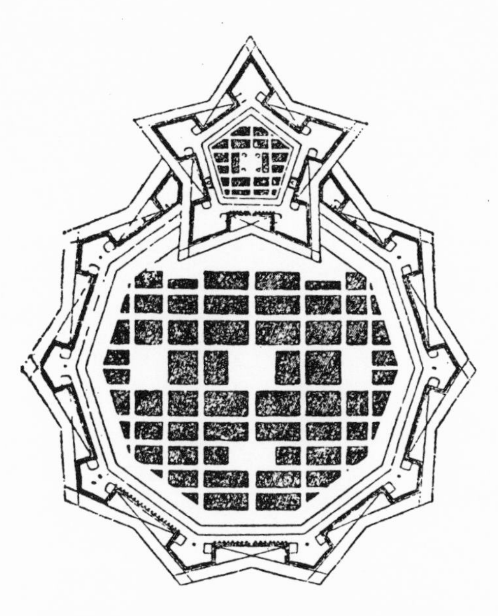

FIG. 29. PLAN FOR AN IDEAL CITY, *ca.* 1567, BY PIETRO CATANEO

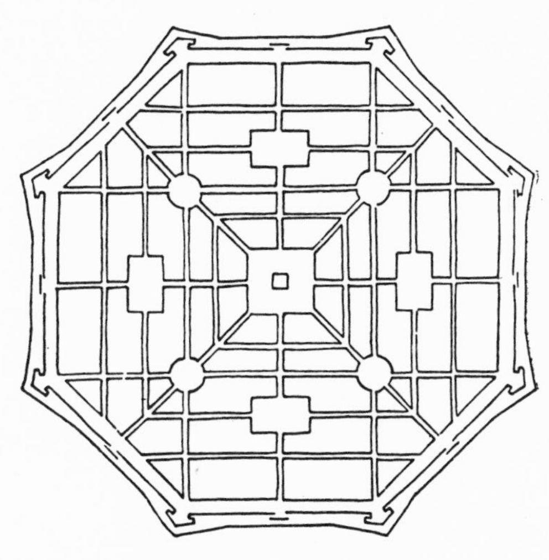

FIG. 30. PLAN FOR AN IDEAL CITY, 1598, BY VASARI IL GIOVANE

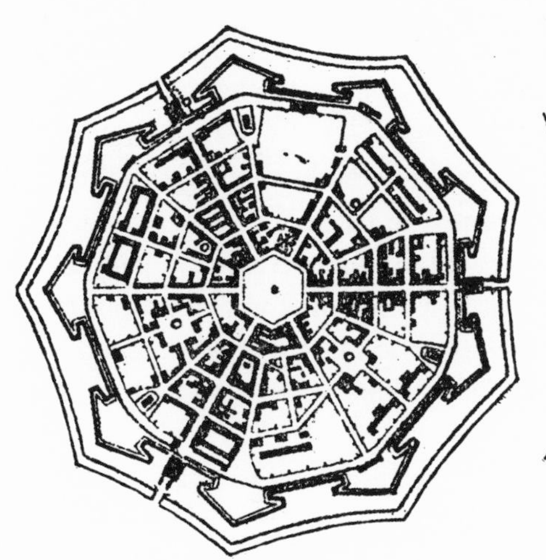

FIG. 31. PALMA NUOVA, 1593. PLAN

FIG. 32. PLAN FOR AN IDEAL CITY, *ca.* 1615, BY VINCENZO SCAMOZZI

in the cloister gardens of monasteries. But it remained an isolated phenomenon at that time.

Now, in the first half of the sixteenth century, the generation of Bramante, Raphael, and Giulio Romano created gardens whose organizations combined the concept of the medieval cloister garden, vastly enlarged, with the ideas proffered in the treatises from Alberti's work on. The great Cortile of the Belvedere of the Vatican (*ca.* 1506), by Bramante, Perruzzi, Antonio da Sangallo, Girolamo da Carpi, and eventually Pirro Ligorio; the gardens of the Villa Madama (*ca.* 1516), by Raphael and Giulio Romano; the gardens of the Palazzo Farnese (1530–80), by Antonio da Sangallo and Vignola—all are characterized by the use of three architectural elements: terraces to overcome differences in level; flower beds, patterned in definite designs; and, most important, the strict emphasis on axial organization. This axiality, in connection with the rhythmically staggered terraces and architectural niches, as, e.g., in the Belvedere of the Vatican and in the Villa Madama gardens, brings about a gradual transition to adjacent architecture and ties garden planning and town planning most closely together. The same principle dictates the planning of the gardens of Caprarola by Antonio da Sangallo and Perruzzi (1543); the parks of Vignola's Villa Lante (1560); and the layout of Giulio Romano's Palazzo del Té in Mantua (1523–35). Sometimes the flower beds, geometrically shaped (parterres), are arranged exactly like city blocks with squares in between.

The botanical garden in Padua, the first of its kind, laid out in 1545 following the ideas of Francesco Bonafede, surprises one by its close resemblance to the radio-centric, circular projects in contemporaneous city planning treatises. A quadrangle is enclosed in the regular circle of the garden layout, both connected by the two intersecting roads as axes. A very late echo of this plan may be recognized in the Prato della Valle, which is close to the botanical garden in Padua (see p. 161).

The most impressive work of landscaping architecture in the sixteenth century is, of course, the park of the Villa d'Este near Tivoli, laid out by Pirro Ligorio in 1549 for the Cardinal Ippolito d'Este. It represents a grandiose system of axes in terms of roads, planted alleys, waterfalls, fountains, and basins. These axes define the direction of stairs and ramps, create terraces, cut through bosquets, and connect canals, fountains, and waterfalls. The whole park rather resembles a town with various quarters where each section shows its own architectural character. And all these quarters are integrated into an overall axial scheme of natural growth and man-made order. The influence of these gardens through the seventeenth century equals the influence of Versailles in the eighteenth century. From now on, landscaping and town planning are closely related and reflect identical aesthetic concepts.

Eventually the theoretical ideas of Alberti and Filarete were executed with only slight variations. Palma Nuova, built as a Venetian fort in 1593, probably by Vincenzo Scamozzi, became the first realization of the erstwhile utopian ideas of Renaissance theoreticians (Fig. 31). The defensive function explains its structure. The inner quarters of the town are organized around a central square from which six streets radiate. Smaller streets start farther away from the center. Palma Nuova as it is executed differs from Scamozzi's ideal city as published in his work.[1] In his theoretical scheme (Fig. 32) the central square was surrounded by four subordinated quadrangular squares which are connected with it through gridiron systems and not by radial streets as in Palma Nuova, a system repeated almost identically in northern Europe in the little fort of Coevorden (see p. 126). More important, however, than Scamozzi's plans for an ideal city and the execution of Palma Nuova is his statement that a city should not be a product of nature but the result of planning. In this planning, "artistic considerations should supersede even the technical needs of fortifications"—a completely new concept.

Quite obviously Scamozzi's importance is based not on the invention of any new forms but rather on the integration of various elements conceived by his predecessors. Consideration of military needs explains an organization which made it possible that all sections of the city could be reached and controlled from the central square.

In Palma Nuova it is no longer the delight in ornamental graphic play but the three-dimensional realization of the design that is the determining factor. The volume of houses, which line the streets and surround the squares, balances the framed open space: *Körperform* (form of mass) against *Raumform* (form of space). The whole town corresponds to the interior of the central domed building transferred into the open space. The Bramante-Raphael-Sangallo-Perruzzi-Michelangelo project of St. Peter's in Rome and Palladio's

[1] It is surprising to find that both the 1678 German translation of Scamozzi's work and the French translation of 1713 do not include the chapter on city planning.

Villa Rotonda in Vicenza are as much the predecessors of the plan for Palma Nuova as are the theoretical suggestions of Alberti and Filarete. The central square is the focus of a strictly radial organization of the town, as is the space under St. Peter's cupola in the first projects for that church and that of the Villa Rotonda. In all instances the individual space units—such as bays, niches, and domed crossing in the church; the central hall in the villa; streets, blocks, and main square in the town—are conceived as elements of an identical order. Actually the star square, so favored in the seventeenth and eighteenth centuries (see p. 210) can be traced to this scheme.

The layout of Palma Nuova was to experience a late revival even on the American continent, in Circleville, Ohio, possibly stimulated by the mounds of pre-Columbian Indians on the same site. The land was bought in 1810 and the town was built exactly following the example of Palma Nuova and the ideas of Scamozzi, complete with central domed octagonal building on the central square from which eight streets radiated, the whole scheme surrounded by a regular gridiron. Unfortunately, this highly original solution was transformed after 1837, step by step, into a regular overall gridiron.

In his later writings, Scamozzi modified the plan of Palma Nuova still further by combining the polygon with the gridiron scheme, yet retaining the radially symmetrical distribution of separate smaller squares, streets, and other subordinated elements.

One hundred years later, Granmichele, built in 1693 for Carlo Caraffa in lieu of the destroyed town of Occhiola near Catania, was a combination of Scamozzi's ideal city and his executed city of Palma Nuova. Again there appears the central square with radiating streets, in combination with six independent gridiron systems, each organized around a smaller secondary square (Fig. 33).

During the last decades of the sixteenth century, more and more treatises and textbooks on the construction of fortifications were published. Although the theoreticians primarily considered military needs in their suggestions, the plan for the interior of these fortresses was never neglected. A central square with or without a central tower in combination with a rectangular gridiron block defines the scheme of many cities laid out in the sixteenth century. There is Gattinara, which after its destruction in 1524 was immediately rebuilt as a regular rectangle by Mercurinus Arborius de Gattinara. There, in the center of the town at the meeting point of the two axes, a square is created by cutting away rectangular sections of the four central blocks. This layout is all the more noteworthy since it represents a definite break from the medieval concept in which the space of the closed square just filled the area skipped by the regular blocks, as in the bastides and eastern German settlements. Arcades frame the square of Gattinara as in Vigevano and Leghorn

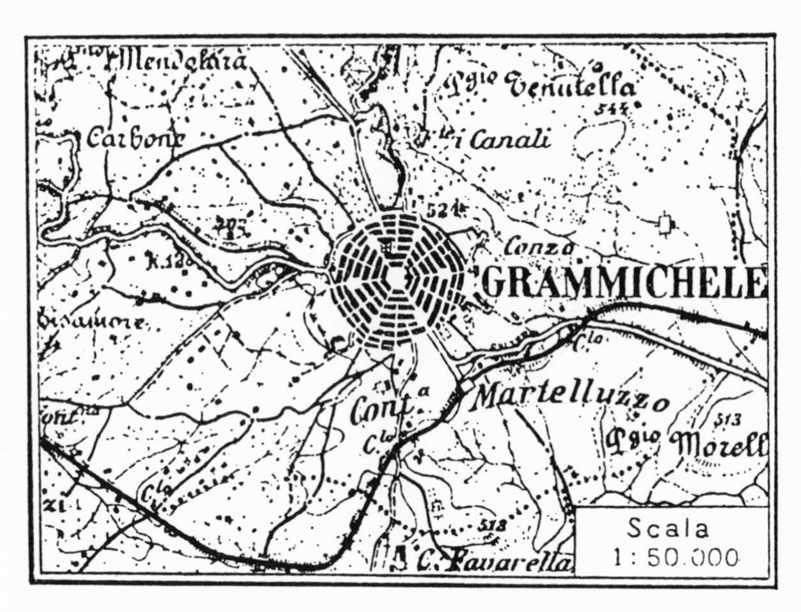

FIG. 33. GRANMICHELE. PLAN
From *L'Universo* (1920)

(see pp. 112–13). Although the surrounding houses are not completely identical, they are so much alike that they increase the impression of uniformity.

In Valletta, laid out in 1564–66 for the Order of the Knights of Malta, two central squares are arranged within a gridiron system, adjacent to each other and to the main street. The plan, however, is less rigid than in Gattinara, since the town is located on a hilly peninsula where specific topographical conditions had to be considered.

From this time on Cataneo's and Scamozzi's ideas were repeated endlessly, either literally or with variations. The designs of these "city planners" turned again into a mere play of ornamental patterns. Although their projects are without any importance for the development of a spatial concept, the titles of the best known treatises from the end of the sixteenth century may at least be mentioned: Antonio Lupicini, *Architettura militare*, Florence, 1582; Girolamo Maggi and Giacomo Castriotti, *Della fortificazione della città . . .*, Book III, Venice, 1583 and 1584; Buonaiuto Lorini, *Delle fortificatione libri cinque*, Venice, 1592; Giovanni Battista di Bartolomeo Bellucci, *Nuove inventione de' fabbricar fortezze di varie forme*, Venice, 1598; Francesco de Marchi, *Del' architettura militare*, Book III, Brescia, 1599; Gabriello Busca, *L'architettura militare*, Milan, 1619. In all these works, the continuous repetition of a stereotyped pattern of a square bespeaks the mechanization of an idea which had lost its original three-dimensional meaning.

So far, so good! However, some important three-dimensional creations of the Renaissance developed more or less independently of theoretical thinking; intuition rather than systematization inspired these crystallizations of the human spirit in space.

In Italy fewer visible achievements of the Renaissance period in city planning still exist than one would expect in comparison with the unique abundance of contemporaneous painting, sculpture, and architecture. In the great squares of Italy, the ancient Mediterranean tradition of space exemplified by the Hellenistic agoras and the Roman fora lived on. Here the impact of the man-made townscape could—and still can—compete with the experience of the God-made landscape, both impressing upon man a transcendental awareness of space.

The common stylistic trends of Italian Renaissance squares can be defined only in very broad terms:

1. The desire for spatial unity, to which all other architectural tendencies are subordinated. This holds true even for a parvis where now, quite in accordance with the typical tendency of the Renaissance for balancing accents, the dominant role of the main structure is reduced. In the Middle Ages as well as later on in baroque times the governing mass of the church was much more strongly emphasized.

2. The frequent employment of arcades as connecting architectural elements in order to increase the unity of the façades surrounding the

square. Identical arcades for all houses now repeat one motif, whereas during the Middle Ages each house had its individual arcades. The impression of such arcaded squares in their purest form, as, e.g., in Vigevano, corresponds to that of the inner courtyards of Florentine and Roman Renaissance palaces translated into a larger scale. Generally, these protective arcades help to dignify even rather indifferent façades and to introduce a persuasive rhythm to the open area of the square.

3. The use of monuments, fountains, flagpoles, etc., for organizing the space of the square, whether it be closed, dominated, or nuclear. In the Middle Ages such structures were treated as individual freestanding structures, without relation to the square as a whole.

No common trait, however, can be found in the preference for any specific proportions or relationship of width and length of the square. The suggestions of Vitruvius, Alberti, and Palladio are nowhere followed.

Before analyzing some of the most significant Italian Renaissance squares, a unique creation must be mentioned where medieval and Renaissance elements fuse: the Piazza Piccolomini in Pienza (Pl. 31A). Bernardo Rossellino had been commissioned by Pope Pius II to rebuild the latter's birthplace, the former village of Corsignano, from 1458 to 1462. The center of this newly founded quattrocento town Pienza is a square with the dimensions of a typical medieval small-town market, but surrounded by the rather pretentious Renaissance edifices of the cathedral, the episcopal palace, and the Palazzo Piccolomini. The inner courtyard of the last is even larger than the whole square. The obliquely directed façades of the two palaces frame the front of the church as do later on the sides of the Campidoglio and of St. Peter's in Rome. This trick of perspective represents in no way an anticipation of later baroque tendencies, since in Pienza the artistic aim was merely to enlarge the impression of square and façade beyond their actual size. Later solutions elsewhere suggest to the spectator primarily a movement toward the dominating structure.

What a contrast between the square in Pienza, a hybrid of two stylistic concepts, and the spatial appearance of a real Renaissance square as first conceived by Brunelleschi, the Piazza di SS. Annunziata in Florence! It was he who designed, in 1409, the motif of the arcades in front of the Foundlings' Hospital on the southwest side of the Piazza di SS. Annunziata, executed in

1421–51 (Pl. 31B). These elegant arcades set the pattern also for the opposite side of the square where they were repeated later by Antonio da Sangallo the Elder in the loggia to the church SS. Annunziata, and taken up again by Giovanni Caccini in 1601–4 in the enlargement of the entrance hall of the church after the earlier design of Sangallo. The airy Renaissance arcade in its continuous flux is felt primarily as a unifying frame around the void of the square while, as was said before, the medieval arcade belongs visually rather to the mass of the individual building of which it is a part. But now, in the Renaissance, the arcades expand the space of the square and integrate the volume of the structure and the spatial void before it.

The equestrian statue of Ferdinand I by Giovanni da Bologna (1608) and the two fountains by Pietro Tacca (1629) contribute to the unified and balanced appearance of the square, which not until two centuries after it was begun realized the original concept of Brunelleschi. His visionary concept was one of strictest axiality and of space channeled into definite form. The cupola of the cathedral in the distance, the equestrian statue, and the central arcade of the church SS. Annunziata create one axis. The continuous surface of the paved floor of the square contributes further to spatial unity. As in his architecture, Brunelleschi also expressed in city planning the spatial concept of the Renaissance in its purest form.

The Renaissance squares which, in contrast to that of SS. Annunziata in Florence, were completed during that period are not imaginable without Brunelleschi's example. The Piazza Ducale in Vigevano, a small town not too far from Milan and hardly ever visited by tourists, must be considered the first complete Renaissance square. It was actually constructed according to a definite program. In contrast to Pienza, in Vigevano not the surrounding structures but the space proper of the square indicates the *Formwillen* (forming tendency) of the Renaissance (Pl. 32). The Piazza Ducale was executed under Lodovico il Moro by Ambrogio di Curtis, possibly (?) in collaboration with Bramante and Leonardo da Vinci, between 1492 and 1498. The project foresaw the razing of previous structures without compromising with any given conditions and without any consideration of the existing web of streets. The continuity of the façades with identical arcades, identical windows, and identical height of eaves and roofs is not interrupted, except for the fourth side, closed in the seventeenth century by the baroque cathedral. The arcades conceal even the exits to the streets leading in various directions. The ideal of Renaissance *concinnitas* (harmonious balance) is achieved by complete spatial continuity and unification of all contributing elements, including even the pattern of the pavement.

Two other Italian Renaissance squares were, like Vigevano, planned in their totality and executed accordingly. On the piazza before the Chiesa della Casa Santa in Loreto the monumental two-storied arcades of the College of the Jesuits and of the Palazzo Apostolico were probably designed by Bramante and executed by Antonio da Sangallo (Pl. 33). Unfortunately, only three sides of the square were completed corresponding to the plan. The fourth side was not dealt with accordingly. The solemn static rhythm of the arcades was designed to induce a balanced state in the people before they entered the church with its miraculous sanctuary. It was not meant to induce an immediate motion toward the edifice, as is so often the intention in later baroque times. The fountain, erected around 1620, represents a nucleus for the milling crowd on the square rather than a guiding post in the direction toward the church.

A similar solution, even more static and thus expressing the true aim of all Renaissance art, is given in the Piazza Vittorio Emanuele in Leghorn. The arcaded square before the cathedral (consecrated in 1606), stimulated clearly by the earlier example of Gattinara, appears as the final expansion of an avenue leading straight through the square toward the main portal of the church. Two streets intersect the square symmetrically at an angle of 90°, thus increasing the effect of an arresting *fermata* before the church structure.

Strangely enough, the most famous Renaissance squares in Italy do not follow the scheme of the typical closed squares of this period as represented by Vigevano, Loreto, Leghorn, and the later Piazza di SS. Annunziata in Florence. Neither are their layouts and appearance derived from the rationalized intellectual solutions of Gattinara, Valletta, or Palma Nuova. They owe their final shape rather to a gradual development from the Middle Ages to the Renaissance, when they took on the characteristics which made them the heart of their cities.

If ever a square was to become the symbol for a whole city, it certainly was St. Mark's Square (the Piazza di San Marco) in Venice, the "ballroom of Europe." In its present appearance it is the result of many additions and changes, of which the most important took place between 1536 and 1640 and around 1810 (Pl. 34A). Around the year 1000, the square already served as market place and at the same time as parvis of St. Mark's, which, begun in 830, had originally been merely the palace chapel of the Doges. The square had been enlarged in the twelfth century under the Doge Sebastiano Ziani, by filling in a small canal and razing previous buildings. As we know from Bellini's painting (Pl. 34B), among other sources, in the fifteenth century the square was surrounded on all sides by uneven brick-arcaded façades. The Campanile had been erected in 888, primarily as a nautical signpost. Its wooden construction was rebuilt in 1329 in bricks. After its collapse in 1902, the Campanile was reerected in its original form, and it must be admitted that the smoothness of the twentieth-century bricks and the neatness of their seams emphasize the overpowering size of the Campanile in comparison with the smaller proportions of the church façade.

The clock tower with its passageway as entrance to Venice's main street, the Merceria, was constructed in 1499 by Caducci. At about the same time Pietro Lombardi and Bartolommeo Buon the Younger built on the north side the Procuratie Vecchie (1480–1517), the old administration offices. The decisive step toward Renaissance concepts was taken by Jacopo Sansovino in 1536–37 by razing previously existing buildings opposite the Procuratie Vecchie, pushing back the building line, and designing his new library (completed by Scamozzi in 1584). By this change the Campanile became isolated as the hinge between the Piazza and the smaller Piazzetta. Continuing the building line of the north façade of Sansovino's library, Vincenzo Scamozzi in 1584 began the Procuratie Nuove (new administration offices), completed by Baldassare Longhena in 1640. Finally, the square's fourth side, opposite St. Mark's, was closed by the Fabbrica Nuova, erected for Eugene Beauharnais by Soli in 1810. This structure bridges the difference in height between the old and the new Procuratie. The flagpoles before St. Mark's were designed by Alessandro Leopardi in 1505, and contribute strongly to the spatial appearance of the Piazza, as does the geometrical pattern of the stone floor, laid out by Andrea Tirale in 1722–35. The Palace of the Doges, built from 1309 to 1424, parallel to the façade of St. Mark's, although receding, creates with its regal horizontals the main mass, framing the Piazzetta on one long side, opposite Scamozzi's library. Two granite columns at the south side of the Piazzetta, the lion's column of 1189 and the column of St. Theodore of 1329, close the Piazzetta as a kind of fourth side. As much as the obliqueness of the north and south sides of the Piazza increases the effect of the Napoleonic Fabbrica Nuova, it cannot be denied that in the opposite direction it minimizes the dimensions of the façade of St. Mark's.

Again and again, tourists, especially from northern countries, describe St. Mark's Square as a "courtyard." As odd as this clumsy misnomer seems to be, it contains a grain of truth: without a doubt, Sansovino and Scamozzi tried in Venice to translate the space form of the Florentine palace courtyard into a larger scale. In order to achieve a certain similarity to such sixteenth-century squares as those in Vigevano, Loreto, and Leghorn, and before SS. Annunziata in Florence, squares which fulfilled the spatial ideas of the High Renaissance so completely, Sansovino and Scamozzi sacrificed the grandeur of St. Mark's, whose façade appears rather small in relation to the overwhelming height of the old Campanile. The oblique directions of the old and new Procuratie, with their façades converging toward the Napoleonic Fabbrica opposite the church façade and diverging from the church, isolate the church façade rather than tie it in as the fourth side. Naturally the beholder, standing in front of the church, perceives the Piazza as much deeper than from the opposite direction, contrary to the effect of the converging sides of the squares of Pienza, the Campidoglio, and of the later St. Peter's Square in Rome. And yet, the combination of Piazza, Piazzetta, and the third smaller square at the northwest corner of St. Mark's fuse into one of the greatest space impressions of all time, comparable in their symphonic effect only to the Imperial Fora in Rome.

The Piazza della Signoria, Florence's civic center for more than six centuries, is actually a medieval creation as to time of origin and erstwhile appearance (Pl. 35). From medieval times the population of Florence had grown relatively rapidly: by 1348 it was 51,000; by 1400 it had already reached 60,000; by 1470, after a temporary decline because of the plague, it was 70,000. When Arnolfo di Cambio began the Palazzo Vecchio (della Signoria) in 1288, palaces and small churches in its environment had been razed and additional lots were still bought as late as 1319 and 1355. Thus a void was consciously created into which the mass of the Palazzo Vecchio protruded. The angular form of that area, into which streets from all sides and in different directions cut, was not alien to medieval feelings, but it was completely contrary to everything in which the Renaissance believed. During the sixteenth century, therefore, sculptural furnishings turned the multilateral and unbalanced area of the medieval square into two separate rectangular spatial units whose small irregularities then became aesthetically irrelevant. And a third spatial unit was added through Giorgio Vasari's erection of the Uffizi Gallery (1560–74), which opened toward the Piazza della Signoria. However, the Uffizi did not become part of the square proper but functioned merely as a passageway. Clearly, it was the perspective effect Vasari sought to achieve through the uniformity of façades, similar to the separate vista of a street on the contemporary stage.

Nearby is the Loggia dei Lanzi, already begun in 1376, probably after a design of Orcagna; its large openings anticipated the new spirit in form and proportion. Thus Michelangelo's later project for continuing the system of the Loggia's arcades around the whole piazza actually would have made the square into a most perfect Renaissance square—but it was never carried through. Then, in 1504, Michelangelo's *David* was placed to the left of the Signoria's entrance after long discussions in which, among other experts, Leonardo da Vinci and Giuliano da Sangallo also participated. Beyond its intrinsic sculptural power, this statue (today only a copy stands there) became the starting point for the location of further sculptural monuments which in their totality were to create a visual fourth wall for both space units which were yet to develop. The row was strengthened to the right of the Palazzo Vecchio's portal by the addition in 1534 of Baccio Bandinelli's *Hercules and Cacus* group, continued at the left by Donatello's bronze *Judith*, and fortified further by Bartolomeo Ammanati's large Neptune Fountain, erected in 1557 at an angle of 45° before the corner of the palace. As the last monument, the equestrian statue of Cosimo I by Giovanni da Bologna was located in the center of the imaginary borderline of both squares. Small compared with the surrounding buildings and topically unrelated, these sculptural masses, together with the clean-cut, severe front of the cubic palazzo, nonetheless introduced a barrier so strong visually that the two newly created space units correspond in their proportions and shapes at least to a certain degree to the ideals of the Renaissance.

Giovanni da Bologna's dominant Neptune's Fountain erected in 1567 on the Piazza del Nettuno in Bologna fulfills a function similar to that of the sculptures on the Florentine piazza, serving as separation between the Piazza Maggiore (formerly the Piazza Vittorio Emanuele II) and the Piazza Nettuno (see p. 90). However, in our opinion, these three combined squares, the Piazza Maggiore, Piazza Nettuno, and Piazza di Re Enzio, which surround the thirteenth-century Palazzo di Re Enzio and the Palazzo del Podestà (begun in 1201) are definitely of medieval character. This impression is not changed by the placing of the fountain by Giovanni da Bologna. None of them becomes a square in the Renaissance concept. They merely surround the central structure of the two combined palaces as separate units, and, unlike the space units in Florence, do not fuse into a larger visual organization but rather help to isolate the volume of the town hall.

Two medieval squares changed their character completely through monuments which were erected during the Renaissance. In spite of all the medieval churches and houses which surround them they definitely must be considered creations of the Renaissance: the Piazza del Santo in Padua and the Piazza di SS. Giovanni e Paolo in Venice. Actually these monuments, Donatello's *Gattamelata*, erected in 1453 in Padua, and Verrocchio's *Colleoni*, erected in 1493 in Venice, turned mere voids, previously irregular and without any spatial continuum, into highly organized squares. In both instances, the spectator is magically drawn from every viewpoint, at every angle, toward the monument, which thus becomes the nucleus of a definite space form; the squares are typical nuclear squares.

In Padua, two streets along the west and north sides of the Church of San Antonio di Padua, the Santo, meet at an angle of 90° and are broadened at their intersection through the elimination of a previously existing churchyard (Pl. 36). These two open areas fused into a spatially unified square only after the statue of the *Gattamelata* was erected. The visual axis of the monument became a pivotal center of gravity, located as it was diagonally between the corner of the church and the inner right angle of the opposite houses, tying together the irregular, almost contradictory masses of these structures. In this way a definitely determined space has been created. The pedestal of the monument has just the right volume and height to balance the protrusions and recessions of the church and of the façades opposite. At the same time, it isolates the figure of the *Gattamelata* and sets it off from the hurly-burly of street life just high enough to let the figure of horse and rider be seen from almost every corner of the square as a clearly outlined silhouette against the sky. The magnetic and unifying effect of the statue is so strong that nobody, strolling over the square, becomes aware of the bizarre irregularity of its confines and of the disparity of both parts of the area. Actually it is only the location of the statue which changes the open areas around the cathedral from medieval haphazardness into an organized Renaissance form.

Andrea Verrocchio faced a similar task of unification through a monumental nucleus when in 1479 he was commissioned to erect the statue of the *condottiere* Colleoni on the Piazza di SS. Giovanni e Paolo in Venice (Pl. 37). The relatively small campo which stretches before the west façade and along the south side of the church opens on a canal. Originally, the square was more narrowly limited because the structure of a charitable association, the so-called *scuola*, and a churchyard were adjacent to the south wall of the church. Here again the monument is located at an angle of 45° toward the southwest corner of the church, visually completely isolated. The very high pedestal, completed in 1493 by Alessandro Leopardi, adds enough volume to the equestrian statue so that it becomes the center of gravity in the same way as the *Gattamelata* in Padua. The position of the monument parallels the longitudinal axis of the church, both being directed toward the canal. The surrounding structures, closer to the monument than in Padua, are irregular in every respect: the west front of the church, rather tall, is immediately joined to the much lower Scuola di San Marco at a right angle; then again at an angle of 90° stretches the complete flatness of the canal; and at the fourth side, a row of small private houses of different heights is interrupted by a small street. The incongruities and discrepancies, increased through entirely heterogeneous architectural forms, are visually suppressed and at the same time dominated by the nucleus of the monument to which everything on and around the piazza refers. The statue with its pedestal subdivides the free space into cubes which dovetail and in their totality exercise a strict and compelling directive force upon the spectator.

The erection of the *Gattamelata* and the *Colleoni* in the fifteenth century created the visual shape and spatial expanse of the two nuclear squares in Padua and Venice. In spite of all remnants from earlier periods which had to be incorporated into their organization, these squares emanate the new spirit of the Renaissance. The history of their origins explains why they are so thoroughly different from two other Italian Renaissance squares where the Renaissance masters had not to face so many incongruous elements of the past, the Piazza Farnese in Rome and the Piazza dei Cavalli in Piacenza.

The Piazza Farnese (Pl. 38A) opens parvis-like in front of the Palazzo of

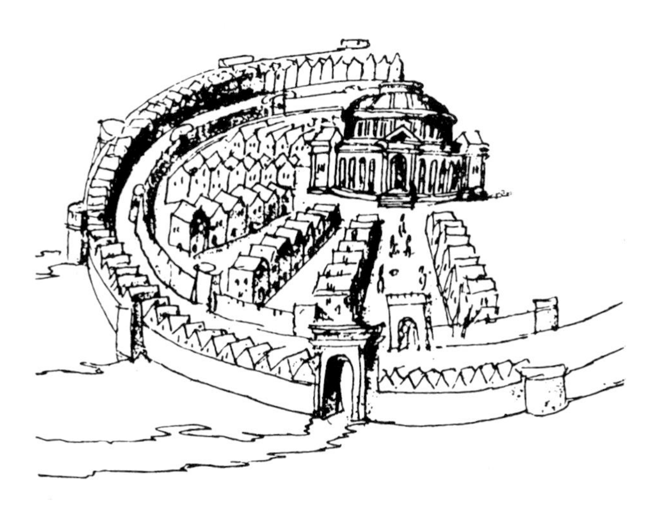

A: PLAN FOR AN IDEAL CITY, *ca.* 1500. ATTRIBUTED TO FRA GIOCONDO

B: CASSONE PAINTING BY LUCIANO DA LAURANA (FORMERLY ATTRIBUTED TO PIERO DELLA FRANCESCA), *ca.* 1500
URBINO, PALAZZO DUCALE
Photo Alinari

C: CASSONE PAINTING ATTRIBUTED TO LUCIANO DA LAURANA
WALTERS ART GALLERY, BALTIMORE, MARYLAND

STAGE SETTING FOR A TRAGIC SCENE BY SEBASTIANO SERLIO

Courtesy Metropolitan Museum of Art

A: PIENZA. PIAZZA PIO II (PICCOLOMINI)
Photo Angeli, Terni

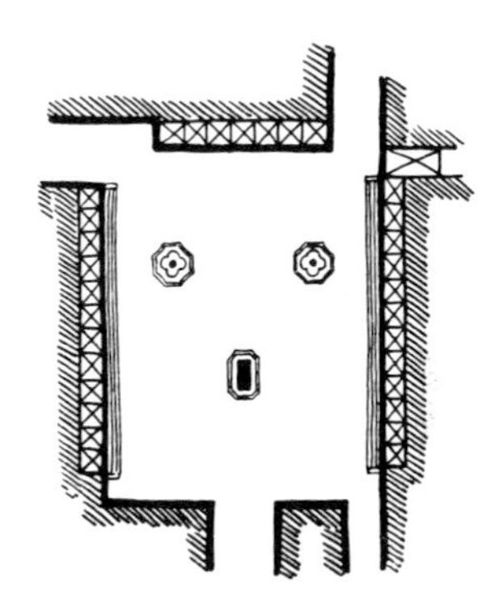

B: FLORENCE
PIAZZA DI SS. ANNUNZIATA. PLAN

COPPER ENGRAVING BY GIUSEPPE ZOCCHI, EIGHTEENTH CENTURY

VIGEVANO. PIAZZA DUCALE FROM THE DUOMO

TOWARD THE DUOMO

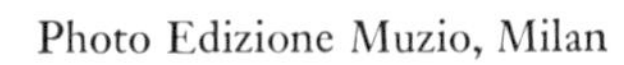
Photo Edizione Muzio, Milan

LORETO. PIAZZA BEFORE THE CHIESA DELLA CASA SANTA

ABOVE: AERIAL VIEW

Photo Ministero Aeronautico

LEFT: GROUND VIEW

Photo ENIT; courtesy Italian State Tourist Office, New York

A: VENICE
ST. MARK'S SQUARE AND
THE PIAZZETTA

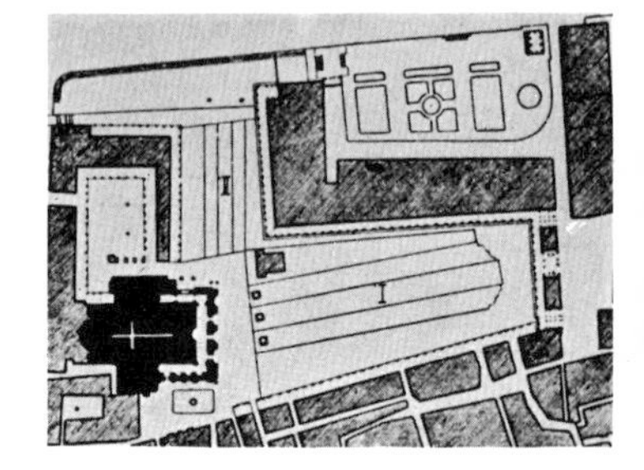

AERIAL VIEW
Photo ENIT; courtesy Italian State Tourist Office, New York

PLAN
From Sitte,
The Art of Building Cities

B: PROCESSION ON ST. MARK'S SQUARE, VENICE
PAINTING BY GENTILE BELLINI, 1496. VENICE, ACADEMIA
Photo Böhm, Venice

FLORENCE. PIAZZA DELLA SIGNORIA

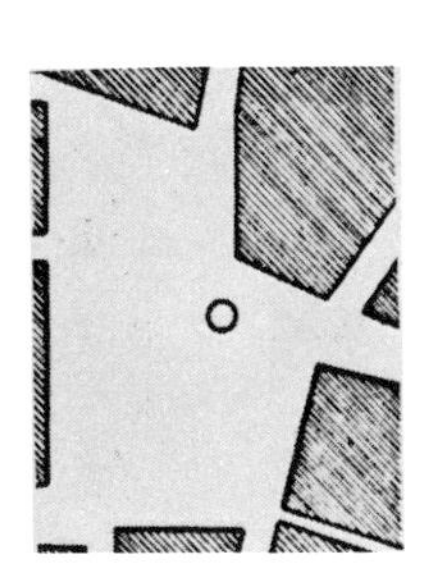

PLAN

From Sitte, *The Art of Building Cities*

VIEW

Photo Gino Giusti, Florence

EXECUTION OF SAVONAROLA AND HIS COMPANIONS ON THE PIAZZA DELLA SIGNORIA, FLORENCE
PAINTING, ANONYMOUS, FIFTEENTH CENTURY. FLORENCE, MUSEO SAN MARCO Photo Alinari

PIAZZA DEL SANTO, WITH ST. ANTHONY'S BASILICA

AERIAL VIEW

Photo ENIT; courtesy
Italian State Tourist Office, New York

PADUA

PIAZZA DEL SANTO. PLAN

From Sitte, *The Art of Building Cities*

PLAN

COPPER ENGRAVING BY ANTONIO VISENTINI, 1747, AFTER CANALETTO

VENICE. PIAZZA DI SS. GIOVANNI E PAOLO

VIEW

Photo G. Brocca, Venice

A: ROME. PIAZZA FARNESE. COPPER ENGRAVING BY GIUSEPPE VASI

From *Raccoltà delle piu belle vedute antiche e moderne di Roma*

B: PIACENZA. PIAZZA DEI CAVALLI

VIEW — Photo Edizione L.F.P.

PLAN — From Brinckmann, *Platz und Monument*

A: ANTWERP. GRAND' PLACE

B: BRUSSELS. GRAND' PLACE

FRITZLAR. MARKET SQUARE

Photo Sepp Jäger; courtesy German Tourist Information Office, New York

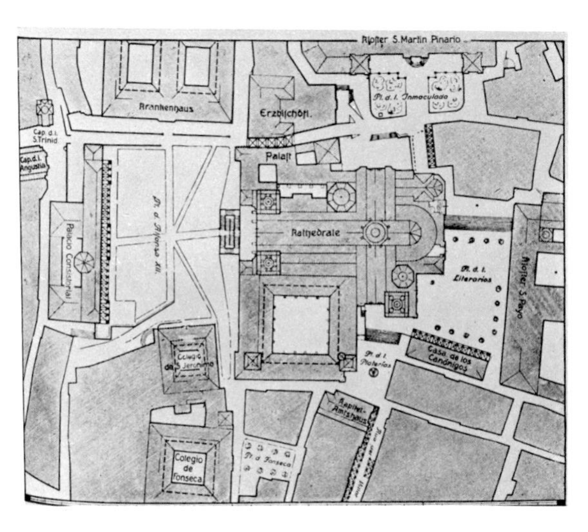

SANTIAGO DE COMPOSTELA

CATHEDRAL AND SURROUNDINGS. PLAN

From Jürgens, "Zur Städtebaukunde Spaniens," *Zeitschrift für Bauwesen*

PLAZUELA DE LAS PLATERIAS

PLATE 42

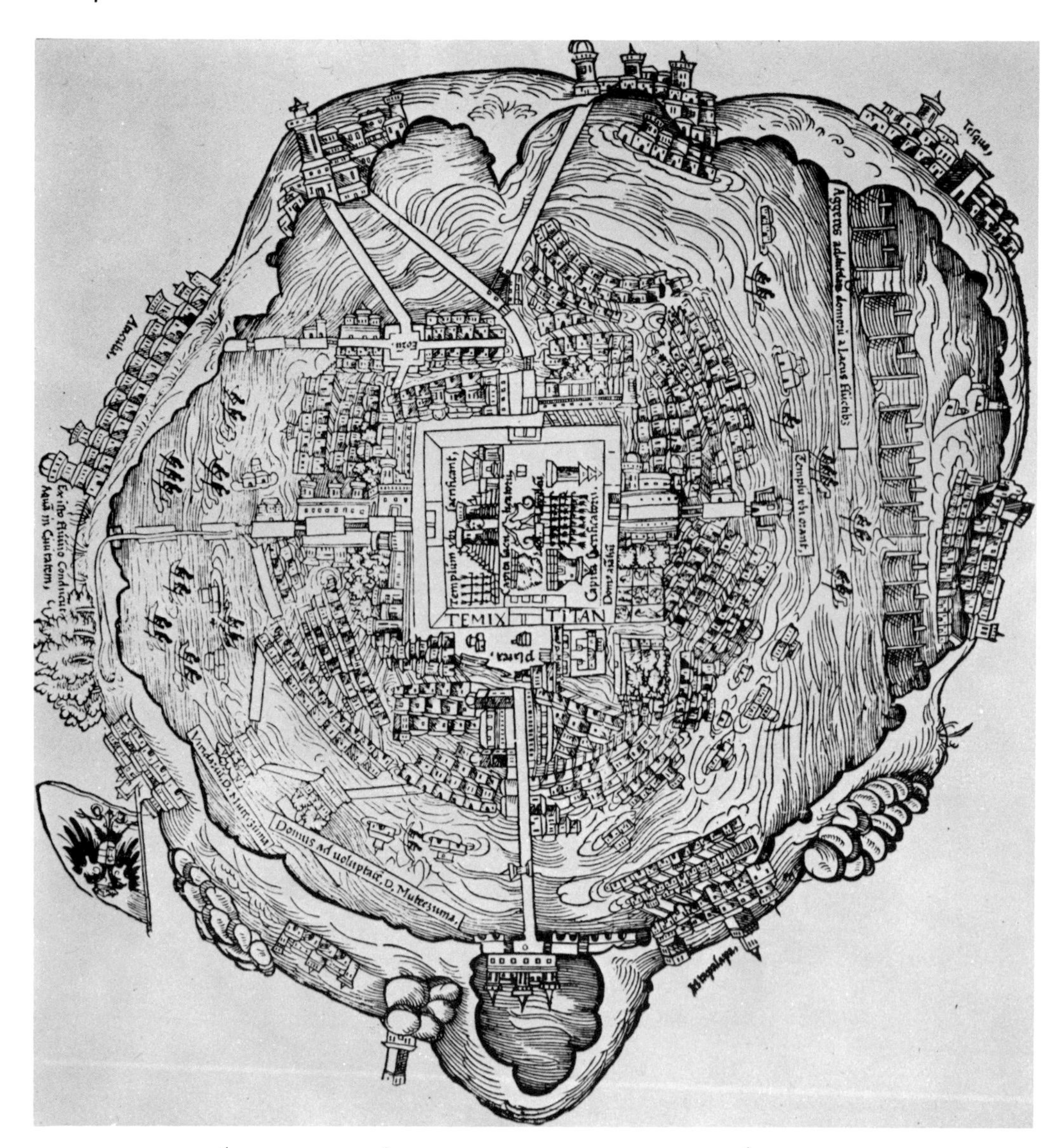

TENOCHTITLAN (MEXICO CITY). PLAN ATTRIBUTED TO CORTÉS

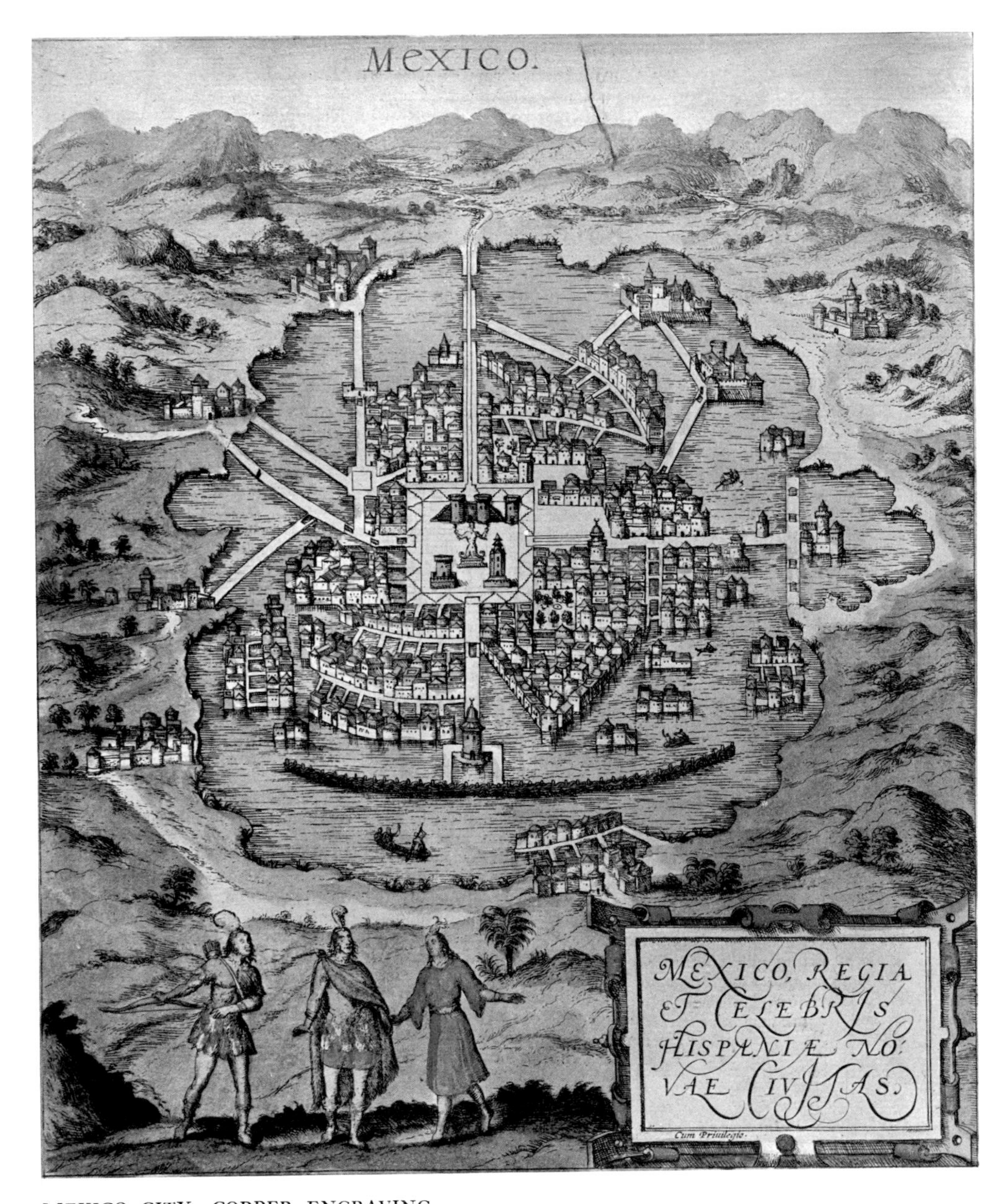

MEXICO CITY. COPPER ENGRAVING

From Braun and Hogenberg, *Civitates Orbis Terrarum.* Photo Pál Kelemen

CUZCO, PERU. COPPER ENGRAVING

From Braun and Hogenberg, *Civitates Orbis Terrarum.* Photo Pál Kelemen

the same name, which was begun by Antonio da Sangallo and continued after his death in 1546 by Michelangelo, who also planned the square. His project was never executed completely; only the part in front of the palace was completed. The rectangular square is closed and the axis of the main street, running into it, leads directly toward the main portal and is continued inside the building. This axis, the Via Marna, sets out at the Campo dei Fiori, which represents somewhat an anteroom for the piazza proper. There two fountains, erected by Girolamo Rainaldi in 1612 and employing ancient basins from the Thermae of Caracalla, leave the center of the square free. Two parallel streets isolate the palace. The houses surrounding the square are of unequal height but are all lower than the palace, which in this way becomes the dominant structure to which the quiet, uniform space of the piazza is subordinated. Michelangelo planned the continuation of the axis through the palace into a second courtyard and in a bridge toward the Villa Farnesina. This project was not executed; substituted for it was Giacomo della Porta's Loggia, erected in 1589. Had Michelangelo's idea been realized, the axis Campo dei Fiori-piazza-vestibule-first (inner) courtyard-corridor-second courtyard-bridge would have exercised such a suction into depth that the sequence of space units rather than the volume of the isolated cube of the palace proper would have developed into the leading motif.

Michelangelo's unique place in history as the link between the High Renaissance and the baroque era is nowhere more evident than in this project for the Palazzo Farnese and its surroundings. This same genius, who had started even earlier on the first great baroque city planning organization, the Campidoglio (see p. 146), appears here as a High Renaissance master in his emphasis on the typical Renaissance tendencies toward symmetry and complete balance. This stylistic ambivalence shows how Michelangelo was completely free from any dogmatic bias in translating his visions into spatial reality.

To a certain degree the Piazza Farnese had been anticipated by the Piazza dei Cavalli in Piacenza (Pl. 38B). This town, a foundation of Augustan times, has still preserved its old gridiron scheme almost completely. The square, taking up the place of some former *insulae*, is located tangential to the crossing of the *cardo* and *decumanus* and is dominated by the thirteenth-century Palazzo Municipale with its imposing arcades. The piazza shows the characteristics of a Renaissance square although its dominant building is of medieval origin and its most striking features, the two framing equestrian statues by Francesco Mocchi, were not erected until 1622–24. These two monuments, located exactly in the continuation of the lateral building lines of the Palazzo, together with the low stone posts (bollards) which keep the traffic off the square proper, limit its space visually and create the impression of a well-defined Renaissance parvis in spite of the actually irregular fronts of all three sides.

A similar effect is achieved in Lucca on the Piazza San Michele (mid-twelfth century) where a row of bollards, in this instance based on a level two steps higher than the surrounding street, creates an isolated space for pedestrians.

FRENCH AND GERMAN THEORIES AND UTOPIAS

During the last third of the sixteenth century, theoreticians in the north also began developing ideas on city planning and the first treatises were published, foremost among them the writings of J. A. Du Cerceau and Jacques Perret. The ideal plans of Italian writers had been circulated in France through drawings and copies by craftsmen, artisans, and builders. Du Cerceau correspondingly developed grandiose plans of tremendous castles with their surroundings which may well be considered as layouts of complete towns, and suggested also a closed circular square in connection with the Pont Neuf in Paris (Fig. 34). Perret, on the other hand, in his designs was more interested in playing with all possible types of squares, from the hexagon to the twenty-four cornered polygon (Fig. 35). In his playful pedantry and frantic desire for centralized symmetry he went so far as to locate the stalls of butchers and fishmongers in corresponding places. Another series of projects, though less important, was published at the same time by Errard, a bizarre combination of all kinds of polygons in connection with both the radial and the gridiron schemes.

Characteristic of all French projects through those of Ledoux in the eighteenth century is an anxious adherence to a most elaborate symmetry.

In Germany, in the sixteenth century, only the ideas of Albrecht Dürer are original. The first clearly designed project is named the *Stadt eines Königs* (town of a king), which shows a quadrangular periphery with the castle in the center of a quadrangular square (Fig. 36). The sides of this

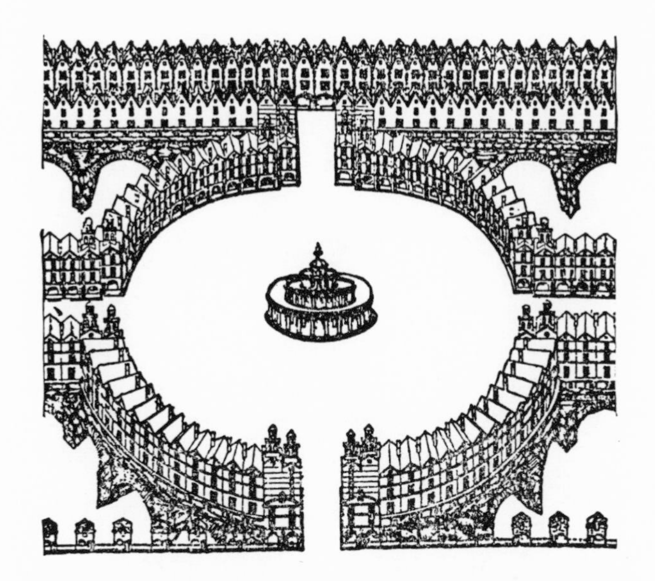

FIG. 34. ROUND SQUARE AT THE PONT NEUF, PARIS. PROJECT, SECOND PART OF THE SIXTEENTH CENTURY, BY J. A. DU CERCEAU

From Gantner, *Grundformen der europäischen Stadt*

FIG. 35. PLAN FOR AN IDEAL CITY, *ca.* 1601, BY JACQUES PERRET

central square are continued as the main streets between rectangular blocks of houses. Dürer's main interest in this project was in solving fortification problems, without special attention to aesthetic considerations. As in all his work, his ideas on proportion dominate the plan. But these proportions are

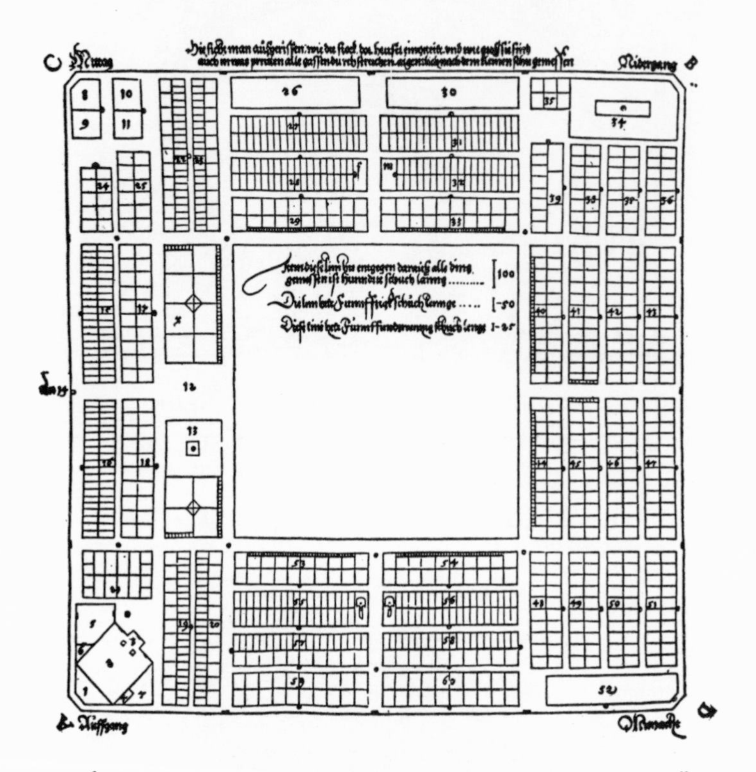

FIG. 36. PROJECT FOR AN IDEAL CITY, BY ALBRECHT DÜRER
Courtesy New York Public Library

definitely applied to the two-dimensional projection rather than to the three-dimensional realization of the town. Without any doubt Dürer by this time was at least familiar with Alberti's and Filarete's work, but in spite of his own quotation from Vitruvius, it seems doubtful whether his ideas were inspired by these humanistic scources. Francesco di Giorgio Martini's plans, although conceived around 1500, were not published until the nineteenth century, so that Dürer could hardly have known them.

However, it is not unlikely that the German masters could have been stimulated from another source. In 1524, the letters of Hernán Cortés were published in Nuremberg and they contained a drawing of Tenochtitlan (Mexico City) (see p. 137). It was probably this map, published three years prior to Dürer's work, which stimulated the German master. This drawing represented a rather free, imaginative depiction of the layout inasmuch as the real scheme of the town was filled in with houses in European fashion. However, it is clearly recognizable that the nucleus of the town was a free space of quadrangular shape from which four streets started, one in the middle of each side of the square, obviously the old Aztec scheme. In the center of the open square was probably the place for sacrifices, accentuated by a pyramid. The plan corresponds roughly to the state of Mexico City around 1521, when the old square still existed, and prior to the transformation of the original scheme by complete Europeanization later.

After Dürer, German theoreticians did not show much originality. Heinrich von Schille proved at least some independence by designing a layout of a quadrangular town without a central square, thus deviating from all

FIG. 37. PLAN FOR AN IDEAL CITY, 1598, BY DANIEL SPECKLE

Italian authors. Best known of all German theoreticians of this period was Daniel Speckle, who was definitely more interested in the sociology of town life than in its visual architectural organization, which he depicted in the usual octagonal radial scheme (Fig. 37). Both of these men, like all other German theoreticians, primarily emphasized technical problems of fortification. So did a great number of German theoreticians who flourished around the mid-seventeenth century. Their concepts were so rigidly bound to the ideas of the Italian Renaissance and so inferior to the great concepts of the French seventeenth and eighteenth centuries that it may suffice to mention their names here in direct connection with their sixteenth-century predecessors in Germany. There were H. Hasemann, W. Dillich, N. Goldmann, J. Furttenbach the Elder, and M. Dögen. None of them possessed any spatial imagination. They were merely designers of ornamental patterns with a certain flair for fortification problems. Without any genuine interest in three-dimensional structure, they had understanding neither for the sociological meaning of the square for public life nor for its possibilities as a work of architecture. They endlessly varied Dürer's and Cataneo's schemes. The underlying lack of creative power of those German generations becomes most obvious in the designs of Joseph Furttenbach the Younger who toyed with the elements of city planning by projecting his ideas as backgrounds for the theater (scenic designs). In his literary comments he explains the practical purpose of each building on the stage in the most amusing way, full of romantic fantasy but without any visual persuasiveness. The last three of this long sequence of dogmatic and pedantic technicians were Christoph Heer, L. C. Sturm, and Christian Rieger, who in the eighteenth century still repeated and varied the artistically worthless patterns of their predecessors.

REALIZATIONS IN SPACE IN CENTRAL AND NORTHERN EUROPE

In France, as in Italy, the principle of regular organization emphasizing one or more axes, marking a definite break from medieval feeling, appeared in garden architecture prior to systematic town planning. These gardens were mostly laid out in front of and around the typical French Renaissance châteaux of the first half of the sixteenth century, such as Anet, built by Philibert de l'Orme for Diane de Poitiers; Blois; Chambord; Dampierre, etc. The original plan for the Jardin des Tuileries in Paris, designed by de l'Orme for Catherine de Medici (before 1570) also showed the relation of the main garden axis and the castle. The great and unified plan for the Tuileries emerged only under Louis XIV. Most of these plans are preserved in engravings by Jacques Du Cerceau. In contrast to Italy, canals became a decisive element in planning, whereas less interest existed in the effects of rhythmically stepped terraces. Always the main axis of parks created a direct connection between built and planted architecture. This employment of axial coordination was refined in the work of the French theoreticians half a century later and was realized in actual town planning.

The national and civil wars of the sixteenth and seventeenth centuries which led eventually to the birth of the great modern nations of Europe favored the foundation of new settlements in France and Belgium. Most of these new towns were built before the great French treatises of the Renaissance had been published, but after the basic Italian ones had appeared.

Thus, for instance, the small town of Vitry-le-François was built in 1545 according to a definite plan by Girolamo Marini under the sponsorship of Francis I, to replace the earlier town of Vitry-en-Perthois, destroyed in 1544. Unfortunately this second town was completely destroyed in World War II. As in Gattinara, a quadrangular square, the Place d'Armes, was located in the center of the town, but without a central structure. The town proper was laid out in the traditional gridiron scheme and within a quadrangular periphery strongly reminiscent of Monpazier (see p. 72).

Out of the great number of new fortifications in the northeastern section of France, part of which is Belgian today, Mariembourg and Philippeville, the latter built by Philip II, may be mentioned. Both were begun around 1550 and completed toward the end of the century; they resemble Vitry-le-François in so far as the whole layout of their fortifications is based on the central square. However, in contrast to Vitry-le-François, the streets of these towns radiate starlike from the center. The bastions are located at the corners of the periphery (in Mariembourg a quadrangle, in Philippeville a pentagon), and respectively four and five of the radiating streets lead directly from the central square to the bastions. In both instances, aesthetic and functional considerations are fused most fortunately.

Cataneo's (1554), Maggi's (1584), and Marchi's (1599) treatises had appeared almost at the same time. One must therefore assume that these publications represented essentially a condensation of ideas already generally known and practiced at this time. All over Europe a great number of architects and engineers projected and, as in Mariembourg and Philippeville, sometimes realized such plans.

Charleroi, erected as a fortress by Vauban in 1666 under Louis XIV, represents a belated echo of Philippeville and Mariembourg, as the last radio-centric Renaissance scheme in the seventeenth century, at a time when otherwise baroque ideas had already superseded the earlier Renaissance concepts. But through the sixteenth century the newly founded cities in the north, in France, Belgium, and the Netherlands, followed faithfully the schemes of Italian and French theoreticians of the period.

At least twice complete realizations of previously published theoretical patterns were actually executed in the north, as they were realized in the south in the towns of Granmichele, Palma Nuova, Gattinara, and Valletta.

Coevorden, a small Dutch fort founded shortly after 1600, like Palma Nuova repeats the ideas of Vincenzo Scamozzi: streets radiate from a central square toward the sides of the regular heptagonal periphery; the only essential difference being the small citadel which was built within its circumference, in contrast to the uninterrupted symmetrical regularity of Palma Nuova.

Much more interesting than Coevorden is Freudenstadt, a foundation of Protestant refugees in southwestern Germany, built in 1599 and rebuilt after a fire in 1632 by Heinrich Schickhardt (Fig. 38). The influence of Dürer's

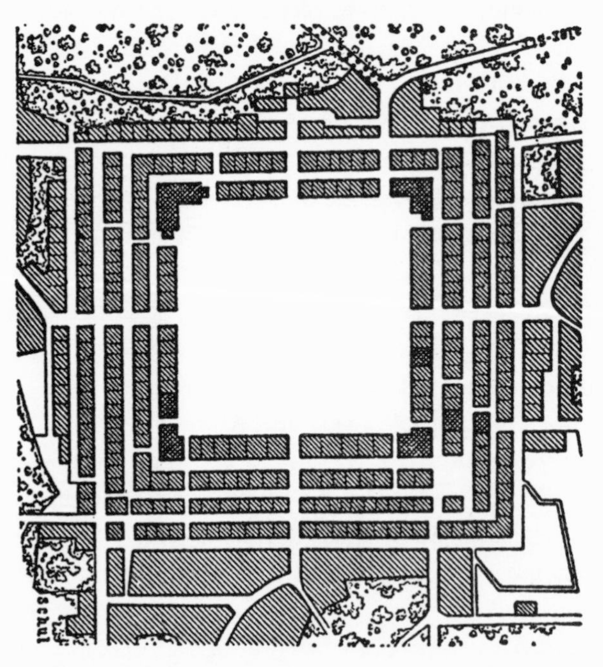

FIG. 38. FREUDENSTADT. PLAN BY HEINRICH SCHICKHARDT, 1632

project is obvious. As in his design, the quadrangular central square represents the main feature of the town, whose periphery is also quadrangular. The streets are laid out parallel to the four sides of the square except for the two main streets which run into the market square. The famous church is built in a right angle as a result of town planning considerations and is in itself a wonderful example of Protestant ecclesiastical architecture, with the pulpit as the focal point in the corner of the rectangle. The church frames one corner of the square whose other three corners are equally occupied by angular buildings, one of them the town hall. In Freudenstadt the square had a definite spatial shape as a closed quadrangle of relatively large dimensions. This was the only town in Germany where the square evoked something of a three-dimensional impression. Unfortunately today this effect is destroyed by planted greenery and haphazardly dispersed houses.

These new German foundations of the seventeenth century and also those of the eighteenth century (see p. 207) demonstrate a dogmatically defined relationship between street and square in extremely schematic symmetry. The form of the individual house is rather unessential since it is as far as possible subordinated to the unified front of street and square. Roofs, eaves, protrusions, and recessions are equalized, arcades are employed, the façade of monumental buildings is repeated, etc. And yet, in spite of the theoretically favorable shapes of the single elements of street and square which should increase the three-dimensional character, hardly anywhere is an aesthetically effective space created with the sole exception of Freudenstadt.

In this connection the small town of Hanau deserves mention since it is so typical for this period. There, a very old medieval town was enlarged in 1597 by a new expansion which was much larger than the original town. Planned for Flemish refugees, the new fortified settlement was laid out as a half-octagon, corresponding to the then ubiquitous Italian and French schemes. Within the gridiron pattern, the regularly distributed squares assume the areas of individual blocks.

The influence of the great Italian writers spread over practically all of Europe, although sometimes not until one or two centuries after the first publication of the original treatises.

In Denmark, King Christian (1588–1648) founded a number of towns taking up the ideas of the Italian Renaissance masters. The proposal for a new quarter of Copenhagen shows the polygonal scheme with an octagonal center square and streets radiating from there. Another project, a plan for Christianshavn by Johan Semp, also with central square and radiating streets, was later changed into the simpler gridiron scheme, but the idea of the central square was kept.

Even in Russia, many foundations of the eighteenth century still represent more or less successful realizations of Renaissance schemes. Thus, the radiocentric pattern of Palma Nuova and Granmichele is mirrored in a plan for Lyoubim (1788), and the quadrangular organization of Freudenstadt with its central square is echoed in the plan of Semyonov (1781) and to a lesser degree in Bogorodsk (1784), to mention only a few examples.

In central and northern Europe, the few existing genuine Renaissance squares, such as those of Vitry-le-François, Mariemburg, Charleroi, etc., in France; Freudenstadt in Germany; Coevorden in the Netherlands; and Christianshavn in Denmark, represent realizations of theoretical Italian schemes, similar to Palma Nuova, Granmichele, Gattinara, etc., in Italy. Original free creations comparable to St. Mark's Square in Venice, the Piazza della Signoria in Florence, etc., independent of all theories, appear only in Flanders. Furthermore, such famous squares as those in Arras, Augsburg, Danzig, Berne, etc., had actually developed in the Middle Ages, even if most of the surrounding buildings, monuments, fountains, etc., stem from the sixteenth century. Thus these squares are often wrongly labeled Renaissance squares. The style of the framing architecture as it appears today is less decisive for their spatial appearance than their structural layout, which is definitely medieval.

But in Flanders, post-medieval squares exist whose structure depends neither on theoretical Renaissance treatises nor on a prior medieval layout such as determined the Grand' Place in Bruges. Whereas in Bruges the economic climax had been reached in the fifteenth century, the beginning of transatlantic trade made Antwerp (125,000 inhabitants in 1568!) the leader of international commerce in the sixteenth century. There a large program of amelioration was initiated shortly before 1550 under Gilbert van Schonebeke. Beyond the planning of new quarters and the improvement of existing ones, the rather irregular group consisting of the cathedral, the small parvis before it, the Groote Markt, the Place aux Gants, and the Place Verte was brought into a more regular shape by the erection of the new town hall (1561–65 by Cornelis de Vriendt) and of numerous guild houses during the sixteenth century (Pl. 39A). Similarity of proportion and of architectural decor, especially the identical direction of all houses with their gables toward the square, produces at least an impression of a somewhat organized space corresponding more to Renaissance concepts than to earlier medieval picturesqueness.

Among the Flemish squares most outspoken in Renaissance character is the Grand' Place in Brussels, essentially formed in the sixteenth and seventeenth centuries (Pl. 39B). Here the square appears even more balanced than in Antwerp, because of its larger dimensions, the greater regularity of its ground plan (almost a completely perfect rectangle), and the correspondence of town hall and the opposite Maison du Roi. In spite of minor variations in architectural details, the identity of material and of coloration—warm, dark-gray sandstone with ornamental forms heavily gilded—creates a unique congruity in the appearance of the surrounding guild houses. The square had served as market place during the Middle Ages. It has continued as such ever since, although many other squares in Brussels functioned as special markets besides, e.g., the "Sablon" as horse market. However, through the gradually increasing number of guild houses the Grand' Place became the civic center of the town—a characteristic example of a change of function in spite of the continuation of the original commercial activities up to the present. The town hall with its frontal tower, originally a fifteenth-century structure like the tower in Bruges, was partially rebuilt after a conflagration in the following century. The Maison du Roi, a genuine Renaissance structure, built in 1515–25 by Anton Keldermans and other architects, replaced the earlier medieval Broodhuis. Similarly, although many of the guild houses were of earlier origin, their façades date from the sixteenth, and partially from the seventeenth, century. The Maison du Roi, parts of the town hall, and most of the guild houses were again destroyed by fire after the siege of Brussels by the French in 1695, but were reerected immediately afterwards in their original structural form, though partially with baroque ornamentation. This restoration was of great historical importance in so far as here—probably for the first time in Europe—the whole process of restoring was carefully regulated by city ordinances, in full consciousness of the unique beauty of the whole complex as it had existed before the conflagration. The balanced effect of the Grand' Place originates from the homogeneity of the surrounding façades rather than from its original overall spatial organization.

Besides Antwerp and Brussels, a number of genuine Renaissance squares still exist in Flanders, although on a smaller scale. Among them the Groote Markt in Veurne (Furnes) is not only the best preserved but also the most typical in its unified appearance. It shows all the characteristics of Antwerp and Brussels: the orientation of all houses with their gables toward the square, the combination of small narrow houses with the monumental town hall (1596–1612), Châtellenie (1612–18), and "Butcher's Hall" (1615), etc. The stylistic unity is even more obvious here since all houses, private and public alike, are pure Renaissance creations. The belfry (completed in 1624) and the older church of St. Walpurga, although not directly connected with the square proper, create a powerful background when seen from the square.

Summing up: in the north of Europe these Flemish squares are the only free creations which show a real Renaissance character. The few realizations of contemporary theoretical designs are on too small a scale and too artificially constructed to evoke any spatial sensation.

Nonetheless, even these Flemish Renaissance squares, such as those in Antwerp, Brussels, and Veurne, cannot be compared in their spatial impact with contemporaneous Italian squares. For in Italy, the awareness of space is primary; in Flanders, it is the architectural beauty of the enclosing structures in their continuity which strikes us first. It is a two-dimensional impression which only gradually develops in a quasi-additive way into a three-dimensional experience. In other words, the lack of tradition in the development of external space, so characteristic for the north, robs even the most beautiful and stylistically genuine Flemish creations of the main quality of Italian Renaissance squares, the complete and closely knit unity of space. In Italy, the elements which compose the square are inseparable and seem therefore to be of secondary importance. In Flanders, the spatial impression is built up gradually by successive accumulation of single visual impressions.

German squares of the Renaissance period, which in the north would cover the time from about 1500 to 1650, are as much or as little "Renaissance" in character as the famous German Renaissance buildings of this era. The town halls of Rothenburg (1573–78) and Augsburg (1615–20), the Armory in Danzig (1602–5), the castle of Heidelberg (1556–1612), the beautiful burgher houses in Nuremberg, Hildesheim, Bremen, Strasbourg, etc.—they all show the German vernacular adaptation of the style; but nonetheless they still appear rather medieval in structure, in scale, and especially in proportions. For the distribution of masses, the fenestration, and the interior spaces still breathe a medieval narrowness. The same holds true for the open expanses within the town. Thus most German squares, which because of their monuments or façades of adjacent buildings are so often called Renaissance squares, have been discussed here as medieval creations. Their shape and their proportions prove unambiguously their medieval origin, and statues, fountains, and other later additions do not change the generic spatial concept.

Thus only a very few German squares of this period truly reveal the "new spirit." In these rare instances a certain uniformity of adjacent houses and a regularity of the free area have repressed inherent medieval features. And it is not only the mere addition of figures and fountains which effects a harmonious appearance almost comparable to that of the squares in Flanders.

Typical for many middle-sized German towns which at the end of the Middle Ages were of greater importance than today is the almost regular market square in Fritzlar in Oberhesse (Pl. 40). Its free area is small and removed from the interurban traffic; a market column (*Rittersäule*) was erected there in 1564. The surrounding houses are timberwork structures from the fifteenth and sixteenth centuries of rather uniform appearance. Not intended for civic representation—there are no important administrative buildings around it—the square in its quiet dignity serves well its function as market place.

In contrast to such modest examples in central Germany, the originally medieval squares of rival North German Hanseatic towns often became monuments of civic pride through their transformations in Renaissance times. In the fourteenth century, Danzig, for instance, originally a Slavic settlement, was enlarged under the Teutonic Knights through the addition of the so-called Rechtsstadt. It soon joined the North German Hanseatic League and gained in economic and political importance. The construction of the Lange Markt (Fig. 39) through a broadening of the main artery of the town, the Lang-Gasse, was clearly a result of the city's new importance. At the smaller side, a town hall was erected in the fourteenth century, and at about the same time, in a rectangle adjacent to it, the Artushof, another public building. These buildings and the houses surrounding the Lange Markt were all "modernized" from the end of the fifteenth century to the end of the sixteenth century. The new façades, remodeled in Renaissance taste, fused with the regular layout of the square into a true Renaissance space form. The geometric shape of the layout is part of the regular planning scheme of all foundations of the Teutonic Knights. From the Grüne Tor, on one small side of the square, the view opens toward the opposite small side with the town hall, whose tower becomes the dominant accent of the square, and the Neptune Fountain, a typical piece of Renaissance decoration which was erected in front of the town hall in 1633. The visual mag-

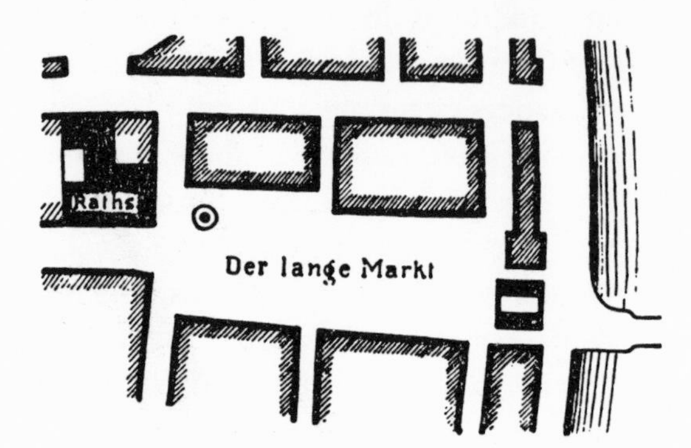

FIG. 39. DANZIG. LANGE MARKT. PLAN

netism of this backdrop is increased further through the slight slope of the ground and the staggered rhythm of the narrow-chested medieval houses in their newly acquired Renaissance costumes.

REALIZATIONS IN SPACE IN SPAIN AND THE NEW WORLD

Italian visitors traveling through Spain in the seventeenth century still complained in their letters home how "disorderly" Spanish cities were. Such a reaction was quite understandable since most of the Spanish towns had been built in the Middle Ages under the Moorish occupation. Hence the streets amidst the clusters of houses were crooked and narrow and entwined into each other without any regular pattern—of typical Oriental character. There was one exception, Barcelona, which in its layout showed then, and still preserves, the character of its Roman period. When the Spanish kings gradually reconquered the peninsula, they did not change the layout of the existing towns, whose fortifications had been laid out in accordance with the rules of Vegetius (see p. 101), followed everywhere in Europe throughout the Middle Ages. Of these towns, some of them already conquered from the

Moors in the twelfth century, only Avila was rebuilt with more regular streets. In all the medieval towns, existing plazas were rather small and irregular. Even the Plaza Mayor in Salamanca (see p. 229), since the eighteenth century one of the most monumental squares in Spain, was still completely unorganized during the seventeenth century.

Amidst the irregular maze of streets sometimes very small rectangular areas appear arbitrarily located, without any attempt at integration. They served in former days as places for tournaments. While these small voids can hardly be considered genuine squares, the open spaces in front of the cathedrals must be taken as such. These irregular squares, whose ground plan is still medieval today, mostly show great differences in level which are conquered by grandiose open staircases. In other words, their irregularity is three-dimensional, in ground plan as well as in level. Through these staircases the church is connected with the regular street level and yet separated from secular life. Such a complex spatial impression cannot be labeled medieval, Renaissance, or baroque so much as specifically "Spanish," even if similar combinations of squares and staircases may be occasionally encountered in other countries (see, e.g., Erfurt, Vienna, Rome).

The long-lasting and far-reaching influence of this complete lack of structural space organization in medieval Spain becomes most obvious in Santiago de Compostela, which is typical also for many smaller Spanish developments (Pl. 41). Its famous cathedral, a goal for pilgrimages from the whole Christian world, was consecrated in 1211. Individual parts of the edifice and the façade underwent continuous remodeling, and thus the whole complex is an almost complete sample chart of architectural styles through the late baroque, each of them in a specifically Spanish variation. The magnificent west façade, *el obradoiro*, conceived by Fernando Casa y Novoa in 1783, with the famous staircase in front, leads onto the Plaza de Alfonso XII, which is surrounded by such heterogeneous buildings as the hospital, the Palacio Consistorial, and the Colegio de San Jeronimo, all originating from different centuries. This plaza is the only one of the five medieval squares around the cathedral that to a certain degree was regularized in the eighteenth century. These squares, with entrances to the church proper and to the adjacent *colegios*, monasteries, ecclesiastical and secular palaces, served for the gatherings of pilgrims. However, they do not create a unified group of combined squares. Differing widely as to size, orientation, and level, they are only loosely interconnected by small passageways, by staircases, ramps, and covered corridors. Never have so many squares contributed so little to the architectural form of the buidings which they surround. The Plazuela de las Platerias in front of the southern transept and the Torre de la Trinidad displays a picturesque intimacy. Broad stairs lead from it toward the church, serving simultaneously as a transition to the following square behind the apse of the cathedral, the larger Plaza de la Literarios. Here again a further difference in level is overcome by other stairs. From this upper level in turn angular passageways link with the Plaza de la Immaculada on the north side of the church, in front of the monastery of San Martin Pinario. However, as was mentioned above, the whole complex of cathedral, monasteries, palaces, staircases, arcades, and squares cannot be perceived as an integration of related spaces and volumes, but merely as an accumulation of separate, individual space and volume units, each in itself a three-dimensional creation of peculiar beauty.

In contrast to these picturesque spatial mosaics, one truly regular plan was realized in the late fifteenth century under Ferdinand II and Isabella in the encampment town of Santafé (1491). This town was laid out as a fortified rectangle to house the armies which besieged (and later conquered) Granada, the last of the Moorish strongholds. Its scheme repeated the gridiron system of the Roman castrum and the layout of the French bastides of the thirteenth century. Bastides were also constructed in northern Spain in the thirteenth century during the reconquest of the northern parts of the peninsula from the Moors. This bastide scheme, of which Santafé may be considered the final example, was to become tremendously influential on the layout of the colonial towns of "new" Spain. Actually these colonial towns in the newly conquered territories of Mexico, Central America, and South America, from the time of Columbus onward, became much more "modern" during the sixteenth century than the towns of the motherland.

Not before the end of the sixteenth century did the treatises of the great Italian theoreticians exercise a certain influence on Spanish town planning, leading to the production of national variations on the original Italian ideas. The treatise of Fray Lorenzo de San Nicolás, *Arte y uso de arquitectura* (Madrid, 1633, 1664), proves that the work of the great Italians, from Alberti to Lupicini, was generally known. Fray Lorenzo supplemented these condensations by exact *ordenanzas* taken from the building laws of the city fathers of Toledo.

Genuine Renaissance plazas are rather few in Spain. Best known among them is the Lonja del Monasterio of the Escorial in the province of Madrid (Fig. 40). Philip II, in fulfillment of a vow, erected a monumental structure which symbolized a combination of secular and ecclesiastical absolutism, as forbidding in its architectural forms as the mountains which surround it. The Escorial, planned in tremendous dimensions, contains a monastery, with

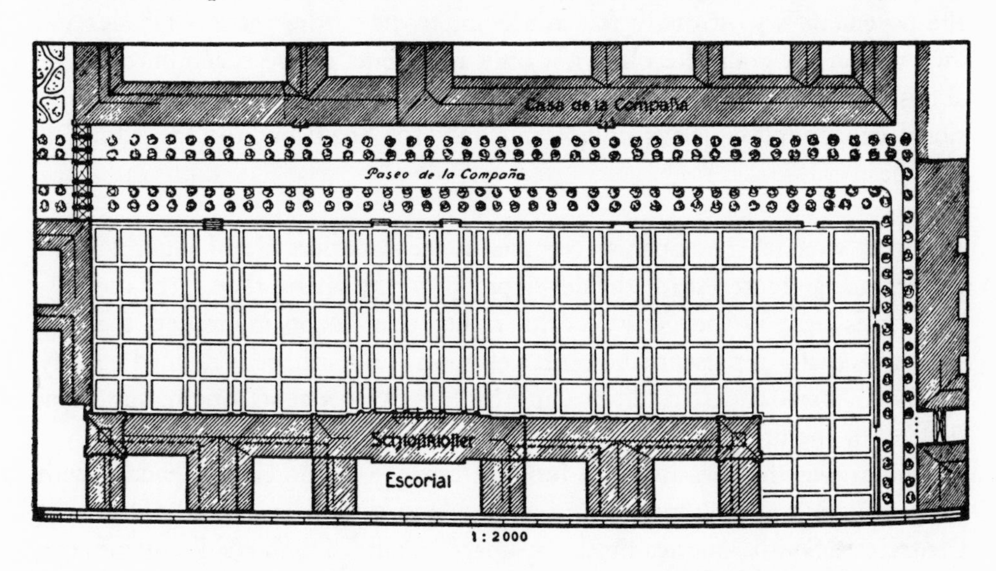

FIG. 40. ESCORIAL, MADRID. LONJA DEL MONASTERIO. PLAN
From Jürgens, "Zur Städtebaukunde Spaniens," *Zeitschrift für Bauwesen*

a church and a mausoleum for the Spanish kings, a theological seminary, and the residential palace. The whole complex was begun by Juan Bautista de Toledo in 1558, and after his death was completed by his favorite pupil, Juan de Herrera, in 1584. However, Juan Gómez de Mora and other architects continued adding and altering certain parts for more than two centuries through the reign of Ferdinand VII at the beginning of the nineteenth century. The enormous monastery-palace is strictly axial in its layout and as symmetrical as the divergent purposes of its construction allowed. Its architecture employed the stone material of the surrounding rocks and is extremely severe, entirely unlike contemporary Italian Renaissance architecture. The same austerity governs the shape of the strictly rectangular plaza which stretches on the slope in front of the west façade as an artificial platform. Opposite this façade the free area is framed by the Casa de la Compaña, housing the servants of the court. Before this building four parallel rows of trees help to mitigate the strict severity of the plaza, which is still further increased through the rigid quadrangular pattern of the granite pavement and the uncompromising façade. There are few squares in the world, even considering St. Mark's Square in Venice and the Campidoglio in Rome, where the pavement is so strongly felt as a counterpart to the vertical façades and vice versa. The courtlike plaza not only represents closed space but may be almost called imprisoned space. In its compactness it provides a three-dimensional experience which is unique not only for Spain but for the whole of Europe.

THE NEW WORLD.[2] The Spanish colonies in the Americas are of much greater importance and interest for the development of the square than is the motherland. It is here in the New World, rather than in Spain proper, that the "plaza" actually represents the center of civic life. Its shape is defined equally by Indian preconquest traditions and by Spanish concepts originating from the end of the fifteenth and the beginning of the sixteenth century.

Seldom was the invasion of a foreign territory so closely connected with the foundation of new towns as was the conquest of Mexico and of parts of Central and South America by the Spaniards from Columbus's discoveries onward. Initial colonization and urbanization were almost identical. Most towns were carefully planned and only a few grew naturally. At the end of the first century of the Spanish conquest hundreds of new settlements had been erected as a result of plentiful resources in material, labor, and space, providing housing for the settlers and for those Indians who were allowed to dwell in town. The majority of the natives were compelled to live outside. Numerous drawings and maps of Mexican towns around 1580 are preserved, some of them, interestingly enough, executed by Indian artists. The only parallel in the history of urbanization would be the Teutonic Knights' conquest of the eastern German provinces and Poland, although this was on a much smaller scale. Colonial foundations around the Mediterranean, first by the Greeks, later by the Romans, can hardly be compared since they involved a relatively limited region only.

[2] I am much obliged to Pál Kelemen for his most valuable advice and specific information on this section.

When the Spaniards came to Mexico, a definitely urban civilization of Mayan, Toltec, and Aztec origins already existed. The plan of Aztec towns was roughly rectangular without necessarily implying a completely regular gridiron. The rectilinear pattern evolved from the division of land among the clans. A central plaza was destined for communal gatherings, probably also as market place, and simultaneously represented the courtyard of the central temple. The social standing of the inhabitants was manifested by the respective nearness of their houses to the plaza.

Tenochtitlan, today Mexico City, was founded in 1325 by the Aztecs as an island settlement. Cortés describes the appearance of the city in his letters, first published in Seville in 1522, then in Nuremberg (see p. 123) and Venice in 1524, and later on republished in many free variations, as, for instance, by George Braun and Franz Hogenberg (1576) (Pls. 42–43). The great number of editions proves the general interest Europe took in the new development. At the time of its conquest, Tenochtitlan had about 300,000 inhabitants. All main roads, partially paralleled by canals, converged on the central square, the later Plaza Mayor. Smaller squares existed in various districts for each clan. Although Hernán Cortés completely destroyed the temples of the town in 1524, its general layout was preserved within the new city erected by him. This new city was laid out in a regular gridiron plan with the former square at the central intersection of its two main axes, framed by the cathedral, public buildings, and probably by arcades, as described by Cervantes de Salazar in 1554 and in Motolinia's *Memoriales*. The square proper was little changed from the original Aztec scheme, which had been centered around the main temple. Although the old Aztec town obviously had no gridiron scheme but was composed of streets, straight or irregular, and of causeways, the location and shape of the Aztec plaza fitted perfectly the gridiron scheme introduced by Cortés. It must be emphasized that at this time Spain, being still of medieval character, had no town—with the one notable exception of Santafé—with such a rectangular square.

This gridiron scheme of Mexico City, facilitating the apportionment of lots to the colonists, can be found in almost all the foundations of New Spain and in South America; for instance, in Puebla (1531), and even in one of the earliest foundations on the islands, in Santo Domingo, built twenty-four years earlier by Governor Nicolás de Ovando. The scheme of Santo Domingo, as well as that of the later Mexico City, was probably stimulated by the layout of the Spanish camp settlement at Santafé in Spain proper, which was known to Cortés.

Soon the Spanish government began sending out exact instructions for the layout of the new colonial towns to the local rulers, among them Pedrarias Dávila and later Cortés. Codified in 1523, these instructions, the "Laws of the Indies," were based on the revived ideas of Graeco-Roman post-Hippodamic concepts; they provided for free spaces for the location of plazas, houses of equal height, etc. The treatises of the Italian theoreticians, which later in the century would become of such decisive influence on the planning of colonial towns, were not yet generally known in Spain. It was only after 1523, when Charles V began to send more and more explicit building laws to New Spain, that these concepts of Renaissance writers began to affect planning there. And even then it was the ideas of Vitruvius, as interpreted by the Humanists around the court of Charles V, rather than the original treatises of contemporary Italians which predominated, especially Vitruvius' hygienic advice and such architectural details as his recommendation of arcades. It is known, for instance, that a copy of Vitruvius was in the possession of a bookdealer in Mexico City in 1550 and that later another bookdealer in Mexico received within a single shipment of books four copies of Vitruvius' works, four of Alberti's, and two of Serlio's.

The building laws of the Emperor were confirmed and modified in 1573 by Philip II, who veered from Vitruvian concepts to those of the Italian theoreticians. The influence of learning and theory in architecture and city planning now became as strong in the New World as it was around the Mediterranean.

The scheme of urbanization in Central and South American regions, although somewhat later, was similar to the Mexican development and showed the same relationship between preconquest foundations and Spanish colonizing activities. Thus it is only natural that location, function, and sociological meaning of the square are also comparable. As in Mexico, the distance of the individual property from the plaza was a gauge for the social standing of the owner.

Chichén Itzá and Tulum in Yucatan, founded respectively in the fourth and fifth centuries B.C. as Mayan cities, and later rebuilt and inhabited by the Toltecs, originally also had their large temple plazas, and even a sequence of such plazas, in axial organization. As a religious center complete with temples and pyramids, Chichén Itzá's squares definitely have a ceremonial character, but they are public gathering places, too. The houses of the city proper must be imagined as being very primitive, built of reeds with thatched roofs or of adobe in contrast to the monumental stone structures of the religious center. Since no traces of these houses or huts are left, the extension of the gridiron scheme is hypothetical. The focal point of Mayan civilization in Guatemala, the town of Tikal, and other towns such as Copán, Palenque, and Uxmal, were similarly organized with a large plaza in their center, without, however, any clear spatial relationship between the open areas and the rather irregularly dispersed monumental buildings. The plaza in Tikal, a religious center, seems to be typical for the spatial concepts of this civilization. It was dominated by two huge pyramidal temples and was flanked by smaller temples and shrines.

In South American towns—for instance, in Bogotá, Colombia; Santiago, Chile; and La Paz, Bolivia, all foundations of the first half of the sixteenth century—basically the same layout was employed as in Mexico City. Two examples from Peru may illustrate the point. In pre-Columbian Chanchan, the capital of the Chimus, rivals of the better known Incas, the center was a rectangle which was composed of eleven sections, each enclosed by a wall. The city probably had 200,000 inhabitants in the fifteenth century; its overall plan was generally rectangular but certain irregularities did not allow a complete gridiron. A similar layout prevailed in Cuzco (Pl. 44), where in colonial times even arcades were employed, and in a great number of small Peruvian towns. Even smaller villages in remote river valleys, as in the Colca River valley, show the same scheme: the streets laid out in a rectangular pattern centered around a plaza.

This native scheme was taken up also by the Spanish conqueror Francisco Pizarro in his layout for the Cuidad de los Reyes, today Lima, the capital of Peru, founded in 1535. Unlike Tenochtitlan (Mexico City), Lima was an entirely new town, and therefore the combination of gridiron plan and central square was the result of conscious planning without any concessions to existing local conditions.

The so-called reduction towns of the Jesuits in Paraguay, founded from the end of the sixteenth century onward and destroyed after the expulsion of the Jesuits in 1767, at least deserve mention. As in Mexico and Peru, these baroque foundations in Paraguay took their cue from the local Indian tradition. The plaza was the nucleus of the town and all houses in blocks of small dimensions centered on it. The rectangular square was always dominated by the mission church and on its opposite side was a statue of the Virgin Mary.

The civilizations of the various Northern Indian tribes, in the Southwest, the East, the Plains, and the Mississippi Valley, were not comparable to those of the Mexican, Central American, or South American Indians. The Northern form of settlement consisted for some tribes merely of rows of caves, for others of villages and towns ranging in size from two acres to twelve acres. These settlements in the open comprised agglomerations of rectangular or oval masses of contiguous rooms, arranged in two or three tiers, grouped around one or more patios. Free spaces with ceremonial chambers (Kivas) half sunken in their midst may perhaps be considered as primordial squares—without definite shape or any spatial meaning.

No squares, either planned or developed from Pre-Columbian Indian civilizations, existed in the northern part of the present United States.

THE RENAISSANCE CONCEPT OF EXTERNAL SPACE

Quite naturally, squares which had grown from medieval beginnings and developed their final shape only during the Renaissance differed in their appearance from those actually newly planned during the fifteenth and sixteenth centuries. But both types share certain characteristics which define them as Renaissance creations more clearly than do any architectural ornamentations of the period. In spite of differences in scale, proportion, and architectural frame between Vigevano and Padua, Brussels and Danzig, the Escorial and Mexico City, man-made order and the attempts to establish definite spatial limits are the basic rule of all these Renaissance squares.

An Italian Renaissance church and a typical Italian square, a sixteenth-century hall church in the north and a northern square of the same period show a greater similarity to each other in their spatial concept than do squares and buildings of the Gothic period. This steadily increasing parallelism in the concept of inner and outer space was not merely born out of a common new psychological attitude. It was also influenced directly or indirectly by something which came about only with the Renaissance: architectural theories. Soon after the initial publication of those basic treatises, their gospel spread throughout the civilized world. Architects and builders studied the original texts or their translations. The wider public, the burghers of the town council, for example, had at least vague ideas of what seemed now, in the fifteenth and sixteenth centuries, to have become fashionable and pleasing to the general taste. During the late medieval centuries, spatial indefiniteness and fluidity of outline had prevailed. From the end of the fifteenth century on, three-dimensional distinctness corresponded to structural clarity. Definite laws and rules directed the limits of space and volume. Purity of stereometric form was in itself considered "beautiful."

Peculiarly, the yearning of the Renaissance for the clearest possible visual articulation of volume and space was realized in two contrasting ways: within the street, this articulation referred primarily to *volume;* the individual structures were independent and isolated. Thus the street itself is conceived as an agglomeration of heterogeneous buildings and not as an artistic unit. But the square, on the other hand, is unified, its single elements tied together by all possible architectural means, and here it is the *space* which is articulated.

This contrast may be explained very easily: in the street, space as such was not yet felt; it represented to Renaissance man merely a row of individually different palaces, in short, a sequence of volumes. To present these volumes as clearly as possible, Alberti recommended the fluctuating curve of the winding street. He motivated this suggestion also by functional reasons, namely, climatic needs brought about by the passing seasons, but also by aesthetic considerations. He believed that the variation of surprising, always new vistas and perspective effects represented architectural values important for the whole town. In the *cassone* paintings of Laurana and Francesco di Giorgio Martini and even much later in Serlio's stage designs around the middle of the sixteenth century, no two buildings are alike and each house has its own *separate* arcade.

But the square, in contrast to the street, was already perceived as space, and therefore the individual volumes of the surrounding buildings were subordinated to its spatial unity by *continuous* arcades and other connecting architectural elements.

The new attitude toward the visual arts reflected the then prevailing Neo-Platonic ideas of such contemporaries of Leone Battista Alberti as Nicholas of Cusa (1401–64) and Marsilio Ficino (1433–99), men who interpreted mathematical figures as symbols of divine harmony. The general demand for planned organization and regular shape was quite logically extended also to the layout of streets and squares. The motivation for this was twofold: on the one hand, those revived Neo-Platonic ideas just referred to, and on the other hand, rational considerations of hygiene, traffic, and other functional demands, such as governed Leonardo da Vinci in his plans for a two-leveled ideal town (1484).

To what degree internal and external space, both equally moldable and definite, were thought of as coexisting matters of aesthetic creation in the Renaissance becomes obvious through Brunelleschi's introduction of the double shell for the cupola of the Cathedral of Santa Maria del Fiore in Florence. The cupola shapes space internally and externally. The surfaces of its volume are defined through this double function: the inner shell shapes interior space; the outer shell expresses the volume within the outer space and thereby makes the beholder conscious of the existence of this outer space. The curves of the two different shells are constructed corresponding to their different functions.

Brunelleschi's cupola certainly has nothing to do with a square directly. Nonetheless, it documents the new approach to the concept of external space. It is more than a coincidence that the same master conceived the basic idea of the Piazza di SS. Annunziata in Florence, one of the first typical Renaissance squares.

V · TOWN AND SQUARE FROM THE SEVENTEENTH TO THE NINETEENTH CENTURY

DRAMATIZATION and the suggestion of movement have been generally accepted as characteristics of the baroque style since the publication of Heinrich Wölfflin's *Renaissance and Baroque* half a century ago. Numerous authors have developed this concept further and have applied it to painting, sculpture, and architecture as against the more static *concinnitas* of the Renaissance, the almost uniform style of which had prevailed in Italian architecture until about the mid-sixteenth century.

The period of transition from the High Renaissance to the baroque is marked by the founding of the Vitruvian Academy in Rome in 1542 and by the publication of Sebastiano Serlio's *Libri Cinque d'Architettura . . .*, Venice, 1531 and 1559; Giacomo Barozzi Vignola's *Regola delle Cinque Ordine d'Architettura . . .*, Rome, 1563; and Andrea Palladio's *I Quattro Libri dell' Architettura*, Venice, 1570. The Academy and these treatises codified High Renaissance concepts, but at the same time prepared the way for stylistic developments of the seventeenth and eighteenth centuries.

However, the border line between the High Renaissance and the baroque period is fluid. It becomes more and more evident that chronological periods and specific aesthetic attitudes do not coincide automatically, that the subdivision of history into definite periods always results in oversimplification. Such terms as "baroque" and "classicism" may be applied to specific art forms and remain meaningful. But if they refer to such basic categories as space and volume they become equivocal and demand more specific definition, especially for the seventeenth and eighteenth centuries. It is necessary, in a specific instance, to determine whether the word "baroque" or "classicism" pertains to a historical period or to specific aesthetic qualities.

The meaning of the term baroque is twofold. Historically, the baroque era stretches from about Michelangelo's death in 1564 to the middle of the eighteenth century, when the period of neoclassicism or classical revival sets in. What is historically called baroque is divided aesthetically into two tendencies. On the one hand, there is the baroque derived from Michelangelo, exaggerating and contorting the more placid forms of the High Renaissance, accentuating individual parts within a whole, dramatizing and emphasizing volumes and masses. On the other hand, during the same centuries there was manifested the classicistic approach, based on Palladio and the Vitruvian Academy, leaning heavily on ancient examples, regular, reticent in expression, sometimes of a certain dryness which often leads to the reproach of "academicism." These opposing tendencies, Michelangelo's emotional, individualistic concept and Palladio's rational, classicistic attitude, became so outspoken in the works of their successors that it seems almost impossible—certainly impractical for the general understanding—to cover both trends by one heading: "baroque," referring merely to chronology. During the seventeenth and eighteenth centuries both tendencies ran parallel and occasionally fused in the works of individual architects.

The space concept of baroque city planning as it appears in the shape of baroque squares may be compared but not identified with the concept of space in a painting by Rubens, in a sculpture by Bernini, or in the interior of a baroque church.

The specific spatial elements which characterize baroque town planning have rarely been analyzed. Some authors have touched on these problems, but even Lavedan in his comprehensive *Histoire de l'Urbanisme* is as little interested in them as Sitte and Unwin were. This lack of interest might be explained by the impression created all over Europe in the seventeenth and eighteenth centuries by the great French classicistic tradition of the *places royales* as the epitome of city planning. Hence the other expression of the baroque style, the Berninesque trend, receded in the conceptions of the writers of these centuries.

"The beautiful and serious game of space" was played primarily in Italy and France. Its instruments in both countries were squares and axes. In the shaping of squares—and never before had so many been planned—the treatment of space was similar to, but not at all identical with, the concept of space in architecture proper. The dynamic masses and volumes now employed in town planning corresponded to the glories of the flesh and other material splendors in painting and sculpture. And these masses appeared to move and to suggest movement to the spectator most intensely—while at the same time they seemed to arrest this suggested movement. "Arrested movement" represents the climax of baroque city planning in Italy in the same way as the direction and the breaking up of currents of light in Spanish, Mexican, and German churches express the climax of baroque interiors. In both of these "super-baroque" developments it is the new relationship and integration of mass and volume and a new employment of light and shadow which add a fresh element to those form-shaping factors which had defined the earlier baroque.

To understand exactly the meaning of "arrested movement," one does best to compare works of the late sixteenth century, the early baroque—e.g., Michelangelo's Piazza di Campidoglio and the original Piazza del Popolo in Rome—with creations of the seventeenth century.

BAROQUE SQUARES IN ITALY

During the baroque centuries the development of city planning in Italy was as clearly centered in Rome as what that of contemporary architecture. In order to evaluate the architectural and city planning activities in Rome during the baroque period, some figures about its still relatively small population should be mentioned: in 1458, it numbered 35,000; in 1526, 55,000; in 1580, 80,000; and in 1656, 124,000. The great Popes from Sixtus V (1586) to Alexander VIII (1691) wanted to glorify the Papal See as the nucleus of the spiritual and worldly power of the Counter Reformation. In this endeavor they were fortunate enough to find great artists worthy of this enterprise whose temperament exactly fit this task. Foremost among them, of course, was Bernini, a man of unique creativity and inventiveness equally as sculptor, architect, and city planner. The spirit of Michelangelo, the "father of the baroque," still hovered above the Eternal City, and his direct and indirect influence after his death can hardly be overestimated. And as if fate had predestined Rome as the cradle of the baroque and as the stage of its climax, the topographical conditions of this hilly town simply called for the development of dynamic vistas. One has only to visualize how Michelangelo employed these nature-given circumstances in the shaping of the Capitol.

As the final form of St. Mark's Square in Venice had depended partially on the employment of structures previously erected, so the Campidoglio, the square before the Capitol in Rome (Pl. 45A and B), was not an entirely free and spontaneous creation of Michelangelo's. He was bound by two already existing structures on top of the Capitoline Hill: the ancient Capitol (Palazzo dei Senatori, remodeled after 1144, again in 1299, and once more reconstructed in 1389 under Pope Boniface IX as a kind of medieval town hall) and the Palazzo dei Conservatori, built under Pope Nicholas V in 1450.

One is not always aware that the Campidoglio definitely and entirely represents a *civic* institution, that this square, although topographically isolated like a Greek acropolis or some medieval cathedral with its local immunity area, is not at all a "sacred area" and has no religious connotations whatsoever. During the Middle Ages, after the ninth century, the Capitol had become the seat of the municipal prefect and had thus gained political importance for the administration of small, medieval Rome. In 1451, Pope Nicholas V already began to think of remodeling the existing structures, especially the Palazzo dei Conservatori and the towers of the Palazzo dei Senatori, the Tabularium. But it was almost one century later, in 1538, that Pope Paul III commissioned Michelangelo with this monumental task as an overall project.

Michelangelo first leveled the irregular top of the Capitoline Hill and brought from the Lateran the famous equestrian statue of Marcus Aurelius, which owed its preservation throughout the Middle Ages to the fact that it was erroneously believed to represent Constantine the Great. Michelangelo envisioned the future piazza as a trapezoid since the two existing buildings were placed at an oblique angle to each other. Thus he planned a third *palazzo*, the present Capitoline Museum, facing the Palazzo dei Conservatori, and at the same angle to the Capitol. Projected in 1562, it was executed in 1644–55 by Girolamo Rainaldi. Although the difference in width between the Capitol building and the smaller entrance side of the trapezoid is about fourteen yards, the spectator hardly becomes aware of it. Moreover, the perspective helps to monumentalize the Palazzo dei Senatori. This stage effect already suggests a movement toward the background, a typically baroque trait. The strongly emphasized horizontals of the two lateral palaces are set lower than the corresponding horizontals of the façade of the Palazzo dei Senatori. Thus the height of the latter—eight yards above the eaves of the lateral structures—is visually increased. It is still more accentuated through the vertical of the tower behind.

The staircase in front of the Palazzo dei Senatori was erected by Michelangelo during his lifetime, although he had originally provided for a larger sculpture than the *Roma* now located there. Michelangelo's façade of the Palazzo dei Senatori, changed in many details by Giacomo della Porta, was completed in 1598–1612 by the same Girolamo Rainaldi who at the end of his life built the Capitoline Museum. The façade of the Palazzo dei Conservatori, opposite the Capitoline Museum, had been built by Giacomo della Porta and Martino Lunghi in 1563–64. Numerous drawings and copper engravings by contemporary artists who visited Rome tell us about the successive stages during the building period (Pl. 45c).

We have deemed it necessary in the descriptive analysis of the square on the Campidoglio to mention so many data referring to individual buildings in order to prove that in spite of the one and a half centuries needed for its completion, Michelangelo's original concept was essentially preserved and determines the appearance of the square even today.

In the overall appearance of the Campidoglio, the verticals of the Corinthian columns tie together all three structures. So do the lateral arcades which face each other. Michelangelo had taken over the motif of the arcades from the Piazza di SS. Annunziata in Florence, from Vigevano, etc. But here it serves quite another function than on those closed Renaissance squares. There the arcades intensified by continuous repetition the static balance of the enclosed space, whereas on the Campidoglio they accelerate the movement toward the background structure.

The shorter entrance side, facing the Palazzo dei Senatori, is closed by a balustrade adorned by the ancient statues of the Dioscuri; it functions as an imaginary fourth wall through which the reservoir of bounded space of the square proper seeps out gently. The access from the ramp of the staircase, the so-called Cordonata, projected by Michelangelo in 1544 and built with slight changes by Giacomo della Porta in 1578, prepares one for the movement into depth. The pavement, whose oval pattern centers around the statue of Marcus Aurelius, climbs slightly toward the pedestal and further increases the spatial sensation. Michelangelo envisioned the Piazza di Campidoglio as a monumental stage set and employed all artistic means to suggest movement into depth and to create the impression of gradually increasing volumes which frame the space in between. The desire for static balance encountered in earlier Renaissance spatial creations no longer exists. For the first time the baroque concept of dynamic motion in space is introduced, although still interwoven with Renaissance ideas, such as the repetition of identical motifs (arcades, the Corinthian order, etc.). But there it is—and the Piazza di Campidoglio represents the exact transition from the one concept to the other.

If this square looms much larger in our memory than it does in actuality, it bespeaks the power of its scenic organization. Seen from the Cordonata toward the Palazzo dei Senatori, the piazza, small as it is, seemingly gains in depth and, as said before, lifts and monumentalizes the Palazzo dei Senatori for the viewer approaching the piazza. In the opposite direction, from the Palazzo dei Senatori toward the balustrade and the opening of the staircase, the vista toward the city appears effectively framed and kept together. Thus the illusionistic effect of the perspective stage device works in both directions, similar to the way in which Bernini later employed it on St. Peter's Square in Rome and as it already existed on St. Mark's Square in Venice. Michelangelo used all his artistic powers to suggest movement and to dramatize the backdrop—both typically baroque devices. Yet this movement which is forced upon the spectator is still straight and not arrested.

Movement in one direction was also the principal motif of the Piazza del Popolo in Rome as it existed in its original form (Pl. 46). This, the first comprehensive baroque town planning project, was not confined to a single square but comprised a whole section of the Eternal City. It was laid out in 1589 under Pope Sixtus V, who determined the whole organization by setting up an obelisk as the hub of the radiating streets. The basic system (the converging Via di Ripetta, the Via del Corso [originally called the Via Flaminia], and the Via del Babuino) had already existed in antiquity, though in a less regular form, comprising the whole quarter between the Pincian Hill and the Tiber River.

The piazza was the receptacle for those visitors to Rome who entered the Eternal City from the Via Flaminia, as did the overwhelming majority during the Middle Ages and the Renaissance centuries. It extended from the Porta del Popolo (executed by Vignola in 1589) and represented the center from which the three streets radiated in fanlike form. At the beginning of the nineteenth century, the trapezoid layout of the piazza was to undergo a change: Berthault planned some projects around 1812 but the piazza received its present-day form in 1816–20 through the Italian architect Giuseppe Valadier (see p. 162).

In its original trapezoid shape, stretching from the Porta del Popolo toward the two symmetrically located, domed churches of Santa Maria in Monte Santo and Santa Maria dei Miracoli, the square showed its directive force most clearly. Both churches were begun after designs by Carlo Rainaldi in 1662–67, and were completed by Carlo Fontana and Bernini respectively; their dominating combined volume accentuated the square's function as a place of gathering and dispersal. The stream of incoming travelers entered the square through the Porta del Popolo and was dispersed over the city in three different directions through the three streets that radiated from the square. In this process the two churches served as a sort of triumphal arch entrance. This current was visualized as moving uninterruptedly in one direction, as on the Campidoglio, directed by the gradual broadening of the trapezoid, and checked by no barrier, no arrest. Palladio's stage plan for the Teatro Olimpico in Vicenza, similar to the layout of the Piazza del Popolo, may have been an additional source of stimulation, but it certainly was not a model for emulation, since the three streets had already existed for many centuries prior to the baroque organization.

The stimulative power of the fan motif of the Piazza del Popolo becomes evident through its many repetitions and variants from Vaux-le-Vicomte and Versailles to Christopher Wren's plan for London. As to corresponding developments of the eighteenth century, such as the square in Aranjuez, the basic scheme of Karlsruhe, the Friedrichstadt in Berlin, the Place de l'Odéon in Paris, and elements of L'Enfant's plan for Washington, D.C., it would be difficult to decide whether the original idea of the Piazza del Popolo in Rome or its further glorification in Versailles was the stronger influence.

The Campidoglio and the Piazza del Popolo show the beginning of the baroque space concept with emphasis on directed movement. However, in both examples this directed movement differs still from dynamic spatial acceleration, the sensation of suspense and surprise which was to become the ultimate aim of architectural organization, based on the concept of arrested movement.

Six Roman squares express best what seemed the ideal relationship between space and movement to the artists of the late baroque: St. Peter's Square (the Piazza di San Pietro), the Piazza Navona, the Piazza di Spagna, and—on a smaller scale—the squares in front of Santa Maria della Pace, San Ignazio, and the Trevi Fountain.

St. Peter's Square (Pl. 48A), like the Piazza del Popolo, is a dominated square; actually, in spite of its gigantic dimensions, it is a regular parvis in its inseparable connection with the façade of St. Peter's—the "Christian Propylaea" to the most sacred area of the Papal See.

The original plan for a completely centralized, domed church as conceived by Bramante, Raphael, Peruzzi, Antonio da Sangallo, and eventually by Michelangelo was changed through the lengthening of the nave into a Latin cross by Maderna in 1606. The façade of St. Peter's was completed in 1614, and the scale of its colossal columns became the point of reference for the proportions of Giovanni Lorenzo Bernini's square.

The story of St. Peter's Square is too well known to be repeated here at full length. In competition with Francesco Rainaldi and other leading contemporary architects, Bernini developed a series of projects rather wide in range. One ground plan, for instance, emulated the figure of the Crucified with the contortions of the arms as the pincers of the colonnades, the head outlining the basilica proper, etc.; in another sketch, with two-storied colonnades, buildings to the left of the church corresponded exactly to the Vatican on the right (Pls. 47 and 48B). The final plan commissioned by Pope Alexander VII was executed by Bernini between 1656 and 1667. In formulating his design, Bernini had to take into consideration the location of the gigantic obelisk erected by Domenico Fontana in 1586 and the fountain on the right-hand side (erected by Maderna in 1613; its counterpart was finished only after the completion of the square).

Bernini conceived of the square as being subdivided into three units: the *piazza retta,* immediately before the church façade; the *piazza obliqua,* appearing as an ellipsoid through the pattern of the pavement, but actually constructed as two half-circles and a rectangle in between; and the third, the Piazza Rusticucci, never brought into a definite artistic shape and today part of Mussolini's avenue linking St. Peter's with the Tiber River (Pl. 48C).

The Piazza Rusticucci collected and directed approaching visitors toward the *piazza obliqua.* Carlo Fontana's later project of a triumphal arch and

ROME. CAMPIDOGLIO

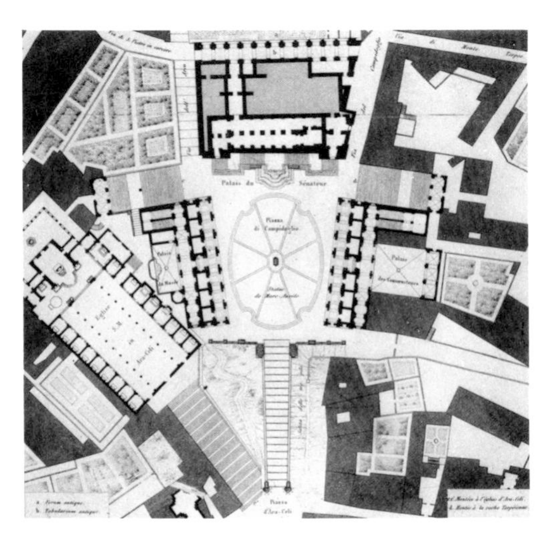

A: PLAN

From Letarouilly, *Edifices de Rome moderne*

B: AERIAL VIEW

Photo Ministero della Difesa Aeronautica

C: ETCHING

BY GIOVANNI BATTISTA PIRANESI

Courtesy Metropolitan Museum of Art,
Dick Fund, 1937

ROME. PIAZZA DEL POPOLO

COPPER ENGRAVING BY GIUSEPPE VASI

From *Raccoltà delle piu belle vedute antiche e moderne di Roma*

PIAZZA DEL POPOLO AND SURROUNDINGS, 1748. PLAN

From *Nuova Pianta de Roma . . . da Giambattista Noli*

VIEW

ROME. ST. PETER'S AND THE SQUARE

PROJECT BY LORENZO BERNINI

From Norton, *Bernini and Other Studies in the History of Art*

ETCHING BY GIOVANNI BATTISTA PIRANESI

Courtesy Metropolitan Museum of Art

ROME. ST. PETER'S AND THE SQUARE

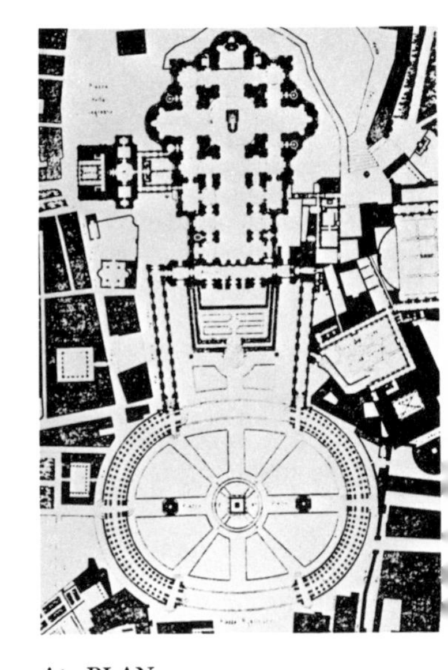

A: PLAN

From Sitte,
The Art of Building Cities

B: AERIAL VIEW

Photo Edizione Belvedere

C: VIEW FROM THE CUPOLA OF ST. PETER'S ACROSS THE SQUARE, BEFORE THE OPENING OF THE AXIS TOWARD THE TIBER RIVER

Photo E. Richter, Rome

A: ROME
PIAZZA NAVONA

ETCHING BY GIOVANNI BATTISTA PIRANESI
Courtesy Metropolitan Museum of Art

AERIAL VIEW
Photo Alinari; courtesy Ministero Aeronautico U.S.P.

B: LUCCA. PIAZZA DELL' ANFITEATRO ROMANO. AERIAL VIEW

PLATE 50

ROME. PIAZZA

BEFORE THE CHURCH OF SANTA MARIA DELLA PACE

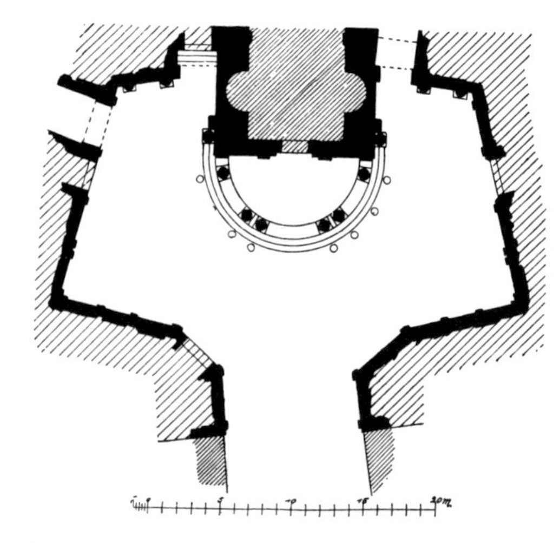

PLAN

From Brinckmann, *Platz und Monument*

COPPER ENGRAVING BY GIUSEPPE VASI

From *Raccoltà delle piu belle vedute antiche e moderne di Roma*

ROME. PIAZZA BEFORE THE CHURCH OF SAN IGNAZIO

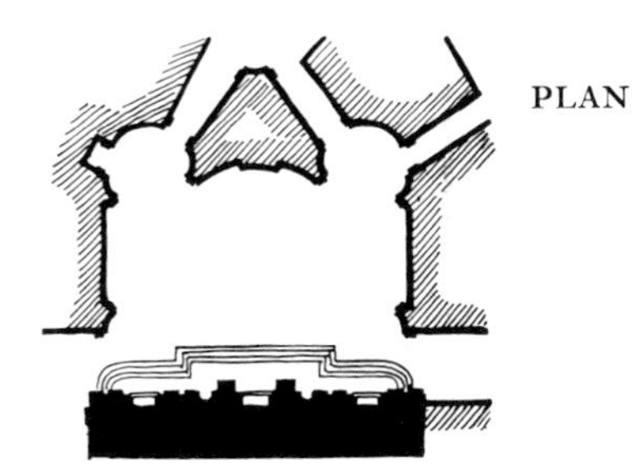

PLAN

VIEW FROM THE CHURCH Photo Ernest Nash

ROME. PIAZZA AND SCALA DI SPAGNA

VIEW

Photo Edizione Enrico Verdesi, Rome

AERIAL VIEW

Photo El Al Israel Airlines, Ltd.

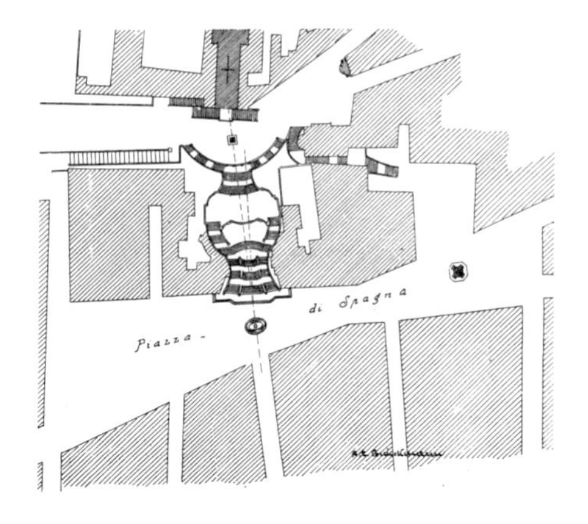

PLAN

From Brinckmann, *Platz und Monument*

A: ROME
PORTO DI RIPETTA
COPPER ENGRAVING BY
GIUSEPPE VASI

B: AJACCIO, CORSICA. CITY SQUARE. INK AND WASH DRAWING BY GIUSEPPE VALADIER, 1780–1800

Photo Cooper Union Museum, New York

A: ROME. CORNER AT THE VIA QUATTRO FONTANE, WITH FOUNTAIN
COPPER ENGRAVING BY G. B. FALDA From *Le Fontane di Roma*

B: TURIN. PIAZZA SAN CARLO Photo Alinari

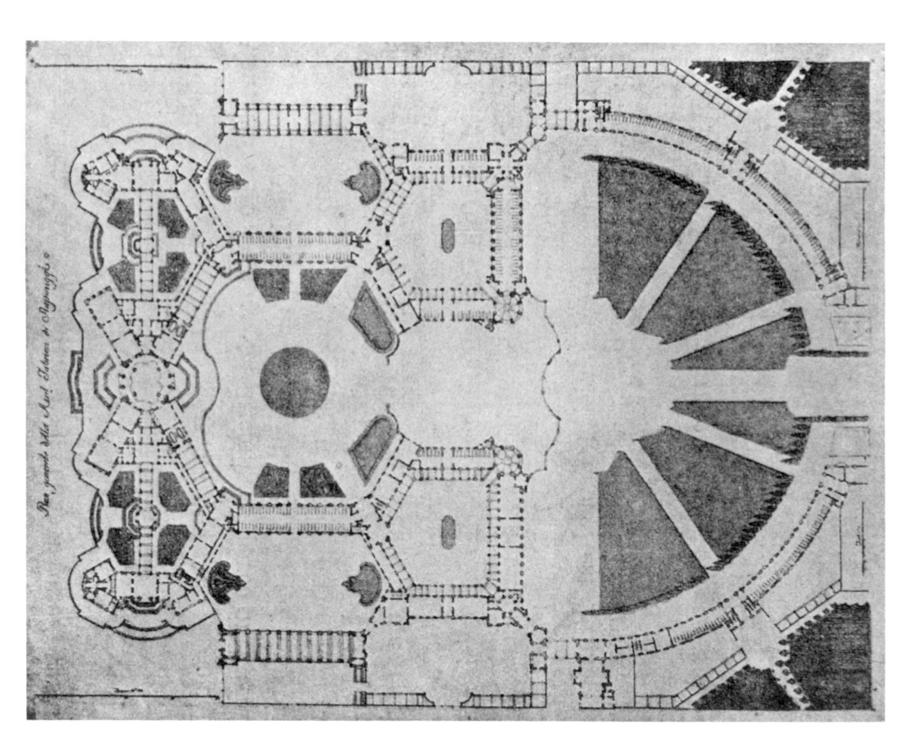

PLAN

CASTLE OF STUPINIGI

AERIAL VIEW

From Zevi, *Architecture as Space*

A: CASERTA. PLAN OF PARK, SQUARE, AND CASTLE. COPPER ENGRAVING
From Chierici, *La reggia di Caserta*

B: VILLA MANIN, PASSARIANO. AERIAL VIEW
From Zevi, *Architecture as Space*

A: ROME. PIAZZA DEL POPOLO. VIEW FROM THE PINCIAN HILL
Photo E. Richter, Rome

B: NAPLES. PIAZZA DEL PLEBISCITO Photo Alinari

TURIN. PIAZZA VITTORIO VENETO

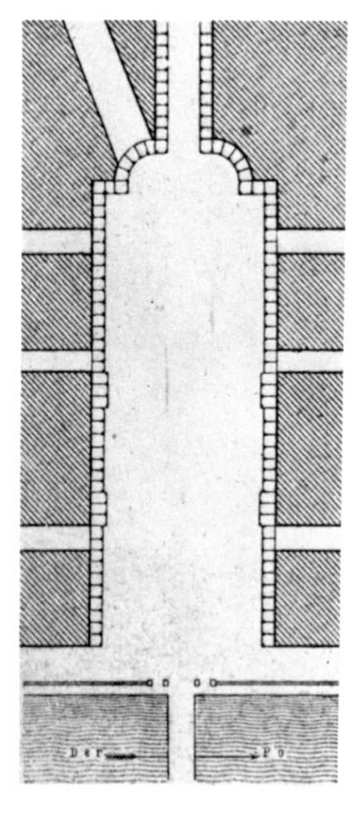

PLAN

From Stübben, *Der Städtebau*

VIEW

Photo Edizione S.A.C.A.T., Turin

A: CHARLEVILLE. PLACE DUCALE

Photo Éditions A.T.M.O., Mézières

B: RICHELIEU. PLAN

From Tassin, *Les Plans et Profiles des Toutes les principales Villes et Lieux . . .*

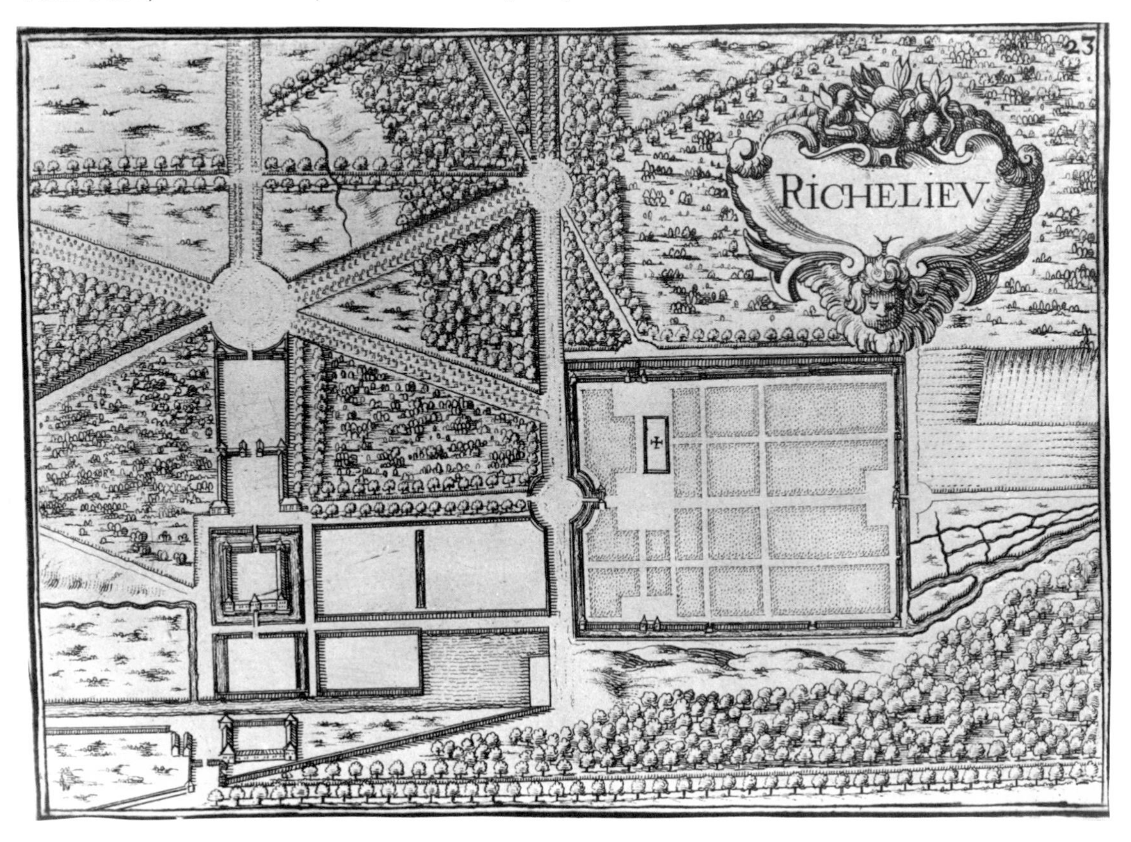

VERSAILLES

LES AVENUES. COPPER ENGRAVING

From Perelle, *Les Avenues de Versailles;*
courtesy Metropolitan Museum of Art, Rogers Fund, 1921

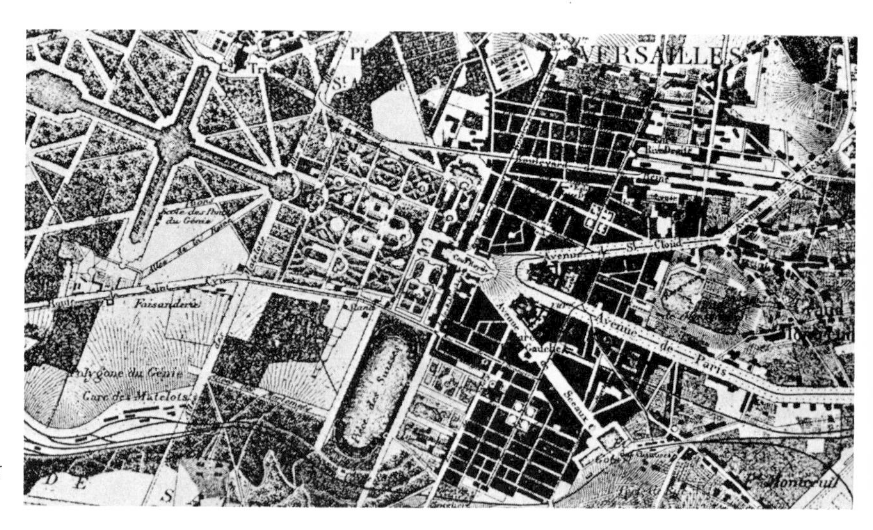

PLAN

clock tower opposite St. Peter's façade and at equal distances from the obelisk would have closed the area. However, this project would have sacrificed completely the dramatization and surprise Bernini had aimed at and would have made the façade of St. Peter's a mere decorative backdrop instead.

Surprisingly, the long main axis of the *piazza obliqua* does not lead toward the church but runs north and south, parallel to St. Peter's main façade. This change in direction astonished Bernini's contemporaries most and aroused their criticism. Actually this very arrangement arrests the movement toward the church, thus creating the spatial tension so desirable from the viewpoint of the late baroque. Bernini laid the *piazza obliqua* at right angles to the main spatial thrust because he wanted to achieve a kind of brake in the movement toward the façade—not because of the existing structures. He emphasized the longer north-south axis through the arrangement of fountain-obelisk-fountain in one line, and especially through the sloping of the piazza toward its center. The pattern of the pavement with its spikes radiating from the obelisk is of more than two-dimensional importance; it also ties together the colonnades and the verticals of obelisk and fountains and makes the floor appear as a flat shell. The open colonnades around the *piazza obliqua* consist of four concentric rows of Doric columns whose diameters increase, and the floor of the colonnades rises toward the outer rim—again a play with optical illusion. Where these open, pincerlike colonnades of the *piazza obliqua* meet with the closed corridors framing the *piazza retta* there is a kind of narrows; a second visual barrier or imaginary stop is created. The *piazza retta* then rises toward the church, and this difference in level is accelerated through the steps which protrude more than eighty yards into the piazza. Most decisive is the oblique direction of both side-wings, diverging in the direction of the church—a device similar to that employed by Michelangelo in the Campidoglio. Since anyone approaching the church naturally supposes that the framing wings meet the façade at right angles, Maderna's much too broad front (the ratio of width to height is 2.7:1) is perceived automatically as narrower than it actually is. This concentrating effect is further increased through the compactness of the closed lateral corridors, whose height decreases slightly toward the façade.

Bernini's ingenious concept of the square was highly praised and equally severely criticized by his contemporaries—a criticism hardly understandable today. The spatial effect of the whole sequence—street-Piazza Rusticucci-

piazza obliqua-piazza retta—amounts to a change from limited expansion to release arrested by the row of fountain-obelisk-fountain. Gradual concentration through the narrowing wings leads to a second visual barrier and beyond to final concentration on the façade. The basic and entirely original idea is the pincerlike frame of the colonnades which directs the movement unambiguously toward the façade. And in this way Bernini reduces for the approaching viewer the mistake of Maderna. Through the latter's lengthening of the nave, the gigantic façade overlapped the tambour of the cupola so completely in perspective that the dome seems to sit immediately on the roof. Bernini himself gave up his original idea of closing the square completely through a structure at the far end opposite the façade of the basilica.

The means by which Bernini achieved the suggestive three-dimensional force of the *piazza retta*, which is directed toward the church, are threefold: first, there is the contrast between the height of the basilica and of the closed colonnades (less than one half of the height of the façade proper). Secondly, there is the oblique direction of both arms diverging toward the façade, a motif employed in the reversed sense by Michelangelo at the Campidoglio and anticipated to a certain degree in Pienza. Finally, marked differences in level help the spatial effect: the rising of the *piazza retta* by about four yards in contrast to the decline of the *piazza obliqua* toward the obelisk in the center by almost two yards.

Sometimes fate is kind to the city planner: Bernini, who in all his work, be it sculpture, architecture, stage design, or city planning, emphasized dynamic movement at the expense of everything else, found in Rome an area predestined for the perfect realization of his ideals. Thus Bernini could create one of the most beautiful squares in the world, the Piazza Navona, out of an ancient circus whose contours were marked by surrounding houses. To appreciate fully the originality of Bernini's transformation of these given data, one has only to compare this square with the Piazza dell' Anfiteatro Romano in Lucca (Anfiteatro Mercato) (Pl. 49B) which also occupies the site of an ancient circus and follows its form. This latter square, although pure in its oval outline, appears to be rather a courtlike enclosure; it represents simply a void, surrounded by houses, and does not evoke any impression of willfully, aesthetically shaped space.

How different is the Piazza Navona (Pl. 49A)! Baroque artists discovered in the seventeenth century the eminent fitness of the area of Domitian's ancient circus, with its emphasis on the longitudinal direction, for the creation of an impressive square, and Girolamo and Carlo Rainaldi in collaboration with Francesco Borromini built there the Church of Sant' Agnese (1652–77), whose façade became an essential element for the piazza. The expansion of the church façade in broad horizontals and especially the location of the cupola, rising immediately behind the façade in contrast to all other baroque churches, prove that the architects were fully aware of the narrow width of the square. They counted on *oblique* perspectives obtainable from various spots on the piazza rather than on the usual central perspective. Connected with the church on either side were small *palazzi* whose architecture was integrated with that of the church. The Church of San Giacomo degli Spagnuoli (of 1450) on the opposite long side became completely subordinated to the overall spatial organization by Bernini.

But it is the furnishing of the Piazza Navona by Bernini that actually defines its spatial form. Bernini placed the Fountain of the Rivers (1647–51), crowned by the ancient obelisk of Domitian, on the longitudinal axis of the square but off the central axis of Sant' Agnese; in this way the effect of the curved façade was not diminished. The southerly Fountain of the Moor already existed at the end of the sixteenth century and Bernini merely remodeled it through the addition of his sculptures; the Fountain of Neptune on the north side with its sculptures was also projected by Bernini but was executed from his models only in the nineteenth century. Through this arrangement of the three fountains Bernini changed the direction of movement of the passers-by, so that instead of merely passing along an avenue, they had their attention directed toward the façade of the church.

The singularly festive character of the Piazza Navona has always been apparent; it is based on the contrast between the dynamic sculptural volumes of the three fountains with their display of cascading waters and the relatively quiet and neutral frame of the surrounding houses, hardly interrupted by incoming streets. Only the façade of Sant' Agnese takes up the colorful orchestration of the three focal points on the square. Small wonder that in the eighteenth century during the Roman carnival this exceptionally festive piazza was often flooded to create a naval spectacle, with gondolas replacing the carriages of nobility. After all, during the seventeenth and eighteenth centuries no sharply defined border lines existed between city planning and architecture, between architecture and decoration, between decoration and stage design, between stage design and landscape architecture—a concept hard for modern man to imagine in an era of highly rationalized functionalism.

This interplay between the creations of city planner and stage designer makes late baroque squares so often appear like stage settings. This is not the accidental result of picturesque street scenes and the colorful life of the people, but because these squares were planned as such. While the impact of the earlier St. Peter's Square and the Piazza del Popolo is more that of a severe, august, monumental grandeur, the squares of Santa Maria della Pace and of San Ignazio and the Piazza di Spagna show the most intricate combination of city planning and stage design, still more so than the Piazza Navona. After all, it is more than mere chance or a chronological coincidence that stage designers like Andrea Pozzo (1642–1709), Ferdinando Bibiena (1657–1743), and Francesco Bibiena (1659–1739) worked together with the then leading architects, both groups doubtlessly influencing each other strongly. Even one generation later, Piranesi in his etchings created visions of public squares and monumental perspectives which elaborated on the ideas of these preceding architects and stage designers.

Much as this period indulged in the employment and display of large masses and vast expanses, its characteristic tendencies expressed themselves just as originally in some solutions of a smaller scale, such as the little squares in front of the churches of Santa Maria della Pace and San Ignazio. These squares are actually parvises dominated by church façades and inseparably tied to them. Here also, within small areas, we experience the same arrested movement and the spatial staccato which distinguished the organization of the larger squares. In both instances people entering the squares from the neighboring streets are not led directly to the church entrance, but their movement is diverted and broken by the fluctuating frame of the surrounding houses.

The Church of Santa Maria della Pace in Rome was first built in 1480 under Pope Sixtus IV and was remodeled in 1657 by Pietro da Cortona, who also shaped the small area of the piazza before it (Pl. 50). This square, one of the most original baroque squares in Rome, is limited by the church façade and the architecture of the surrounding houses, which is in tune with the architectural details of the church. The principal street runs into the piazza at an oblique angle opposite the church; two smaller streets unobtrusively cut in close to the façade. Out of these given, rather chaotic conditions only a baroque architect could create a unified spatial shape. The two stories of the church façade form contrasting curves, the upper part bent backwards while the lower part with its semicircular porch protrudes into the square. The mutual penetration of volumes is mirrored in the ground plan of the square. The symmetry of the wings extending from the church façade is entirely unfunctional, the right wing framing the entrance to a street, the left pasted before a closed wall. The fake opening is repeated on the right side of the piazza. In this way the unification of the area and the correspondence of its individual architectural elements are achieved—only to be broken up again and almost negated by the protruding porch and the staggering forms and angles of the piazza's confines.

Very similar is the stagelike effect of the small piazza before the Jesuit church of San Ignazio (begun in 1626 by Orazio Grassi; façade erected by Algardi in 1649; completed after Grassi's design in 1686) (Pl. 51), an extraordinary example of a closed and at the same time a dominated square. The architectural elements of the surrounding houses are dictated by the overwhelming façade of the church, second only to Il Gesù in size and decoration. The triangular building opposite the church, functioning as its counterpart, represents little more than a stage wing, although it actually contains small apartments. Niches, created by the curved walls of the houses opposite, conceal the incoming streets so that the façades seem to be uninterrupted. Again, as with the square before Santa Maria della Pace, the symmetry is maintained by fake openings. Because of the size of the church front with its stairs, the street in front of the façade becomes visually negligible, which makes the square appear completely closed. The subdivisions of this seemingly uninterrupted space envelope make the square appear larger than it actually is. The curvature of the eaves against the sky seems to form a ceiling of a definite pattern. If ever the idea of baroque space with its fluid limits overflowing into each other is realized, it is here on this civic stage—as much so as inside the church.

The Piazza di Spagna with its 137 steps (by Alessandro Specchi and Francesco de' Santis, 1721–25) represents the climax of stage effects in Roman city planning on a larger scale (Pl. 52). Here, nature lent a helpful hand to the spatial vision of the planner, who had to cope originally with a relatively narrow area without definite confines, an area which since the seventeenth century has been the gathering place for foreigners in Rome.

The triangular area of the piazza, into which five streets run, serves as the starting point for the stairs which lead to the Church of Santa Trinità dei Monti (built in 1459; façade erected by Domenico Fontana in 1595; rebuilt in 1816). Lorenzo Bernini's father, Pietro, had built a fountain in the shape of a boat, the so-called Barcaccia (1627–29), repeating an ancient motif, and had sunk it into the pavement of the piazza. From this fountain the stairs climb straight up the hill, continuing the direction of the incoming Via Condotti. Stopped by the obelisk at the top, the stairs run into the center of the church façade at an oblique angle. The slight deviation from the axis of the church is not perceptible in three-dimensional reality; it can be seen only on the ground plan. The unique spatial and visual experience is the integration of staircase and piazza. Actually the staircase, the link between two topographically different levels, becomes the square. The remaining part of the piazza is irrelevant. The Scala di Spagna is the only example in the history of city planning where a staircase does not merely lead to a square in front of a monumental structure, but where the stairs themselves become the visual and spatial center.

The free-flowing stairs are framed at both sides by houses of average height and articulated through landings which interrupt the successive steps. After the initial four sections of curved steps a larger landing provides a major stop around which the stairs divide. A platform extending over the whole width collects the movement to split it again into two ramps which end on the upper street level in front of the church.

The three-dimensional organization of the staircase-piazza with its curved subdivisions, clearly marked by banks and balustrades, inserts a *fermata* in movement with each subdivision which shifts the direction of the advancing spectator and his vista continuously. This organization represents the last stage of the late baroque: the introduction of a forceful bilateral countermovement, which is more than a mere arrest, against the earlier unilateral movement which was the ideal of the seventeenth century.

For centuries the most abundant flower market in Rome has been displayed at the foot of the Scala di Spagna, thus reflecting the popular awareness of the dramatic backdrop character of the staircase, mellowed as it is by the unique qualities of Roman colors and light.

The originality of this spatial concept found its echo in imitations all over Europe—quite naturally always unsuccessful. There was no substitute for Roman grandeur. Even in Russia, in the small town of Kerch, a nineteenth-century architect attempted a similar combination of staircase and square.

In designing the Scala di Spagna, Alessandro Specchi used the motif of bifurcating stairs which he had employed before, in 1703, in the smaller piazza of the Porto di Ripetta in front of the Church S. Girolamo degli Schiavoni (built by Martino Lunghi around 1588) (Pl. 53A). Here the difference between the level of the church and the rim of the Tiber River is overcome by curved bifurcating stairs in connection with the small protruding platform. The whole square-stairs combination—no longer in existence—is known to us only through contemporaneous engravings.

The typical baroque character of this solution becomes evident by a comparison with a project which Giuseppe Valadier designed one hundred years later for an almost identical "marina" (Pl. 53B). The classicist employs all architectural means possible to stabilize the spatial relations between the square and the water and to avoid carefully any kind of three-dimensional movement.

The piazza in front of the Fontana di Trevi (1735–62, erected by Niccolo Salvi and the sculptor Pietro Bracci after an earlier project by Bernini), an overwhelming interplay of architecture (static), sculpture (semistatic), and water (fluid), melting into one brilliantly orchestrated three-dimensional composition, represents a last echo and condensation of these three-dimensional concepts of the late baroque (see Pl. 3B). The gable wall of the Palazzo Poli, more than fifty yards broad, offers the background for an illusory façade whose columns and niches, architraves and aedicula are genuine but whose window openings are faked, partially painted, partially in relief. From this façade's gigantic central niche Neptune descends in his chariot, drawn by prancing horses and led by Tritons. The façade with its severe architectural order rises from seemingly natural rock which at the same time serves as the playground for the dramatic and lively performance of the sculptural figures and animals—all enveloped into the movement of the falling water.

The piazza proper, small as its two-leveled space is, must be perceived as a kind of secular parvis for the fountain. None of the surrounding buildings with the sole exception of the fountain proper is of any influence upon the shape of the square, least of all the Church of SS. Vincenzo e Anastasio (built by Martino Lunghi around 1650), spatially isolated as it is by its oblique position. The "square" is subdivided into an area opposite the fountain, actually not much more than a broadened street, and a level, ten steps below, framing the quiet surface of the basin which arrests the thundering whirl of sculpture, rocks, and water. Since none of the small incoming streets prepares one for the sudden grandiose stage effect, here the element of visual surprise is most effectively employed.

Even mere crossroads (*carrefours*) were worked out as miniature squares, employing architectural elements similar to those that prevailed in the planning of the aforementioned larger squares of Rome. The crossing of the Via del Quirinale and the Via Venti Settembre (Via Quattro Fontane) in Rome, for instance, is developed as a completely symmetrical small space unit. One of the four corners is taken up by the Church San Carlo alle Quattro Fontane, whose façade (1667–82) was one of the last works of Francesco Borromini. The four corners of the streets are cut at an angle of 45° and are decorated with fountains, each of them with a reclining figure, representing a river or virtue respectively, above the basin (Pl. 54A). This motif had first been employed by Domenico Fontana (1543–1607) on his house which occupied one of the four corners. Since this crossroad is situated on the crest of a slight elevation, it creates an opportunity for long vistas in all four directions well in tune with baroque concepts. Thus the crossroad with its four oblique corners takes on the character of a miniature octagonal square.

A very similar solution, also with four fountains and sculptural decor, appears at the Piazza Vigliena or Quattro Canti in Palermo, at the crossing of the Corso Vittorio Emanuele and the Via Maqueda, laid out under the Viceroy Marqués de Vellena in 1609. And once more the same idea was taken up outside of Italy in Potsdam, Germany, at the "Acht Ecken," planned by von Gontard in 1771.

CLASSICISTIC SQUARES IN ITALY

Historically no exact demarcation line can be drawn between baroque and classicism in Italy. The climax of the late baroque must be identified with the three-dimensional work of Lorenzo Bernini, Carlo Rainaldi, Francesco Borromini, Pietro da Cortona, etc., with Rome as its center and with counterparts in the architecture of Turin, Naples, and Genoa. But even while the late baroque prevailed, the influence of Palladio and the Vitruvian Academy expressed itself in more or less pure classicistic examples. This holds true primarily as to individual architecture, but to a lesser degree also to city planning projects. Classicistic solutions became more numerous during the eighteenth century when the trend toward thinking in rational and "academic" concepts increased. The extent and intensity of Italian classicism cannot, however, be compared with the exclusive rule of classicism in France, where its formative force was equally strong in city planning and architecture.

It is hard to believe that the same Bernini who had envisioned St. Peter's Square and the Piazza Navona in Rome, and whose overpowering artistic temperament had stimulated his contemporaries and successors to create the most baroque spatial organizations in such squares as Santa Maria della Pace, San Ignazio, and di Spagna, was able to design a clear-cut, purely classicistic solution. However, the piazza at Ariccia, between the Church of S. Maria dell' Assunta and the Palazzo Chigi, both of which were designed by Bernini in 1664, shows a strict formalism which could not have been surpassed by the most typical solutions of the High Renaissance or even of late French classicism. This refers equally to church and *palazzo* and to the regularity of the square proper. This revival of the severe dignity of the High Renaissance calls quite logically for the location of two symmetrical fountains. In their relation to the church they correspond exactly to those in front of the Palazzo Farnese in Rome. In its small dimensions the square represents a complete reversal of everything the younger Bernini had aimed at.

In the Piazza San Carlo in Turin (Pl. 54B) contradictory stylistic tendencies—baroque and classicistic—fight each other. Its plan was originally conceived by Vittozzi and was executed by the Count of Castellamonte in 1638. Vittozzi had borrowed the baroque idea of twin churches from the Piazza del Popolo in Rome. The twin churches in Turin, San Cristina and San Carlo, each with a campanile, frame the entrance to the main street, the arcaded Via Roma. Only the clock tower of San Carlo was executed originally (the façade of San Cristina was erected in 1718, that of San Carlo in

1836). Arcaded houses surround the square on three sides. The force of the whole town plan of Turin with its ancient Roman castrum scheme was so strong that any later square had to be integrated into it. Thus Vittozzi was compelled to employ a rectangular ground plan, the shape of which contradicted per se the baroque accentuation. In other words, the churches, in spite of their similarity to Santa Maria del Popolo, in no way define the spatial character of the square as they do in Rome.

Three squares in front of large castles show the same amalgamation of native Italian baroque concepts with the invading influence of French classicism: the squares before the Castle of Stupinigi near Turin; the Villa Manin, the palatial residence of one of Venice's last doges, near Udine; and the Palace of Caserta near Naples.

The Castle of Stupinigi (Pl. 55) was begun by Juvara in 1729 and the main part was completed by him in 1733. After Juvara's death in 1736, the architect Conte Benedetto Alfieri took over and designed additional parts, faithful to the spirit of the original. Stupinigi as it appears today—the castle proper, the park, and the adjacent parts of the town—was completed not before 1773, after Alfieri's death. The main body of the castle consists of a central oval from which four wings branch out. In the main axis, in front of the oval, an open hexagon is framed by two- and three-storied buildings and is decorated by two parterres. A second *cour d'honneur* along the same axis opens toward a semicircle of much larger proportions, the real public square, framed by low buildings. The spatial contrast between the *cour d'honneur* and the public square is obviously inspired by Versailles.

The Villa Manin, in Passariano near Udine, is laid out on a smaller scale, following the same principle (Pl. 56B). It was designed by Girolamo Frigimelica (1653–1732) and was built about 1738 by Francesco Maria Prati (1701–74); it was restored in 1763. The large horseshoe of the public square framed by simple arcades opens toward the rectangular U-form of the palace proper with its modest wings. Compared with the Castle of Stupinigi, the layout appears to be conceived in a more classicistic sense—and that refers as much to the built volumes as to the open combination of square and *cour d'honneur*.

The largest classicistic layout in Italy, Caserta (Pl. 56A), between Rome and Naples, mirrors quite obviously the basic idea of Versailles—park, castle, and town conceived as one unit. This is an Italian paraphrase of what was originally a French concept, an interesting integration of a typically Italian feeling for volume with a typically French obedience to a system of governing axes. The castle was begun in 1752 by Luigi Vanvitelli for King Charles III of Naples, and was completed under Ferdinand IV in 1774. The ambition to surpass the dimensions of Versailles is evident; as originally planned it would have become the largest castle of Europe. The dimensions of Vanvitelli's original design were later reduced, yet the main façade of the castle still stretches over a width of about 280 yards. The ground plan of the castle with its four inner courtyards reminds one strongly of the Palace of Diocletian in Spalato. A main axis leads from the castle through the tremendous park to a cascade in the far distance. A large oval square extends in front of the palace, tied to the façade by the two lower wings in imitation of Bernini's closed colonnades before St. Peter's in Rome. This square was destined to become the focal point for a new town besides the already existing town of Caserta, in this respect again analogous to Versailles.

It is astonishing how Vanvitelli combines forms borrowed from Versailles and from St. Peter's, both conceived about one hundred years earlier, and yet is able to create an entirely different visual impression. Exactly as the park, in spite of its tremendous dimensions and the hilly background, looks relatively flat with its bosquets and parterres compared with Versailles and its hedges, trees, and statues, so the Berninesque oval of the square remains isolated and without spatial interrelation with the castle proper, in spite of its physical connection. The basically two-dimensional concepts of late classicism are so entirely different from the three-dimensional late baroque that no emulation of individual architectural forms or even of layout patterns could produce true spatial effects.

The introduction of trees and planted areas into the townscape under the influence of Rousseau's *retournons à la nature* (back to nature) took place during the second part of the eighteenth century and contributed much to the loosening of the baroque and classicistic stereometric forms within the city. This development is reflected, for instance, in the remodeling of the Prato della Valle in Padua in 1775 by Cerato. This "green" was developed as something between a square and a park. Doubtless the layout of the oldest botanical garden in Europe, founded in 1545 in its immediate vicinity, stimulated the plan (see p. 106). Amidst a vast square of roughly triangular shape a large, planted oval island was laid out in the middle of the eighteenth century. Cut by two paths, it periphery is framed by a very wide, flat moat on whose watery surface are reflected the two rows of statues accompanying both its rims—the whole a peaceful refuge for the townspeople. The layout of the Prato della Valle resembled such Italian Renaissance projects as Palma Nuova and Granmichele. It is interesting to observe how the classicistic landscape artist adapted the original architectural shapes of these towns to the green center of a rather large square. No definite boundaries are established, no definite spatial impressions are created.

In some respects this scheme of the Prato della Valle is reminiscent of the

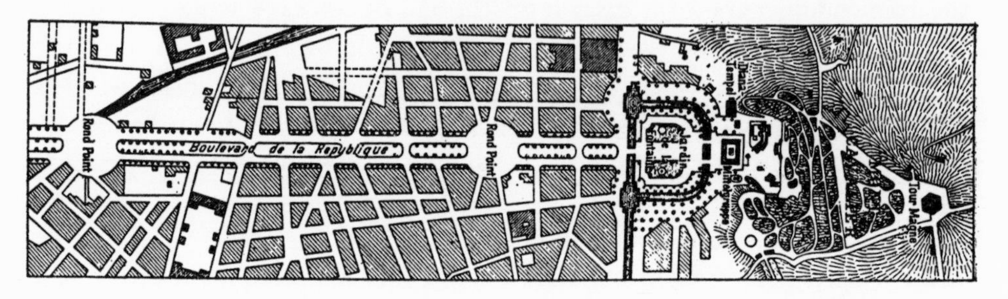

FIG. 41. NÎMES. BOULEVARD DE LA RÉPUBLIQUE (BOULEVARD JEAN JAURÈS) AND JARDIN DE LA FONTAINE. PLAN

From Stübben, "Vom französischen Städtebau," *Städtebauliche Vorträge*

Jardin de la Fontaine in Nîmes, France (Fig. 41). There the central axis of the Boulevard Jean Jaurès ends in an area which was developed into a park-like square by Maréchal in 1740. At the beginning of the eighteenth century, the substructures of an ancient Roman public bath had been excavated, and Maréchal employed them for a complex system of canals, balustrades, stairs, statues, and regular parterres. Here and in Padua the planted areas are so entirely subordinated to architectural elements that both projects are felt as built-up architectural areas. However, since no vertical spatial confines exist, neither area represents a real square.

The Piazza del Popolo in Rome, as was mentioned earlier, had received its basic shape in combination with the previously existing fanlike form of its radiating streets during the period from Pope Sixtus V to Bernini. However, at the beginning of the nineteenth century, between 1816 and 1820, Giuseppe Valadier (1762–1839) changed the outline of the trapezoid square into a larger ellipsoid (Pl. 57A). Now a newly created west-east axis, leading from the Tiber bridge toward the slope of the Pincian Hill, prevailed over the thrust of the previous trapezoid toward the two churches. For this effect Valadier transformed the existing gardens of an Augustinian monastery into a public park on the slopes of the Pincian Hill. In the present stage, houses adjacent to the churches extend the width of the square and change its original directed dynamism into classicistic balance. Evidently the integration of the churches, houses, and obelisk with the ramps, stairs, and greenery up the Pincian Hill appealed to the romantic sentiments of the period rather than the strict tectonic space relations of the previous baroque plan. The inclusion of the landscaped slope of the Pincian Hill as an element of confinement for the square proper is typical of the eighteenth century. One can truly say that Valadier by this integration followed the ideas of English city planners of the late eighteenth century and their concept of the role nature plays within the town.

The hemicycles of green on both sides of the piazza are doubtlessly derived from St. Peter's Square but have taken on an entirely different meaning spatially: idyllic romanticization replaces rigid architectural three-dimensionality.

In Naples the same motif of the hemicycles framing only one side of the square was first employed by Vanvitelli in the Piazza di Dante in 1757. It was taken up again on a larger scale in the more monumental Piazza del Plebiscito (Pl. 57B). In 1817 Ferdinand I of Naples built opposite the Palazzo Reale a half-ellipsoid of Doric colonnades as an extended parvis before the Church of San Francesco di Paolo, an imitation of the Pantheon in Rome erected also in 1817 by Bianci. On this square the two statues of Charles III and Ferdinand I look rather lost against the background of church and colonnades and do not contribute to the formation of space, whereas in Piacenza, for instance, the two equestrian statues represented an essential factor in defining the space.

The motif of the half-circle or half-ellipsoid with colonnades is, of course, derived from Bernini's colonnades for St. Peter's Square. But in this classicistic version in Naples it has the effect of a stage background rather than that of a structural spatial boundary. During the eighteenth century, the same motif was used in Pöppelmann's colonnades at the Zwinger in Dresden (1711–22) and in Nancy's Place du Gouvernement, and, at the beginning of the nineteenth century, in Woronichin's only partially executed projects for the Kasan Cathedral in Leningrad, etc.

Nowhere, however, did colonnades of semicircular or semiellipsoid layout achieve the three-dimensional effect of Bernini's concept or that of the Imperial Fora in Rome. The purpose of such colonnades turned gradually from being a formative spatial structure into a merely decorative motif. Increasing classicistic tendencies, through changes in proportion and lack of architectural integration, diluted the original dynamic force of the curve as spatial framework—and almost abolished it.

Probably the most perfect classicistic square on Italian soil is the Piazza Vittorio Veneto in Turin (Pl. 58; see also Pl. 4A), constructed between 1820 and 1830. The Via di Po, one of the main traffic arteries of the town, laid out already in 1673, runs into a square of extraordinary size, continuing beyond it, over and beyond the Ponte Vittorio Emanuele, toward the Church Gran Madre del Dio (1813–31). This long, straight axis starting at the Piazza Castello is one of the very few streets which cut diagonally into the ancient gridiron scheme of Turin. The motif of the semicircle or niche appears again in the entrance to the Via di Po. The integration of the Via di Po, the Piazza Vittorio Veneto, and the Church Gran Madre del Dio across the bridge reminds one strongly of the axis established in Paris by the Church of the Madeleine-Rue Royale-Place de la Concorde-Pont de la Concorde-Palais Bourbon (see p. 184). The almost identical houses which surround the Piazza Vittorio Veneto are arcaded, as are those over the incoming streets. The same arcades continue through the Via di Po. The floor of the square slopes strongly toward the bridge, the lowest level of the axis. Beyond the river the axis climbs again toward the elevated, central-domed church.

The classicistic simplicity of the sequence—street-square-bridge-church—and the uniformity of the adjacent houses represent the strongest possible contrast to similar sequences planned during the baroque period. The idea of continuous motion still exists, in the words of Milizia, "una progressione crescente di bellezza," but the moment of surprise and of dramatic movement has completely vanished. There are no props or features such as fountains or statues to accentuate specific parts of the straight axis and to arrest the movement. The turbulence of a forceful waterfall has given way to the even flow of a calm, well-channeled river.

TOWN AND SQUARE IN THE SEVENTEENTH AND EIGHTEENTH CENTURIES IN FRANCE

From the very beginning, a rather disciplined and rational attitude directed the projects of French architects. It is this very attitude of rigid formality and of heroic monumentality, as mirrored, for instance, in the paintings of Nicholas Poussin (1594–1665), Charles Le Brun (1619–90), and Claude Lorrain (1600–1682), in the tragedies of Pierre Corneille (1606–84) and Jean Racine (1639–99), which directed the work of French city planners of this period. Their spatial organizations, squares and axes alike, represent unambiguously the academic-classicistic trend of the baroque, in contrast to Italy where both tendencies of the baroque period are expressed in contemporary town planning. The axis with its vista was as important to the French as the three-dimensional spatial effect of the square.

In France, Renaissance architecture developed relatively late through contact with Italian architects, from Fra Giocondo under Louis XII (1462–1515), Serlio and Primaticcio under Francis I (1494–1547), and so on. Hence it was not necessary for the French baroque to overcome traditional, deeply ensconced concepts and firmly established artistic ideas as it was in Italy.

It was the mitigated and more reasoned north Italian form of expression which primarily affected French architecture, and not the Berninesque Roman *maniera grande*. Thus it was Palladio's, Vignola's, and della Porta's influence which directly permeated the visual concepts of the French architects of the first half of the seventeenth century. Building for the king, the gentry, and the Church, men like Jacques Lemercier (1585–1654), Cardinal Richelieu's architect; Louis Le Vau (1612–70), who began Versailles; and especially François Mansart (1598–1666), the architect of the Church of Val-de-Grâce, worked on their tasks in the stylistic language of the great "classic" Italian masters.

The French approach to Italian architecture of this period is reflected best in Daviler's work which mirrored the prevailing ideas of this period in France. Daviler, who elaborated further the ideas of the earlier French theoreticians from around 1600, the Du Cerceaus, Perret, and Errard (see p. 120), was, like these men, firmly bound to the tradition of the great Renaissance theoreticians. But it was not only Daviler who tried to systematize

French architecture of the seventeenth century. Louis Savot and especially François Blondel developed architectural maxims which were still followed in the eighteenth century. While Savot was less interested in specific urban questions, and referred only rarely to the problems of whole squares and streets, Blondel gave distinct layouts of fortifications and whole towns and emphasized the architect's duty to consider also squares and *carrefours*. Claude Perrault, the most famous theoretician of the end of the seventeenth century, was not concerned with problems of town planning.

Any analysis of French squares in the seventeenth and eighteenth centuries cannot overlook the contemporaneous development in gardening and landscaping. Town planning and landscaping had been interrelated in the first half of the sixteenth century, but now this connection became even more outspoken. Thus, for instance, the Jardin des Tuileries in Paris was generally discussed as a work of art. It had been remodeled at the beginning of the seventeenth century under Henry IV by Boyceau, in further development of the original plans of Philibert Delorme, and was still further improved according to the taste of the time by Le Nôtre. Its structure was based on a system of axes. The main axis was later to be extended through to the Arc de Triomphe to become the most representative axial development of Paris for centuries.

In Vaux-le-Vicomte and Versailles, André Le Nôtre realized finally the spatial concepts and the relationship between void and volume which became equally important for the development of landscaping and city planning in the last third of the seventeenth century and throughout the eighteenth century. The difference was simply that in town planning the three-dimensional expanse was limited by masses of stone, in landscaping by growing bushes and trees.

THE BEGINNINGS. The squares of Vitry-le-François (1545), Philippeville, and Mariembourg (both 1550) were realizations of pure Renaissance concepts, as was Charleroi, built by Vauban for Louis XIV more than one century later. At the beginning of the seventeenth century, two closed squares, the Place d'Alliance in Nancy and the Place Ducale in Charleville, continued the Renaissance tradition. However, they lost the intimacy of the smaller, closed Renaissance squares and anticipated in dimensions and proportion the spirit of the baroque era in France, thus becoming models for the later *places royales*.

The Place d'Alliance in Nancy is located in one of the three *faubourgs* added to the medieval town of Nancy in the middle of the sixteenth century and completely incorporated in the town in the seventeenth century. The square occupies half a block of the regular gridiron scheme in the middle of one of these *faubourgs* built by Jérôme Citoni in 1588. The absolute regularity of its layout is still emphasized today by a quadrangle of regularly trimmed trees with a fountain in the center. The houses show identical façades, and the parallel horizontals of their ledges, eaves, and rooftops tie the area of the square, repeating the original pattern of the layout. In contrast to the later Place des Vosges in Paris, the streets at its four corners run into the square unconcealed. In spite of the early date of its planning, the Place d'Alliance must be taken as an immediate predecessor of the Place des Vosges, to a higher degree even than the more pretentious Place Ducale in Charleville. After all, it is only a very small interval of time, from 1588 to 1607, which separates the Place d'Alliance from the Place des Vosges.

The Place Ducale in Charleville (Pl. 59A), planned by Charles de Gonzague and executed in 1608–20, develops its regular quadrangular layout into a spatial form of greatest beauty. Arcaded two-storied houses in brick with sandstone decor are arranged with their eaves toward the square, framing it on all sides. Their steep roofs, resembling clipped pyramids, are separated from each other and increase the impression of total uniformity by the repetition of their extremely characteristic stereometric form. The Place Ducale must also be considered a predecessor of the Place des Vosges in Paris. But while the Place Ducale in Charleville serves as a central *carrefour* with four streets running into it, the later Place des Vosges is completely removed from the traffic of the town.

The total scheme of Charleville is based on the gridiron, and its straight streets connect its central square with six subordinate squares, all of them closed like the Place Ducale itself. Its overall pattern, probably designed by Clement Métézeau, is a fortunate combination of Italian theoretical projects of the latter part of the sixteenth century and such Renaissance realizations as Leghorn and Vigevano. However, the relationship between the volume of the surrounding houses and the central void is different from that in the earlier Renaissance examples. The individual houses are clearly outlined, although the rather identical façades of the single units are connected with each other on the street level by continuing arcades. The town hall, the former Palais Ducale, is even asymmetrically located and differs in its proportions from the adjacent houses. This tension between architectural unification and architectural individualism certainly represents a baroque tendency.

A further step toward the development of the typical *places royales* of the second part of the seventeenth and of the eighteenth century may be recognized in two quasi-feudal foundations, the town of Richelieu (1633–40) and the castle and park of Vaux-le-Vicomte (1656–61). In both town plans, and especially in the layout of their squares, post-Renaissance tendencies become more clearly articulated. Richelieu (Pl. 59B) in the Touraine owes its existence to Cardinal Richelieu, who was born there when it was still a small village. In 1629 he commissioned Jacques Lemercier with the remodeling of his house of birth. But soon he became more ambitious and in 1631 acquired the privilege for the foundation of a completely new fortress town, which was executed in 1633–40. It was the general fashion then with the nobility to expand their houses and castles in the country into larger settlements, definitely a trend toward social responsibility. The town was laid out as a rectangle, surrounded by ramparts and moats, and was only loosely connected with the castle. Inside, a strict axial system was developed. The market square, close to the main entrance of the town, was crossed by the two main streets, exactly as in Charleville. The main axis connected this market square with another square, actually a half square, adjacent to one of the town walls. This main street was framed by twenty-eight residences of uniform appearance, thus creating a spatial unit. Here the new tendency becomes evident, the emphasis on an axis in contrast to the centralizing system of the Renaissance.

The castle and park of Vaux-le-Vicomte, built in 1656–61 by Louis Le Vau for the French Minister of Finances, Fouquet, deserve mention at this point even though no town was laid out there. André Le Nôtre (1613–1700) worked together with Le Vau, and the spatial rhythm developed by the cooperation of landscape architect and architect became decisive for the further development of all French city planning. Actually Louis XIV was so enthusiastic about their common achievement that he assigned the development of the park of Versailles to Le Nôtre. In Vaux-le-Vicomte the axis finally triumphs and extinguishes the last traces of the spatial concepts of the Renaissance. Only now was the tradition of the Italian garden completely overcome in France and replaced by the typical French park. A detailed analysis of the ground plan of the park of Vaux-le-Vicomte would be out of place here. Suffice it to state that everything achieved later on at Versailles was worked out here on a smaller scale. And we are thinking not only of the park of Versailles but also of the town. For the characteristic fanlike form of the town plan of Versailles, derived from the Piazza del Popolo in Rome, was anticipated in the three main alleys of the park opposite the castle of Vaux-le-Vicomte, and with it the shape and sequences of the squares.

The emphasis on axes and the integration of regularly shaped squares, realized by Le Vau and Le Nôtre in the park of Vaux-le-Vicomte and anticipated to a certain degree in the earlier Richelieu, became the governing principle in Versailles. The effect of Versailles (built from 1661 to 1708) on architecture, landscaping, and city planning all over Europe can hardly be overestimated.

Louis XIV had admired Vaux-le-Vicomte so much that out of sheer envy he imprisoned its owner Fouquet and commissioned its artists Le Vau and Le Nôtre, and later also Jules Hardouin Mansart, with the organization of the castle, park, and town of Versailles (Pl. 60). Versailles had been built originally by Louis XIII as a royal rural castle (1626), and Louis XIV liked to arrange his sumptuous entertainments there. The integration of park, palace, and town is so intimate that Le Nôtre, without any doubt the more original of the two artists, was certainly also influential in the planning of the town. Its structure reflects in architectural terms that of the park. The axis of the latter is continued through the interior of the castle into the *cour d'honneur*, whence it stretches through the town. Certain motifs of the park were widely imitated, such as the *rondel*, a focus of radiating avenues, which appeared later on in towns all over Europe in the shape of star squares. This motif had developed in forestry and had been employed occasionally in the late sixteenth century in Italian parks, but it became basic only in Richelieu and in the park of Versailles. The pattern of the fan, so essential in Vaux-le-Vicomte, developed into a decisive figuration in park and town. As in the Piazza del Popolo in Rome three streets radiated from the Porta del Popolo, so in Versailles the streets diverged from the entrances of the castle into both town and park; in each city the *grand perspective* was the leading motif.

The newly founded town of Versailles was entirely artificial. Neither natural nor man-made conditions such as overland traffic lines or fortification needs influenced the site of a town to be settled by nobility and courtiers. The U-shaped layout of the palace dominates the landscaping of the park (as it does later on in Mannheim and Karlsruhe) and the structure of the town alike. The highway, leading straight from the palace to the Champs Élysées and the Louvre in Paris, becomes the backbone of the town plan and continues the axis of the park's Grand Canal and Tapis Vert. The approach to the palace is by three streets—Avenue de Sceaux, Avenue de Paris, and Avenue de St. Cloud—which run into the vast expanse of the Place d'Armes; the sectors between the avenues were filled in by the two identical buildings of the Écuries erected by Jules Hardouin Mansart. The movement is arrested in the Place d'Armes by a grille with sculptural decorations. Behind it, slightly ascending, a second square extends with its central monument framed by two identical structures. Beyond that the incoming stream of visitors is caught between the wings of the palace proper, additions built by Gabriel under Louis XV. Only now is the *cour d'honneur* entered and the visitor is led toward the main entrance of the palace. This organization emphasizes the directive power of the axis so strongly that one becomes less aware of the lateral expanses of the consecutive squares (Pls. 60–61).

A comparison between this approach and the access to St. Peter's in Rome across St. Peter's Square best clarifies the difference between concept and meaning of the square as spatial unit in Roman late baroque and in French classicistic baroque. In Rome, the continuity of movement is interrupted and the faithful are ever reminded of the three-dimensional expansion of the three consecutive squares. In Versailles, the latitude of the squares, gradually decreasing, serves only as potential expansion for the predestined movement toward the main entrance.

The fan motif of Versailles reappeared even in Russia, which under Peter the Great (1682–1725) came into the orbit of European civilization. For her newly founded capital, St. Petersburg, now Leningrad, various plans exist, the first by the Frenchman Le Blond, a pupil of Le Nôtre, who was called there by Peter the Great. Of decisive importance for the appearance of the city was, however, a plan from 1753 by Bartolomeo Rastrelli, an Italian who became the architect of the Empress Elizabeth (1741–62). His scheme is more reminiscent of Versailles than of the Piazza del Popolo: three streets converge on the Admiralty Building. But the vast square in front of this building is rather amorphous, not of the same spatial definiteness as the corresponding Italian and French examples.

In the second part of the eighteenth century, the planning of new towns in Russia or the reshaping of existing ones was organized by a special commission composed of the best Russian architects, who from 1762 to 1796 approved 416 plans. The fan motif then appeared often on Russian soil, although on a much smaller scale than in France, e.g., in Oboyev (1779). In Tver (now Kalinin), a square dating from 1767 is very similar to the Place de l'Odéon in Paris.

Still another factor was influential in the development of the French square in the seventeenth and eighteenth centuries: the erection of numerous fortifications under Louis XIII and Louis XIV, necessitated by the political situation in France, which now became the strongest political and economic power in Europe.

The great engineer into whose hands Louis XIV placed the defense of the expanding frontiers of France can be discussed only briefly. Sébastien de Vauban (1633–1707) was much more interested in giving shape to the varying polygonal outlines of his fortifications than he was in the inner structure of the town. When Vauban remodeled existing settlements, he did not change the old street system of the inner town but confined his work to the construction of its fortifications. In his newly built fortress-towns he took over the simplified gridiron scheme of the French medieval bastides with a quadrangular square in the center, combining it with basic ideas of the Italian sixteenth-century theoreticians. He stuck to this scheme in all of his newly planned towns, of which there were more than thirty and among which Saarlouis (1679) and Neuf-Brisach (after 1698) probably best represent his original ideas (Fig. 42). In both instances the quadrangular square clearly represents the spatial and functional center of the town, as it did in the ancestral bastides and in the Italian ideal projects. Only in one of the very first tasks of his career, in Charleroi, did Vauban employ a radio-centric scheme, creating thereby almost a copy of Philippeville and Mariembourg.

Because of their sheer quantity Vauban's rather schematic plans influenced French city planning in the eighteenth century (as late as 1770 his principles were still discussed in Roland Le Virloys's *Dictionnaire d'Architecture*), but fortunately the integrated spatial concept as expressed first in the Place des Vosges proved a still stronger stimulus.

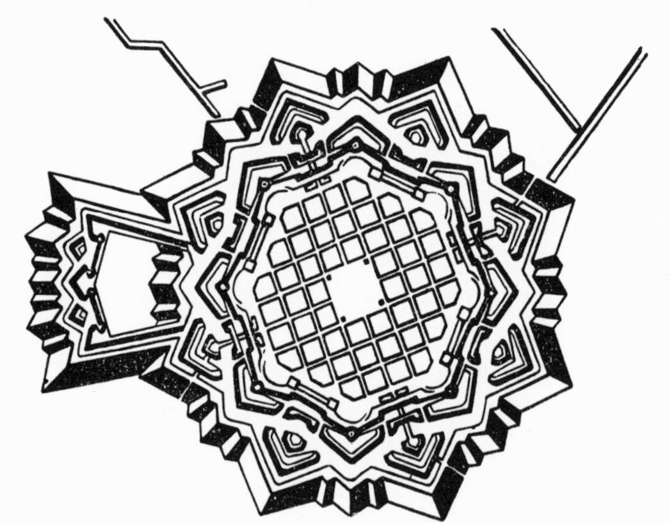

FIG. 42. NEUF-BRISACH. OLD PLAN

From Riese, *Historisch-geographische Beschreibung . . .*

THE PLACES ROYALES OF THE SEVENTEENTH CENTURY. In their spatial and architectural shape the *places royales* of the seventeenth and eighteenth centuries in France crystallize the predominant ideas and underlying philosophies, the political and sociological systems, and the cultural attitude of their time as immediately and as unambiguously as do the great squares of these centuries in Rome. In Rome, the triumph of the resurgent papal power had created grandiose dramatizations and architectural spectacles in richest orchestration for the purposes of emotional stimulation and sheer sensuous delight. In France, directed by "reason" and classical tradition, the dominant power of an absolute monarchy shaped forms of utmost regularity as background for regal pageantries and as documentation of the power of the state and its ruling classes.

In view of this development, it is hard to realize that around 1600 only two public squares existed in Paris—the Place de Grave and the parvis of Notre Dame—in a city which then had a population of some 500,000 people.

In some respects, many types of closed squares throughout the history of town planning may be considered as predecessors of the *place royale:* the late Hellenistic agora; the free area at the crossing of *cardo* and *decumanus* in the Roman castrum; the market square of the bastides and the foundations of the Teutonic Knights; the central squares of utopian towns of the Italian theoreticians; and such actual Renaissance squares as the Piazza di

SS. Annunziata in Florence and the square in Vigevano. But it is only in France that this idea develops into its final form, the most immediate predecessors for which in the sixteenth century are the squares of Vitry-le-François, the Place d'Alliance in Nancy, and the Place Ducale in Charleville. The last two already show almost all the traits which were to become so characteristic of the *places royales* of the seventeenth and eighteenth centuries: mathematically regular layout; complete or nearly complete continuity of the framing façades; uniformity of these façades or at least repetition of basic types; and accentuation of the center, mostly by means of a monument of the ruling sovereign.

The Place des Vosges, the archetype of the *place royale*, was laid out under Henry IV and was probably executed by Claude de Chastillon in 1607–12, almost simultaneously with the Place Ducale in Charleville. At first glance this most beautiful Parisian square seems to continue the Renaissance tradition completely: a regular quadrangular layout, an equestrian statue of Louis XIII in the center (erected in 1629), and the repetition of identical three-storied façades (Pl. 62; see also Pl. 1B). Contrary to Charleville, the Place des Vosges is located away from the traffic, a situation typical for the French squares of the seventeenth century. Entrance and exit for the street leading into the square are carefully concealed by special pavilions, which are incorporated into the continuous row of houses. Again, similar to Charleville, the individual units are separately roofed. The two pavilions are higher and their façades differ slightly from those of the other houses. In this way an axis across the square is established: pavilion-monument-pavilion. Thus an accent which contradicts Renaissance uniformity is introduced into the otherwise uniform balance.

Contrary to Italian Renaissance squares, the Place des Vosges was originally not paved but merely sanded and was used for tournaments; after some years it was covered with a lawn and protected by a fence, a completely new idea unknown to the Italian Renaissance. Now it had become a residential square. The eighteenth-century English concept of greenery in combination with squares was anticipated with this change. But this concept is definitely different from the nineteenth-century pseudoromantic mania for "decorating" all public squares with miniature parks. The difference lies in the fact that here, at the Place des Vosges, at least the planted area is level, an even surface, and still part of the spatial cube. The more or less irregular planting of later times annihilates any possibility of a three-dimensional impression. Today's arrangement of the square with flower beds and grouped trees has somewhat confused the original basic idea.

The Place Nationale in Montauban (Pl. 63A) cannot be considered a genuine *place royale* like the Place des Vosges and those squares built later under Louis XIV. However, it must be mentioned in this context since the influence of the Place des Vosges upon its shape is evident. Montauban, founded in 1144 and located on the Tarn River at the crossing of two important medieval highways, has been mentioned (see p. 92); it was one of the *villes neuves* from the beginning of the Gothic period. Unlike other *villes neuves,* its street plan was irregular, and hence its central square was not an exact quadrangle or rectangle but a trapezoid. The double rows of its arcades represented rather an exception. It is this feature which distinguishes the reconstruction of the old twelfth-century square (Pl. 63B) after it had burned down in the first part of the seventeenth century. When the square was rebuilt around 1650, framing houses with identical façades were erected, two stories above the arcades preserved from Gothic times, with galleries below the roofs and articulated by attached pillars between the windows. The oblique corners of the square were closed by free-standing portals in brick which leave open only very narrow passageways at two diagonal corners.

Like the Place des Vosges, the Place Dauphine (1606) in Paris was laid out under Henry IV prior to the great number of *places royales* of the reign of Louis XIV. However, because of the triangular form of its ground plan it proved less basic for later developments. Its layout is conditioned by the connection of the triangular tip of the Île de la Cité with the Pont Neuf, which was built between 1578 and 1604 under Henry IV by Baptiste Androuet Du Cerceau and Charles Marchand to connect the right and left banks of the Seine River via the Île de la Cité. In connection with the bridge Du Cerceau designed a project for a circular square, into which four streets ran in symmetrical intervals, with a domed structure in the center almost like Bramante's Tempietto in Rome. This thoroughly artificial project could, of course, never be realized under given topographical conditions. It is interesting only in so far as it employed all the well-known Renaissance ideas but at the same time, by the uniformity of all the house façades, anticipated one of the main artistic features of French seventeenth-century city planning.

The Place Dauphine (Fig. 43), as actually executed, is framed by uniform four-story buildings (similar to the Place des Vosges). The row of houses at the base of the triangle has been razed in order to make room for the Palais de Justice with its wide staircase. Originally the square had only two

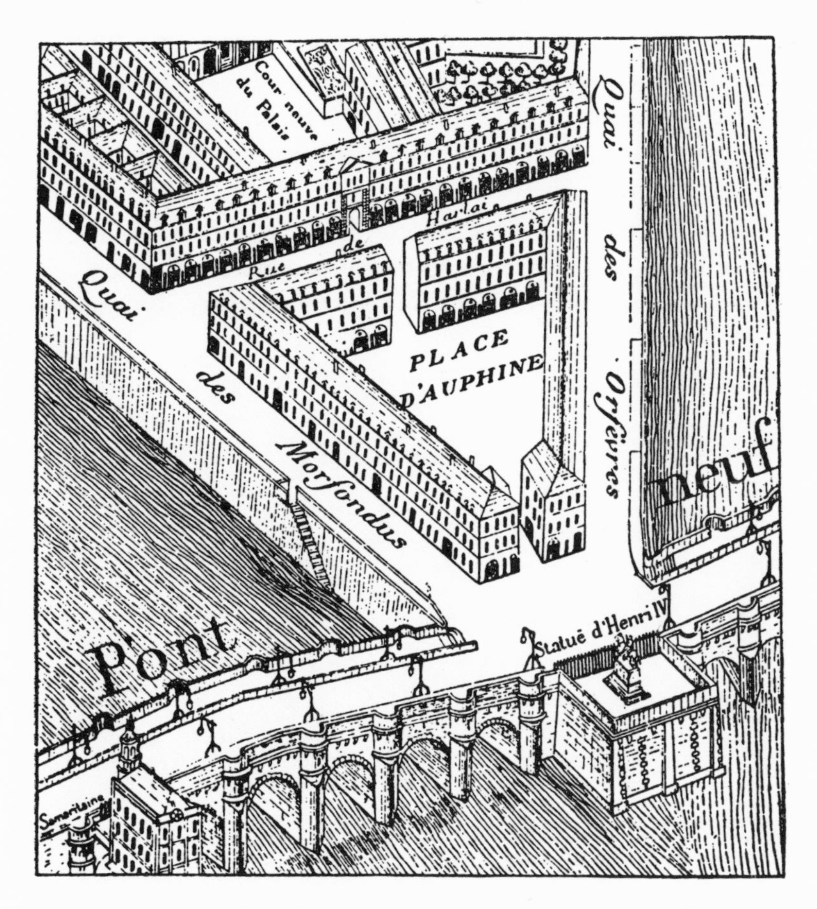

FIG. 43. PARIS. PLACE DAUPHINE. ORIGINAL STATE, FROM THE TURGOT PLAN
From Gantner, *Grundformen der europäischen Stadt*

openings: one, the entrance from the Île de la Cité, and another opposite, toward the bridge where the statue of Henry IV is erected. In other words, the square does not represent a self-contained centralized unit, like the Place des Vosges and all later *places royales*, but refers to an outside structure, the monument. Thus a distinctive direction is forced upon the space.

After these beginnings, the golden age of the *places royales* burst into full bloom under the reign of Louis XIV, more than half a century later. Thus it was that the "Roi Soleil," the Sun King, found added expression for his ambitions in the field of city planning, and the artist who helped in realizing his dreams was Jules Hardouin Mansart.

The spatial structure of Mansart's first great square, the Place des Victoires, executed between 1684 and 1687 under the supervision of Prédot, does not yet represent a clear-cut solution. Basically it is a round square with a monument honoring Louis XIV in the center (the old group was replaced by an equestrian statue of the king in 1822) and six streets running into it (Fig. 44). Only one of them continues in a straight line at the opposite side of the square. As a result, an axis is established which counteracts the otherwise centralized layout. Because of this irregularity one cannot call

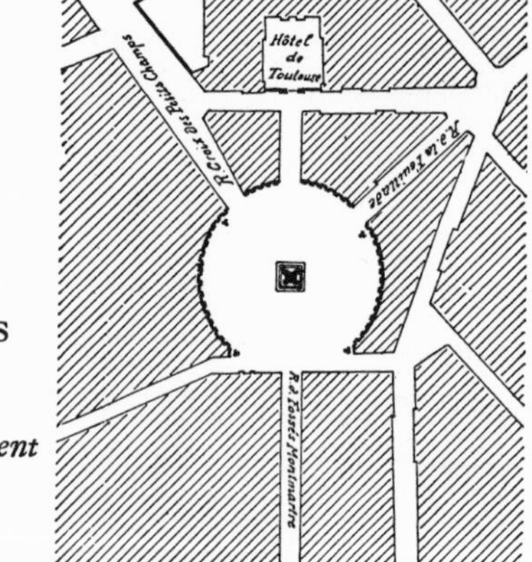

FIG. 44. PARIS. PLACE DES VICTOIRES. PLAN

From Brinckmann, *Platz und Monument*

the Place des Victoires a genuine star square, although its intrinsic idea was probably stimulated by Le Nôtre's garden rondels. In spite of its identical façades, the Place des Victoires does not achieve the impression of a closed square. Its openings toward the surrounding streets (an anticipation of the typical *place percée* of the eighteenth century) are too numerous. It was in all likelihood just this connection between the square and its neighborhood that made the Place des Victoires so much appreciated, especially by the theoreticians of the second part of the eighteenth century.

In contrast to the Place des Victoires, the Place Vendôme clearly represents the epitome of the closed square and, moreover, generally the most conscious space creation of the French classicistic baroque. Originally, Jules Hardouin Mansart was commissioned (in 1677) to design a square around which the royal library, the royal academies, the mint, and some embassies should be united in order to increase the real-estate value of the land belonging to the Duc de Vendôme. However, financial difficulties stopped the work after it had been started in 1685. In 1699 a reduced scheme was developed. That year Girardon's statue of Louis XIV was erected, around which the new square was to come into existence. And now something unique in the history of squares took place: in order to achieve a uniform appearance, in 1701 all the façades around the square were constructed, after the designs of Hardouin Mansart and his disciple Pierre Bullet under the supervision of Prédot. It was only later that the actual houses behind these façades were executed by various architects. This procedure proves the absolute priority of artistic purpose over any functional demands.

The square proper is a rectangle with its corners flattened out at an angle of 45°, which gives the square the shape of an octagon, and is surrounded by houses of identical three-storied height with dormer windows and identical eaves and roofs (Pl. 64A). The corner buildings and the center of the two long sides are emphasized through pediments and columns. Only two small openings, later continued as the Rue Castiglione and the Rue de la Paix, connect the square with the Rue St. Honoré and the Boulevard des Capucines, but without creating any axial movement across the square. In lieu of the statue of Louis XIV, a column was erected in 1806, imitating the Column of Trajan in Rome, crowned by the figure of Napoleon. By its very height of 130 feet in contrast to the 54 feet of the previous equestrian statue, it lowers visually the height of the surrounding buildings and in this way destroys somewhat the original proportions of the square.

It is the completely closed form of the square which was later condemned by theoreticians of the eighteenth century. They considered only an open square, especially the star square integrated into the network of streets, as a representative and artistic solution. But such a square would never convey the definite spatial experience of the Place Vendôme and the earlier Place des Vosges. The latter in its closed form was still accepted in the eighteenth century as artistically satisfactory, but only because it was a residential square. However, the lack of monumental vistas in distance and of integration with its surroundings was then regarded as an artistic misconception for a square destined to represent the grandeur of a whole city. This difference in aesthetic approach is characteristic for the stylistic change from the seventeenth to the eighteenth century in France.

Jules Hardouin Mansart's third great square is located outside Paris: the Place d'Armes (today the Place de la Libération) at Dijon (Pl. 64B). In 1686 he had designed for that town the façade of the Salle des États, the parliament building of Burgundy. The square, too, is his work, in spite of its occasional attribution to his assistants Gittard or Noinville. His original plans, actually a sequence of projects, are still extant. The square represents a semicircle opposite the dominating architecture. In its main axis a statue of Louis XIV was projected (erected only in 1725, today destroyed).

Since the medieval town of Dijon had developed quite irregularly, the problem was to find a solution for the various irregular streets which met the projected square under entirely different angles. The architect-planner solved this problem by concealing the entrances almost completely. Only for the most important street a visible opening was left in the main axis, although this street actually runs into the square at an oblique angle also. The other streets are hidden behind individual open arches which form part of the existing arcades.

In Mansart's first project of 1686, these arcades were isolated; but eventually they became part of the surrounding façades of the adjacent houses as simple arches in relief. Many alterations have changed the appearance of these houses so that today only one quadrant of the old buildings has kept its original shape of two-storied façades. Again the influence of landscape architecture expresses itself clearly in the resemblance of the arcades, originally planned in a semicircle, to half a park rondel. Mansart succeeded marvelously in superimposing this regular shape of a semicircle upon the irregular crossing of the earlier obliquely directed streets. As in Versailles the *cour d'honneur* of the palace and the Place d'Armes create a felicitous combination of two open spaces, so in Dijon the smaller U-shaped *cour d'honneur* of the parliament building is a preparation for the wider expanse of the Place d'Armes. The wrought-iron grille erected between the two emphasizes rather than disrupts the spatial sequence.

Mansart again played with the idea of the semicircle in his projects for the squares in front of the Church Val-de-Grace and of the Dome des Invalides in Paris. However, neither square was executed according to his design. Even prior to Mansart, a semicircular square had been projected under Henry IV for a "Place de France," preserved only in an engraving by Claude de Chastillon of 1610.

Later, in the eighteenth century, the idea of a half-circular square was taken up very often, as, for instance, in the Place de l'Odéon in Paris and in the form of half an octagon in the Place Fontette in Caen (see p. 101).

THE PLACES ROYALES OF THE EIGHTEENTH CENTURY. The *places royales* built under Louis XV in his honor, and mostly with his statue in the center, differed in principle from those laid out under Louis XIV. The concept of the closed square, preferably removed from the traffic, as crystallized first in the Place des Vosges in Paris, no longer monopolized the imagination of the city planners. Now, on the contrary, it was considered an essential quality of the ideal square to be interrelated as closely as possible with the town as a whole. Therefore, it was not the Place des Vosges, the Place Dauphine, or the Place Vendôme which was praised in the eighteenth century but the Place des Victoires, the only one of the earlier *places royales* where the connection between square and streets was visually admitted. This transition, however, came about gradually.

Even the eighteenth-century squares from which streets radiated preserved some features of the seventeenth-century square, namely, the irrelevance of axial direction within the square and the erection of a central monument. In other words, the space of the square still remained autonomous, and the new relationship to streets and vistas outside contributed to the spatial effect of the square proper. Where, as for instance on the Place de la Concorde in Paris or in Nancy (see pp. 183, 187), a visual relation to monumental buildings outside the square existed, the vista served rather as a backdrop for the square proper. It helped to close it visually, even if at a certain distance and not as an immediate continuation of its surrounding architecture.

This new concept is presented most clearly in a collection of engravings of eighteenth-century *places royales* in France, projected or executed, which was published by Patte in Paris in 1765, *Monumens érigés en France à la gloire de Louis XV;* this collection was based essentially on a general competition for a monumental square in honor of Louis XV, with his equestrian statue as center. Patte (1723–1814), the author of this compilation, was an architect in his own right and a well-known theoretician who wrote on Perrault and Boffrand and completed Blondel's *Cours d'Architecture*. In Patte's survey, individual squares as they actually existed in elevations and plans are given, as well as projects never executed, for instance, the one for Rouen. However, the most conclusive documentation of his ideas is his general plan of Paris, which suggests a new organization of the whole inner town. It is definitely and consciously based on squares (Pl. 65) which are considered focal points for new organizations of whole quarters. Among those squares which were actually built are the Place des Vosges, the Place de la Concorde (Louis XV), the Place des Victoires, the Place Vendôme, etc. The most important among the projects not realized was a square opposite the Louvre, including a second Louvre building on the left bank and a complete remodeling of the Île de la Cité with strong axial emphasis.

The legend on Patte's plan with the names of the architects reads like a "who's who" in architecture from the mid-eighteenth century. There are Soufflot, Boffrand, Rousset, Destouches, Constant, Slotz, and Servandoni, all of whom were then in the foreground of building activities. As a whole, the project shows a web of axes leading to monumental star squares distributed all over the city with unchanged quarters in between. The emphasis on axes consisting of wide streets is motivated functionally by needs of traffic and hygiene and aesthetically by the more striking effect of architecturally elaborate buildings. Some ideas anticipated here were actually executed by Haussmann in the nineteenth century in a more or less modified form.

Obviously, the typical square of the seventeenth century with its strictly limited space had gone out of fashion, and the new trend was all for the star center in connection with long axes, in other words, for unlimited space and openness. If there was any landscaping—planting of trees, bushes, and lawn—which now began penetrating the townscape, the green was still controlled. The general corrosion of the spatial effect of a square, suggested by a misapprehension of English landscaping, can be blamed only on the nineteenth century.

The first square typical for the period of Louis XV was done outside Paris: the Place Royale (Place de la Bourse) in Bordeaux (Pl. 66A) today under reconstruction after the bombardment in World War II. It is a so-called marina, a square along a quai parallel to the Garonne River. After an initial project by Robert de Cotte, Jacques Gabriel (1667–1742) designed the square in 1729, it was completed by his son, Jacques Ange Gabriel

(1698–1782), in 1743. The architect was faced with the problem of connecting the extremely irregular streets of the town with a new monumental square. Thus Gabriel planned a rectangle with cut corners, its long side parallel to the river, in essence half an octagon. He developed this motif into a complete octagon later on the Place de la Concorde in Paris (see p. 183). The center of the square in Bordeaux was occupied by a statue of Louis XV by Lemoyne; erected in 1743, the statue was replaced by a fountain in 1869 after its destruction. The public and private buildings around the square are unified by identical façades, alternately receding and protruding, and thus creating a lively play of light and shadow; the center recedes, and at both sides two new, converging streets cut into the square. In this way the connection with the inner town is established. The square was originally set off from the river by a balustrade, which today is replaced by steps. The whole vista was destined to be enjoyed from the riverside and presents a monumental entrance to the town. The basic idea of the Place Royale is again reflected in the Place de Bira-Hakeim, formerly the Place de Bourgogne, also in Bordeaux.

In his general plan of Paris from 1748 Patte reproduces two projects for marinas for the Quai Malaquet (today Malaquais). Comparable to the plan for Bordeaux, although on a smaller scale, these two plans, the one by Slotz, the other by Contant, prove the same desire for symmetrical confinement of space. However, neither of them was ever executed.

The same Jacques Gabriel created in Rennes, after a devastating fire, one of the most interesting combinations of squares in France, the Place du Palais and the Place de la Mairie (1721–30) (Pl. 66B). The smaller, almost regular square of the Place du Palais was developed in front of the already existing seventeenth-century Parliament of Brittany by Salomon Debrosse (1565–1627 or 1618–54?) and was originally decorated with a statue of Louis XIV, replaced today by a fountain. This typical closed square, completed only in the nineteenth century, dominated by the parliament building, is connected diagonally with the larger Place de la Mairie. Also rectangular, the latter stretches in front of the two-winged town hall built by Gabriel, with the statue of Louis XV by J. B. Lemoyne (1744) in its receding central part. Although cut by a street, the square nevertheless represents visually a spatial unit. A second monumental building was probably projected for the other small side of the square. Five parallel rows of trees balance the volume of the town hall—one of the first examples of planting employed as an architectural element within the town.

The originality of this solution results from the spatial relation of the two squares. In contrast to such grouped squares as those in Venice, Padua, Bologna, or Salzburg, there exists no wide opening between both squares in Rennes. Only a narrow passage between the corners of the two buildings adjacent to both squares connects them. In this way extremely interesting perspectives develop from whatever angle the onlooker may enter. This perspective effect is increased further in the Place du Palais through the direction of all the horizontal lines of the buildings which Gabriel erected. They stretch below the corresponding architectural elements of the parliament building and thus increase the architectural impact of the latter—not unlike the effect of the Campidoglio in Rome.

The *places royales* in honor of Louis XV in Rheims and Rouen show a strong similarity to Jacques Gabriel's Place du Palais in Rennes, although they were designed more than a generation later in a period of rising neoclassicism. The first project for Rheims was done by the engineer Le Gendre in 1755; one year later Jacques Germain Soufflot was called in and made an entirely different project with cut corners, half an octagon, obviously stimulated by Gabriel's Place Royale in Bordeaux and the Place de la Concorde in Paris. Then Le Gendre changed the entire project again since a new monumental structure, the Hôtel des Fermes—an obvious copy of the town hall of Nancy—was erected to become the focal point of the whole spatial organization. In its final, executed stage the plan shows a rather pedantic rectangle and a rigid axial system (Pl. 66c). Starting from the square in front of the Hôtel de Ville, the axis is carried through as the Rue Royale and leads to the central monument of Louis XV by Pigalle (today replaced by a modern monument of 1818). It ends in front of the Hôtel des Fermes. The Rue Royale, paralleled by two very short streets, is one of seven streets which cut into the square. These small parallels connect the corners of the Place Royale with two smaller market squares with fountains. Thus the whole scheme consists of two large squares—the square before the Hôtel de Ville (not on Patte's plan) and the Place Royale—and two smaller ones, the two market squares, with the Rue Royale as the axial backbone. The Place Royale, in spite of its many references to streets and the minor squares, nevertheless impresses the viewer as a closed square. The completely unified archi-

VERSAILLES. PALACE. AERIAL VIEW

Courtesy French Government Tourist Office, New York

VIEW Photo Yvon, Paris

PARIS. PLACE DES VOSGES

AERIAL VIEW Photo Éditions Greff, Paris

MONTAUBAN. PLACE NATIONALE

A: VIEW OF THE SQUARE Photo Éditions Tito, Bordeaux

B: ARCADES
Photo Éditions Gaby, Nantes

A: PARIS. PLACE VENDÔME

PLAN

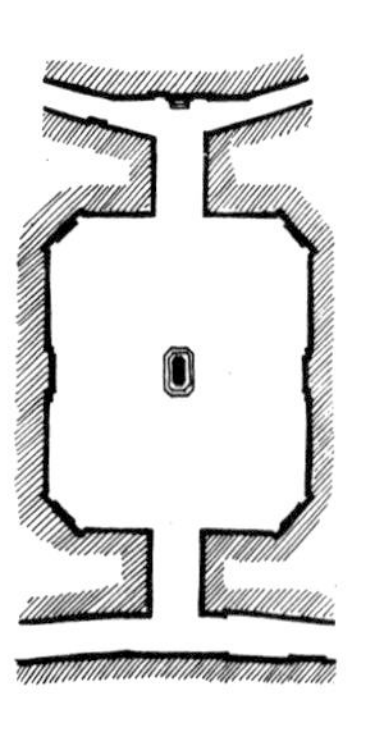

COPPER ENGRAVING, EIGHTEENTH CENTURY From Cain, *La Place Vendôme*

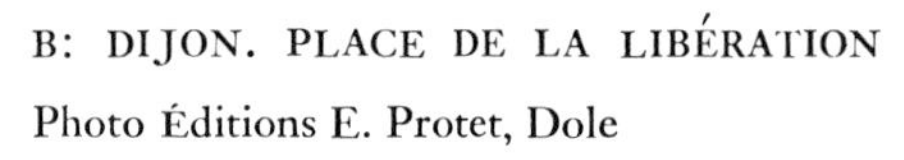
B: DIJON. PLACE DE LA LIBÉRATION

Photo Éditions E. Protet, Dole

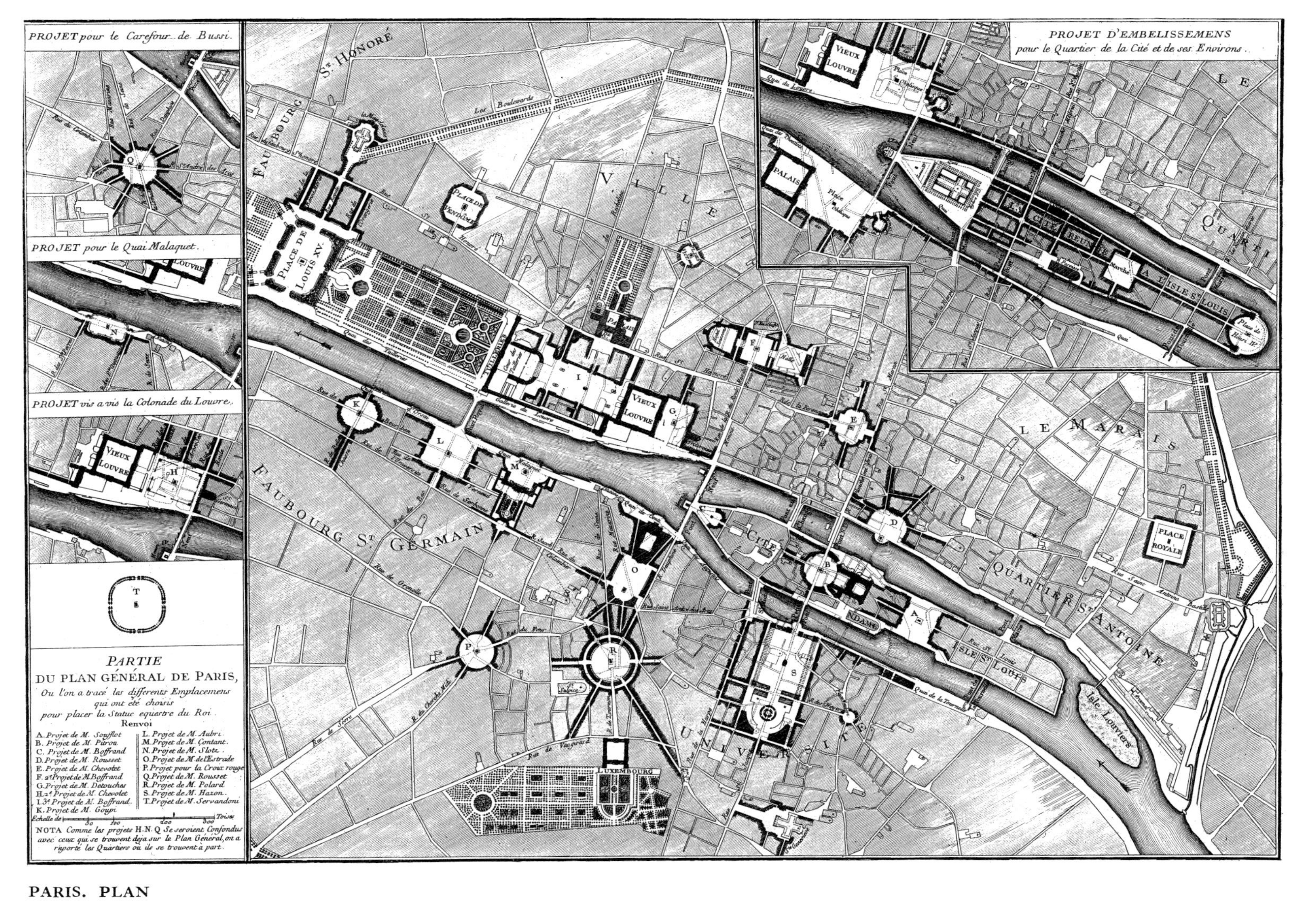

PARIS. PLAN

From Patte, *Monumens érigés en France*

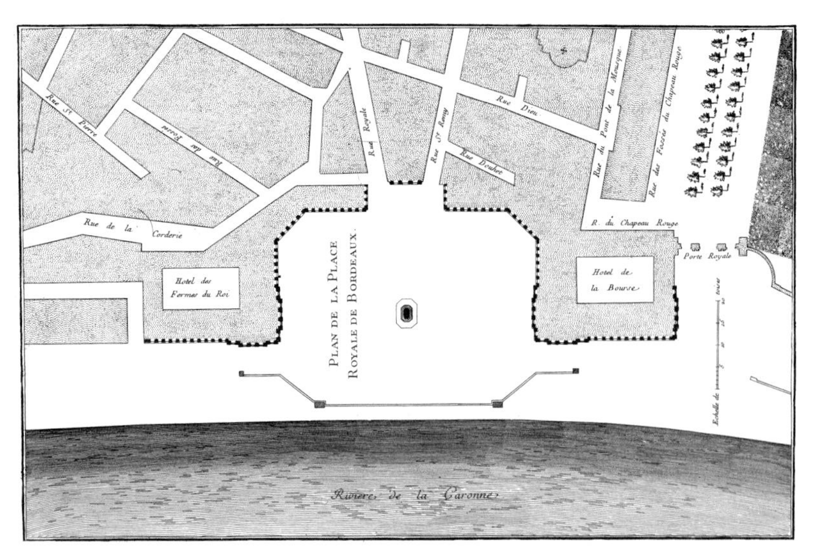

A: BORDEAUX. PLACE ROYALE OR PLACE DE LA BOURSE

PLAN

From Patte, *Monumens érigés en France*

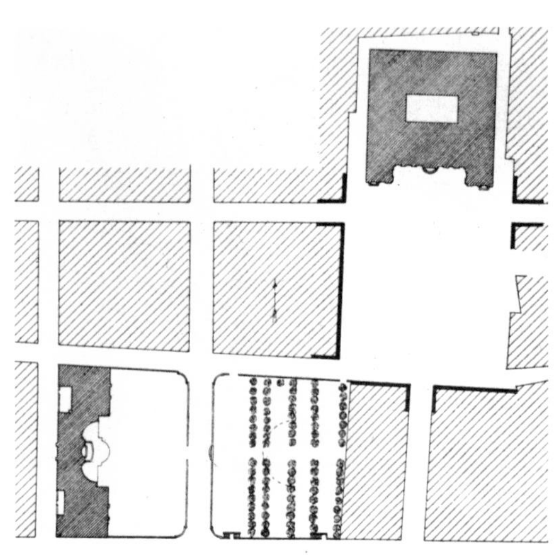

B: RENNES. PLACE DU PALAIS AND PLACE DE LA MAIRIE

PLAN

From Brinckmann, *Platz und Monument*

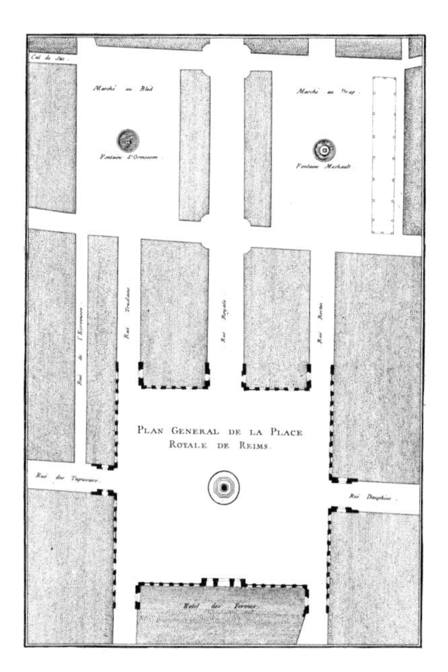

C: RHEIMS PLACE ROYALE

PLAN

From Patte, *Monumens érigés en France*

D: ROUEN. PLACE ROYALE

PLAN

From Patte, *Monumens érigés en France*

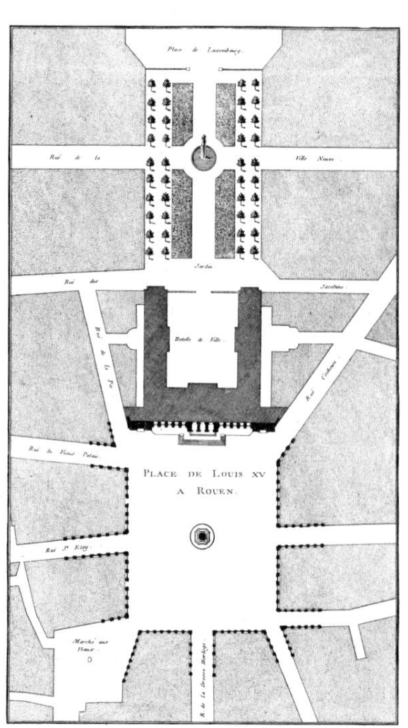

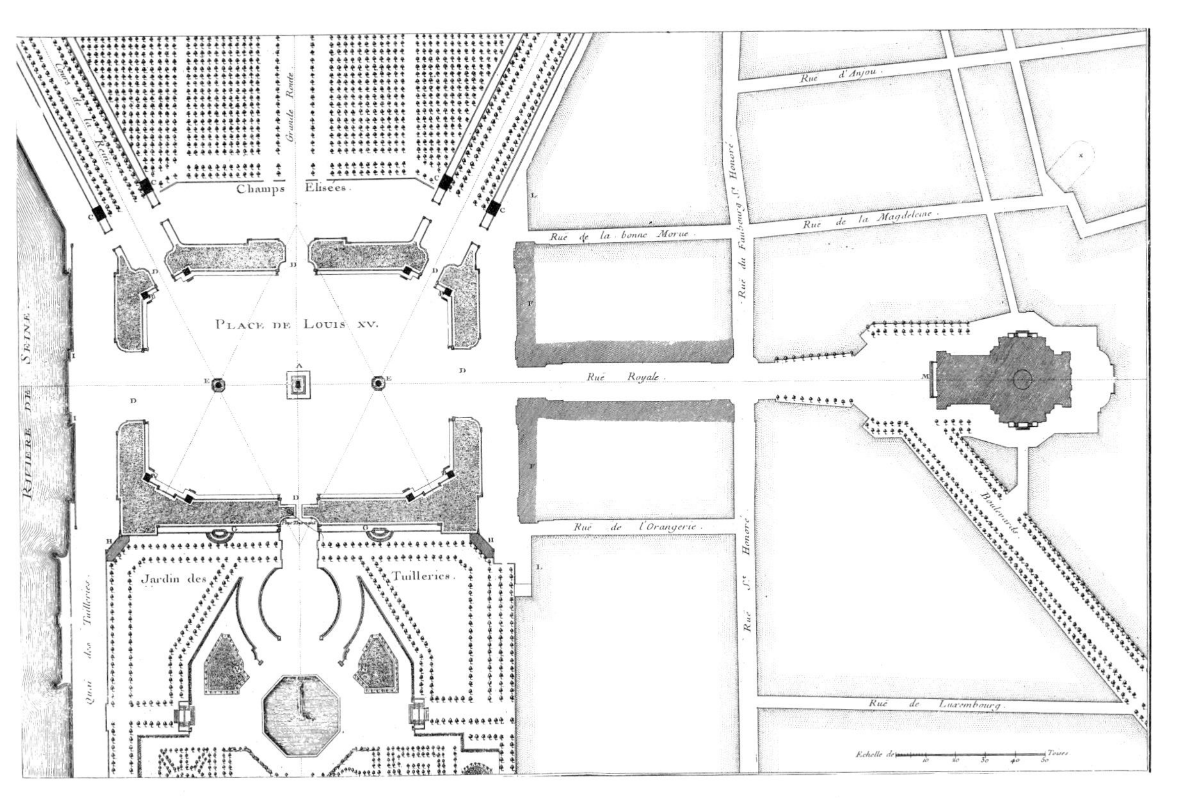

A: PARIS. PLACE DE LA CONCORDE, FORMERLY PLACE LOUIS XV. PLAN

From Patte, *Monumens érigés en France*

B: PLACE DE LA CONCORDE

PAINTING, OIL ON CANVAS (1938–42),

BY PIET MONDRIAN

Collection Harry Holtzman. Photo Oliver Baker; courtesy Sidney Janis Gallery, New York

VIEW FROM THE SQUARE TOWARD THE MADELEINE

Photo Éditions Greff, Paris

PARIS. PLACE DE LA CONCORDE

VIEW VIA THE BRIDGE TOWARD THE SQUARE AND THE MADELEINE

Photo Boudot-Lamotte

VIEW ACROSS THE SQUARE
Photo Estel, Paris

PARIS. PLACE DE LA CONCORDE

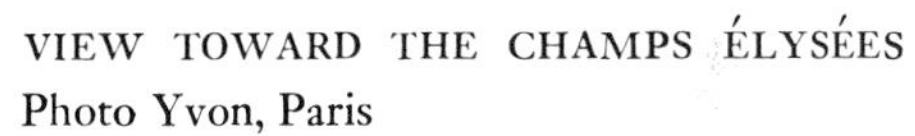

VIEW TOWARD THE CHAMPS ÉLYSÉES
Photo Yvon, Paris

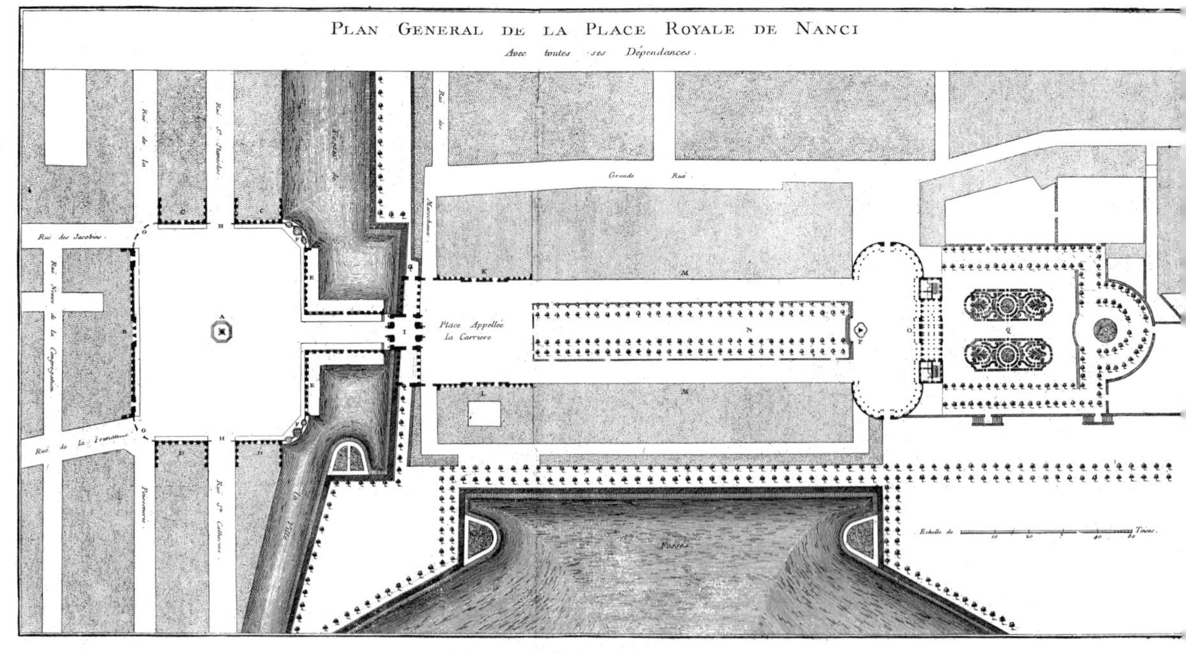

NANCY. A: GENERAL PLAN OF THE PLACE ROYALE

From Patte, *Monumens érigés en France*

B: AERIAL VIEW TOWARD THE PLACE STANISLAS

Photo Éditions Greff, Paris

NANCY

A: PLACE STANISLAS
Photo Éditions V. Roeder, Nancy

B: RUE HÉRÉ TOWARD THE HEMICYCLE
Photo Éditions V. Roeder, Nancy

C: HEMICYCLE OF THE PLACE DE LA CARRIÈRE
Photo Éditions V. Roeder, Nancy

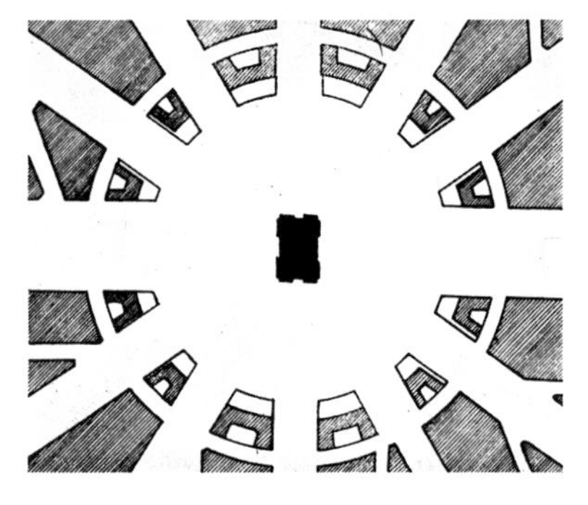

A: PARIS. PLACE DE L'ÉTOILE

PLAN

From Sitte, *The Art of Building Cities*

AERIAL VIEW

Photo Archives Photographiques Paris

B: CHAUX-DE-FONDS

PROJECT OF LEDOUX

From Ledoux, *L'Architecture considerée sous le rapport de l'Art, des Moeurs, et de la Législation*

tecture of the arcaded houses and the regularity of the layout compensate for the distracting effect of the street exits. The final harmony and regularity that the eighteenth-century projects foresaw was not achieved until 1910, when the fourth side of the Place Royale was completed.

Very similar to this solution in Rheims is Lecarpentier's project for the Place Royale in Rouen (Pl. 66D), as published by Patte; however, it was never executed.

Still another square, closely related to those in Rennes, Rheims, and the project for Rouen, must be mentioned in this discussion although it is located outside France: the Place Royale in Brussels. It took the place of an area which had stretched in front of a palace of the Dukes of Brabant burned down at the beginning of the eighteenth century. The design of the present-day square dates back largely to 1776 and stems from Barré and Barnabe Guimard, who also supervised the execution. The rectangle of the square is cut by the Rue de la Régence, which continued the Rue Royale, the main link between the older sections of Brussels and those of the eighteenth century. Since the dimensions of the Place Royale are relatively small, the square represents rather a monumental enlargement of the Rue Royale than an independent square, and yet it appears as a closed spatial unit—definitely comparable to Rennes and Rheims. This effect is achieved through the complete architectural identity of the eight palaces which surround it and of the four arcades which close the open spaces between them at the corners, comparable to the grilles of Nancy. The Church of St. Jacques-sur-Caudenberg at one long side of the square is completely integrated into the architecture of the framing palaces. Opposite the church the Rue Montagne-de-la-Cour runs into the square and offers a picturesque vista over the lower parts of the town. The monument to Godfrey of Bouillon in the center of the Place Royale, substituting for an older monument, unfortunately destroys part of the spatial impact of the square. Nevertheless, the Place Royale in Brussels may be considered as one of the last typical eighteenth-century creations, and if it lacks the grandeur of its French examples, it charms the spectator by its perfect architectural uniformity and the definiteness of its spatial shape.

The two most famous and grandiose city planning solutions of the eighteenth century in France were the unique Place de la Concorde in Paris and the sequence of squares in Nancy.

The Place de la Concorde (Pl. 67A) definitely represents the climax of the *places royales* of the eighteenth century. Today, with all its later changes and additions, it is still the square which signifies the spirit and meaning of Paris in the most impressive form—unique in its grandeur and monumentality. To a certain degree it was anticipated by the two squares in Bordeaux and Rennes dating from the first third of the century. When Le Gendre and Soufflot worked on their project for Rheims in 1755, Jacques Ange Gabriel, the son of Jacques Gabriel, began preparing the designs for the Place de la Concorde. Its area had been leveled two years before, but construction was not inaugurated until 1763 and was actually completed in 1772. After a competition in 1748 among the members of the Academy, Louis XV commissioned Jacques Ange Gabriel in 1755 to work out the final plan by combining the nineteen projects submitted. The intention of all these projects was to create *the* monumental square of Paris by integrating urban elements and landscape—entirely contrary to the sentiments of the seventeenth century. As mentioned above, open space in contrast to closed space was the new ideal and its realization was assured by the inclusion of nature. Out of these sentiments the king presented the city of Paris with the open land adjacent to the Jardin des Tuileries, the Seine River, and the Champs Élysées, and the quarter around the projected church of the Madeleine. Thus the new square could expand on three sides into open space. The location of Bouchardon's statue of the king, begun in 1754, marks the crossing of the two main axes: in the east-west direction, the extension of the main alley of Le Nôtre's Tuileries gardens to the entrance of the Champs Élysées; in the north-south direction, from the Madeleine through the Rue Royale toward the Seine River (Pls. 68–69).

In order to define more firmly the large area of the square, Gabriel introduced various architectural elements. In the east he built a terrace and balustrades, separating the sloping expanse of the Tuileries gardens from the square. In the north he erected the Gardes Meubles (1760–65, the present Ministère de la Marine and Hôtel Grillon) symmetrically flanking the entrance to the Rue Royale. Their façades represent free variations of the Louvre façade. Most decisive, however, was a trench, fifteen feet deep, its bottom covered by lawn, which ran parallel to the four sides of the square, its inner corners oblique. It was crossed by six bridges which connected the inner area with all exits from the square. Thus the vast expanse of the square was narrowed down to dimensions which could be perceived as a spatial unit.

The Place de la Concorde became the representative stage on which France celebrated her festive events, celebrations which are partially preserved for posterity in copper engravings. The most splendid pageantry was unfolded with the fireworks on the occasion of the marriage of the Dauphin to Marie Antoinette in 1770. Little did the royal couple know that the same square would witness their decapitation twenty-three years later. To realize the enormous crowd attending such festivities on the square, it may be mentioned that on the former occasion 132 spectators were killed—a dubious record not surpassed by the even larger gatherings on St. Peter's Square in Rome. The French Revolution replaced Bouchardon's statue of Louis XV in the center of the square with the guillotine, whose victims on this very spot numbered 2,625, among them besides the king and queen almost all the great figures of the Revolution, such as Philippe Egalité, Charlotte Corday, Danton, and Robespierre.

The following decades saw the gradual transformation of the prerevolutionary square of the eighteenth century into its present-day shape. Of greatest importance aesthetically was the Pont de la Concorde, which Jean-Rodolphe Perronet (1708–94) had begun in 1787 and for which stones from the destroyed Bastille were later used. In itself a great work of architecture, the bridge became an essential element of the square, extending as it does the axis from the Madeleine to the Palais Bourbon (today the Chamber of Deputies) on the left bank of the Seine River.

The idea of linking a bridge with a square on either or both ends had been anticipated by Perronet with two other bridges, although on a less monumental scale. Both of them, the bridges over the Loire at Orléans (1751–61) and at Tours (1772–86), run into small squares surrounded by uniform house façades, with streets continuing the direction of the roadway of the bridge.

A similar relationship between bridge and square may be seen in Schlüter's project for a square in front of the royal castle in Berlin, the so-called Schloss-Freiheit (see p. 215). And the same motif was taken up again in the most grandiose manner in Turin with the Ponte Vittorio Emanuele (see p. 164).

Today the Pont de la Concorde serves a double function: it gathers the traffic on the left bank to sluice it in a regulated current onto the square, whereas from the opposite direction its broad surface creates a magnificent background for the obelisk of Luxor, erected in 1836 on the spot of statue and guillotine.

The final and most decisive alteration took place in 1854 when the trench surrounding the square was filled in and only its inner balustrade remained, rather forlorn and meaningless today since it helps neither to accentuate the space nor to regulate the traffic. At the same time, the famous eight statues representing French cities were erected and the German architect Hittorff gave the final shape to the square by the erection of the two fountains which fall into the axis of Madeleine-obelisk-bridge. This arrangement of the obelisk and fountains was obviously stimulated by the similar organization on St. Peter's Square in Rome. There, however, spatial nuclei are created while here, on the Place de la Concorde, only a directional perspective effect is accomplished.

With the completion of the Church of the Madeleine (built by Contant Ivry in 1806–42) a further indirect strengthening of the spatial structure of the square was achieved: the pediment of the church lies higher than the eaves of the uniform houses along the Rue Royale, so that the Madeleine's actual distance from the square is visually shortened and, although distant, it becomes part of the square's framing architecture.

The spatial impact of the Place de la Concorde is entirely different from that of the seventeenth-century squares in France and Italy and cannot, of course, be perceived as directly and immediately as that of a closed square. Its tremendous dimensions, its location along the Seine River which makes it almost a marina, and its openness on three sides do not actually create a definite space but rather a field of complex spatial relations: *perspectives, not edifices, are its boundaries*. How intense, nevertheless, its peculiar beauty and aesthetic effect are may best be described in the words of an old Parisian "amateur," a figure in Arthur Koestler's *The Age of Longing* —a description which at the same time is a perfect characterization of the timelessness of any great city planning idea:

Do you know how long it took to make the Place de la Concorde into that miracle of townscape-planning that it is? Three centuries, my friends. It was begun by Gabriel under the Fourteenth Louis, continued by the Fifteenth, carried on by the Revolution, continued by Napoleon, completed by Louis-Philippe. And it was one plan, one vision, which continued to materialise through the centuries, regardless of political upheavals, fires, famines, wars and plagues. . . . It is quite common that a building, like a cathedral or a palace, is being restored, reshaped and so on, for three centuries or more. But the Concorde is not a building, it is a square. It is an expanse of organised space. And when you stand on it, you see that the space has been organized around it for a mile to the West up to the Arch of Triumph, and half a mile to the North up to the Madeleine, and across the Seine to the Palais Bourbon. If you look northward, you see seventeenth century palazzi and between them, receding in a perfect flight of perspective, a Greek temple built in the early nineteenth. An abominable idea! But the effect is one of perfect beauty, because the detail dissolves in the whole, and the various periods fuse in harmonious con-ti-nu-ity. And if you look to the South, across the bridge built out of the slabs of a dungeon, you see another antique façade, on the Palais Bourbon, made to match that to the North. But the joke is that the Bourbon Palais faces the other way, and this façade was stuck on its buttocks two hundred years after it was built. Another abomination! And to the West, the Champs Elysées with that monstrous triumphal arch at its end! Yet the effect of the whole is perfection itself. But to build perfection out of so much ugly detail, you must have a vision which embraces centuries, which digests the past and makes the future grow out of it.[1]

Mondrian's abstraction of the Place de la Concorde (Pl. 67B) shows the impact of the square upon another, later generation. It is interesting to note that, although the regularity of the layout is somewhat reflected in the painter's geometric image, the vitality of the square's three-dimensional reality is by no means conveyed.

The sequence of squares in Nancy, created during the same decade as the Place de la Concorde, represents an entirely original solution of spatial problems in city planning. The integration of three autonomous units into a total spatial configuration is as suggestive and persuasive in Nancy as it is in Pergamum, Rome, Venice, Bologna, and Salzburg—in each instance the solution is equally expressive of the spirit of its period.

When Stanislas Leszczynski, the erstwhile King of Poland, was made Duke of Lorraine and Bar by his son-in-law Louis XV in 1737, he resided first in Lunéville and later in Nancy. In his political frustration Stanislas tried to expand and transform Nancy, until then a combination of a regularly planned medieval and a Renaissance town, into a European capital according to the concept of the eighteenth century. The commission was

[1] Arthur Koestler, *The Age of Longing* (New York, 1951), pp. 12–13. Reprinted by permission of the Macmillan Company.

given to Héré de Corny (1705–63) in 1753. The nucleus of his project became the axis of three connected squares: Place Stanislas, Place de la Carrière, and the Hemicycle. Only one existing building, erected by Boffrand in 1715 and today the Palais de Justice, had to be considered in Héré's new project (Pl. 70A).

The rectangular Place Royale, today's Place Stanislas (Pls. 70B and 71A), corresponds exactly in its measurements to the *places royales* in Bordeaux and Rennes. It is dominated on its long side by the Hôtel de Ville, and slopes gently toward the other squares. Identical façades frame the square on its shorter sides. Intricate, transparent grilles in gilded wrought-iron work, designed by Lamour, close the square in elegant curves at its corners. In this way the square is separated visually from the incoming streets right and left of the Hôtel de Ville. On the opposite side, combined with decorative corner fountains by Guibal, the grilles allow a view into the park, which was once a canal. A statue of Louis XV, also by Guibal, was erected as usual in the center, to be replaced after its destruction during the Revolution by a monument honoring Stanislas Leszczynski. Two arcaded blocks of lesser height, carefully calculated in their reduced proportions, create the transition toward the Rue Héré, the small and short annex of the Place Royale (Pl. 71B).

The Triumphal Arch (1757) closing this section of the area opens at the other side toward the second square, the Place de la Carrière. Here, Boffrand's existing structure dictated the shape of the uniform houses which frame the promenade. Four rows of regularly trimmed trees parallel the middle axis of the square. This axis is stopped by the longitudinal axis of the third ellipsoid square, the so-called Hemicycle (Pl. 71C), which meets the promenade at an angle of 90 degrees. The colonnades which enclose this square in half-circles continue the architectural system of the government buildings in the background and create, as a third unit in the general sequence of squares, a parvis before their façades.

The differences between the basic layouts of the individual squares, each of which is an independent, closed spatial unit, fuse into a comprehensive town planning pattern—not only on the drawing board but in three-dimensional actuality. Relatively minor architectural elements, such as the grilles at the Place Royale and the Triumphal Arch at the Place de la Carrière, help to bring about a complete spatial continuity. The rhythmical alternation of smaller and larger, higher and lower structures in their relative proportions, of the framing façades, and of the perforations of grilles, Triumphal Arch, and colonnades increases and intensifies the overall impression of spatial suspense to a degree that may be experienced elsewhere only in the baroque squares of seventeenth-century Rome.

CLASSICISTIC SQUARES. Soon after the middle of the eighteenth century the stylistic development in France turned more and more toward what is generally termed "classicism." This change—so obvious in painting and sculpture—expressed itself in city planning in a different concept of space. In architecture proper, the classicistic trend had reigned in France even during the baroque period. From Perrault's Louvre façade to Jacques Ange Gabriel's Garde Meubles at the Place de la Concorde, the Palladian spirit had prevailed with its desire for discipline, regularity, and rigid lawfulness. However, the *concept of space was then baroque;* the feeling for the three-dimensional expanse and the shape of its confines was as vital as in contemporary Italy—although expressing itself in a different way architecturally. Now, during the last third of the century, "neoclassicism" corroded this feeling. The susceptibility for the third dimension diminished till it finally vanished entirely at the beginning of the nineteenth century, the "flat" century which was interested only in two-dimensional design.

The triumph of reason became complete; architecture and city planning followed essentially structural concepts. A logical, almost functional approach rather than the desire to express three-dimensional imagination directed the creative process. The leading theoreticians of this period, from Laugier to Durand, continually referred to logic and general philosophical principles—and they were taken very seriously by artists and public alike. Simplicity in contrast to richness and variety of expression became the ideal, and it was this ideal which writers and artists saw primarily in the works of antiquity. The beginning of systematic archaeological studies in Greece and the excavations in Pompeii and Herculaneum from the middle of the eighteenth century stimulated the study of antiquity again—led, in fact, to another Renaissance, although one that was dryer and more theoretical—and influenced all aesthetic considerations.

Accordingly, the straight line became predominant in architecture and hence rectangularity in city planning—in other words, the gridiron scheme.

Thus, quite naturally, the *street,* conceived of as a continuous perspective, mostly of similar units, became more important than the square. In the opinion of this period, utmost clarity suggests to the mind structural truth and creates automatically therewith aesthetic pleasure, which now actually became identical with mere intellectual satisfaction. No wonder that at this time the city of Turin (see p. 159) was generally admired all over Europe, since there the ancient castrum plan was continued and enlarged through the seventeenth and eighteenth centuries. The high point of this development was reached under Napoleon in Paris. There the Rue de Rivoli proves better than anything else the victory of linear perspective and the complete neglect of spatial articulation. The thoroughness of this change in concept is proved by Durand's suggestion for the remodeling of the Place de la Concorde. According to his idea, Gabriel's great spatial concept would have been turned into a lifeless and boring scheme, the only advantage of which would have been its geometrically neat pattern.

The idea of combining a square with a promenade, as in Nancy, was taken up again in Nantes. Here the combination of three squares was first conceived by Jean Baptiste Cenaray, who in his program went back to still earlier projects (mainly De Vigny's). These earlier ideas were eventually realized with slight modifications through the building activities of a real-estate speculator named Graslin whose enterprises changed the appearance of Nantes decisively. His plans were finally executed by Mathurin Crucy. The combination of the three squares, the Place Royale, the Place Graslin, and the Course de la République (today the Course Cambronne) lacks any structural or spatial integration. From the Place Royale, the main traffic artery, the Rue Crebillon, leads to the Place Graslin (Fig. 45), entering it at an oblique angle as do the other streets which radiate from it. Another street opposite the façade of the theater serves as a link to the Course de la République, though without an axial relationship between the squares. The Place Graslin, completed in 1785, consists of a half-circle attached to a small rectangle in front of the theater (built by Mathurin Crucy in 1788). It represents a faint echo of the Place d'Armes in Dijon and is somewhat similar to the contemporary Place de l'Odéon in Paris. The theater dominates the slightly sloping square, which is surrounded by extremely plain, typical classicistic façades, brought into harmony with the theater by the identical height of all the horizontals. These horizontals are repeated in the

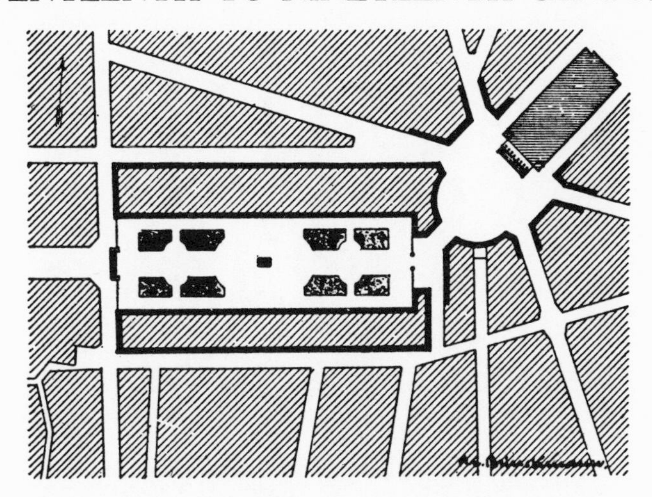

FIG. 45. NANTES. PLACE GRASLIN AND COURSE DE LA RÉPUBLIQUE. PLAN
From Brinckmann, *Die Baukunst des 17. und 18. Jahrhunderts*

façades framing both sides of the Course de la République (1789), an outspoken residential square like so many of the same period in England. The rather small distance between the comparatively high houses on both sides makes the closed rectangle appear more a promenade than a square. The complete lack of axial relationships in the spatial connection of these three squares is obvious. This lack is all the more astonishing since it contrasts so sharply with the tradition established by the grandiose city planning schemes of the first two thirds of the century.

The Place Fontette in Caen, dominated by the Palais de Justice erected by Lefevre in 1787, shows a great similarity in its basic layout with the Place Graslin in Nantes as a kind of civic parvis in front of a public building. However, here the main approach leads directly across the semi-octagonal square to the public building, thus establishing a central axis.

The purest example of a semicircular classicistic square is the Place de l'Odéon (1779–82) in Paris (Fig. 46). Whereas in Nantes the half-circle was combined with a small rectangle immediately in front of the theater, and in Caen the semicircle was broken into half an octagon, in Paris the square consists of a geometrically exact half-circle. The five incoming streets subdivide its periphery symmetrically. The façades of the surrounding houses are even more reticent than those surrounding the other two classicistic squares. Aesthetically and traffic-wise the Place de l'Odéon and the streets

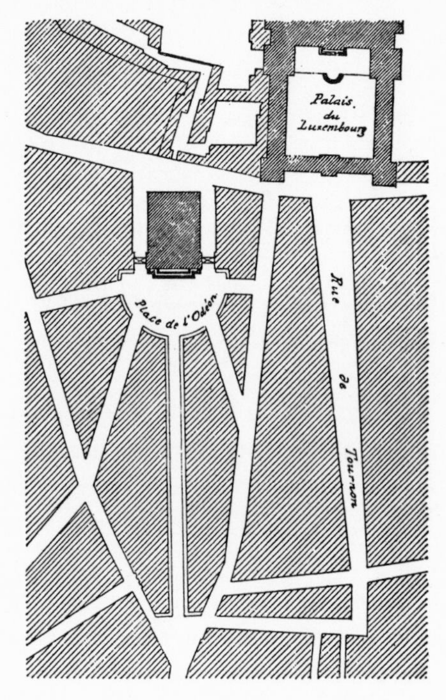

FIG. 46. PARIS. PLACE DE L'ODÉON. PLAN
From Brinckmann, *Platz und Monument*

leading to it bring regularity and clarity into the rather crooked network of an old Parisian quarter. In letters and diaries of the end of the century the Place de l'Odéon is often praised for offering a dignified entrance to the building it fronts—quite in contrast to the location of other theaters of this period in Paris.

As was stated before, the eighteenth century conceived of a square not as closed space, as did the seventeenth century, but rather as a center for expanding space, its frame well pierced. The primary idea was to create and organize the best possible intra-urban integration between the square and its surrounding quarters. The Place de l'Étoile, planned at the very end of the century, realizes this idea in the most monumental way.

As early as 1685 the "rondel," Le Nôtre's motif in landscaping, was transferred into urban planning with Mansart's Place des Victoires. Although not quite consistently carried through, this nevertheless was the only seventeenth-century Parisian square whose layout was still acclaimed in the eighteenth century. Already in Patte's anthology of projects from the middle of the century for the beautification of Paris in honor of Louis XV, a great number of genuine star squares were projected, though none of them were executed. Most interesting among these projects is Rousset's Carrefour de Bussy, a complete circle, with a statue of Louis XV in the center, from which ten streets radiate (see Pl. 65). But Rousset still surrounds his square with an almost continuous architectural frame, decorated by triumphal arches and fountains. In other words, this project represents an intermediary step from the closed square, which appeals to a feeling for definite space, to the complete openness of the Place de l'Étoile without any immediate spatial effects.

To understand the function of the Place de l'Étoile in the overall plan of Paris one must recall that already in 1666 Le Nôtre had developed the main axis through the Tuileries gardens in continuation of the main axis of the Louvre. As at Versailles, he continued his axis up-hill, what is the present-day Champs Élysées, as the center lane of a three-pronged fan through the adjacent forest (the Place de la Concorde did not yet exist). Various ideas were suggested during the eighteenth century to accentuate the crest of the hill as the final vista; to mention only one, there was Ribart's famous, rather grotesque building in the shape of an elephant (1758). Under Napoleon, Chalgrin and Raymond were finally victorious in a competition for a triumphal arch (1805). Chalgrin started the work, which after his death was completed in 1836 under Louis Philippe.

The Place de l'Étoile with the Arch of Triumph, which was to become one of Paris's symbols, can no longer be considered a square in our sense (Pl. 72A). The overall area is much too large to be perceived as a whole, especially since the width of each of the twelve uniform blocks of houses is less than that of the incoming twelve streets. Even the trees, planted in concentric rings in front of the houses, cannot keep together the open void. Advantageous as this layout may be for the effect of the arch proper, it counteracts the establishment of any spatial relations. Thus the square becomes merely a monumental crossroads, whereas its nucleus, the Arch of Triumph, dominates most impressively the Champs Élysées and the other avenues. This organization stimulated similar smaller patterns all over Europe throughout the nineteenth century when the star square turned into merely a traffic center.

It was the most important French architect of the second half of the eighteenth century who finally abolished three-dimensionality in town planning. Claude Nicolas Ledoux (1736–1806), greater as artist and more radical in his thinking than any other French architect of his period, through his executed work, his theory, and his utopian projects completely erased the small vestiges of spatial feeling in town planning that the general development of neoclassicism had still left. In architecture, this lack of interest in three-dimensional interrelationship turned into revolutionary creativeness since it enabled him to visualize and shape each structure as an isolated work of clearly articulated form, defined by its functional purpose and expressed in almost abstract geometrical terms. Quite naturally such a concept brought to an end any possibility of conceiving of a group of buildings and even less of an entire town quarter as a totality in three dimensions. Ledoux's ambition was twofold: to create the "simplest" expression of the practical purpose of each single structure in basic stereometric shapes and to achieve the best possible provisions for the well-being of the people. In short, a mathematical formula for the realization of utilitarian, social, and especially recreational concepts. With these ideas he anticipated many architectural trends of today, from architectural functionalism to the planning of garden cities.

His projects (1775–79) for the *salines* (salt mines) of Chaux-de-Fonds (Pl. 72B), a town in the Swiss canton of Neuchâtel intended as the industrial center for the mining and processing of mineral salts, prove the point. They are published in Ledoux's treatise on site plans as well as in explicit designs for individual buildings. His first project foresaw only one tremendous building on a quadrangular layout with many subdivisions, reminiscent of the pattern play of the French theoreticians of the late sixteenth and early seventeenth centuries. His second project, however—the last comprehensive plan for an ideal city prior to the twentieth century and at the same time the first project for an industrial workers' settlement—was partially executed, with some remainders still extant. The nucleus is a tremendous ellipsoid area whose long axis is part of an existing highway from Besançon; along this axis buildings for special functions are erected. The periphery of the area is studded with individual structures of uniform types, each with orchard and kitchen garden. But this periphery in no way represents a frame for or a confinement of space, in contrast to John Wood's earlier ellipsoid Royal Crescent in Bath (see p. 204). The ring of houses in Chaux-de-Fonds is paralleled by an ellipsoid boulevard of trees. Outside stretches a garden city with trees, planted streets, and carefully planned buildings in simplified classicistic forms, such as market halls, public baths, churches, hospital, cemetery, plant for cannon manufacturing, administration building, etc.

The concept of this ideal city is solely planimetric, hence the whole has correctly been called "architecture in relief." The grouping of equivalent units of variegated layouts around the inner ellipsoid and the plain juxtaposition of independent single elements create no spatial references.

Summing up, Ledoux's ideal city shows merely a multitude of consciously and intentionally isolated individual volumes, lacking any spatial coherence. The nucleus represents but the center of a two-dimensional pattern. Intellectual rationalization triumphs over the baroque concept of spatial integration. The conflict between traditionalism and innovation, so outspoken in Ledoux's works, is solved in this project for Chaux-de-Fonds in favor of the new two-dimensionality which was to become the leading principle through the nineteenth century. It means the total negation of the square as a structural element in town planning.

THE INTERNATIONALIZATION OF FRENCH AND ITALIAN CONCEPTS

As has been stated so often, French taste, if not French style, monopolized the whole of Europe throughout the eighteenth century. Europe had become intellectually and artistically a colony of France. The obvious reason was not only France's political and economic superiority but also the general trend favoring rationalization of the creative process and its reglementation by academic rules. For the emotional exuberance of the baroque was essentially limited to Italy proper, extending to a certain degree into Austria and southern Germany. Everywhere else outside Italy theoretical thinking, aesthetic treatises, and discussions were based on Vitruvian and Palladian concepts. These general concepts were taken for granted among all those who commissioned public building—princes and aristocrats, mayors, and affluent amateurs. Consequently, the strict regularity and rigid formalism of the French space concept were generally accepted and the *places royales* of France, as well as the architecture of Versailles, were now copied or imitated with minor national variations all over Europe.

The countries outside Italy and France where noteworthy squares were created during the seventeenth and eighteenth centuries were England and Germany, while the fringe countries of Central Europe, Denmark, Spain, and Portugal shared only to a lesser degree in the general development. Some very few examples in Belgium and Russia were mentioned before.

In the Netherlands, no specific spatial developments emerged. Her sometimes very picturesque small squares stemmed mostly from the Middle Ages, for the middle-class attitude of her people—so characteristic for all classes of her population—did not demand great representative show places and vistas. The Dutch spatial feeling found its most fitting expression in their interiors, depicted so truthfully in the masterworks of the golden age of Dutch painting. Even the narrow streets of Dutch towns represent aesthetically nothing else than open-air interiors.

ENGLAND. The only country which did not fall prey to the overwhelming splendor of French building and planning was England. She was almost immune toward it since through all periods of her history England had never developed any true feeling for space in architecture. Even the interiors of her great Gothic cathedrals, impressive as they are, are creations of an interplay of form, volume, and light rather than of spatial relations. Up to the present English architecture and sculpture have remained essentially volume-bound, without any intention to shape space as such. England's innate romantic feelings found their most adequate expression during the Middle Ages and during the various succeeding Gothic revivals. Even during her most classicistic period, these inclinations were never completely suppressed—one need think only of Christopher Wren's Oxford Gothic and Horace Walpole's Strawberry Hill. In the eighteenth century, artificial waterfalls and even more artificial ruins, make-believe bark huts, and Chinese pagodas in her parks expressed more genuinely her artistic imagination and subconscious daydreams than did the orderly Georgian façades. As contemporaneous literary sources prove, an assembly of picturesque forms always appealed more strongly to the Englishman of the eighteenth century than the most beautifully shaped spatial form.

Closely integrated with this trend of public taste in architecture was the intimacy with nature in its "natural" form, in contrast to the well-groomed French parks, architecturally so clearly defined. The development of English gardens and parks in the eighteenth century mirrors this general English attitude, as does the ever-increasing tendency to draw nature into the townscape in the form of greens and planting. In the permanent fight between the sprawling forms of natural growth and the rigidity of architectural elements, the latter succumbed and with it the possibilities for creating definite spatial shapes weakened.

Even the classicistic attitude of an Inigo Jones and a Sir Christopher Wren could not suppress completely the latent romantic medieval tendencies of the nation. As imposing as their work may be, it nonetheless remains somewhat of an alien body and represents merely an aristocratic layer over the multitude and variety of ordinary English structures. The academicism of the *Vitruvius Britannicus* in all its editions certainly does not give an overall picture of English building in the respective decades it covers. Even in the second part of the eighteenth century, the influence of the Society of Dilettanti and of the publications of James Stuart and Nicholas Revett was limited to the highbrows.

What holds true for Wren's architecture is valid also for his town planning projects. Sir Christopher Wren's famous plan for rebuilding the City of London after the conflagration of 1666 (Fig. 47) remained largely on paper. In this plan he considered neither any previous boundaries between individual lots nor existing foundations of buildings. Small wonder then that it was obstructed by the resistance of real-estate interests and

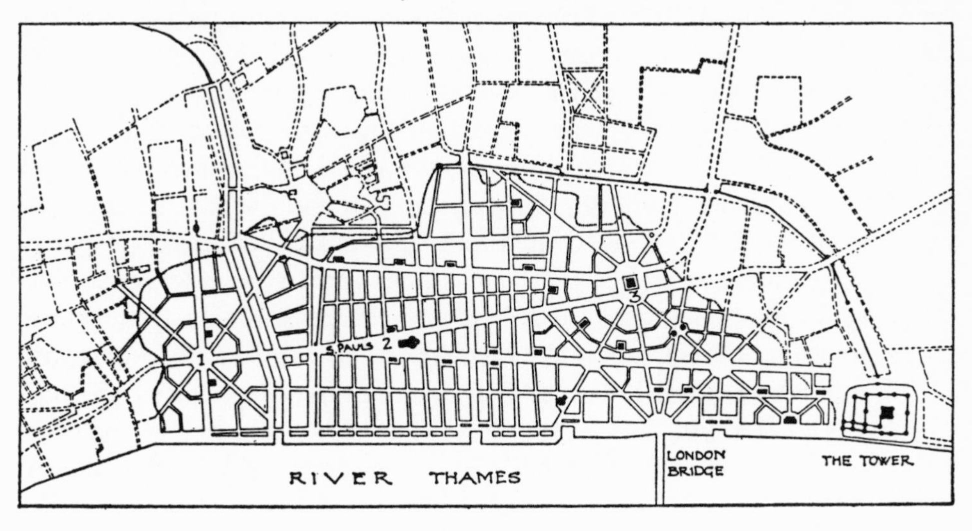

FIG. 47. LONDON. SIR CHRISTOPHER WREN'S PLAN, 1666

consequently not accepted by the king. However, at least it was possible for Wren to reerect fifty of the eighty-nine churches that had burned down. In evaluating the project one should bear in mind that it coincided approximately with Le Nôtre's project for Versailles and Bernini's St. Peter's Square in Rome (Wren had visited Paris, where he was shown Bernini's drawings for the Louvre). His plan would have changed completely the character of medieval London, of which, after all, an essential part had survived the fire. And it was a very medieval London—more medieval than most contemporary continental towns—as may be seen from Wenceslaus Hollar's engraving of the town plan (1658) before the great fire.

Wren's plan, not too different from the more schematic and geometrical project of his friend and competitor Sir John Evelyn which exists in three versions, was prepared within a few days after the disastrous event. It was based essentially on an integrated system of star squares, cut by extended axes. The western part was developed as a rather strict gridiron system, a principle on which, by the way, also a third competitor, the mathematician Robert Hooke, had based his project entirely. The influence of sixteenth- and seventeenth-century Italian theoreticians and of executed squares in Italy is obvious, especially that of the Piazza del Popolo in Rome. However, Wren's imagination, not geared to the concept of space, could not visualize what a monumental square actually means for the organization of a quarter. The largest square was characteristically provided for the Royal Exchange, whose structure would have risen in its center, flanked by a triumphal arch. Ten streets were to radiate from there, tied together by concentric streets. Characteristically, the narrow triangular square in front of St. Paul's, where two main axes converge, is definitely much less important to Wren than the square before and around the Royal Exchange. Commissioners appointed by Crown and City established three categories of streets of different width and suggested standard types of houses. Toward the south, London Bridge led to a semicircular square from which six streets again radiated, not unlike Mansart's solution for the Place d'Armes in Dijon and the projected Place de France in Paris on Chastillon's engraving of 1610. The dogmatic schematism of Wren's plan could not be mollified by reminiscences of such Roman and French motifs as fan shapes, the employment of star squares, etc.; the whole was a product of intellectual considerations rather than of the spatial imagination of an actual city planner.

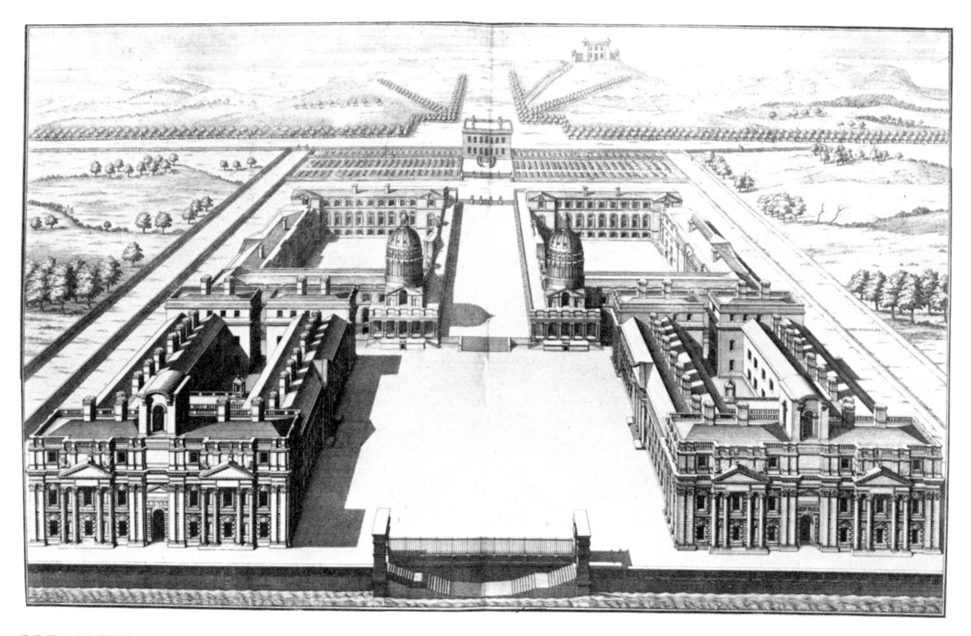

OLD VIEW

From Campbell, *Vitruvius Britannicus*

GREENWICH HOSPITAL

MODERN VIEW FROM THE THAMES RIVER

Courtesy British Information Services, New York

LONDON
COVENT GARDEN "PIAZZA"
ETCHING BY WENCESLAUS HOLLAR,
SEVENTEENTH CENTURY
Courtesy British Museum

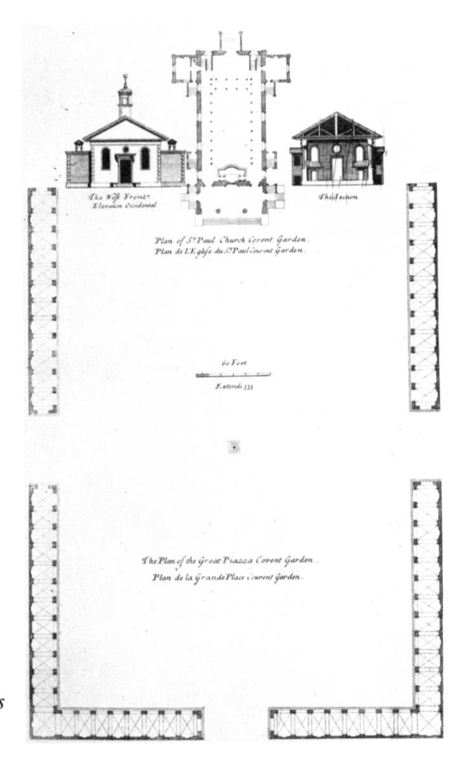

COVENT GARDEN. PLAN
From Campbell, *Vitruvius Britannicus*

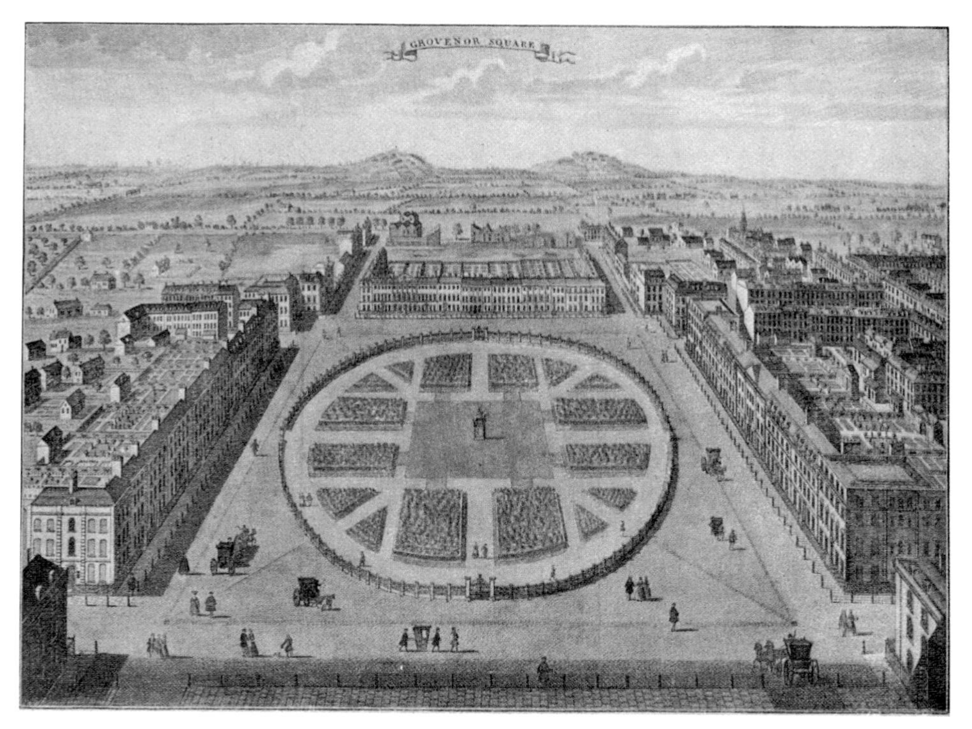

A: GROSVENOR SQUARE IN 1754. OLD PRINT
Courtesy British Information Services, New York

LONDON

B: ST. JAMES'S SQUARE IN 1773. OLD PRINT
Courtesy British Information Services, New York

A: LONDON
PARK CRESCENT
PART OF JOHN NASH'S
PLANNING SCHEME
Courtesy British Information Services, New York

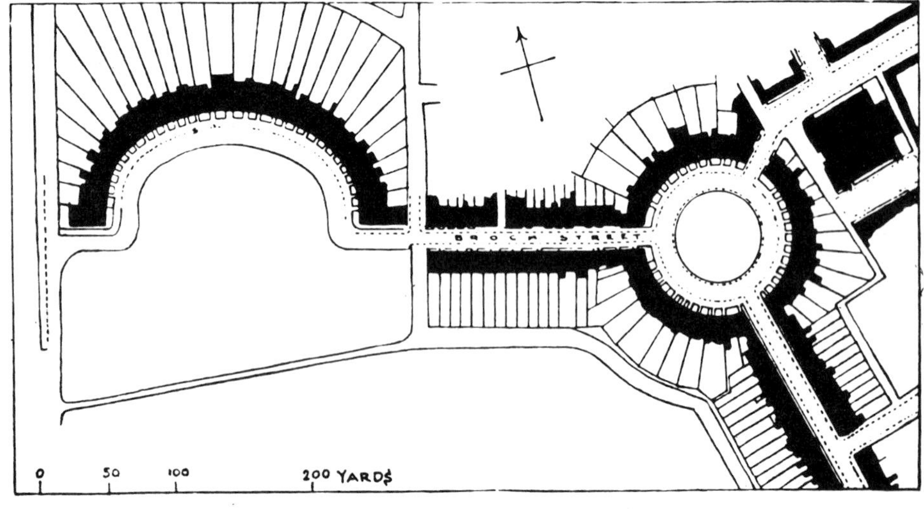

B: BATH
ROYAL
CRESCENT
AND
CIRCUS
PLAN
From Triggs, *Town Planning*

C. BATH
ROYAL
CRESCENT
Photo Valentine and Sons, London

A: THE CIRCUS. GENERAL VIEW
AQUATINT BY JOHN R. COZENS, 1773

B: ROYAL CRESCENT AND ST. JAMES'S SQUARE. AERIAL VIEW
Courtesy British Information Services, New York

MANNHEIM

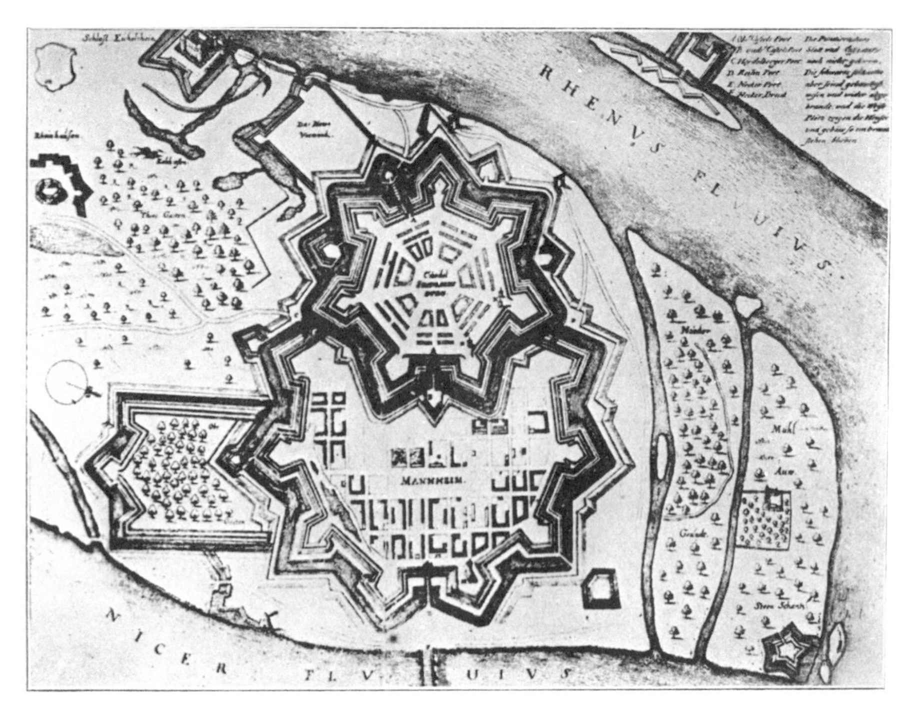

PLAN, SEVENTEENTH CENTURY
From Martin Zeiller, *Topographia . . .*

MARKET SQUARE. AERIAL VIEW
Photo Junkers Luftbild

LUDWIGSBURG. MARKET SQUARE

AERIAL VIEW

Photo Aero-Lux, Frankfurt am Main

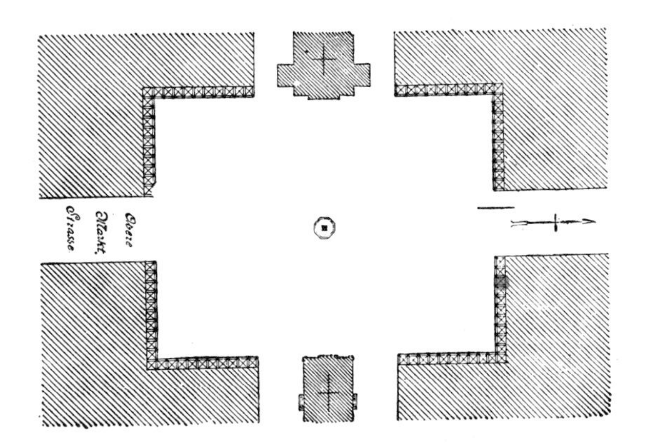

PLAN

From Brinckmann, *Platz und Monument*

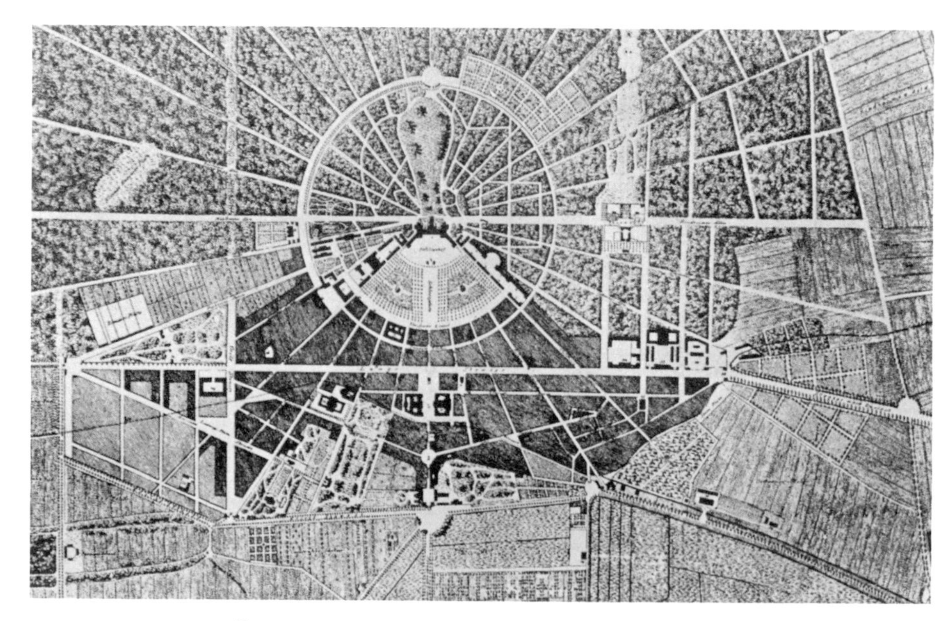

A: PLAN FROM 1822

KARLSRUHE

B: MARKET SQUARE WITH TOWN HALL AND CHURCH
Photo Junkers Luftbild

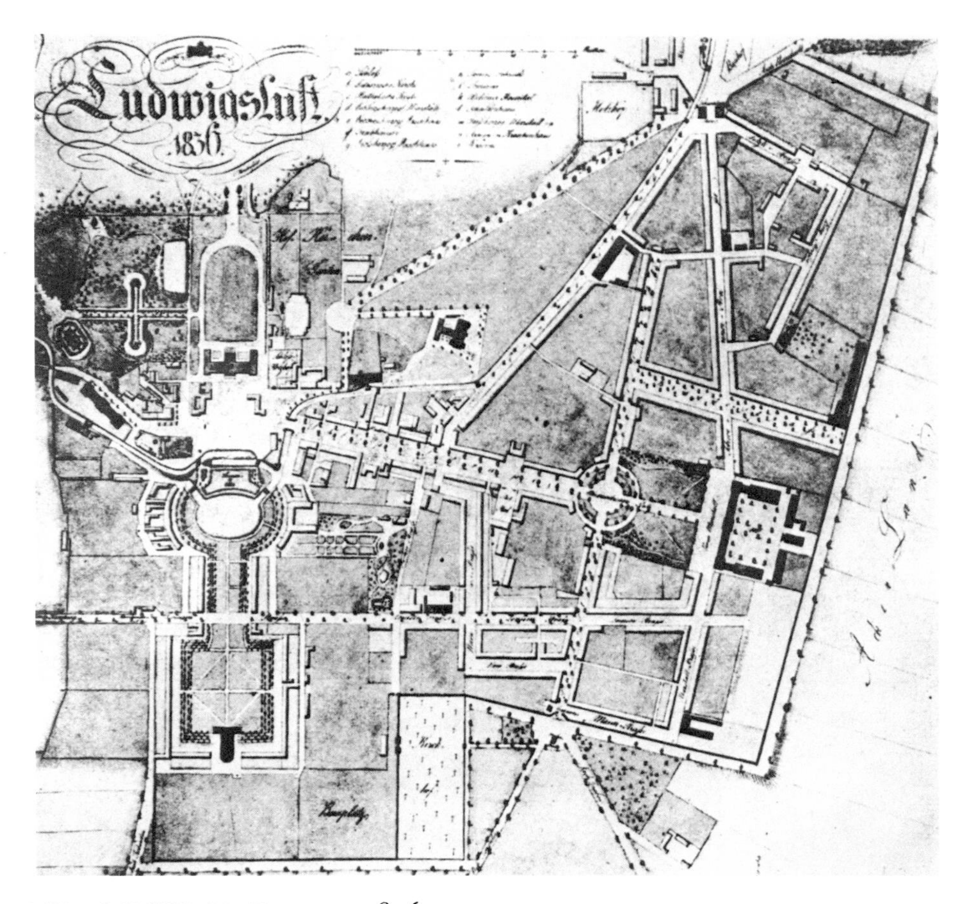

LUDWIGSLUST. PLAN FROM 1836

From Dobert, *Bauten und Baumeister in Ludwigslust*

A: PROJECT FOR A PLACE ROYALE BY ANDREAS SCHLÜTER. ENGRAVING

From Broebes, *Vues des Palais et maisons de plaisance de S. M. le Roi de Prusse, 1702*

BERLIN

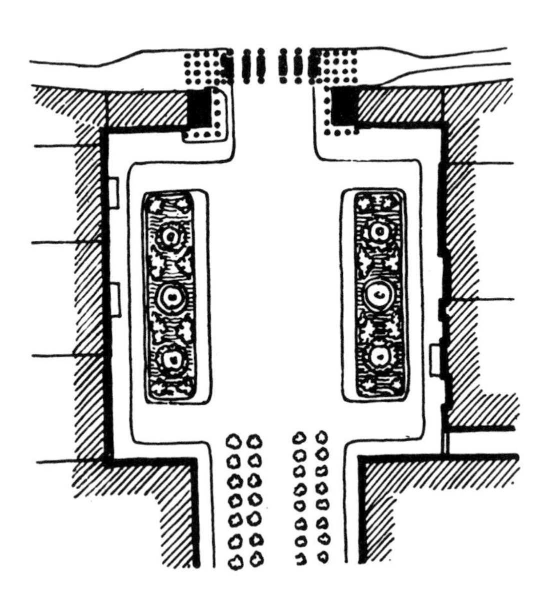

B: PARISER PLATZ. PLAN

A: LEIPZIGER PLATZ. AERIAL VIEW Photo Junkers Luftbild

BERLIN

B: BELLE-ALLIANCE PLATZ
PAINTING BY AN ANONYMOUS ARTIST
AFTER THE ARCHITECT'S DESIGN
From Kuntze, *Das alte Berlin*

A: AM HOFE. ENGRAVING BY SALOMON KLEINER, 1725

VIENNA

B: HOHE MARKT

Courtesy Information Department, Austrian Consulate General, New York

VIENNA. REGENSBURGER HOF. AFTER SALOMON KLEINER'S ORIGINAL OF 1725; ENGRAVING BY ZINKE

GROUP OF SQUARES

AROUND THE CATHEDRAL. PLAN

From Sitte, *The Art of Building Cities*

CATHEDRAL SQUARE

Photo Landesbildstelle Salzburg; courtesy Information Department, Austrian Consulate General, New York

SALZBURG

RESIDENCE SQUARE; TWO VIEWS

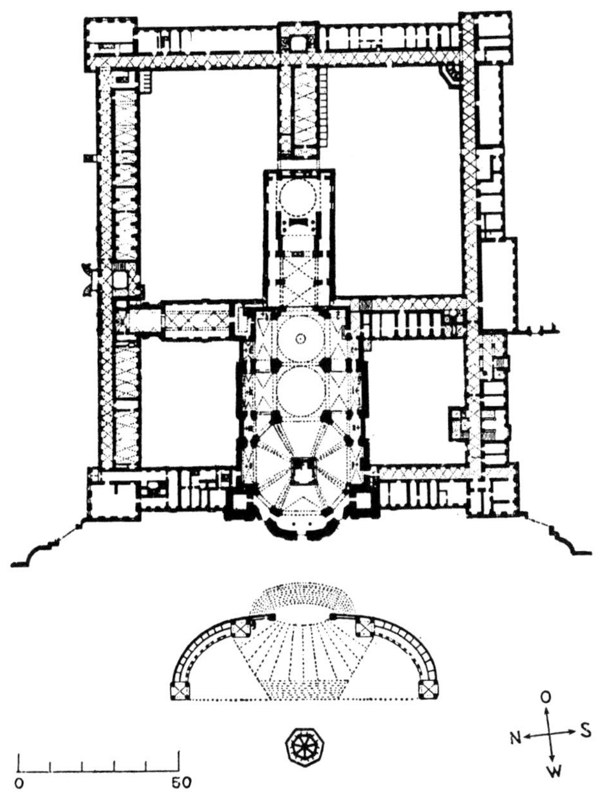

PLAN OF THE MONASTERY

EINSIEDELN

VIEW TOWARD THE MONASTERY

Photo Jean Gaberell A.G., Thalwil

A: KONGENS NYTORV From Thurah, *Den Danske Vitruvius*

COPENHAGEN

B: AMALIENBORG SQUARE

Photo Aistrup; courtesy Royal Danish Ministry for Foreign Affairs, Copenhagen

Greenwich Hospital (today the Royal Naval College of Greenwich) and its Grand Square are largely the work of Sir Christopher (Pl. 73). The "Queen's House," some distance from the river, had been erected by Inigo Jones between 1618 and 1635. Close to the Thames River, John Webb had begun building a palace in 1662, when the old Tudor palace there had been razed. Two more structures followed after 1696, and the last was completed later in the eighteenth century. With Inigo Jones's "Queen's House" in the background, the composition of Greenwich Hospital represents a triumph of a somewhat academic symmetry enjoyable in its two-dimensional plan rather than by actual spatial effects. Its exaggerated depth cannot be reconciled with the basic concept of a marina approachable from the Thames River—one has only to remember the Ripetta in Rome, the Place Royale in Bordeaux, etc. Thus the impression comes closer to that of an inner court opening toward the river than of a real square in connection with the river embankment. As always Wren was interested more in the forms of individual structures than in the shape of the resulting open space.

Good or bad as it may be, however, the Grand Square of Greenwich Hospital is in no way typical of an English square. The term "English square" evokes quite different associations. The typical English residential square —and the vast majority of all English squares are residential squares—may be defined as a green framed by architecture, just as the French park and formal garden have been characterized as architecture built of greenery. But it had not always been like that; when the first squares were established in London they were not yet planted. Only in the eighteenth century did the adulation of nature by the English become so strong that they felt almost a moral obligation to plant every free area.

While in Italy the private gardens of town palaces and of suburban villas had gradually become part and parcel of the townscape, and while at the same time in France the planted areas of the Tuileries, of the Place Dauphine, of the Jardin du Palais Royale, and finally of the Place de la Concorde were strictly formal, distinctly controlled by their architectural frame, this relationship took on other forms in England. English squares developed from the tendency of the British toward "gracious living," bourgeois comfort, and, above anything else, the highest degree of privacy. There existed no aesthetic desire for spatial accents within the totality of the town. These squares were as "private" as anything outside the private home could be.

That the greens were so often fenced in, with keys available only to the owners of adjacent houses, clearly illustrates the situation—a feeble echo of which is still perserved in New York City's Gramercy Park.

In London, about fifteen such squares already existed in the eighteenth century. Some of them developed out of old village greens of communities which were gradually incorporated into the town of London. Many more stemmed from the partial conversion of old baronial estates.

The very first square was that before Covent Garden, erected around 1630, which Inigo Jones had laid out as a piazza of seven acres (Pl. 74). He was commissioned by the Earl of Bedford, the first among the great landowners in London to split up his lands for real-estate enterprises. There can be no doubt that the large piazza in Leghorn and the Place des Vosges in Paris, both of which Inigo Jones had seen, had influenced him. The very term *piazza* for Covent Garden, together with the strictly geometric pattern of its layout, proves the ambition of the architect to compete with these well-known continental squares. Therefore it actually became the least English of all London squares. Nothing is left today of its original appearance except the church. Only an etching by Wenceslaus Hollar from 1639 and the ground plan in Campbell's *Vitruvius Britannicus* make a reconstruction of the original effect possible.

As was the case with the cathedral in Leghorn, so Inigo Jones's St. Paul's Church (not to be confused with St. Paul's Cathedral), flanked by two smaller buildings, dominated the square, in spite of its modest dimensions and reticent classicistic forms. Arcades were to surround three sides of the square, but only two sides were executed since the south side was never built. The houses, uniform in Inigo Jones's project, did not follow this program either. As to the mastery of space, this square cannot be compared with its predecessors on the continent. The height of the surrounding houses —essentially Dutch, three-storied, and narrow—does not suffice to frame visually the free area, whose inner rectangle soon turned into a busy market place. The structures besides the church on the small side are not homogeneous enough to tie the whole together. So it is Inigo Jones's *scheme rather than its realization* that initiated the sequence of squares in London.

To live in private houses around a square soon became fashionable, an aristocratic privilege. Consequently, during the later part of the seventeenth century an ever-increasing number of squares was laid out. The spatial impact of these residential squares is not strong enough to merit an individual analysis of each of them here, as delightful as it has been and still is to reside in their atmosphere. The importance of London squares definitely lies not in their architectural or town planning aspects but in their potentialities as recreational centers for their neighborhoods—a statement which in no way should deny their visual charm which contributes so much to London's total overall appearance.

The original shape of Leicester Square, laid out in 1635, is hardly recognizable today in the square's present disorderly appearance. Entirely different from the academic concept of Covent Garden, Leicester Square was the first of the long sequence of typical, very similar London squares. Their shapes are of the utmost simplicity: a rectangle or a quadrangle of moderate dimensions, the incoming streets symmetrically distributed, meeting the square either at the corners or in the middle of the sides. The green repeats the outline of the square or, more often, stretches in circular, oval, or octagonal form. It consumes the greatest part of the open area, so that the sidewalks remain relatively narrow. The surrounding houses are inconspicuous, similar though not uniform in type, and create in their totality a continuous frame. Only two squares were actually framed by uniform structures: Grosvenor Square (begun in 1695 but completed only in the eighteenth century), whose oval green was originally laid out as a distinct formal garden (Pl. 75A); and possibly St. James's Square (1684) with its octagonal center (Pl. 75B).

London squares, although sometimes topographically rather near to each other, are always closed entities, without any spatial relationship among them: no connecting axis, no angular grouping, no vista planned from one to another or into the neighboring quarter. Thus, for instance, the various squares in and around Bloomsbury, an area originally owned by the Earl of Southampton, such as Bloomsbury Square (laid out in 1665), Bedford Square (1775), Queen's Square, Red Lion Square, and later on also Russel Square (1801), were without any organic connection.

In other words, the concept of these squares represents the greatest imaginable contrast to contemporaneous French squares and continental squares under French influence. There, representative display and, if possible, monumentality were the artistic aim, based on integration of the area into the total structure of the city, as exemplified by Patte's plan of Paris. In London the aim was privacy, the privacy of the pedestrian, residential comfort, and seclusion from the life of the surrounding neighborhood. There can be no doubt that architecturally, and also emotionally, the basic concept of these squares was rooted in the collegiate squares of the Middle Ages.

At the end of the eighteenth and in the early nineteenth century, a new type of square appears in London's townscape. In these squares architecture and landscape are so integrated that they balance each other and neither one prevails over the other. Planted and built elements mold the space equally, a concept which must be traced to John Wood's Royal Crescent and Circus in Bath. By the end of the eighteenth century, the brothers Robert and James Adam and particularly John Nash had employed uniformity of house façades as the main means for their architectural effects in such spatial units as Portland Place (Robert Adam, completed by James Adam, 1778), Fitzroy Square (Robert Adam), and the Adelphi Terraces (Adam brothers). In 1812 John Nash conceived of a town planning idea which combined monumentality with the free forms of nature: Park Crescent, adjacent to Regent's Park. Again the project was based on a grand real-estate speculation. The combination of real-estate enterprise, contracting, constructing, and planning activities created the possibility of thinking in terms of larger units and of continuous blocks, with unified façades and large open spaces.

When the entrepreneur who had first started to erect the initial structures went broke as a consequence of the Napoleonic Wars, building was interrupted to be taken up again in 1815 by a new entrepreneur. Originally Park Crescent was imagined as a closed circus consisting of two semicircles. If completed, it would have been the greatest circle in Europe. However, this idea was abandoned in 1822. It became a semicircular square with the green of Regent's Park stretching into it. The two large quadrants of the half-circle with double-columned Ionic colonnades encircling the whole perimeter are paralleled by a very narrow paved strip, immediately adjacent to the peninsula of lawn and green (Pl. 76A). Incoming Portland Place creates an axis of symmetry for the approaching spectator, and the vista toward the park opens behind the Crescent proper. Thus a complete integration of nature and architecture is achieved. Here for once the forms of nature do not interfere with the clear articulation of enclosed space.

Henceforth the concept of the crescent became a London tradition; it was taken up in many London squares of the nineteenth century, of which the noblest example, Pelham Crescent in South Kensington, was built by George Basevi in 1820–30.

This particularly English architectural feature, the crescent, had its origin in Bath. The spa of Bath appears in the history of English civilization at various times: there the Romans had constructed expansive public baths to take advantage of the hot mineral springs. In Saxon times the town became an important religious center. Chaucer mentioned it, and from the period of Queen Anne it became the rendezvous of the mundane world, of court and aristocracy alike. From then on Bath was a distinct locale in English literature of the eighteenth century, and almost all the famous literary figures spent some time there. Since it had become fashionable to own a house in Bath, the Earl of Pulteney parceled out part of his estate, as the Duke of Vendôme had once done in Paris. He commissioned one single architect to create a whole new town as an elegant resort.

John Wood the Elder, architect, real-estate man, and builder at the same time, was given the task of planning a whole community in 1725. He was already well known for the design of Prior Park in the immediate vicinity of Bath, the layout of which represents a unique combination of landscape and architecture—an English counterpart to the Italian landscaped architecture of the Villa d'Este in Tivoli near Rome. Palladian motifs, including the erection of a true Palladian bridge, and the romantic, picturesque tendencies of English eighteenth-century landscaping fuse into a combination of alluring charm. Suggestive perspectives, emulating sceneries of seventeenth- and eighteenth-century paintings and stage designs, alternate with dignified Palladian structures.

In his artistic ingenuity John Wood felt immediately that the principle of Prior Park could not be employed in the new town of Bath, as charming as the interplay of romantic and classical motifs had been there. Thus he created a rigid classicistic scheme of architectural frames with precise spatial accents. He was aware that the irregular, steep slope toward the meandering river Avon could be mastered only by definite cubic shapes and that free-flowing masses could not overcome the variety of growing natural forms. So, in 1727, he first leveled the area for Queen Square, which was designed with a planted area in its center, not unlike contemporary London squares. One of the four streets at its corners, Gay Street, ascended toward a second, circular square, the Circus. The latter was composed of three circular segments, separated from each other by three streets. The Circus, destined originally for sportive events for a selected society, was begun in 1754, the year the older Wood died, and was completed by his son about 1764. The sequence of open or half-open areas continued through Brock Street to the Royal Crescent (1767–75), an almost amphitheatrical ellipsoid framing a wide lawn. In contrast to the reticent classicism of the uniform façades which surround the Circus, the architecture at the Royal Crescent becomes grandiloquent with its colossal order of Ionic columns rising above the ground floor (Pls. 76B, 76C, and 77).

The curve of the Royal Crescent opens toward the natural beauties of the valley. Its architectural shape means for the spectator essentially an anchorage in space. Here, architecture, skirting the greater expanse of natural growth, does not lose its own dignity in its ambition for an almost Roman grandeur. Without adapting its forms to nature it blends organically into it.

The principle of opening crescents, squares, and even streets toward the countryside wherever possible was the basic idea of Wood's project. This system of squares, of ascending and descending streets, was continued also to higher sites after the death of the younger Wood. Thus St. James's Square (see Pl. 77B, upper center) repeats the form of Queen Square, and the undulating Lansdown Crescent (1794) by John Palmer varies the basic principle of the Royal Crescent in more playful, flexible forms. The more modest curves of the Camden (1788, by John Eveleigh) and Norfolk Crescents repeat the same motif. At the end of the eighteenth century, when Ledoux designed Chaux-de-Fonds, first Robert Adam, in 1777–82, and then Baldwin and Eveleigh planned a new system at the opposite bank of the river – in the sequence of Laura Place, Great Pulteney Street, and Sidney Gardens, continuing the axis of Pulteney Bridge, which was built by Robert Adam in 1770. This whole scheme appears rather dry and typically classicistic, without the advantage of enlivening differences in level which characterized the uphill eighteenth-century town.

The effect of squares and crescents in Bath is something quite original and in absolute contrast to the sequences of squares and streets organized in regular axial systems, such as the Imperial Fora in Rome or the contemporary plan of Nancy. It differs equally from the nonaxial combinations in Bologna, Salzburg (see pp. 89, 221), etc. The function of squares and terraces in eighteenth-century Bath can only be compared with the part the same elements played in a Hellenistic town such as Pergamum. Only there and in Bath do squares and terraces (crescents) simultaneously represent fully developed spatial units and topographically fixed points of three-dimensional reference. In this way they connect the inner urban space with the outer space of nature. In other words, one can establish a scale of expanding spaces to be defined architecturally: the interior of a building, defined by floor, walls, and ceiling; square and street, defined by the continuous row of houses, pavement, and the sky; nature, defined by adjacent architecture and its expansion within topographical limits.

Bath is an excellent example of the last category, a dream in space, materialized in the concord of the region's typical warm yellow limestone and green lawns.

In spite of all its venerable medieval remainders, Edinburgh, Scotland's capital, owes its urbanistic individuality, like Bath, to the eighteenth century. As in Bath, the fusion of landscape and man-made organized space is also its main characteristic. About four decades after John Wood had started on his project for Bath, James Craig won a competition in 1767 for a new quarter of Edinburgh to be laid out above its existing older parts (Fig. 48). In his project he molded the natural slopes of the site and employed them

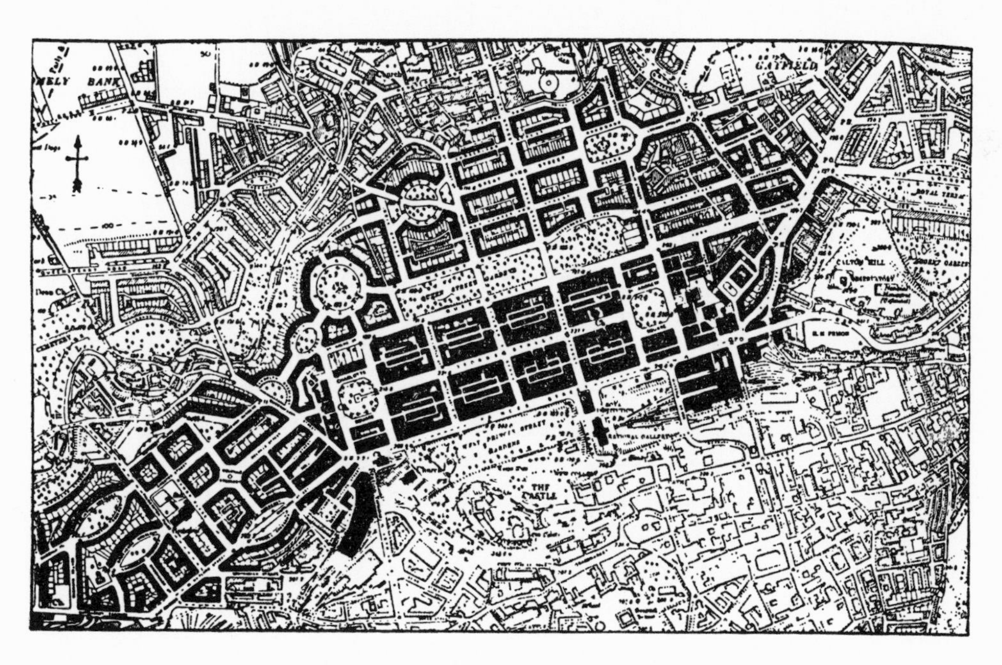

FIG. 48. EDINBURGH. PLAN

consciously for building up panoramic vistas. Three streets of identical length, level in themselves, stretch parallel. George Street, the broadest, is the central artery and runs on the crest. Princes Street, toward the south, and Queens Street, toward the north, are located lower. Since both are built up on one side only, they allow a free view down the slopes. Two smaller streets accompany the three main streets and together with seven cross streets produce regular gridiron blocks. Charlotte Square and St. Andrew's Square, which terminate George Street at its ends, have, contrary to the squares in Bath, no spatial importance as such. Visually, however, they offer the necessary distance to accentuate the classicistic architecture of Robert Adam's St. George's Church (1791) on one side and of the Royal Bank on the other side. The classicistic attitude of the Adam brothers, who shaped stylistically the character of the streets of the new town of Edinburgh, was responsible for its further extension as developed after 1809. Thomas Hamilton and William Henry Playfair took up the ideas of John Wood, Craig, and the Adamses and played around with circuses and crescents. The Royal Circus, Moray Place, Ainslie Place, Randolph Crescent, etc., repeat the familiar shape between 1820 and 1830, without matching, however, either the unpretentious dignity of London squares or the unique amalgamation of landscape and town in Bath. The peculiar beauty of eighteenth-century English concepts faded out as soon as spatial elements became mere patterns and were no longer parts of a unique three-dimensional vision.

GERMANY. During the seventeenth and eighteenth centuries, the French influence upon Germany was certainly much stronger than on England. Italian ideas manifested themselves less; when they did appear it was predominantly in southern Germany and Austria. The Thirty Years War had destroyed a large number of towns and interrupted whatever may have existed of an artistic tradition. The so-called "German Renaissance" had been little more than a continuation of late Gothic spatial and rhythmic organization, thinly disguised behind curtains of Renaissance ornamentation. Thus there was little left of truly original creations to resist the overwhelming influence of Versailles and the *places royales* on the one hand and of the didactic French treatises on the other.

The town of the medieval burgher had gone, and it was the innumerable, more or less powerful German princes, margraves, and grand dukes who dictated the forms of architectural expression—house, street, and square—always with an eye on the grandiose French examples. They certainly believed that culture meant "the transmission of organized experience in form of tradition," as Julian Huxley defined it two centuries later; and they were not restrained by the fact that these architectural and city planning achievements were, after all, the expression of a foreign culture. Thus they tried to imitate the French example, not only in palaces they erected for themselves, but also in layouts of towns connected with those palaces for their subjects. The residential town of the prince was built mainly for his entourage and for his many civil service employees. Only secondarily it served the general citizenry, or, in some instances, the settlement of political and religious refugees like the French Huguenots and the Austrian Protestants. Those towns in their relatively small dimensions still preserved a rather rural character and centered sociologically and architecturally around the palace. The castle and the blocks of private houses—no longer individual structures but unified in rows—formed one homogeneous architectural pattern. Space began to be regularized and a certain degree of bourgeois monumentality was accomplished. Broader streets led to vistas toward palace, town hall, and church. The square in front of such structures represented the terminus of a street and at the same time the spatial frame for the respective structures.

It needed, however, almost a whole century after the last original town plan in Germany had been realized, in Freudenstadt in 1599 (see p. 126), before those princely towns were founded on a larger scale and in larger numbers.

One town in Germany, however, owes its appearance as much to the seventeenth century as to the eighteenth century: Mannheim, located at the confluence of the Neckar and Rhine rivers. It was founded and fortified on the site of a previously existing village in 1606 by Elector Frederick IV of the Palatinate. Its layout conformed completely with Cataneo's scheme, the essential feature of which was the inclusion of a special citadel into the plan of the fortified city. Jacques Perret, whose treatise had been published only five years previously in 1601, functioned as mediator between the late Italian Renaissance tradition and its realization in Germany.

This settlement of Mannheim consisted of an octagonal citadel with radiating streets and an octagonal central square, fortified by ramparts and trenches against the adjacent town as well as against the surrounding open country. The town proper was a larger fortified polygon, its streets organized in a gridiron scheme in which the market occupied the central area of six blocks (Pl. 78). Mannheim underwent many changes during the Thirty Years War and afterwards, until finally, in 1689, the citadel and town were razed and burned by Vauban, to be rebuilt and newly fortified by Coehoorn in 1699. Elector Carl Philip and his successor Carl Theodore made it their residential town from 1720 to 1778. At the site of the old citadel a palatial castle was erected in 1720–26 by Clemens de Froimont, and was later enlarged in 1749–60. Earlier, around 1670, plans for a castle had been designed by Jean Marot, before Louis XIV had invaded the Palatinate, an event which made the realization of the project impossible. Marot's project, of course, represented one of the many variations of the scheme of Versailles: the *cour d'honneur* was planned as an ellipsoid, opening toward an adjacent public square, and set off against it by a grille as in Versailles. In actuality, the town proper, now stretching immediately in front of the castle, was laid out in a regular gridiron scheme, without consideration of the polygonal periphery stemming from the old seventeenth-century town. This gridiron scheme, unique in Europe for such expansion, has often been mentioned as the prototype for the grids of eighteenth-century towns in the United States. Nor is it by chance that Mannheim is the only town in Europe where the streets are identified by numbers and letters instead of having individual names.

There are three squares within the scheme of eighteenth-century Mannheim. One of them stretches before the castle, a combination of *cour d'honneur* and broad public area into which seven parallel streets run. In this way the castle becomes the final point in a vista. Although the castle does not dominate the town as a whole, as in Versailles with its angular perspectives and as in Karlsruhe, its visual dominance is still strong enough to counteract the monotonous bleakness of the gridiron scheme. Two further squares are laid out to the right and left side of a wider central street, the Paradeplatz and the Market Square, each of them occupying the area of one block. However, since all streets in both directions end at the periphery (today they continue into the nineteenth-century expansion) and since the squares are lateral to the main street, no genuine axis in the eighteenth-century sense was established.

While the Paradeplatz does not offer any aesthetic sensation, the Market

Square is accentuated on one side by a monumental architecture by Rischer, the town hall (1701–11) combined with the Catholic church (1706–20), both united by a common tower as symbols of worldly and spiritual power. Their masses are as alike as their façades. An identical fenestration throws light into the one large interior of the church as well as into the multitude of rooms of the town hall, a fact that would arouse the anger of any dogmatic functionalist. The spatial effect of the square is defined by the mass of this double structure, the fountain of 1771 in the center of the square, and the contrast of the closed space of the square to the continuous movement in the adjacent streets.

During the same period, Ludwigsburg near Stuttgart was to become the residential town of the Duke Eberhard Ludwig of Württemberg. It was planned in connection with an already existing castle built by J. F. Nette in 1704–9 and enlarged later by Donato Frisoni. After 1710 Nette also laid out the town symmetrically along a main street leading toward the castle. However, only one side of this symmetrical organization was realized. In this way the axis of the executed part of the town and that of the castle and its garden in front meet at an angle of 90°, not unlike the plan of Richelieu. This scheme contrasts with the almost contemporaneous plans of the princely residences of Mannheim and Karlsruhe. The center of the existing part of Ludwigsburg's almost regular gridiron layout is taken up by a very original square, created by Nette in 1724 (Pl. 79). It is framed by uniform two-storied houses with continuous arcades. Their horizontal isomorphism is interrupted at two opposite sides by the verticalism of a Protestant and a Catholic church, built in 1718 and 1726 respectively by Paolo Retti after designs of Frisoni. The aesthetic effect of the square with its contrast of horizontals and verticals reminds one of the earlier squares of Charleville and Covent Garden.

Built only a few years later, Karlsruhe differs basically from Mannheim. Karlsruhe was also founded as the residential town of a prince and was shaped by the playful whim of an absolute ruler. As Mannheim represents an exact realization of the gridiron scheme, so Karlsruhe represents the perfect radial pattern (Pl. 80A). When Jacob Friedrich von Betzendorf, on the order of Margrave Karl Wilhelm, laid out the circular scheme in 1715–19, he placed a tower, the Bleiturm, in its center. From this point thirty-two alleys radiated, twenty-three toward and through a forest, the remaining ones intended as streets for the projected town. The castle itself was begun in 1716, with its central part attached to the tower, the two side wings aligning themselves with the corresponding radii. The *cour d'honneur* and the park sector were too large to allow the development of any specific spatially impressive form, although the radial streets, originally framed by modest two-storied houses, converged before the castle and its court. The subjects of the absolute ruler were thus directed visually and psychologically toward the center of worldly power. The revival of the traditional Renaissance pattern of Palma Nuova and Granmichele and of the projects of Errard becomes evident, as does the analogy to the concepts of Le Nôtre in Versailles.

However, the strict rigidity of the star system was abandoned through later changes, changes which made the Karl Friedrichstrasse the main axis, thus adding an element of directed classicistic symmetry to the original Renaissance system. This change began with the remodeling of the castle proper from 1752 to 1781 by the architect Leopoldo Retti, inspired and helped by the greatest German baroque architect, Johann Balthasar Neumann, who had designed two projects. The definite turn toward classicism came about when an international competition was held in 1787. Then the architect Pedetti in his project developed the market square into a clearly defined spatial expansion, surrounded by ultra-academic government buildings, two domed churches like those on the Piazza del Popolo in Rome, and adorned by monuments—all this in a conventional classicistic vernacular, without any genuine three-dimensional feeling. Though this design was never executed, it nevertheless stimulated a new, conscious emphasis on direction. The development of this axis in symmetrical sections would have added a new accent within the town proper, abolishing the exclusive domination of the castle over the whole town. The axis and the market square were actually built later by Friedrich Weinbrenner. Like Pedetti, Weinbrenner also originally planned two symmetrical churches and three-storied, uniform arcades in front of all houses of the main street starting from solemn propylaea. Today, the axis consists of the main street, without arcades, and the market square with church and town hall opposite each other (Pl. 80B). In the center of the square a monument has been erected in the form of a pyramid. Town hall and church are contrasted by the horizontals of lower private buildings. Two blocks beyond the market square a small rondel interrupts the main axis, which ends in a broad street rectangular to the whole scheme.

In spite of the propylaea, arcades, and double churches never having been built, the whole organization as it appears today proves the classicistic longing for purity of form. It does not represent merely a sterile geometric pattern; actually the sequence of squares creates perspective vistas which are enlivened by the change in proportions from street to square. The monumentalization of the main axis in contrast to the existing castle shifts the accent without destroying the inner connection between castle and town.

As in Mannheim and Karlsruhe, the square also plays a decisive part within the organization of the whole layout in the numerous other small princely residential towns which were founded during the eighteenth century in Germany. Since it is impossible to analyze all of them here, only three will be discussed. They are symptomatic of the spatial feeling of the eighteenth century: either the grouping around a central square or the emphasis on axial development becomes the decisive element of planning.

The original plan of Neustrelitz in Mecklenburg, founded as a residential town for the dukes of Mecklenburg in 1733, showed a strictly centralized market square, quadrangular in shape and without a central structure, from which the streets radiated as in Karlsruhe. Today it is obscured through later changes.

Carlsruhe in Silesia was founded in 1743 for Karl Christian Erdmann, Duke of Württemberg-Oels, as one of the last settlements to be planned and founded in Germany. Today it is still not much more than a village with a castle in its center. The whole town consists of one circular square from which eight streets radiate. Only one sector is reserved for the princely park, contrary to the town's namesake in Baden. The layout, which incidentally is literally repeated in Hamina, Finland, represents one of the clearest and purest realizations of the old Renaissance scheme.

By far the most interesting among these small residential towns is one from the second part of the eighteenth century, Ludwigslust in Mecklenburg, founded by Duke Christian Ludwig II in 1747; the castle was not built until 1772–75. Here the various squares are not only the center of clearly defined geometric patterns but are actually inseparably integrated into the whole town plan. Le Geay, Busch, and von Seydewitz succeeded each other as architects, erecting various buildings for the court in reticent classicistic forms without changing the basic layout. As in Baden's Karlsruhe the final shape was eventually formed by the classicistic style of Friedrich Weinbrenner, so here, in Ludwigslust, the architect Barca defined the appearance of the whole town in the purest classicistic manner. He took over the two long main axes, which meet each other at the Schloss Platz, from the original layout of the eighteenth century. In imitation of the French scheme, the one axis originates from the castle with its large square, the Schloss Platz, before it. Stairs lead down from there to a large oval basin, and their direction is continued in a long alley to the Hofkirche, which becomes the final vista of this long axis. A second alley starting from the Schloss Platz leads to the palatial stables and is interrupted by one large circular square. The latter was originally an ellipsoid but the classicist Barca changed this typically baroque form into a rondel. The modest houses and structures for the court fit completely into the framework of water basin, canals, and greens, and a perfect fusion of the eighteenth-century layout with the classicistic architecture of the early nineteenth century is achieved (Pl. 81).

While in all these examples, from Mannheim and Karlsruhe to Neustrelitz and Ludwigslust, the castle with its *cour d'honneur* and public square became the nucleus of urban organization, an even greater number of princely residences exist where the courtyard remains merely an element of architecture and not a factor in city planning. In these instances the *cour d'honneur* proper is without any influence upon the town as a whole.

The *cours d'honneur* of Würzburg, Coblenz, and many other German princely residences clearly represent self-contained and limited cubes of space, simply architectural space-volume relationships. The space of the courtyard seems to be cut off from the surrounding volume and framed in crystal-clear architectural form.

In Würzburg (Fig. 49), an outstanding example of this relationship, the extraordinarily deep *cour d'honneur* of the palace can be seen and felt merely as part of the residence which embraces it in a pincerlike manner. The overpowering influence of Versailles upon the castle is undeniable. The castle was erected in 1720–44 by Johann Balthasar Neumann for the Fürstbischof Johann Philipp von Schönborn; but in contrast to Versailles, no spatial integration exists here between the *cour d'honneur* and the public square adjoining it. The square existed as a very irregular open area before the castle was built. Neumann reshaped it into a rectangle, but its wide expanse still belongs visually and spatially to the late medieval town rather than to the later baroque creation. In Versailles, the sequence Avenue de Paris-public square-exterior *cour d'honneur*-interior *cour d'honneur* is completely framed by symmetrical buildings, the symmetrical balustrade, and the side wings of the palace; the approaching viewer is directed straight toward the main entrance of the castle. In Würzburg, no common axis exists; the square in its main direction represents rather a broadening of a lateral street.

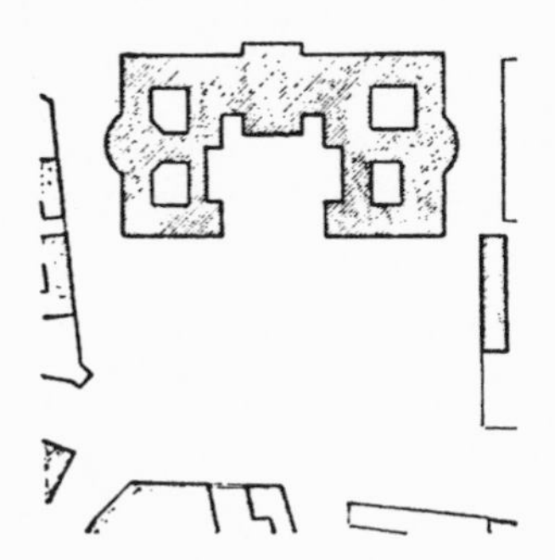

FIG. 49. WÜRZBURG. SQUARE BEFORE THE RESIDENCE. PLAN
From Sitte, *The Art of Building Cities*

This lack of spatial integration, so characteristic of Würzburg, is also evident in a large number of other contemporary princely residences. Original and creative as the architects of the German baroque were, it seems obvious that, in contrast to eighteenth-century French masters, their plastic imagination shaped *volume in space* rather than *space confined by volumes* such as squares. For example, such castles as those of Pommersfelden (1711–18, designed by Maximilian von Welsch and executed by Johann Dientzenhofer for Lothar Franz von Schönborn); Bruchsal (1720–52, designed by Maximilian von Welsch for Damian Hugo von Schönborn); and the classicistic castle of Coblenz (begun in 1777 by Michael d'Ixnard for Elector Clemens Wenzeslaus von Trier, and executed after 1779, on a rather reduced scale, by Antoine François Peyre)—all show the typical *cour d'honneur*. These courts, however, function merely as clear-cut elements of the overall architecture of the castle and never as the beginning of a far-reaching spatial integration in connection with the general urban development.

Some eighteenth-century squares in Germany, however, developed independent of any newly built castles. In these instances individual seventeenth- and eighteenth-century squares in Paris set the pattern. Ansbach, Erlangen-Neustadt, the little town of Karlshafen an der Weser, Kassel, and especially the eighteenth-century quarters of Berlin with their new squares are typical.

Shortly before and after the turn of the seventeenth century, a new period of planning additional parts in existing towns began in Germany. First, in 1665, there was a project for a new quarter of the small residential town of Ansbach to be settled by French Huguenots. Its layout represented an interesting combination of the German town of Freudenstadt from 1632 and of the French town of Charleville from 1608–20: a checkerboard scheme with one larger square in the center and smaller ones in each of the four corners. Peculiarly the five squares were not formed by empty blocks but were created by receding corners of the built-over blocks themselves. The squares would thus have appeared tightly closed in spite of the four streets running into each square. However, this rather playful project was never executed.

Only one year later another haven for French Protestants was actually founded: a new quarter in Erlangen, the Neustadt, was connected with the medieval town. It was laid out by Johann Moritz Richter. When in 1706 the older quarters burned down, this section of the town was rebuilt in the usual checkerboard scheme. Within the combined new and old towns several squares were arranged, a very large one in front of the castle (today the Schlossplatz), another, the Holzmarkt, as market square—all axially connected. Originally all surrounding houses were two-storied. In spite of the much smaller dimensions in Erlangen, the influence of French *places royales* is clearly recognizable, and from now on this influence increases continuously.

Two other foundations in Germany stem from the same period when the French trend for regularity found its echo in Germany, although in rather free variations. In Karlshafen on the Weser River, the architect Paul du Ry together with the German engineer Conradi laid out the traditional gridiron scheme in 1699, again in order to settle French Huguenots. The inner part of the central square is occupied by a large harbor basin linked with the Weser River and surrounded by low embankments. Thus the surface of the water substitutes for a paved floor in the three-dimensional expansion of the square, not unlike the better-known and far larger Innen-

A: SALAMANCA. PLAZA MAYOR
Photo Kindel

B: BURGOS. PLAZA MAYOR
Photo Laurent

GERONA. STEPS LEADING TOWARD THE CATHEDRAL

Photo Mas, Barcelona

A: PRAÇA DO COMÉRCIO. AERIAL VIEW
Photo Pan American World Airways System, New York

LISBON

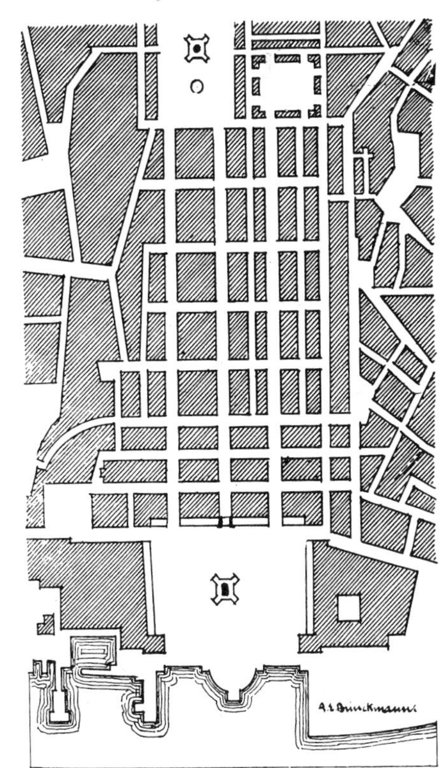

B: CIDADE BAIXA. PLAN

LISBON. THE ROCIO (PRAÇA DE DOM PEDRO IV). AERIAL VIEW

Photo Pan American World Airways System, New York

Alster in Hamburg. In its time, the specific charm of town and square in Karlshafen were highly praised by a contemporary writer, Stefan Winterberg. In his *Oratio Panegyrica* he describes how the whole town appears to be one single house because of its complete uniformity.

The same Paul du Ry also planned the Oberneustadt of Kassel during the last decade of the seventeenth century for expelled Protestants and within it the rectangular Friedrichsplatz, which is too large to evoke any definite spatial reaction. Almost one century later, his grandson Simon Louis du Ry designed a rondel, the Königsplatz, stimulated doubtlessly by Parisian squares and by Patte's publication. It was to be surrounded by houses of equal height, and its present-day appearance still creates a spatial center which commands the perspectives of the six streets which radiate from it, one of them connecting it with the older Friedrichsplatz.

Compared with other and much smaller residential towns and capitals of German principalities and duchies, Berlin, Prussia's capital, did not mirror her political weight in grandiose architectural or city planning developments. Only a project by Andreas Schlüter (1664–1714), one of the greatest German sculptors and architects, showed ambitions to beautify this still provincial town. Unfortunately it was never executed. Thus, in spite of the genius of this great baroque artist and in spite of the fact that the royal castle and some private palaces bear testimony to his art, Berlin has never become a baroque city. Its profile has rather been shaped by the later periods of the typical Zopf style and of classicism.

In 1702, Schlüter had planned a monumental square in the axis of the Lange Brücke as a continuation of the Königstrasse (Pl. 82A). This bridge was built by Johann Arnold Nering in 1692–95 and was monumentalized by one of the most original equestrian statues of the baroque, that of the Great Elector by Schlüter. As the focal point of the square opposite the bridge, a domed church, reminiscent of Roman baroque churches, was to be erected and the sides of the square were to be flanked by Schlüter's royal castle on the one side and a corresponding architecture to house the royal stables on the other side.

The strict axiality of this square with its dominating church architecture would have presented, by its partially Roman, partially French character, a space concept entirely alien to the small town, which was still of provincial character in spite of its 60,000 inhabitants. Berlin never developed into a city organized by axes, notwithstanding its one monumental avenue, Unter den Linden, planned in 1673.

The town had been fortified under the Great Elector (1640–88), and foreign architects, foremost among them the Dutchman Nering, had erected some larger buildings. But the decisive development took place under the first King of Prussia, Friedrich I (1688–1713), who had not only commissioned Schlüter for monumental tasks like the royal castle, palaces of nobility, and the monument to his predecessor, but had also added whole new quarters like the Friedrichstadt, planned in a gridiron scheme. Under the following king, Friedrich Wilhelm I, three pedantically geometric squares were laid out: the Quarré (later the Pariser Platz) in the form of a regular quadrangle; the Rondell (later the Belle-Alliance Platz), based on a circular plan; and the Octagon (later the Leipziger Platz), laid out as an octagon; all of these were constructed between 1734 and 1737. No individual architects can be associated with the basic layouts of these squares since their designs were just another task of public administration for the king in his Spartan austerity. Originally they were planned as being surrounded by uniform houses, but the parsimony of the king did not allow their simultaneous erection and thus their spatial effect cannot be compared with other German squares of that time.

The Pariser Platz with its gate terminates the avenue Unter den Linden toward the encircling town wall (Pls. 3A and 82B). The dimensions of the square in relation to the width of the Unter den Linden are too small to evoke any monumental impression per se. Only with the erection of the Brandenburg Gate in 1789–93, by Carl Gotthard Langhans (1733–1808), and its two adjoining smaller buildings was a truly monumental vista created. This gate was to become much more than a pale classicistic imitation of the Propylaea in Athens, for its very proportions dignified the otherwise indifferent architecture around the square. It served not merely as a decorative triumphal arch but opened as a real gateway with a view into the great adjoining section, the Tiergarten.

The Octagon, today's Leipziger Platz (Pl. 83A), repeated the pattern of the Place Hoche in Versailles and, in different proportions, the Place Vendôme in Paris, a scheme which was taken up again in Amalienborg Square in Copenhagen (see p. 225). Actually it is the only architecturally meaningful square among the three then planned in Berlin. Its monumentality was generally recognized, as may be deduced from two later projects for this square: Friedrich Gilly's plan for a monumental tomb for Frederick the Great (1797) and Carl Friedrich Schinkel's project for a tremendous Gothic cathedral to be erected at the same site (1811). However, neither was ever executed. The spatial effect of the Leipziger Platz was completely destroyed by meaningless planting during the nineteenth century, as happened so often.

The third gate-square of this period, the Rondell (today's Belle-Alliance Platz), represents an almost amusing example of the influence of Italian and French city planning on artistically less developed nations during the eighteenth century. One might almost call it a bourgeois version of the Piazza del Popolo in Rome, with three streets also starting from it and the gate leading into the open country (Pl. 83B). As in the two aforementioned Berlin squares, the surrounding uniform houses were never executed but instead only rather heterogeneous structures were erected; nor was the fountain in the center ever realized. Only as late as 1843 was a decorative column erected to stress the center. At the Belle-Alliance Platz, too, the basic layout, monumental in its two-dimensional projection, did not work out three-dimensionally. It is as if the dry middle-class atmosphere of Berlin, untouched by international contacts, had impeded a true development of imported ideas of design. In other non-Prussian towns of equal size in Germany it was the spirit of cultured and ambitious princes that made artistic development flourish.

Different in every respect is the Gendarmen Markt in Berlin, located in the newly founded Friedrichstadt. Although it is a closed rectangle in its ground plan, no definite spatial limits are perceivable since the dimensions of the square are too vast. On this former Linden Markt two churches had been erected, in 1701 and 1708 respectively—the Französischer Dom by Cayart and Quesnay, and the Deutscher Dom by Gruenberg—which in no way were tied into an overall organization. In the second part of the eighteenth century, Frederick the Great aimed at giving the square a monumental appearance and had Carl von Gontard superimpose two domed towers above the existing church buildings (in 1780–85)—without any inner structural connection. The example of the two churches on the Piazza del Popolo is undeniable but no organic connection between square and architecture was achieved here on the Gendarmen Markt. Again, the surrounding houses planned uniformly by Gontard were never erected and the Prussian St. Mark's Square of which Frederick the Great had dreamed never came true. Nor was a pretentious project of 1772 by Bourdet, consisting of four monumental entrance gates into the closed square, ever realized. Even the addition of a third building between the churches, a theater by Bouman the Elder in 1774, which was later replaced by Langhans's theater in 1801–10, and eventually by Carl Friedrich Schinkel's Schauspielhaus, could never bring about the desired spatial effect. Theoretically the complex of these three structures should have created a typical nuclear square. The discrepancy between the expanse of the open area, the height of the cupolas, and the irregularity and relative smallness of the surrounding buildings worked against any predominance of the nuclear volumes, before the area of the square was spoiled by the landscaping and monuments of the nineteenth century.

Two squares in Munich, located close to each other, offer very characteristic examples of the development of nineteenth-century classicism in Germany. Karl Fischer designed, during the first third of that century, the circular Karolinen Platz, surrounded by small private houses, partially still extant. The whole concept shows the typical reluctant shyness of early German classicism. Its lack of pretension expresses itself in the spatial appearance of the square—unobtrusive and completely natural—with its reticent proportions and only loosely arrayed individual buildings. The obelisk in the center was erected in 1833.

Quite to the contrary, the nearby Königs Platz, in the same axis of the Briennerstrasse, was developed as a pet project of King Ludwig I from 1816 to 1848, using the fullest orchestration to impress the beholder. The rectangular layout of the square, with its pompous classicistic buildings at three sides—the Propyläen (1848–62), the Glyptothek, and the Kunstsammlungs-Gebäude—proves a conscious planning for striking monumentality. The final result presents actually a dehydrated classicistic showpiece where only the architectural forms count and no overall space-volume relations exist. The general influence of Ledoux and Gilly, from the late eighteenth century, cannot be denied, though in both architects' work the space effect is decisive. It must be admitted, however, that, in contrast to the original incongruous nineteenth-century green, the uniform pavement of today, enforced by

Hitler's ambition for monumentality, ties the framing structures together somewhat.

AUSTRIA AND SWITZERLAND. All these squares in Germany had been planned under the suggestive stimulation of the "classical" French examples. A small number of squares in southeastern Germany, Austria, and Switzerland, however, were obviously influenced by the great Italian baroque tradition of the seventeenth century. This influence becomes most obvious in Vienna. There the network of streets in the inner city is so thoroughly medieval that there was hardly a possibility for any spatial developments comparable to Italian standards. Nonetheless, the city of the Hapsburgs had the ambition of competing with other capitals of Europe.

The Graben, for instance, an ancient Roman moat, had originally marked the limits of the town toward the southwest and had served in the Middle Ages as the most important market place of the town; mention is made of it as early as 1294. In spite of its very limited width and its rather irregular boundaries, it was newly furnished in the seventeenth century with three monuments. A column, the Dreifaltigkeitssäule (1687–93), one of the most characteristic works of Austrian baroque sculpture, by Burnacini and Johann Bernhard Fischer von Erlach, was erected between two fountains. At first glance, this organization reminds one of the Piazza Navona in Rome, in spite of entirely different dimensions. In order to imitate the relationship of Sant' Agnese and the Piazza Navona, Vienna's oldest church, St. Peter's, was rebuilt in 1702–33, probably by Fischer von Erlach. This attempt was doomed to fail, however, since the Viennese church does not border the square proper as does Sant' Agnese on the Piazza Navona, but is separated from it by a small parvis. Notwithstanding all these endeavors, the Graben remains a medieval thoroughfare with baroque decoration.

The same pattern is employed on another square in the inner town, the Am Hofe. Again, an originally medieval square where pageants and tournaments had unfolded their splendor was modernized in the fashion of the seventeenth century: the fifteenth-century Gothic church, Zu den Neun Chören der Engel, was changed into a baroque structure in 1607, and its baroque appearance was completed by Carlone's façade of 1662; the Bürgerliche Zeughaus and other older structures underwent similar changes in the baroque spirit. Again the scheme of the Piazza Navona was imitated by placing three monuments to accentuate the long axis: the Mariensäule by Balthasar Herold (1667) and two fountains. Later engravings, such as the one by Salomon Kleiner from 1725 (Pls. 84A and 85) where the irregular layout, the obliqueness of the sides, and especially the narrow width are suppressed by means of a grotesquely wrong perspective, indicate an awareness of the shortcomings of such architectural plagiarism when applied to inadequate spatial means.

In two other instances in Vienna, the attempt to lend a baroque appearance to a spatially indifferent and inarticulated square was made. On the Hohe Markt, Fischer von Erlach, together with Carradini, erected the Joseph's Fountain and thus changed the ancient Roman forum into a very small nuclear square, surrounded by uniform eighteenth-century houses. The space functions here merely as an envelope for the volume of the fountain (Pl. 84B). On the Neue Markt, which is not much more than a widened street, it is again only the fountain by Raphael Donner (1739) that counts.

Vienna with its squares proves most convincingly that later period furnishings alone, even if done by the greatest contemporary artists like Fischer von Erlach, Donner, etc., could not overcome the given spatial limitations set by earlier centuries.

The great courtyard of the Zwinger in Dresden, built in 1711–22 by Matthäus Daniel Pöppelmann, under Augustus II (1670–1733), belongs rather to this Austrian baroque world than to its local environment. Pöppelmann envisioned the whole as a kind of stage architecture, a one-storied gallery, accentuated by seven two-storied pavilions, and serving simultaneously as an orangery. Located in the vicinity of the oldest Elbe bridge, the Augustus Brücke (built originally in 1119, later rebuilt), of the Catholic Court Church and the Opera House (formerly a theater), and of the later Guard House, the area of the Zwinger is in no way related to those individual structures—a proof that this princely courtyard was considered as an independent enclosure, and therefore not as an element of town planning. It was meant merely as a kind of monumentalized, permanent grandstand for the spectators of court festivities, ballets, pageants, and tournaments—one of those grandstands, mostly provisional wooden structures, to be encountered in almost all German capitals at the beginning of the eighteenth century. The influence of Bernini's colonnades for St. Peter's Square, perhaps also of Jean Marot's project for the castle of Mannheim—both true public squares—on the design of the Zwinger cannot be denied. Thus the Zwinger is often considered a public square, while actually it represents an independent structure with a large inner open area—to a certain extent comparable to the English collegiate squares in their identically ambivalent spatial character.

Vienna and Dresden prove the impact of Italian baroque on squares north of the Alps. Certainly they cannot compete with the achievements of Italian town planning in spatial and aesthetic perfection. In Vienna, the tensely knit web of a thoroughly medieval plan did not allow the three-dimensional expansion necessary for the formation of grand squares; in Dresden, the specific destination of the Zwinger as part of a princely residence made a meaningful structural integration with the town as a whole impossible.

Occasionally, however, the fusion of Italian and northern trends creates impressive townscapes, for instance, the group of squares around the cathedral in Salzburg, Austria, and the grandiose entrance terraces to the monastery in Einsiedeln, Switzerland.

During the seventeenth century Salzburg became the fountainhead of Italian influence in Austria and Germany. Vincenzo Scamozzi, called to Salzburg from Venice, began the rebuilding of the cathedral in 1611 and was the first to introduce the spatial concepts and the stylistic vernacular of the Italian baroque into Austria on the largest possible scale. Although Antonio Solari reduced Scamozzi's originally more grandiose design for the cathedral in 1614, its structure and the completed façade of 1654 were still impressive enough to become the centerpiece of the three squares which surround the church. The Archbishop Wolf Dietrich (1587–1612) was responsible for the organization of these three squares, for which end he had razed older houses and an earlier church at the same spot.

The Cathedral Square, known the world over through the staging of the Salzburg Festival, was chosen for this purpose because it is completely closed, stretching in front of the church toward the west (Pl. 86). Its actual connection with the two adjacent squares is visually disguised through two-storied colonnades, which frame the church on both sides. They serve as links between the church façade and the lateral residence on the one side, and the cloisters of St. Peter's on the other side. At the west, similar colonnades close the square toward the axial Franziskaner Gasse. The center of the square is marked by a column, the Mariensäule, by Wolfgang and Johannes Hagenauer of 1771.

Two other squares stretch along the north and south sides of the cathedral, both larger than the Cathedral Square proper: the Residence Square and the Capital Square. The Capital Square on the south side corresponds roughly to the Residence Square and is decorated by the Kapitel Schwemme, an imitation of Roman fountains. The Residence Square is flanked by the Residence (1592–1724); opposite this is the Neugebäude, begun in 1788. In the center of the square is the rather tall Hofbrunnen by Antonio Dario (1680), who worked also on the Residence. This square is connected by a wide opening with still another square, the Mozart Square, on which is located the composer's house of birth and which includes his monument in the center. The wide-open connection between the Residence Square and the Mozart Square contrasts with the rather narrow and camouflaged exit to the Cathedral Square in the diagonal corner.

This configuration of three, or rather four, squares in Salzburg differs in principle from the axial sequences in Copenhagen (see p. 225) and Nancy as much as it does from the grouped squares in Venice and Bologna. The integration of the individual spatial units in Salzburg is complete, achieved paradoxically by spatial and visual contrasts. The Cathedral Square appears as a completely closed parvis, whereas the others by their very expanse create a spatial transition between townscape and surrounding landscape. Mountainous contours become the background vista. Although the colonnades close the Cathedral Square visually, they lend to this area at the same time a feeling of potential movement toward the two other squares; they are not at all "Raumtrümmer mit Rückansichten" (space fragments with rear views), as Brinckmann calls them. Thus a suspended tension is brought forth through the contrast between free overall movement and the definiteness of spatial enclosure on the Cathedral Square, a fluctuation and shift of vistas which is typical of Austrian baroque feeling.

Salzburg and its architectural atmosphere no doubt strongly influenced the planning and development of the monastery, the Stiftskirche, and the square in Einsiedeln in Switzerland, an old center of pilgrimages (Pl. 87). In the galaxy of Italian, German, and Austrian baroque artists active at Einsiedeln we encounter the names of many artists who also had worked in

Salzburg. The monastery was founded as early as 934; it was continually remodeled and rebuilt. The present structure is the sixth consecutive one on the same site above the small town. During the second half of the seventeenth century some parts were begun which were later incorporated in the final plan of Brother Caspar Moosbrugger (1656–1723), who started planning the present building in 1703. After his death the work was continued in 1724 by his brother Johannes Moosbrugger and other architects. The façade of the Stiftskirche, which in its typical baroque curvature may have been influenced by Fischer von Erlach's Salzburger Kollegienkirche, was completed in 1758. This façade accentuates the center of the very long west side of the monastery, itself a very elaborate and complex organization with four inner courtyards and cloisters. The incline of the hill, gradually sloping before the west side of the monastery, is overcome by a combination of wide, curved ramps, arcades, and steps, the last in direct continuation of the long axis of the church. In front of these steps, twice interrupted by ramps, the pilgrims would drink from a little fountain by Hans Georg Kuen (erected in 1684–86) with a statue of the Virgin by Domenico Pozzi from about 1748. The arcades, behind which are little shops for devotional gifts, embrace the central ramp in a wide half-circle and are crowned by sculpturally decorated rails.

The whole area appears as a typical baroque stage setting for the unfolding processions of pilgrims. Quite obviously it is not a parvis in the traditional sense of the word, that is, a mere anteroom before a church, but instead represents a spatial rhythmization of naturally given topographical conditions. And as in Salzburg, the whole organization turns into a transition from architecture to landscape. Although the baroque employs its own stylistic devices here, other earlier combinations of squares and staircases immediately come to mind, such as Kos, Erfurt, and above all S. Trinità al Monte in Rome.

DENMARK. The trend toward classicism, so characteristic of eighteenth-century planning in northern Germany, is also typical of the Scandinavian countries. There the decisive development took place in Denmark. The Swedes never succeeded in a clear organization of their capital Stockholm, neither of the town as a whole nor in the creation of any squares of artistic importance. The various successive plans for Stockholm from 1640 on left no remarkable traces on the city, and Stockholm had to wait until the twentieth century for a successful amalgamation of town vista and surrounding landscape.

In Denmark, the interest in town planning had begun in the seventeenth century under Christian IV (ruled 1588 to 1648) and had led to specific laws concerning urban organization at an earlier date than in other Central European countries. Technical and aesthetic stimulation came essentially from Holland, whence architects and engineers were called, although the achievements in town planning in that country were certainly not outstanding.

Small fortified towns with regular gridiron layouts and quadrangular squares, strongly reminiscent of the thirteenth-century French bastides, were founded by the king, such as Christianstad (1614), Christiansand (1641), and Fredericia in Jutland, which was completed under his son. In Norway, which then belonged to Denmark, Christian IV had Christiania (today Oslo) rebuilt in 1624; it was fortified and was laid out on a gridiron scheme. How widespread this scheme was in the north is proved by the contemporaneous foundation of Goteborg, in Sweden, by King Gustavus Adolphus. In all these towns the squares were never more than free areas interrupting the rows of regular city blocks, without any artistic pretension and, of course, also without any spatial impact.

The only interesting foundation made by Christian IV was a small fortress, Glückstadt, then Danish, today in northern Germany. It was destined as a settlement for political refugees during the Thirty Years War. Laid out by a Frenchman, Pacherval, it realized faithfully, in 1629, the radio-centric schemes of Perret and Errard some years after their publication. It was the last of three radio-centric towns planned under Christian IV, and the only one actually executed.

The two other similar projects concerned expansions for Denmark's capital Copenhagen: Christianshavn (1617) and New Copenhagen (1629). The first, designed by Johan Semp as an independent fortress on a small island opposite the old capital, was planned as an incomplete nonagon with bastions at each corner. From the central square main arteries radiated. Noteworthy is the fact that the secondary streets ran parallel to the sides of the central square between the radiating avenues. Because of this specific organization the scheme reminds one very much of Freudenstadt in Germany.

Christian IV had planned the whole of Copenhagen to be rebuilt into a radial town of which Christianshavn would have been only one section. Another part would have been New Copenhagen, also a radio-centric project with an octagonal square as center, designed by Richard Douchette in 1629. However, while neither monumental vision was executed, these quarters were later built in regular gridiron schemes, like all other towns founded under Christian IV with the one exception of Glückstadt.

Later in the century, under King Christian V (ruled 1670 to 1699), an attempt was made to create something like a royal square in Copenhagen—Kongens Nytorv—obviously with the intention of imitating French and Italian examples (Pl. 88A). However, the attempt never came off. At the east side of a large free area, owned by the king, a palace was begun in 1672 (now Charlottenborg) for the illegitimate son of the king, Ulric Frederik Gyldenløve. In front of it, a statue of the king was erected by Lamoureux in 1688, around which concentric rows of trees were planted in the manner of a Dutch garden. Twelve streets ran at different irregular angles into the "square." Although the elements for a genuine square—palace, statue, and regular landscaping—were given, the irregular placing of additional, entirely incongruous buildings destroyed any possibility of a unified appearance and still less any definite spatial shape of the enclosure. The square, today one of the liveliest traffic centers in Copenhagen, is still as irregular as it ever was, especially since the original, regular landscaping has given way to the confusion of modern times. An interval of two generations following this unsuccessful attempt was needed before Denmark's capital developed its true *place royale*—and one of the most beautiful squares in Europe to boot—Amalienborg.

It certainly is no exaggeration to rank Amalienborg Square (Pl. 88B), although it is on a smaller scale, with the Imperial Fora, St. Mark's Square and Piazzetta in Venice, St. Peter's Square in Rome, and Nancy, as one of the most perfect realizations of grouped squares. The sequence of separate space units becomes a comprehensive spatial figuration. It is hard to believe that the master of Amalienborg, the Danish architect Nicolai Eidtveg (1701–54), had never seen Paris, so closely related is his creation to the *places royales* in France. It breathes grandeur, a northern Puritan grandeur, but still grandeur!

In 1749, during the reign of Frederick V, Eidtveg began building four identical two-storied palaces with attics and high roofs for members of the Danish nobility. They became the basic structures of an octagonal square whose other four sides were occupied by smaller, lower buildings with corner pavilions. These pavilions flanked the entrance of two streets, the Amaliengade and Fredericksgade, crossing here at angles of 90 degrees. In the center of the square, Jacques François Sally, in 1771, placed an equestrian monument to King Frederick V (ruled 1746 to 1766). The Fredericksgade opens a vista toward the harbor on the one side and in the opposite direction connects the Amalienborg Square with a small quadrangle on which Jardin, in 1749, built the monumental Frederickskirke (the Marble Church)—not quite as originally planned by Eidtveg. The church was completed only in the last quarter of the nineteenth century. The axial sequence reminds one of the relationship between the Place de la Concorde and the Madeleine church. Although the octagonal layout had been employed before in the Place Hoche in Versailles, the Place Vendôme in Paris, and the Leipziger Platz in Berlin, here another, different spatial effect is achieved: the regular alternation between the height of the four monumental palaces on the one hand and of the subordinated smaller entrance pavilions on the other hand creates a fluctuating rhythm which lends a certain visual freedom to the square. This freedom corresponds exactly to the French ideals of the eighteenth century, when the compactness of the previous seventeenth-century squares was criticized. A monumental effect is created through the extension of the visual axis of the Fredericksgade. It is the sequence from harbor to monument and finally the continuation of the Fredericksgade to the imposing cupola of the Frederickskirke which makes the beholder aware of the relatively limited dimensions of the whole organization.

SPAIN AND PORTUGAL. In a survey of great European squares of the seventeenth and eighteenth centuries, Spain, like the Netherlands, is of only secondary importance. Relatively few of her squares mirror the general European trends of this period. By the very reasons which left Spain separated from typical European developments during the Renaissance, European squares from the seventeenth and eighteenth centuries did not much influence the overall appearance of Spanish towns. It was seemingly very difficult for the Spaniards of later centuries to disentangle the clusters of crooked, entwined streets which the Moors had left.

Generally the ordinary plazas of Spanish towns are located approximately in the center of the town. The arcades which surround most of them rarely provide a definite architectural framework.

Only two squares in Spain fit roughly the basic ideas of the seventeenth and eighteenth centuries elsewhere in Europe: the Plaza Mayor in Madrid and the Plaza Mayor in Salamanca. In 1617, Philip III began remodeling the very irregular market square in the center of Madrid, which by then had become the capital of Spain. Juan Gómez de Mora laid out a completely regular rectangle, the Pandería of 1590, along an already existing building, razing older structures to do so. The regular shape of the area, in strong contrast to the irregular network of adjacent medieval streets, is obviously influenced by the prototype of all *places royales*, the Place des Vosges in Paris. However, no statue emphasized the center here (the present monument of Philip III by Giovanni da Bologna was erected only in 1848). Seven streets run into the square under various angles at irregularly distributed points. Nevertheless, a certain unity is achieved by the equal height of the almost uniform six-storied houses with their arcades which not only surround the square, covering the street entrances, but are also continued into some of the streets. Whereas the Parisian example represents the center of a residential quarter, the Plaza Mayor in Madrid is an impressive stage on which tournaments and bullfights, autos-da-fé and canonizations (e.g., of Ignatius of Loyola) took place under the enthusiastic applause of some 50,000 spectators, as contemporaries proudly recorded. Today, its festive appearance has been destroyed completely by landscaping, a change so typical of the nineteenth century.

In the eighteenth century, Madrid tried once more to compete with Parisian squares, but none of the various interesting projects was ever executed. These projects centered essentially around the royal castle. The large project of Ventura Rodriguez (*ca.* 1755–60) is known only through contemporaneous descriptions, whereas the layout of a project by Sacchetti of 1757 is still preserved (Fig. 50). In its strict axiality this latter plan is obviously influenced by the sequence of squares in Nancy. It differs from Nancy only by its arcades, which frame the main avenue and which are continued around both squares before the palace. The scheme definitely appears as a totally alien concept within the layout of Madrid as it had grown throughout the centuries.

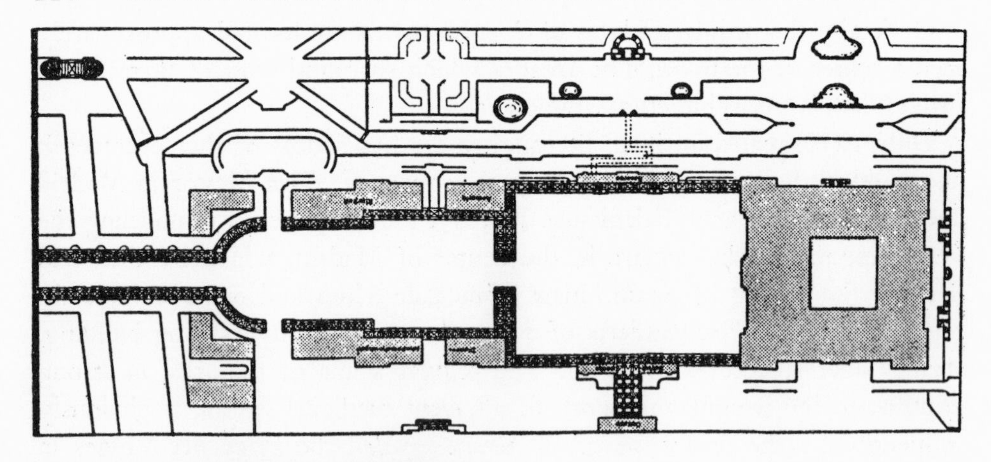

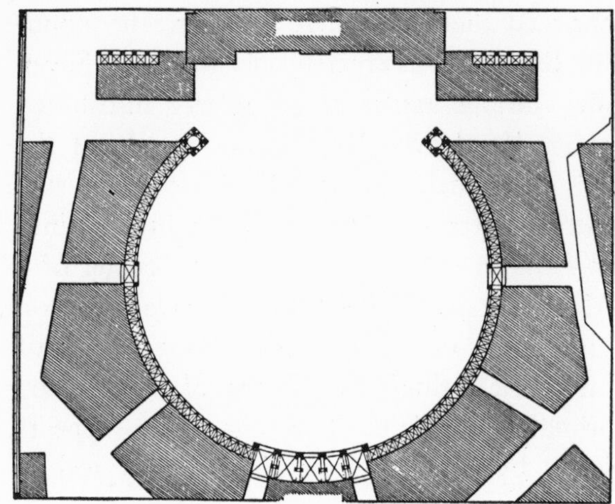

FIG. 50. MADRID. PROJECTS FOR REMODELING THE QUARTERS AROUND THE ROYAL CASTLE BY (ABOVE) SACCHETTI (1757) AND (LEFT) ISIDORO VELASQUEZ AND LUIS DE OLIVIETTA (1830)

From Jürgens, *Spanische Städte*

In the first decade of the nineteenth century, Joseph Bonaparte, during his brief reign, tried also to remodel Madrid along French ideas by embellishing it with new squares. However, he did not succeed in making any essential change, acquiring only the nickname *Rey Plazuelas* (the king of squares) through his endeavors.

Still more out of place in this Spanish environment was an attempt by Isidoro Velasquez and Luis de Olivietta from 1830 (Fig. 50). They tried to change the area in front of the palace into a pale imitation of the Place des Victoires in Paris and attempted to combine the star square with the qualities of a representative closed area, comparable in its festive character to the earlier Plaza Mayor in Madrid and Salamanca.

Salamanca's Plaza Mayor, dating from 1720–33, is generally regarded as Spain's most beautiful square (Pl. 89A). It had preserved its medieval irregularity until the early eighteenth century. Resembling contemporary Parisian examples, it is framed by uniform four-storied houses with arcades by Andreas Garcia de Quinones (after 1720); the town hall by Nicolas Churriguera (died 1725) is slightly higher. The square owes its monumental splendor to the strict discipline of its surrounding structures: the continuous repetition of horizontals which are contrasted with the vertical motif of ornamental Bourbon lilies on the balustrades of the roofs. Streets run into the square without destroying its closed character since their entrances are hidden behind the arcades. Contrary to the French *places royales*, no statue accentuates the center. In the immediate vicinity toward the east is the Plaza de la Verdura, the market place, which fulfills the function of business and administrative center, so that the Plaza Mayor still remains the representative square of the town today.

The Plaza Mayor in Burgos (Pl. 89B) probably is most typically Spanish because here the irregularity of the old medieval quarters is still preserved in its ground plan, a pentagon with uneven sides. Located at the outer edge of the town, behind one of the old town gates, the square was gradually remodeled in the seventeenth century by surounding it with almost uniform houses. Their façades are of the utmost simplicity, connected with each other by plain arcades. In this way a closed area is created whose actual irregularity does not become immediately evident because of a statue of Charles III, erected in its center in 1784. The reticent classicism of the surrounding architecture proves that the French influence had affected the appearance of the square only in larger cities. The small provincial town of Burgos, already in decay in the seventeenth century, obviously subordinated the appearance of her largest square to the towering monumentality of her famous Gothic cathedral, visible from the square and dominating it, in spite of its location about two blocks away.

The only overall town planning development of the eighteenth century in Spain started from a castle built in Aranjuez by Philip V in 1727. Aranjuez had been a favorite *buen retiro* of the Spanish court already under the Emperor Charles V, and his successors had their hunting ground there and had created large parks and gardens. Philip V's palace of 1727, destroyed by fire, was rebuilt by Ferdinand VI in 1748, and was once more enlarged by

Charles III in 1775–78. This palace, the site of many important events in Spain's history, became the hub for two fanlike developments in the layout of town and park at Aranjuez (Fig. 51). From the U-shaped court of the Palacio Real six alleys radiate and subdivide the park with its world-famous fountains and water displays, the whole emulating the layout of the park of Versailles. On the other side of the palace, the small town, planned by

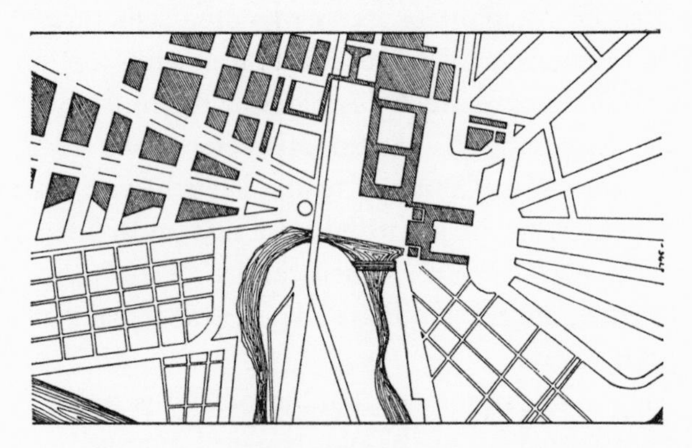

FIG. 51. ARANJUEZ. PLAN OF PALACE AND SURROUNDINGS

Ferdinand VI in 1750 for 20,000 inhabitants, but never fully developed, is cut by three main avenues. They converge, corresponding to the fan pattern of the park, in front of the palace on a rather shapeless square. The principle of the organization reminds one of the almost contemporary plan of Mannheim, both being equally dependent on the great French example.

The actual main square of Aranjuez, the Plaza de la Libertad, is independent of the axis of the castle. The square is framed on both long sides of the regular rectangle by almost uniform houses with arcades except for a small part which borders the gardens of Isabella II. Identical arcades close the south side in slight curves, with the Chapel of San Antonio in the center. The north side is open and connects the Plaza de la Libertad with the small square before the palace, the Parterre de Palacio. The dimensions of the square are too large, compared with the relatively low structures which surround it, to achieve a unified spatial impression in spite of its regularity and the nuclear fountain in its middle axis.

Often the configuration of church and parvis on different levels, so characteristic of medieval Spain (see p. 133), found its true articulation only in the seventeenth and eighteenth centuries. In Gerona, for instance, a grandiose open staircase leads immediately from the landing before the west façade of the cathedral (dating from the fourteenth and fifteenth centuries) down to its parvis (Pl. 90). However, these stairs were added only in 1607. Their three flights are interrupted by balustraded landings. The movement is channeled downward toward the parvis, but at the same time temporarily arrested. Since this monumental staircase occupies the larger part of the free area before the church, it becomes an integral part of the square proper and lifts the church far above the everyday life of the town. The whole scheme, though on a much smaller scale, is comparable to the Scala di Spagna in Rome.

The most beautiful and the most important square on the Iberian peninsula is not Spanish, but Portuguese. To call it at the same time also the most characteristic Portuguese square would be misleading since it is essentially French, a typical *place royale*. The Praça do Comércio in Lisbon, on the banks of the Tagus River, has often been compared with two other marinas, the Piazzetta in Venice and the Place de la Bourse in Bordeaux, the earliest among the *places royales* of Louis XV. Actually it resembles the latter more, while sharing with the Piazzetta only the open vista over the adjacent surface of water (Pl. 91A).

After the catastrophic destruction of Lisbon by earthquake and conflagration in 1755, King Joseph I (ruled 1750 to 1777), under the guidance of his minister, the ingenious Marquês de Pombal, began immediately the reconstruction of its central part, the Cidade Baixa. Pombal developed exact plans which changed completely the character of the town located between the estuary of the Tagus River and the surrounding hills. A gridiron scheme was laid out between two monumental squares, the Praça do Comércio and the Praça de Dom Pedro IV, with the Rua Augusta as the backbone leading from the center of the Praça do Comércio northward toward the Praça de Dom Pedro, paralleled by two other streets, the Rua d'Ouro and the Rua da Prato (Pl. 91B). Precise building laws provided for such details as leveling the terrain, the width of the avenues and cross streets, and the proportions of public and private buildings. In 1758 actual reconstruction began under the leadership of two architects, Eugenio dos Santos Carvalho (Praça do Comércio) and Carlos Mardell (Praça de Dom Pedro IV).

Three-storied uniform buildings with continuous arcades surround the Praça do Comércio on three sides. Higher pavilion-like structures terminate the row of lateral buildings toward the quai; a triumphal arch in the center of the northern building, opposite the water, accentuates the entrance to the

Rua Augusta. The fourth side opens toward the river, with facilities for disembarkation. The public and representative character of this square as gateway to the city is established by the function of the surrounding buildings as government offices for various departments, court of justice, courthouse, etc. In the center of the square a monument to Joseph I was erected by Joaquim Machado in 1775.

The monumentality of the Praça do Comércio results from the relationship between the rather tall central monument and the relatively limited height of the surrounding buildings. In this way a visual impression is achieved which paradoxically may be described as openness of a closed square, by means of which a perfect transition is made from the horizontal surface of the water to the man-made structure of the town and the amphitheater of the hills behind. There are very few squares (among them, the Piazza in Venice, St. Peter's Square in Rome) where the horizontal area of the floor is of the same decisive importance for the total spatial effect.

The Praça do Comércio and smaller sections of post-earthquake Lisbon were imitated with slight modifications in the Portuguese colonies in South America, e.g., in Rio de Janeiro, in the same way as plans of North American settlements frequently show partial reminiscences of the "old" country.

Lisbon's Praça de Dom Pedro IV, better known as the Rocio ("Rolling Square," because of the wavy pattern of its mosaic pavement, which was taken up on a larger scale later in Rio de Janeiro), is the commercial center of the town, in contrast to the representative and administrative function of the Praça do Comércio (Pl. 92). The Rua Augusta and the Rua d'Ouro, which link this square with the Praça do Comércio, enter it at the outer corners. Here also the Marquês de Pombal had planned uniform structures. Today the surrounding houses have at least kept similar proportions and equal fenestration. The oblong square with its two fountains and the central column impresses the spectator less through its spatial qualities than by the prominence of the two-dimensional patterns of its pavement.

BAROQUE AND CLASSICISTIC CONCEPTS OF EXTERNAL SPACE

The problem arises whether the two stylistic trends which began in the second half of the sixteenth century, the Michelangelesque-Berninesque baroque and Palladian-French academic classicism, expressed themselves in spatial concepts of *entirely different nature* or whether actually *a common and basic element* can be discovered beyond their stated differences.

To answer this question it is necessary to summarize once more the different trends of development in space, in the creation of squares within their given environment.

From its very beginning, the so-called Roman baroque, from Michelangelo to Specchi, and its various national variations showed the desire to mold space as a free-flowing continuum with a gradually increasing emphasis on visual arrests—*fermatas*. This continuum, seemingly infinite, is to be perceived through a sequence of different vistas (from the Campidoglio to the Piazza di Spagna). Individual architectural elements, although always self-sufficient and never fragmentary, are yet interconnected by extended views, the one farther away always based on the existence of the one closer by. The purpose of this interconnection is to astonish the spectator by the unexpected, to surprise him by all means, and yet not to let him lose the feeling of spatial unity which comprises everything visible. Because of the forced acceleration of visual perception, this baroque interpretation of spatial unity is, though in a different way, stronger and more suggestive than the quiet, balanced unity and static entity typical of the Renaissance. The continuously shifting interplay of light and shadow contributes further to the "hide-and-seek" of spatial impressions.

All these effects are based on the possibility of *movement*. Thus the dimension of time is added as a decisive factor—in contrast to the timelessness of the Renaissance equilibrium. Now space is actually liberated and is perceived not in any finite form but, so to say, in successive stages of development, in the process of becoming three-dimensional. This movement is directed by individual architectural elements and the multitude of their spatial relations. Such elements are, for instance, the direction of the incoming streets; the position of monuments and fountains; differences in level; and, last but not least, the fluctuating building lines and staggered volumes of the surrounding structures. Their aesthetic impact is intensified, if possible, by the illusion of seemingly increased depth, by the visual penetration into the third dimension, created by all the techniques of a refined stage design. Of course, this appeal to visual imagination, so natural and widespread during the seventeenth and eighteenth centuries, demanded a highly conscious perception. Subjective spatial interpretation, so often suggested in painting and sculpture of the same period, was challenged.

Psychologically those Roman squares and their variations and imitations in other countries provided an infinite number of aesthetic stimuli. And since sensory responses are related to specific somatic states, the result of the continuous shift of vistas—something like a visual shock treatment—meant an increase of nervous and physical tension, identical with the psychological effect of contemporary church interiors.

In sharp contrast to this dramatization of spatial consciousness, classicistic architects and city planners do not aim at an increase, but at a *reduction*, of physical and nervous tension. Their intent is a somatic equilibrium as accomplished in squares from the Piazza di San Carlo in Turin to the Piazza del Plebiscito in Naples, from the Place Ducale in Charleville to the Place des Vosges in Paris and the squares in Nancy and Amalienborg—to mention only some examples. This equilibrium is entirely different from the static balance of the Renaissance. The contrast between spatial void and its three-dimensional boundaries is stressed by conscious, regular design based mostly on geometric figuration, a rectangle, a square, or a circle. Order in planning, reflecting the centralistic, nay, absolutistic, tendencies of the state, does not allow any spatial deviation, nor any play with infinite vistas. The legitimacy of the reasonably expected takes the place of the surprise of unexpected vistas, the finite takes the place of the infinite of Roman provenience.

The artistic means of producing these more formalized effects of three-dimensional limitation are, first, the integration of clear-cut horizontal and vertical planes as basic elements of visual perception, and second, in town planning and landscaping alike, the dominance of the axis. Both make you aware of where you stand and where your next step will lead you, regulating your kinesthetic reactions. The clarity and simplicity of this concept explain why not only ingenious town planners but even plain real-estate speculators could bring forth within the frame of such a solid tradition decent solutions such as occurred in England at the end of the eighteenth century.

The axis as backbone of the spatial structure—*la culte de l'axe*—prevails over the square and organizes the environment in the classicistic vision, as does the square in the Berninesque baroque. And it is the axis which leads the eye into the far distance. In such a context, squares integrated into an axial organization lose their quality as primary stimuli of space consciousness and become rather extensions of the longitudinal axis. Or squares may merely represent final stops, as stages for one or more monumental buildings.

Even in contact with nature, the axis is the compelling force; architecture and natural growth are equally subordinated and square and rondel alike become simply the means for retarding or stopping the visual flight. They do not represent spatial entities in themselves.

Only the completely closed square, such as, for instance, the Place Vendôme in Paris or Amalienborg Square, and the small squares of German residential towns are independent spatial units. In contrast to Roman baroque design, in the classicistic concept the three-dimensionality of the square, carefully shaped and balanced, does not suppose any movement but implies rest, a place set off from the hubbub of normal town life, comparable to the seclusion of an interior.

Thus it is only logical that out of the classicistic prevalence of the axis, *the street, and no longer the square*, evolves in the nineteenth century into the leading element in town planning, from Percier and Fontaine's Rue de Rivoli to Haussmann's boulevards in Paris. When under Napoleon some utopian town projects were planned, they were no longer based on the square as spatial center. These rather unimportant and unoriginal plans, comparable in their schematism to the late work of Errard and Speckle, merely standardize the measurements of squares, streets, and uniform houses. As an anticlimax to both the baroque and the preclassicistic development of the seventeenth and eighteenth centuries, the awareness of the third dimension vanishes almost completely during the flat nineteenth century.

Now, after this brief summarization of the essential differences between baroque and classicistic spatial developments, the crucial opening question of this chapter may be answered: does there yet exist any common denominator in aesthetic purpose and consequently in spatial appearance of both stylistic trends beyond the echoes of mere temporal coincidence?

Such basic traits *do exist:* actually all squares of the seventeenth and eighteenth centuries are created consciously and in full awareness of the void, the hollow space. Though the molding of this hollow space follows contrasting principles in baroque and classicistic concepts, the difference between both structural developments is still less outspoken than the difference from Renaissance squares, when the volumes of framing buildings dictated the shape of the void.

Furthermore, both stylistic trends expressed rather directly contemporary emotional attitudes. These emotional attitudes were not purified through firmly established theoretical rules, as was true for the Renaissance period. Theoretical principles had never been established for Roman baroque squares and their derivations, and the theoretical codes of classicism were formulated after the main achievements in town planning had already been accomplished.

And finally, the shape of baroque and classicistic squares is in both instances based on the experience of progression in time. While the aesthetic effect of baroque squares with their continuously changing aspects supposes the accumulation of contrasts, building up a polarity of climactic sequences in time, the form of classicistic squares evolves from a gradual summing up of visual impressions, experienced in time, step by step, corresponding to straight linear progression; the onlooker is led to a logically expected stop and final rest.

Thus some essential aesthetic factors in both stylistic forms of spatial expression are similar, although certainly not identical. Differences of spatial shape and architectural form do not always mean such a basic contrast as appears at first glance. The aforementioned common traits explain, for instance, how Bernini, the foremost protagonist of the late baroque, could envision such a typically classicistic project as the square in Ariccia. They explain also the fusion of both trends in many individual works of Italian and French architecture, town planning, and even landscaping.

Quite generally the meaning of the square as a spatial experience can be grasped only by those who are aware of the phenomenon that the human reaction toward the form and dimensions of shaped and molded space changes continuously. This change happens not only from century to century, from country to country, but even within one period and one nation; and it means more than a mere alteration of "taste." It is not dependent on contemporary abstract doctrines and philosophies, although it is certainly influenced by them. It is elemental. It grows from a specific and characteristic mode of human behavior and attitude, articulated in specific forms by the creative process either of an anonymous collective, as in the Middle Ages, or of an individual artist, as in the Renaissance and during later centuries. In each instance it represents an integrated complex of reason, feeling, and will.

VI · EARLY AMERICAN PUBLIC SQUARES

by Carl Feiss, A.I.A., A.I.P.

The urban development in the United States differs so basically from the European, where the heritage of twenty or more centuries shows itself still very strongly even in creations of the seventeenth and eighteenth centuries, that the author did not consider himself sufficiently equipped to analyze the evolution of the American town and square. Thus he feels especially indebted to one of the leading scholars in this specific field, his colleague and friend Carl Feiss, for contributing the following chapter and in this way rounding out the whole story. P.Z.

THE SETTLEMENT of the New World was accomplished in a large part by urban peoples from the nations and principalities of Renaissance and baroque Europe. The problem of designing appropriate new towns to fit the low shores, the vast forests, the banks of deep, swift rivers, and the high, arid terraces of monumental mountain ranges was for these early settlers an unaccustomed and, within the technology of their period, an incomprehensible task. These settlers, courageous but not trained in theory and with only feeble traces of tradition, made many tragic errors of judgment. They often found impractical solutions of site selection and town design in their search for elemental answers to the complexities of survival in strange climates and soils; in their contest with hostile human, animal, and insect hosts; and in the then unknowable and fatal miasmas of swamp, forest, and jungle. But throughout the epic history of this pioneer world there runs a utopian dream of a setting for a civilized society which survives disaster, disease, and despair, lawlessness and loneliness. Even in the most primitive village outpost some common instinct or inherent cultural survival created certain amenities of an urban character, simple in themselves, but sufficient to distinguish such a village from that of the indigenous savage which it was shortly to replace. Of these amenities the town square was the most common, and in time it became the most important.

THE USES OF THE SQUARE

The settlers of the Americas brought with them to the wilderness their immediate memories of the cities from which they came. They well remembered the medieval market square, the parvis before the cathedral, the *plaza mayor*, the *place* or the parade before the palace or the town hall. Within the limits of their skills, their imaginations, and the special character of their individual cultural traditions, they built new towns from the Gulf of St. Lawrence to the coast of Chile. Among all of these, even the most humble, it is hard to find an early plan that did not incorporate a public open space or square for both a utilitarian purpose and an ornamental amenity.

Since the square always and everywhere serves many functions, it is not surprising to find that in the Americas, too, the square has multiple uses. But often, as in the Old World, several squares were developed in these early plans, and to each were assigned special duties. The most frequent uses and typical functions of squares from the very first settlements and continuing throughout the pioneer period in the United States were:

1. The communal use of a fenced, open area for grazing and for storing cattle at night. These "commons" were in the center of the towns for the convenience of guarding against straying and depredation.

2. The community use of a central square for the drilling of militia and for public gatherings (the Parade).

3. The use of the square as a site on which faced, or on which were placed, ecclesiastical and public buildings. Such squares were often decorated with trees and ornamental lawns, frequently in formal design relationships. In New England, such squares are best known as "the Green."

4. The use of the square as a purely ornamental and social amenity or for creating or improving a view.

5. The use of the square for a market. This is less common than the other uses and much less common than in Europe or Latin America, and is usually combined with other functions.

In many instances, squares appeared on early town plans with no use assigned to them. They were merely open spaces in the real-estate subdivision plat. Obviously it was an instinctive feeling on the part of the designers that the heart of a new town should be the square, whether or not they thought of any or all of the uses listed above. But as new records turn up, we discover that most squares had a planned purpose from the beginning, even though they did not have specific buildings planned for them at the time they were staked out in the first clearing.

The squares of the towns in the United States have played many important roles in our history. Often their names are bywords in story and in the common mind. The public does not think of the square as a mathematical open space but rather as an area in a city associated with events, uses, or individuals. These are frequently romantic associations, deeply entrenched in our culture, such as those which belong to Independence Square, the Lexington Green, the Boston Common. To the Clevelander, for instance, the Public Square is the heart of his town today just as much as it was when it was laid out 160 years ago. And the Green in New Haven, Jackson Square in New Orleans, and limitless others stand in the minds of the residents of these cities as the symbol of the city itself. So both in national and local history the square is an important entity and deserves our attention as a part of our culture. But for some curious reason, perhaps because they are taken for granted, the American squares have little recorded history and are subject to misuse and neglect.

In the writing of this brief summary of American squares, the author has made no attempt to do more than indicate a few important *types* of squares, many familiar by name to the reader. There is much more material of value than can be recorded here on important squares which deserve our attention. Therefore our discussion deals mainly with the *character* of American squares and not so much with geographic location and history. Also, while dates are given, character rather than chronology is the emphasis. This is not so much a treatise on history as it is a suggestive review of one element of our heritage of early planned communities.

THE SETTING OF THE SQUARE

From the very beginning, the settlers of what was to be the United States seem to have had an interest in the romantic beauty of the wilderness landscape, in particular views over water. While it was natural that new towns would be located on or near navigable streams or potable water, frequently town squares were located in such a way as to take advantage of a water view and serve as a formal town landing as well. Those squares, although less pretentious and less formal, may be compared with so-called marinas in Europe, such as the Place Royale in Bordeaux, the Porto di Ripetta in Rome, etc.

Perhaps the earliest of these squares in the United States is to be found at St. Augustine, Florida (Pl. 93A). When the town was rebuilt after Sir Francis Drake's attack in 1586, a waterside plaza developed which was unique in Spanish colonial plans. Here the town landing, the church (1790), and the customs house, as well as other important buildings, were laid out informally around an open-ended plaza to form an attractive little townscape as one approached by boat. A more formal example is the Place d'Armes, now Jackson Square, in New Orleans (Pl. 94A). When this was laid out (in 1718), the Mississippi River could be seen from ground level and the cathedral with its flanking public buildings at the far side of the parade ground had a fine view of the broad stream. Today the levee and buildings at the south side of the square have obliterated one of the original features in the design, although later elements have created an architectural setting that was not conceived of in the early years.

When Edenton, North Carolina, was laid out in 1700, there were two planned rectangular squares, placed perpendicular to the broad and picturesque waters of Albemarle Sound and equidistant from a central street at the end of which was the main boat landing. One square was the Parade Ground and the other became the charming Court House Green (1750). The latter remains intact today as it was built and the view from the steps of the old courthouse down the lawn and out over the island-strewn Sound is one of the most felicitous to be found in any early settlement.

Even in as primitive a little settlement as Gallipolis, Ohio (Pl. 96A), after the tragic collapse of the French settlement, Fortescue Cummings wrote on July 26, 1807, "A spacious square is laid out in the center on which they are now making bricks to build a court house." The fine little courthouse unfortunately is now gone, but the square, large and handsome, with one broad side to the sweep of the Ohio River, is a proud feature of the still Gallic little town.

But of all the river-view squares, the most charming and most spectacular is the Parade at Hudson, New York, from 1795 (Pl. 94B). There are three squares in Hudson, all part of a remarkably formal plan strangely reminiscent of that of Williamsburg, though probably only by coincidence. The Parade at the western end of the long axis is at the top of a rocky bluff and was designed to provide a view of the Hudson River for the little acropolis city. The whole river lies below and the beautiful west bank spreads out to the distant horizon. The Parade was a popular place in the early nineteenth century; it was set aside by the founders of the city "as a public walk or Mall, and for no other purpose whatsoever." However, an octagonal, two-story refreshment pavilion was built on it in the early 1800s, the upper part being a covered gallery from which to look at the view. On the ground floor, a contemporary advertisement boasts, were "tables furnished with newspapers, where the news can be read and public events discussed with as much summer comfort, as in any room on the continent." The turtle soup available was also a local pride. In the center of the Parade was a Quaker "Wedding Stone" surrounded by a circle of trees, and at a later date at the north end was located the charming monument to the great Hudson River landscape architect, Andrew Jackson Downing. The Parade today is little changed from its original character and bears testimony to the good judgment of the founders of this small planned city.

Not all open-ended squares face on water. One of the most interesting, the Palace Green at Williamsburg, from 1699, opened on meadow and woodland. This provided the centrally located Palace with a sense of space similar to that found in the great formal English Renaissance houses of the landed gentry. Such houses were frequently placed above a formal green lawn which then opened onto pasture land. If this was the effect intended at Williamsburg, it was an ingenious solution for the setting of a fairy-book house, its formal parterres on one side, with the long approach by way of the square on the other side and open country beyond; the whole flanked by the town on both sides.

Many of the New England greens and squares were open-ended, as at Cohasset and Ipswich. These squares were seldom geometrically square, although they frequently achieved a sense of rectangular space by the location of buildings and trees. The sites chosen in New England often took advantage of natural features. A noteworthy example is the upper green at Ipswich, where a handsome, exposed rock outcropping was used as the base for a formal setting of an important church.

The location of squares in early town planning, despite the frequent use of the gridiron layout, was not stereotyped. The famous Oglethorpe plan for Savannah, Georgia, from 1733, made a unique use of the square in the design, nothing like it having appeared in a town plan before or since. Here, in Savannah, the square by frequent repetition becomes an integral part of the street pattern and creates a series of rhythmically placed openings which give a wonderful sense of space in a solidly built townscape.

William Penn, when he laid out Philadelphia in 1682, also located five squares in a broad formal grid pattern (Fig. 52). Curiously, the early settlers of the town seem to have had no sense of the possibilities of the use of these squares for important buildings or churches. The State House (Independence Hall), erected in 1735, was located without relationship to the

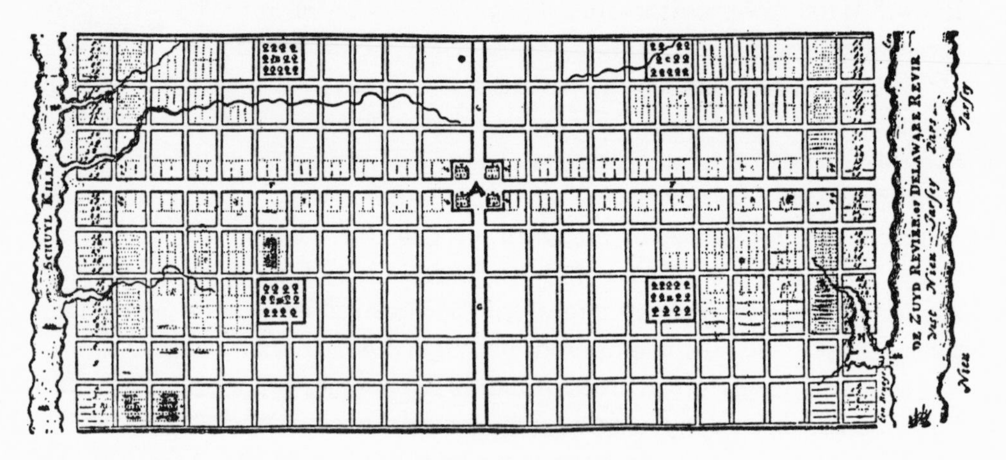

FIG. 52. PHILADELPHIA, PENNSYLVANIA. PLAN BY WILLIAM PENN, 1682

original squares. This was not true at Annapolis (as shown on an early map of 1695), where the two big public circles (instead of squares) were well used. Also the great squares at New Haven and Cleveland were centrally located and historically always important, both as town centers and as sites for important structures.

THE DESIGN OF THE SQUARE

THE NEW ENGLAND GREEN. The best known of the large, irregular type of civic open spaces, the Boston Common, cannot by any stretch of the imagination be called a designed square, although it has always been a major element in the Boston townscape. Even after Park Church and Bulfinch's State House were built above one end of it and the formal buildings were developed on Beacon Hill along the north side, it never quite achieved an architectural unity as did the North Common or Green at Ipswich (Pl. 93B) through the use of equally romantic vestiges of natural elements. Any number of the smaller New England greens were irregular or only partially geometric in plan, but they achieved a unity of design through the careful spotting of churches and meetinghouses, through formal landscaping, and through the regular placing of single private houses of uniform design around them. The preponderant number of New England greens are geometric in shape, ranging from the triangular to elongated and narrow rectangles many blocks in length. Many are purely formal domestic squares, serving as a setting for the prim white houses which frame the central open space.

The New England green developed a character entirely its own with no counterpart in European town square design. While it may have derived in part from Anglo-Saxon village greens, at an early date it developed an individual design quality that remains unique and which influenced the development of townscapes over a vast area of New York State and the Middle West into the Western prairies. This design is a very great contribution to the art of city design but curiously it has received little analysis by town planners.

The major design characteristic of the New England green is its openness. By framing it with single family houses with well-proportioned, gardened side yards, the effect is one of permeability of space through and around the frame without loss of design unity. This unity is achieved consciously by the adoption by fashion or consent of a common architectural idiom, usually the two-story, white-painted wooden house facing the green. Such houses had more or less uniform setbacks from the streets bordering the central open grassed areas, and also provided more or less regular eave and roof lines. A further binding element was the frequent use of white picket fences at the street which created a long horizontal architectural base to the open façade of each side of the square. Also early records, plans, and drawings show that often formal tree planting, usually elms and maples, was a basic element in the design of these greens. This planting plan consisted of regularly placed trees along the sides of the greens and along both sides of the bordering road. On the inside or center these rows were often two deep and on some of the larger plans even three deep. Sometimes, as at Wiscasset, Maine, the entire green was planted with regular rows of trees designed not only to provide an axial approach to a church or meetinghouse but also to provide sub-axes to the handsome entrances of each of the houses framing the green. In time the large trunks of the magnificent trees as well as the high curtain of foliage and branches, even in winter, added to the design unity of the whole. But at all times the effect of openness and lightness was not destroyed. Sunniness and space, human scale, natural beauty combined with a garden quality, formality combined with informality—all join hands in the New England green to make it one of the loveliest of American ideas and an incomparable contribution to the joy of urban living.

In New England there was no set practice as to the location of churches or public buildings in relation to squares or greens. One of the most frequent practices was to place these buildings at one end of a green but still on it. Whether on the green itself or on one of the sides, however, it seems to have been almost as common a practice to place the building broadside to the open space as it was to have the entrances and steeples or towers facing or on the axis. Because of the high and narrow bulk of the buildings, the broadside view made the building more impressive. On the North Common at Ipswich, however, when the old cathedral church broadside to the Common was destroyed, it was replaced by the present lovely Gothic Revival one lodged perpendicular to the long axis (see Pl. 93B).

Fortunately it was not the usual practice to place buildings for public assembly at the center of greens or commons. Because of the length of the green at Cohasset (nearly 1,000 feet), however, the graceful Meeting House of 1747 at the center, axially facing the ocean, does little violence to the sense of space. The velvet expanse of greensward, walled by a giant hedge of ancient elms, gives the beautifully proportioned building with its sharp spire an incomparable setting.

But it is at New Haven that the *ne plus ultra* of central lodgment is to be found. In this largest of all planned New England greens, nearly 1,000 feet on a side, three fine early churches are arranged in a row down the center, all facing the southwest side of the green (Fig. 53). Since 1638 this square has served as the site for churches and other places of assembly, as well as a graveyard. The present effect is both startling and impressive, though the competing skyscrapers around the square and the accompanying destruction of the frame of fine houses has thrown the scale out of kilter. This square probably achieved its fullest development about the middle of the last century when the elms were at their best, and the then neoclassical fronts of Yale University on College Street, along with a frame of white houses, supported the three churches more adequately than they do today. At their peak, the three churches must have created an exciting dominating scheme, and this constituted probably the most impressive group of public buildings on a public open space north of the Delaware River.

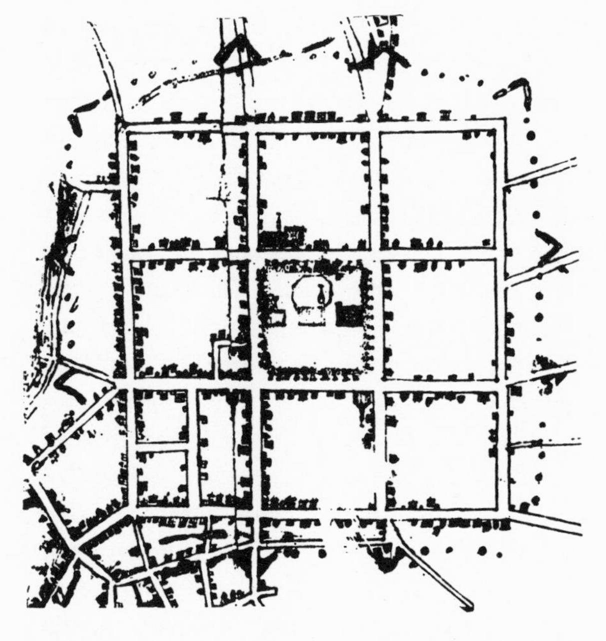

FIG. 53. NEW HAVEN, CONNECTICUT. PLAN FROM 1775 (SECTION)

THE ENCLOSED URBAN SQUARE—A SELECTED GROUP. The enclosed urban square as differentiated from the New England green or open square is a rarity in New England. The best example there is Louisburg Square in Boston. It was laid out by the Mt. Vernon Proprietors in 1826 as a joint ownership venture, similar to Gramercy Square in New York City; construction of houses bordering the square (really a long narrow rectangle) did not actually begin until 1834, and it was not until 1847 that all the gaps were filled in and the square could be said to have been completed. The square stands today with little change from that time. With its complacent and elegant paunchy-bowed brick fronts and handsome formal doors, its iron fence around the little statued park, it is the epitome of prosperous respectability. Its resemblance to the little squares of Bloomsbury is more accidental than planned but it is there all the same. I like to think that the caustic comments about Boston made by President Timothy Dwight of Yale University in 1821 in his *Travels in New England and New York* may have been responsible for this handsome square. He said, in part:

> Boston contains 135 streets, 21 lanes, 18 courts, and it is said a few squares; although I must confess I have never seen anything in it to which I should give that name. . . . It is remarkable that the scheme of forming public squares, so beautiful, and in great towns so conducive to health, should have been almost universally forgotten. Nothing is so cheerful, so delightful or so susceptible of the combined elegance of nature and art.

President Dwight then went on to recommend ten squares for Boston and described their size and design. Too bad that only Louisburg Square was built and then only one half of the size he recommended.

The dull plan for Manhattan Island contains a few alleviating squares, not counting that amazing urban phenomenon, Central Park. Of these squares, the best was Washington Square. The sadly defaced remnants of the beauty and dignity of this once proud square are still to be found on the north side, and by stretching the imagination a good bit, they give some idea of what the square was like in its heyday and what it should have remained. Washington Square was probably at its best in the 1870s when the style of gracious living was at its peak and the handsome rows of dignified houses looked out on a romantic landscape of trees and beds of flowers. In severe neoclassical style, this square more closely resembled the later Bloomsbury squares in London than any other American one with the possible exception of Rittenhouse Square in Philadelphia before it too was ruined by the so-called modern improvements.

Another example of an urban square that has played an important role in town design and in local history and is now defaced beyond repair is Lafayette Square in Washington, D.C. (Pl. 95A). This square, an important element in the L'Enfant plan, was the planned forecourt to the White House, designated the "Palace" in the original plans. On it focuses two great radials, Connecticut and Vermont Avenues, and 16th Street running along the main north-south axis, on which is placed the executive mansion itself.

A: ST. AUGUSTINE, FLORIDA. PLAZA
WOOD ENGRAVING
BY JOHN WARNER BARBER, 1861

B: IPSWICH, MASSACHUSETTS
NORTH COMMON OR GREEN
WOOD ENGRAVING
BY JOHN WARNER BARBER, *ca.* 1838

C: SAVANNAH, GEORGIA
SQUARES AS SEEN FROM BULL STREET, 1861
WOOD ENGRAVING
BY JOHN WARNER BARBER

Reproduced from the Collections of the Library of Congress

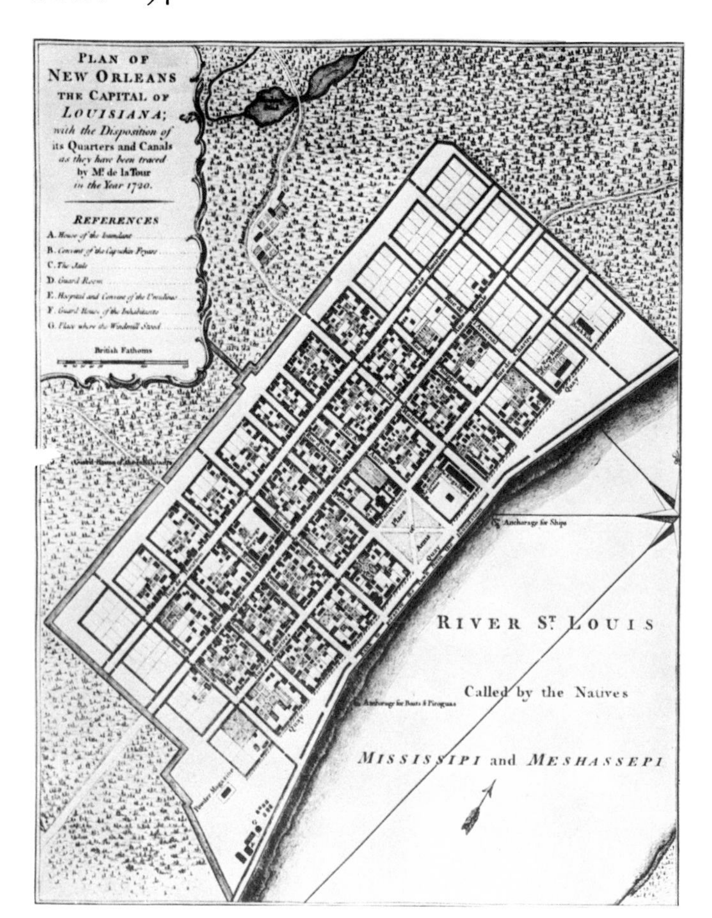

A: NEW ORLEANS. PLAN FROM 1720

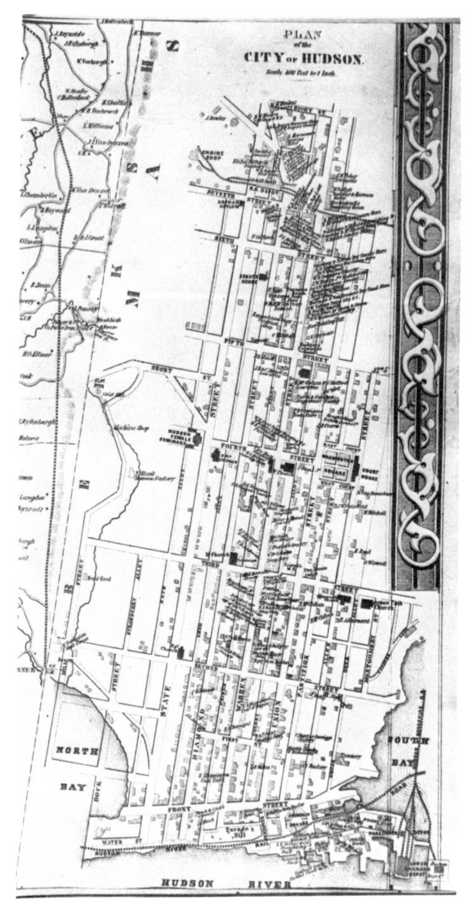

B: HUDSON, NEW YORK. PLAN

WASHINGTON, D.C.

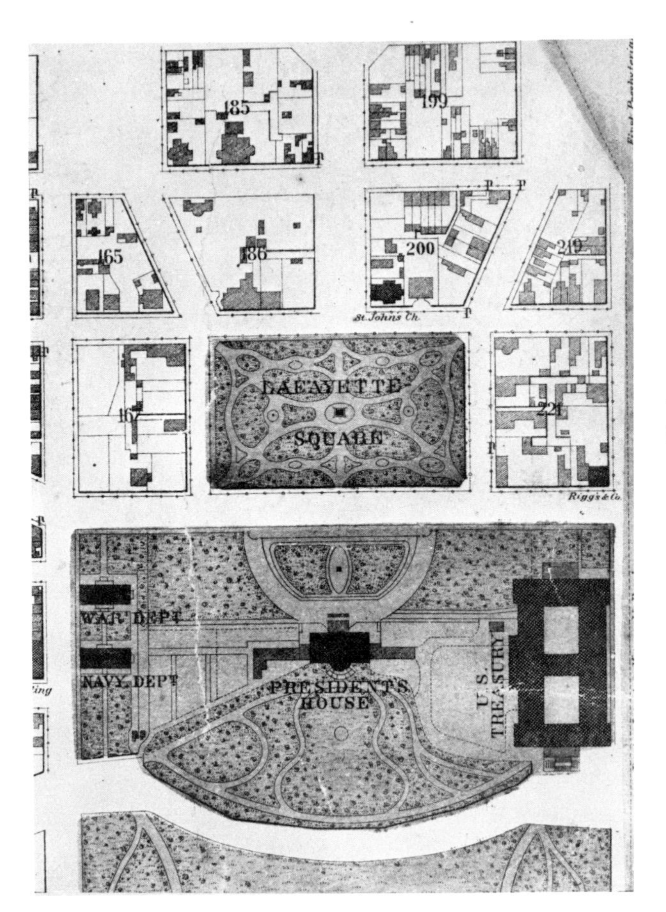

A: LAFAYETTE SQUARE, 1857
From the rare Boschke plan in the National Archives

B: L'ENFANT'S PLAN

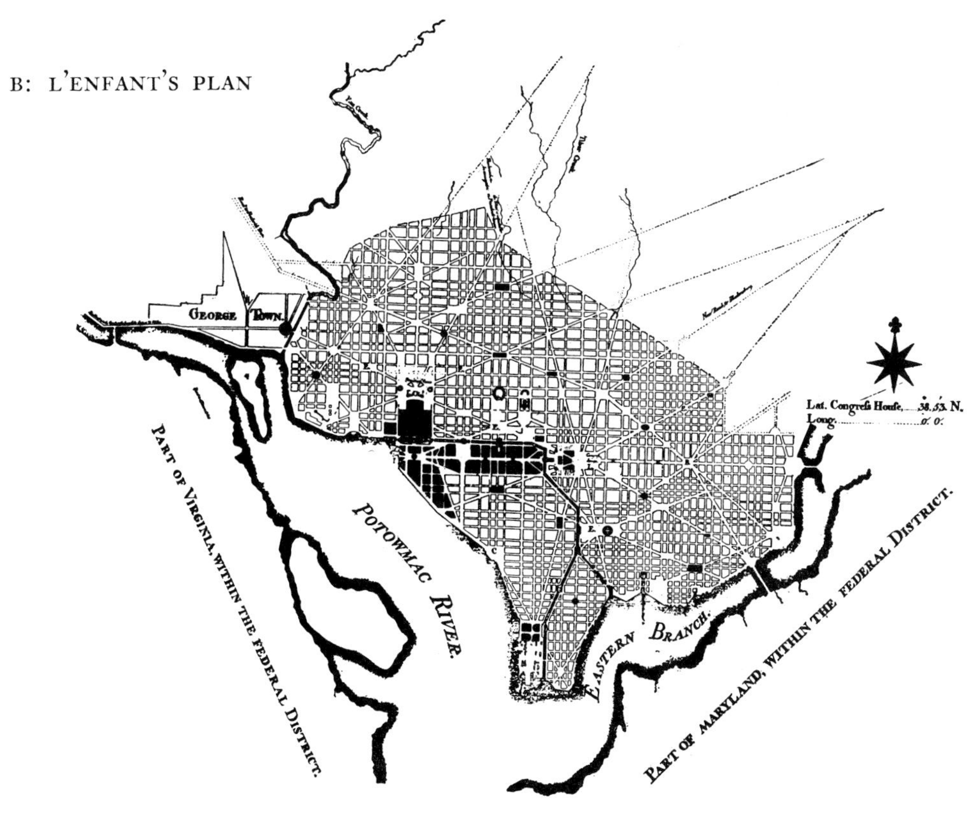

A: GALLIPOLIS, OHIO. AERIAL VIEW

Photo Tawney Studios; courtesy Gallipolis Chamber of Commerce

B: CLEVELAND, OHIO. PUBLIC SQUARE, 1859

From a print in the Library of Congress;
reproduced from the Collections of the Library of Congress

In a microcosm this is the Place d'Armes at the entrance to Versailles. From the beginning the square was a center of the social and political life of the capital. Here Dolly Madison ruled Washington society, and here Henry Clay and Stephen Decatur lived. St. John's Church was built opposite the White House in 1816. Except for this, the square seems never to have been intended for public buildings in competition with the White House itself. Throughout the nineteenth century the square remained in residential use and by 1850 it was called the "lobby of the White House." At its height as a center of political life in the 1870s, while several of its handsome Federal houses, including the surviving Decatur House by Benjamin Latrobe (1819), still stood, a formal and rather turgid frame of pretentious brownstone houses and handsome Victorian mansions bounded the square. Despite all the changes since, Lafayette Square today still represents as pleasant and informal a front door to the home of the ruler of a great nation as is to be found anywhere in the world. Let us hope that it always retains this character!

Perhaps of all the urban squares on the Atlantic seaboard, Mt. Vernon Place and Washington Place in Baltimore constitute the most complete and the finest architectural ensemble. These two places form a cross with the great Washington Monument, designed in 1809 by Robert Mills (and started in 1815), at the crossing. Despite a wide range of styles and a variety of buildings, these intersecting squares on their hill, on which are located the Peabody Institute and the Walters Art Gallery and many charming Greek Revival town houses, create the most sophisticated townscape of all. It still is as dignified and gracious a city square as one can find.

One other famous city square, Jackson Square in New Orleans, belongs in this general category of the enclosed urban square. This beautiful square, laid out between 1720 and 1725 for a parade ground by Adrian de Pauger, assistant engineer to the Sieur de Bienville, did not achieve its zenith until the completion of the two great flanking rows of apartments built by the Baroness Pontalba in 1856. She also succeeded at this time in having the square converted into a public garden. What the baroness created was a proper setting for the St. Louis Cathedral and its two fine flanking buildings, the Cabildo (1795) and the Presbytère (1794–1813). Although the cathedral and the rear of the Mississippi levee diminish somewhat the total effect, the square with its fine gardens and the same Andrew Jackson on his prancing steed as in Lafayette Square in Washington, together with its extraordinary frame of the lacy horizontals of the long galleries of the Pontalba Apartments, has a character and individuality not to be found elsewhere and a charm which is indigenous to New Orleans.

So far we have been talking about some of the closed squares in a few of the larger Eastern and Southern cities. The small town and village squares are less well known but are a significant part of the story. Derived from the villages and town squares of England, Ireland, and Germany, brick settlements of a distinctly urban nature are found in the open country from New Jersey to South Carolina. Unlike the New England village, these communities, particularly the German settlements of Pennsylvania, Maryland, northern Virginia, and southeastern Ohio, used the brick row house as a wall against the open country and the wilderness. Here the town squares turned in on themselves and created a little urban scene in the midst of the vastness of nature. Entering these villages is like entering a house and shutting out the world. Here we find friendly and very domestic little squares with two-story brick houses often painted in individual colors but with a white stone stoop, and built right on the brick sidewalk and the cobbled street. Only occasionally does one find a vestige of a lawn or dooryard. Trees were frequently planted in the paved or unpaved square for shade purposes, since these squares often served as market places, a rarity in New England. But the planting is seldom formal, although even today we may find the trees neatly pollarded as they were in the old country. In some of these villages, particularly as we move to western Pennsylvania and into Maryland, we find the single family house used, rather than the row house. But the concept is still that of the row house. The space between the houses is hardly more than a slit in the wall and the side garden is an incident with the general aesthetic relationships undisturbed. The house still remains on the street and the cornice and roof lines are constants.

While there is a wealth of material to discuss, we will limit ourselves to one example for illustration. Of the many fine little Pennsylvania "Dutch" towns we select Lititz in Lancaster County, founded in 1744. Lititz was settled by the Moravians, as were many of the older "Dutch" towns, and achieved a high order of architectural merit. It was common practice to lay out these settlements with two and sometimes more squares. While one may have been planned for public uses, the others seem to have been intended for a relief in the straight lines of the residential rows. Lititz (Fig. 54) was actually laid out in 1757 by settlers from the Moravian center at Bethlehem, Pennsylvania. The main square, although not large, was designed as a setting for a fine informal group of ecclesiastical buildings. It was placed at the center of the length of Main Street, which runs along one side. A secondary street enters the center of the square on an axis with the Moravian church

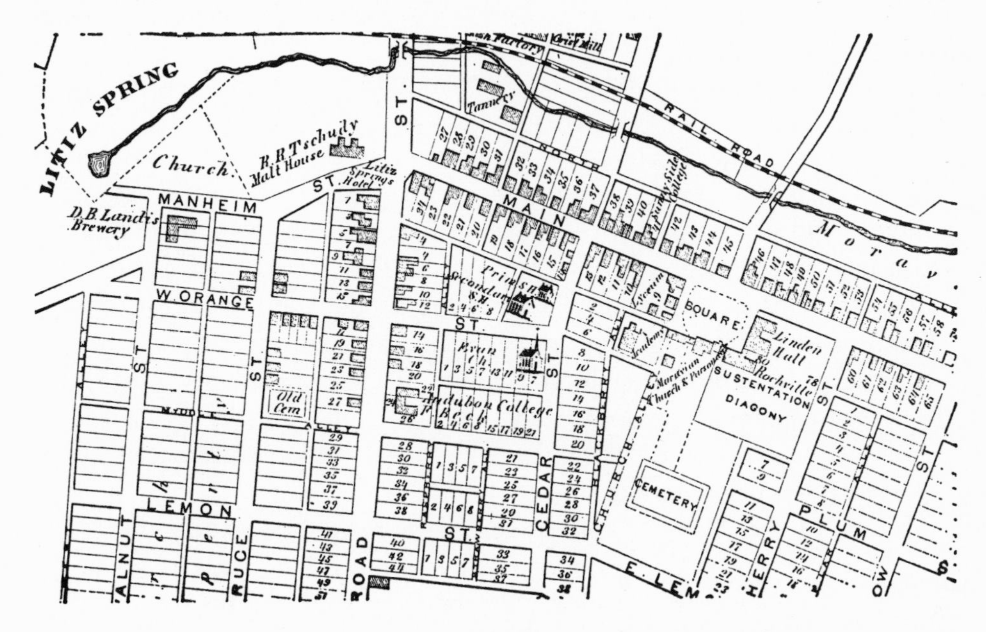

FIG. 54. LITITZ, PENNSYLVANIA. PLAN FROM 1875
From *Lancaster County Atlas*, by Everts and Stewart; reproduced from the Collections of the Library of Congress

and parsonage on the opposite side. By 1787, the main ecclesiastical buildings, including the church, the parsonage, and the large Single Sisters' Home and Single Brothers' Home, had been completed. In the mid-nineteenth century, John Beck, head of the Boy's Academy (a part of the group but just off the square), had this to say in his *Authentic History of Lancaster County:*

It is not saying too much if we state that Lititz is probably the cleanest and neatest village in Lancaster County. The church square around which are located the institutions, church and parsonage, is perhaps not surpassed in beauty by any other spot in the county, such is its splendor in the summer season, that it frequently occurs that travelers stop in their journey to give closer examination than a mere transient notice.

In Virginia, the village square had little significance except in the courthouse towns. Here, however, it achieved a remarkable development, unique in the country. Undoubtedly the formal building group concept which predominates in these squares grew out of the influence of Williamsburg. While several of the handsome early courthouses in the tidewater country stand in isolated rural places, by the latter part of the eighteenth century several squares with courthouses had been built in the center of villages. At Gloucester is to be found intact one of the finest, a miniature walled square within which are the Debtors' Prison (1750), the porticoed Courthouse (1766), and a later Clerk's Office. The usual grouping was a handsome porticoed or arched courthouse at the center, flanked on each side by small law-office buildings and a prison, the whole set in a shaded square of some size and frequently surrounded by a low brick wall. This tradition of design, with many variations to it, continued right down to the late nineteenth century. Several of the Greek and Roman Revival squares are of exceptional merit, particularly the little Acropolis at Palmyra in Fluvanna county (1838) and the walled compound at Goochland (1826–48), undoubtedly influenced by Jefferson's University of Virginia, which was under construction when Goochland was being started.

A tour of the Virginia county seats is a rewarding experience to the connoisseur of town squares and building groups. The scale is small, but dignity and graciousness of character are often achieved by the minimum means. Hilltop sites were frequently used to add monumentality to the groups, and in many of the villages the courthouse square is a rectangle with the broadside to the main street to give it increased size.

Reference has already been made to Edenton, North Carolina, and to Savannah, Georgia. Further mention should be made of the Savannah squares. They are part of a unique concept of town planning about which there has been much speculation. The original plan of Oglethorpe comprised only six blocks, to which more were added later. Exactly as Cortés was stimulated for his gridiron scheme of Mexico City by his experiences in the military encampment town of Santafé in Spain, it may be that Oglethorpe was impressed by the gridiron scheme of the Austrian encampments of Prince Eugene under whom he had served. Prince Eugene's encampments corresponded to the theories of seventeenth-century theoreticians who leaned essentially on Vitruvius, which means on the ancient Roman castrum plan.

Some English plans of the seventeenth century, e.g., Londonderry (1622), reflect similar principles and perhaps they too may have stimulated the Savannah plan. Whatever the derivation or the purpose of the multiple little squares in the Oglethorpe plan, the ultimate effect as a townscape is both curious and attractive. The squares by themselves have no monumentality. They are too small and too separate. They are certainly no benefit to modern through traffic. But they create little islands of neighborliness and intimacy seldom found in a big city and they create pools of light in the geometry of a gridiron plan. John Warner Barber's wood engraving of the squares as seen looking down Bull Street, made in 1861, gives perhaps the best illustration of these squares in an overall effect at the peak of their attractiveness (Pl. 93C). Here is what he said about his drawing:

The engraving embraces the whole length of Bull St. showing the two monuments which are about ¾ of a mile apart. The view is taken southward from the Exchange, a public building on Bay Street, situated on the elevated bank of the Savannah River. Most of the public edifices are on or near the four of five public squares embraced in the view. On the left is seen part of the Custom House, the lower story being the Post Office, on the right is the Pulaski House (a hotel) beyond which rises the spire of the Independent Presbyterian Church. . . . In the central part of the view is seen the monument in Johnson Square in memory of General Greens, 1825. The distant monument is to Pulaski (also on a square).

THE SQUARE WEST OF THE APPALACHIAN MOUNTAINS. As the pioneers moved west into the prairie areas, they brought the East Coast town square with them and modified it to meet their special interests. A great number of Midwestern towns with their squares were based on plans by surveyors who were simultaneously military engineers, educated at West Point and for whom aesthetic considerations were of only secondary interest. However, they may have studied French textbooks and through them indirectly have become familiar with a condensed version of the great European tradition. Of all the many hundreds of fine squares built in the Midwest during the nineteenth century, none was larger or finer than the Public Square in Cleveland (Pl. 96B). Laid out in 1796, this square of ten acres was bisected by an east-west street, now Superior Avenue, of the extraordinary width of 132 feet, probably at that time the widest street in the New World. The Cleveland Public Square had two distinct periods of greatness. The first was during the Federal period in the 1830s when it served as a parade ground and the site for a handsome courthouse and jail as well as a fine church. The city having been settled by migrants from Connecticut and having been established as pretty much the capital of the Western Reserve, it followed the New England architectural tradition. Part of the square for a long time was fenced and used as a pasture, but it was landscaped at an early date. It was the center of the life of the town, and as the town gradually grew into a prosperous Victorian city, to become known as the "Forest City," the character of the Public Square changed also, until by 1876 it was the most perfect expression of Victorian civic art in the country. By this time all buildings had been removed from the square proper, a twenty-five-foot statue to Oliver Hazard Perry graced one quadrant, and the rest of the square was embellished with huge trees, flower beds, and romantic walks. The name of the square was changed to Monument Park and was vividly described by William Payne in *Cleveland Illustrated: A Pictorial Hand-book of the Forest City*.

The influence of this spectacularly romantic square was very great throughout northern Ohio. Sandusky, Elyria, and innumerable other cities redid their squares in this manner. For it would be hard to find a city, town, or village in Ohio, Indiana, and Michigan without its public square dating back to the first settlement plans. Today, while the Public Square is still the center of Cleveland and the high and ugly Terminal Tower shades its southwest corner, it no longer can be called attractive in any sense of the word and awaits a third reincarnation while serving as a traffic maze.

The public square in the Ohio and Indiana settlements was the community center. Many were large and served as spacious trading spots. Gallipolis, Salem, Lisbon, Newark, Mansfield, Terre Haute—the list is long! It was common practice in this region to place a market building, courthouse, or town hall at the center of the square. The effect was excellent, as the squares were large and the buildings in good proportion. It would be hard to say where this practice originated since the examples are relatively few on the Atlantic seaboard, the most noteworthy being at Fayetteville, North Carolina. Avoiding the ungainly effect of the frontalism of a classic temple, the architects of these buildings developed a compact, four-square building type with a pyramidal roof, often surmounted by a cupola. One of the finest of these is still to be seen at Corydon, Indiana, where the first state capitol was designed in this fashion in 1813.

Perhaps the finest of the Ohio squares is the well-known one at Tallmadge, Ohio, laid out in 1803. Here within a four-mile square at the intersection of long diagonal roads from the corners was placed a seven-acre oval in which is located a fine New England colonial church and a meetinghouse. The whole is surrounded by a rectangle of single family houses in the same tradition. It is an open but very central plan and unique in its scale and in its geometric formalism.

THE FRENCH OR L'ENFANT INFLUENCE. The plan of Washington, D.C., is permeated with squares and circles of a wide variety of types and dimensions (Pl. 95B). We have discussed only one of several worthy of mention. It is curious that the influence of the Washington plan was not more widespread. The only three important cities to have their plans influenced by it were Detroit, Buffalo, and Indianapolis. The fantastic Woodward plan of Detroit of 1806 (Woodward had been a councilman in Washington in 1802) allowed for innumerable squares and circles, and some of these still exist in the part of the city which was actually platted in accordance with this plan. But none of the existing squares ever achieved significance outside of the plan. In Buffalo, where Joseph Ellicott mapped the city in 1799 for the Holland Land Company, influenced by advice from his brother Andrew who had worked on the Washington plans, Niagara Square, the center of the four great diagonals of the grand plan, never quite developed the importance of Cleveland's Public Square. But it has retained more dignity as a site for a public monument and the forecourt to the skyscraper city hall. In the Indianapolis plan, instead of a square, Alexander Ralston, another of L'Enfant's assistants, in 1821 used a circle at the center but intercepted the four main diagonals with a solid square within which the circle rests. It was a paper plan but Ralston thought in large sizes. The circle was to be the site of the Governor's House and is 400 feet in diameter. The tremendous Victorian Soldiers and Sailors Monument that occupies the circle today, and once dominated the handsome Victorian crescent building block at the northwest quadrangle, for all of its crudity of design and scale still makes of the circle an impressive center for the town.

On the whole, one can say that L'Enfant's influence on the American square was less than it should have been, but such as it was, it was dreadful.

WESTERN SQUARES. The New England tradition of town design joined forces with other traditions, the French, German, and Spanish, and they crossed the Mississippi together. The Mormons took the town square with them from Independence, Missouri, to Salt Lake and made it the compound for their religious center. The cowboys took the square with them to the cattle towns, so that we find an open frame town like Jackson, Wyoming, with a fine large square in the middle and a hitching rail along one side and the Tetons beyond. And up from Mexico came the padres and the conquistadores and they brought with them the plazas as we find them in old San Diego and Santa Fe (Fig. 55) and in the mission forecourts and compounds. None of these are great squares in the sense that St. Mark's Square in Venice is great

FIG. 55. SANTA FE, NEW MEXICO. OLD PLAN (SECTION)

or that the Place Vendôme in Paris is great or that the Place Stanislas in Nancy is great. These are not the squares of Rome or of St. Petersburg or of Peking. But each means as much to its own culture as do the great squares which are the expression of other cultures.

SUMMARY AND CONCLUSION

We have briefly touched here on one element of the design of the new towns in colonial America and in the United States after it was formed. The square in the United States (and in French Canada) in only rare instances achieved the significance of becoming the main element in civic architecture as it did in most of Latin America. There the canons of settlement and design were rigidly established by the Spanish colonial government and the Church. Nothing in North America approaches the grandeur of the great squares of Mexico City, of Antigua in Guatemala, or of Cuzco, Peru, three out of many.

But even though the North American squares cannot compete with their European brethren of the same period, they constitute an individual expression and a manifestation of the civic arts which must be forever considered a vital part of our heritage.

BIBLIOGRAPHY

The titles listed below represent the basic literature referred to in writing the text. To add here an exhaustive bibliography of all the material consulted would be too tedious and pretentious. The scholar interested in a specific period or in an individual problem will, no doubt, be guided to further source material through those books which are mentioned here. Monographs of the individual places mentioned in the text are cited only if they are pertinent to the specific problems of town and square. Special monographs on individual towns, as helpful as they were in each single instance, are too numerous to be listed in detail.

CHAPTER I. THE SQUARE IN SPACE AND TIME

Abercrombie, Sir Patrick. Town and Country Planning. London, 1944.

Arnheim, Rudolf. Art and Visual Perception. Berkeley, 1954.

Brinckmann, A. E. Baukunst: Die künstlerischen Werte im Werk des Architekten. Tübingen, 1956.

—— Plastik und Raum als Grundformen künstlerischer Gestaltung. Munich, 1924.

Cullen, Gordon. "Common Ground," *Architectural Review*, Vol. CXI, No. 661, 1952.

—— "Focus on Floor," *Architectural Review*, Vol. CXI, No. 661, 1952.

Exploding Metropolis, The. By the Editors of *Fortune*. New York, 1958.

Gallion, Arthur. The Urban Pattern: City Planning and Design. New York, 1950.

Gantner, Josef. Grundformen der europäischen Stadt. Vienna, 1928.

Goldfinger, Ernoe. "Urbanism and Spatial Order," *Architectural Review*, Vol. XC, 1941.

Heart of the City, The. 8th International Congress for Modern Architecture (CIAM 8). Edited by J. Tyrwhitt, I. R. Sert, and E. N. Rogers. New York, 1952.

Hilberseimer, Ludwig. The Nature of Cities. Chicago, 1955.

Hiorns, Frederick R. Town-building in History. London, 1956.

Korn, Arthur. History Builds the Town. London, 1953.

Lavedan, Pierre. Histoire de l'Urbanisme. 2 vols. Paris, 1926, 1941.

Luebke, Hans. Strassen und Plätze im Stadtkörper. Halle, 1932.

Maertens, H. Der optische Massstab. Berlin, 1884.
Sitte, Camillo. The Art of Building Cities. New York, 1945 (original German ed., 1889).
Stübben, Josef. Der Städtebau. Berlin, 1890. Handbuch der Architektur.
Zucker, Paul. Die Brücke. Berlin, 1921.

CHAPTER II. TOWN AND SQUARE IN ANTIQUITY

1. INDIA, MESOPOTAMIA, AND EGYPT

Andrae, Walter. Die Festungswerke von Assur. Leipzig, 1913.
—— Das wiedererstandene Assur. Leipzig, 1938. Deutsche Orient-Gesellschaft, Berlin. Sendschriften No. 9.
Blumenfeld, Hans. "Mohengo-Daro," *Journal of the Society of Architectural Historians*, Jan., 1942.
Borchardt, Ludwig. Excavations at Tell el-Amarna, Egypt, in 1913–1914. Washington, Government Printing Office, 1921. Abstract translation from Mitteilungen der Deutschen Orient-Gesellschaft zu Berlin, No. 55, Dec., 1914.
Coomaraswamey, Ananda. History of Indian and Indonesian Art. New York, 1927.
Dutt, Binode Behari. Town Planning in Ancient India. Calcutta and Simla, 1925.
Finegan, Jack. Light from the Ancient Past. Princeton, 1946. With extensive bibliography.
Frankfort, Henri. The Art and Architecture of the Ancient Orient. Baltimore, 1954. The Pelican History of Art. With comprehensive bibliography.
Haverfield, Francis John. Ancient Town-planning. Oxford, 1913.
Koldewey, Robert. The Excavations at Babylon. Translated by A. S. Johns. London, 1914.
—— Das wiedererstehende Babylon: Die bisherigen Ergebnisse der deutschen Ausgrabungen. 4. erweiterte Aufl. Leipzig, 1925.
Kramrisch, Stella. The Art of India: Traditions of Indian Sculpture, Painting and Architecture. London, 1954.
Lange, Kurt, and Max Hirmer. Egypt: Architecture, Sculpture, Painting in Three Thousand Years. Translated by R. H. Boothroyd. London, 1956. With complete bibliography.
Mackay, Ernest J. H. Early Indus Civilizations. London, 1948. With definitive bibliography.
Marshall, Sir John. Mohengo-Daro and the Indus Civilization. London, 1931.
Olmstead, Albert Ten Eyck. History of Assyria. New York and London, 1923.
Peet, T. Eric, and C. Leonard Woolley. The City of Akhenaten. Part I: Excavations of 1921 and 1922. Egypt Exploration Society, 1923. Part II: Excavations during the Seasons 1926–1932. By H. Frankfort and J. D. S. Pendlebury. Egypt Exploration Society, 1933.

Petrie, W. M. Flinders. Illahun, Kahun and Gurob. London, 1891.
Preusser, Conrad. Die Paläste in Assur. Berlin, 1955. Deutsche Orient-Gesellschaft, Berlin. Wissenschaftliche Veröffentlichungen, 66.
Rowland, Benjamin. The Art and Architecture of India: Buddhist, Hindu, Jain. Baltimore, 1953. The Pelican History of Art.
Smith, Earl Baldwin. Egyptian Architecture as Cultural Expression. London, 1933.
Stanislawski, Dan. "The Origin and Spread of the Grid-Pattern Town," *Geographical Review*, Vol. XXXVI, 1946.
Winlock, Herbert Eustis. Excavations at Deir el Bahri, 1911–1931. New York, 1942.
Zimmer, Heinrich. The Art of Indian Asia. New York, 1955.
—— Myths and Symbols in Indian Art and Civilization. New York, 1946.

2. GREECE

Altertümer von Pergamon. Mitteilungen der Staatlichen Museen zu Berlin. 1930.
Bacon, F. H., ed. Investigations at Assos. Cambridge, Mass., 1902.
Bell, Edward. Prehellenic Architecture in the Aegean. London, 1926.
Borrmann, R. "Die geschlossenen Platzanlagen im Altertum und in neuerer Zeit," *Städtebauliche Vorträge*, Band 5, Heft 8, 1912.
Bosanquet, R. C., and R. M. Dawkins. The Unpublished Objects from the Palaikastro Excavations, 1902–1906. London, 1923. British School of Athens, Supplementary Paper No. 1.
Broneer, Oscar Theodore. Corinth. Vol. I, Part 4: The South Stoa and Its Roman Successors. American School of Classical Studies at Athens. Princeton, 1954.
Collignon, Maxime, and Emmanuele Pontrémoli. Pergame. Paris, 1900.
Conze, Alexander. Die Ergebnisse der Ausgrabungen zu Pergamon. Berlin, 1880–88.
Curtius, Ernst, and Friedrich Adler, eds. Olympia: Die Ergebnisse der von dem Deutschen Reich veranstalteten Ausgrabung. Berlin, 1890–97.
Dinsmoor, William B. The Architecture of Ancient Greece. New York, 1950.
Dörpfeld, Wilhelm. Alt-Athen und seine Agora. Berlin, 1937.
Doxiadis, K. A. "Raumordnung im griechischen Städtebau," *Beiträge zur Raumforschung und Raumordnung*. Heidelberg, 1937.
Erdmann, M. "Hippodamos von Milet und die symmetrische Städtebaukunst der Griechen," *Philologus: Zeitschrift für das klassische Altertum*, Band 42. Göttingen, 1884.
—— Zur Kunde der hellenistischen Städtegründungen. Strasbourg, 1879.
Evans, Sir Arthur J. The Palace of Minos. London, 1921–28.
Fabricius, Knud. "Städtebau der Griechen," in Pauly's Real-Encyclopädie der classischen Altertumswissenschaft. Neue Bearbeitung . . . von Georg Wissowa. 2. Reihe. Stuttgart, 1929.

Fustel de Coulanges, Numa Denis. The Ancient City. New York, 1955.
Fyfe, Theodore. Hellenistic Architecture: An Introductory Study. Cambridge, 1936.
Gardiner, E. Norman. Olympia: Its History and Remains. Oxford, 1925.
Genzmer, Felix. "Die Gestaltung des Strassen- und Platzraums," *Städtebauliche Vorträge*, Band 2, Heft 1, 1909.
—— "Stadtgrundrisse: Ein Rückblick auf eine geschichtliche Entwicklung," *Städtebauliche Vorträge*, Band 4, Heft 1, 1911.
Gerkan, Armin von. Griechische Städteanlagen. Berlin, 1924.
—— Der Nordmarkt und der Hafen an der Löwenbucht. Berlin and Leipzig, 1922.
Glotz, Gustave. The Greek City and Its Institutions. London, 1929.
Hauser, Arnold. The Social History of Art. New York, 1951.
Herzog, Rudolf, ed. Kos: Ergebnisse der Deutschen Ausgrabungen und Forschungen. Band I: Asklepeion. Berlin, 1932.
Hill, Ida Thallon. The Ancient City of Athens. London, 1953.
Hiller von Gaertringen, Friedrich, Freiherr, and P. Wilski. Thera. Vol. III: Stadtgeschichte von Thera. Berlin, 1904.
Hirschfeld, Gustav. "Die Entwicklung des Stadtbildes," *Zeitschrift der Gesellschaft für Erdkunde*. Berlin, 1890.
—— "Zur Typologie griechischer Ansiedelungen im Alterthum," in Historische und philologische Aufsätze Ernst Curtius zu seinem 70. Geburtstag am 2. September 1884 gewidmet. Berlin, 1884.
Hörmann, Hans. Die inneren Propyläen von Eleusis. Berlin and Leipzig, 1932. Archäologisches Institut des Deutschen Reiches. Denkmäler antiker Architektur, Band I.
Hulot, Jean, and Gustave Fougères. Sélinonte. Paris, 1910.
Humann, Karl, and Julius Kohte. Magnesia am Maeander Bericht über die Ergebnisse der Ausgrabungen der Jahre 1891–1893. Berlin, 1904.
Ivanka, E. von. Die aristotelische Politik und die Städtegründungen Alexanders des Grossen. Budapest, 1938.
Jones, A. H. M. The Greek City from Alexander to Justinian. Oxford, 1940.
Judeich, Walter. Topographie von Athen. 2d rev. ed. Munich, 1931. Handbuch der Altertumswissenschaft.
Kaiserlich-Deutsches Archäologisches Institut Mitteilungen. Various papers on Pergamum. Athens, 1902 ff.
Keil, J. "Zur Topographie und Geschichte von Ephesus," *Jahreshefte des Österreichischen Archeologischen Instituts in Wien*, Band XXI–XXII, 1922–24.
Knackfuss, Hubert. Der Südmarkt und die benachbarten Bauanlagen. Berlin, 1924.
Korneman, Ernst. "Polis und Urbs," *Klio*, Vol. V, 1905.
—— Staat und Wirtschaft im Altertum. Breslau, 1929.
Krischen, Fritz. Die griechische Stadt. Berlin, 1938.

Laidlaw, W. A. A History of Delos. Oxford, 1933.

Lapalus Étienne. L'Agora des Italiens. Exploration Archéologique de Délos faite par l'École française d'Athènes. Paris, 1939.

Lehmann, Phyllis Williams. "The Setting of Hellenistic Temples," *Journal of the Society of Architectural Historians*, Vol. XIII, No. 4, 1954. With complete bibliography on Hellenistic temples, etc.

McDonald, W. A. The Political Meeting Places of the Greeks. Baltimore, 1943.

Martienssen, R. D. The Idea of Space in Greek Architecture. Johannesburg, 1956.

Martin, Roland. L'Urbanisme dans la Grèce. Paris, 1956.

—— Recherches sur l'Agora Grècque. Paris, 1951. Bibliothèque des Écoles Françaises d'Athènes et de Rome. Fasc. 174.

Michelis, P. A. "Refinements in Architecture," *Journal of Aesthetics and Art Criticism*, Vol. XIV, No. 1, 1955.

Noack, Ferdinand. Eleusis: Die Baugeschichtliche Entwicklung des Heiligtums. Berlin and Leipzig, 1927.

Pausanias. Description of Greece. Translated by W. H. S. Jones and R. E. Wycherley. 5 vols. London, 1918–35.

Reincke, Gerhard. "Pharos," in Pauly's Real-Encyclopädie der classischen Altertumswissenschaft. Neue Bearbeitung . . . von Georg Wissowa. Vol. XIX, Part 2. Stuttgart, 1938.

Robertson, D. S. Handbook of Greek and Roman Architecture. Cambridge, 1945.

Robinson, David M. Excavations at Olynthus. Baltimore, 1931.

Roussel, Pierre. Délos Colonie Athénienne. Paris, 1916. Bibliothèque des Écoles Françaises d'Athènes et de Rome. Fasc. 3.

Schede, Martin. The Acropolis of Athens. London, 1923.

—— Die Ruinen von Priene. Berlin and Leipzig, 1934.

Scranton, Robert. "Group Design in Greek Architecture," *Art Bulletin*, Vol. XXXI, 1949.

Seure, Georges. Monuments Antiques. . . . Paris, 1910–12. With supplement, Notices Archéologiques . . . by Victor Chapot. Paris, 1920. Publication de l'Institut de France.

Staatliche Museen zu Berlin. Milet: Ergebnisse der Ausgrabungen und Untersuchungen seit dem Jahre 1899. Band 1, Heft 7. Berlin, 1924.

Stillwell, Richard. "The Setting of Classical Greek Temples," *Journal of the Society of Architectural Historians*, Vol. XIII, No. 4, 1954.

Szanto, E. "Agora," in Pauly's Real-Encyclopädie der classischen Altertumswissenschaft. Neue Bearbeitung . . . von Georg Wissowa. Band I. Stuttgart, 1894.

Thiersch, Hermann. Pharos, Antike, Islam und Occident: Ein Beitrag zur Architekturgeschichte. Leipzig and Berlin, 1909.

Thompson, Homer A. Agora and Forum. 10th International Congress of Historical Studies. Rome, 1955.

—— "The Agora at Athens and the Greek Market Place," *Journal of the Society of Architectural Historians,* Vol. XIII, No. 4, 1954.

Tritsch, F. "Die Agora von Elis und die altgriechische Agora," *Jahrbuch des österreichischen Archäologischen Instituts.* Vienna, 1932.

—— "Die Stadtbildung des Altertums und die griechische Polis," *Klio,* Vol. XXII, 1928.

Wiegand, Theodor, and Hans Schrader. Ergebnisse der Ausgrabungen (Pergamon). Berlin, 1904.

—— Priene: Ergebnisse der Ausgrabungen und Untersuchungen in den Jahren 1895–1898. Berlin, 1904.

Wycherley, R. E. How the Greeks Built Cities. New York, 1949.

Wymer, Joseph A. Die Marktplatzanlagen der Griechen und Römer. Munich, 1916.

Zevi, Bruno. "Lo spazio interno delle citta' ellenica," *Urbanistica,* Vol. XIX, No. 3, 1950.

Zschietzschmann, Willy. "Pergamon," in Pauly's Real-Encyclopädie der classischen Altertumswissenschaft. Neue Bearbeitung . . . von Georg Wissowa. Vol. XIX, Part 1. Stuttgart, 1937.

3. ROME

Blankenhagen, Peter H. von. Flavische Architektur und ihre Dekoration. Berlin, 1940.

—— "The Imperial Fora," *Journal of the Society of Architectural Historians,* Vol. XIII, No. 4, 1954.

Boethius, Axel. Die Hellenisierte Italienische Stadt der Römischen Republik. Lund, 1953. Opuscula Athenensia I in Skriften Utgiwua av Svensk institutet i Athen 4, II.

—— Roman and Greek Town Architecture. Göteborg, 1948. *Göteborgs Högskolas Erskrift* 54, 1948, Fasc. 3.

Borrmann, R. "Die geschlossenen Platzanlagen im Altertum und in neuerer Zeit," *Städtebauliche Vorträge,* Band 5, Heft 8, 1912.

Bosanquet, R. C. "Greek and Roman Towns," *Town Planning Review,* Vol. V, 1914.

Calza, Guido. Scavi di Ostia: Topografia Generale. Vol. I. Rome, 1953.

Carrington, R. C. Pompeii. Oxford, 1936. With good bibliography.

Champdor, Albert. Les ruines de Palmyre. 4th ed. Paris, 1953.

Corti, Egon Caesar, Conte. The Destruction and Resurrection of Pompeii and Herculaneum. Translated from the German ed. of 1940. London, 1951.

Domaszewski, Alfred von. Hygini Gromatici liber de munitionibus castrorum, avec commentaire. Leipzig, 1887.

Gerkan, Armin von. Griechische Städteanlagen. Berlin, 1924.

Grenier, A. Bologna villanovienne et étrusque. Paris, 1912.

Holwerda, J. H. Hyginus und die Anlage der Kastelle. Berlin, 1915. Kaiserlich Deutsches Archäeologisches Institut Jahrbuch, Band 30.

Hörnes, Moritz, and Oswald Menghin. Urgeschichte der Bildenden Kunst in Europa. Vienna, 1925.

Huelsen, Christian. The Forum and the Palatine. Translated by Helen H. Tanzer. New York, 1928. With explicit bibliography.

Kaschnitz-Weinberg, Guido. Über die Grundformen der Italisch-Römischen Struktur. Vols. I and II. Munich and Berlin, 1944, 1950. Mitteilungen des Deutschen Archäologischen Instituts.

Kraeling, Carl Hermann, ed. Gerasa, City of the Decapolis. New Haven, American Schools of Oriental Research, 1938.

Lanciani, Rodolfo Amedeo. Ancient and Modern Rome. New York, 1925.

—— The Roman Forum. Rome, 1910.

Lehmann-Hartleben, Karl. "Städtebau in Italien und im Römischen Reich," in Pauly's Real-Encyclopädie der classischen Altertumswissenschaft. Neue Bearbeitung . . . von Georg Wissowa. 2. Reihe, 3. Band. Stuttgart, 1929.

Maiuri, Amedeo. Pompeji: Kultur und Kunst einer antiken Stadt. Berne and Stuttgart, 1939.

Marconi, Pirro. Il Foro Romano. Rome, 1935.

Mau, August. Pompeii: Its Life and Art. Translated by Francis W. Kelsey. New York, 1899.

Peet, T. Eric. The Stone and Bronze Ages in Italy and Sicily. Oxford, 1909.

Pliny the Elder. Historia naturalis. First English translation by Philemon Holland. London, 1601.

—— Historia naturalis. English translation, Natural History, by H. Rackham. 4 vols. Cambridge, Mass., 1938–45.

Polybius. Histories. With an English translation by W. R. Paton. London, 1922–27. The Loeb Classical Library.

Roussel, Pierre. Délos, Colonie Athénienne. Paris, 1916. Bibliothèque des Écoles Françaises d'Athènes et de Rome, Fasc. 3.

Savoja, Umberto. "Turin, the Regular Town," *Town Planning Review,* Vol. XII, No. 3, 1927.

Sogliano, Antonio, Il foro di Pompei. Rome, 1925. Reale Accademia dei Lincei. Memorie. Classe di scienze morali storiche e filologiche. Ser. 6, Vol. 1.

Spengler, Oswald. The Decline of the West, Translated by Charles F. Atkinson. New York, 1927–28.

Stanislawski, Dan. "The Origin and Spread of the Grid-Pattern Town," *Geographical Review,* Vol. XXXVI, 1946.

Swift, Emerson H. Roman Sources of Christian Art. New York, 1951.

Thompson, Homer A. Agora and Forum. 10th International Congress of Historical Studies. Rome, 1955.

Vitruvius. The Ten Books of Architecture. Translated by M. H. Morgan. Cambridge and Oxford, 1914.
Weichardt, Carl. Pompeji vor der Zerstörung. Leipzig, 1898.
Wiegand, Theodor, ed. Palmyra: Ergebnisse der Expeditionen von 1902 und 1917. Berlin, 1932.
Zevi, Bruno. Architecture as Space. New York, 1957.
Zschietzschmann, Willy. Die hellenistische und römische Kunst. Potsdam, 1939. Die antike Kunst, Band II, 2. Teil. Handbuch der Kunstwissenschaft.

CHAPTER III. THE MEDIEVAL TOWN AND SQUARE

Abercrombie, Sir Patrick. Town and Country Planning. London, 1944.
Aronovici, Carol. "Glimpses of Democracy in Medieval Urbanism," *Journal of the Society of Architectural Historians*, Vol. IV, No. 1, 1944.
Beloch, K. Julius. Bevölkerungsgeschichte Italiens. 2 vols. Berlin, 1937, 1940.
Bernoulli, Hans. Die Stadt und ihr Boden. Zurich, 1946.
Borrmann, R. "Vom Städtebau im islamischen Osten," *Städtebauliche Vorträge*, Band 7, Heft 2, 1914.
Börschmann, R. Die Baukunst und religiöse Kultur der Chinesen. Berlin, 1914.
Braunfels, Wolfgang. Mittelalterliche Stadtbaukunst in der Toscana. Berlin, 1953.
Brinckmann, A. E. Platz und Monument als künstlerisches Formproblem. Berlin, 1923.
—— Spätmittelalterliche Stadtanlagen in Süd-Frankreich. Berlin, 1910.
Calza, Guido. Scavi di Ostia: Topografia Generale. Vol. I. Rome, 1953.
Cecchelli, Carlo. I Mosaici della Basilica di S. Maria Maggiore. N.p. 1956.
Collingwood, R. G., and J. N. L. Myres. Roman Britain and the English Settlements. Oxford, 1936.
Creel, Herrlee Glessner. The Birth of China. London, 1936.
Dickinson, Robert E. "The Morphology of the Medieval German Town," *Geographical Review*, Vol. XXXV, 1945.
Flach, J. L'origine historique de l'habitation et des lieux habités en France. Paris, 1899.
Frankl, Paul. Die frühmittelalterliche und romanische Baukunst. Neubabelsberg, 1918. Handbuch der Kunstwissenschaft.
Fritz, Johann. Deutsche Stadtanlagen. Strasbourg, 1894.
Gall, Ernst. Die gotische Baukunst in Frankreich und Deutschland. Teil I: Vorstufen in Nord-Frankreich von der Mitte des 11. bis gegen Ende des 12. Jahrhunderts. Leipzig, 1925.
Gantner, Josef. Grundformen der europäischen Stadt. Vienna, 1928.
Gibberd, Frederick. Town Design. New York, 1953.
Goldfinger, Ernoe. "Urbanism and Spatial Order," *Architectural Review*, Vol. XC, 1941.

Gruber, Karl. Die Gestalt der deutschen Stadt: Ihr Wandel aus der geistigen Ordnung der Zeiten. Munich, 1952.

Grunebaum, G. E. "Studies in Islamic Cultural History (G. F. Housani)," *Journal of the American Oriental Society*, Vol. LXXIV, No. 3, 1954.

Hamm, Ernst. Die deutsche Stadt im Mittelalter. Stuttgart, 1935.

Hartmann-Schaedel. Liber Chronicum. Nuremberg, 1493.

Haverfield, F. J. The Roman Occupation of Britain. Oxford, 1924.

Hübner, Lorenz. Beschreibung der kurbaierischen Haupt- und Residenzstadt München. . . . Munich, 1803.

Jerusalem: The Saga of the Holy City. With an introduction by Benjamin Mazar. Jerusalem, 1954.

Klaiber, Christoph. Die Grundrissbildung der deutschen Stadt im Mittelalter. Berlin, 1912. Beiträge zur Bauwissenschaft.

Laborde, Alexander, comte de. Les manuscrits à Peintures de la cité de Dieu de St. Augustin. Vol. III. Paris, 1909.

La Porte, Paul M. "Architecture to Painting in the Middle Ages," *Journal of the Society of Architectural Historians*, Vol. XII, No. 4, 1953.

Lavedan, Pierre. Historie de l'Urbanisme. 2 vols. Paris, 1926, 1941.

Logie, Gordon. The Urban Scene. London, 1954.

Lynch, Kevin Andrew. "The Form of Cities," *Scientific American*, Vol. CXC, 1954.

Meurer, F. R. Der mittelalterliche Stadtgrundriss im nördlichen Deutschland. Berlin, 1914.

Mielke, Robert. "Die Entwicklung der dörflichen Siedelungen und ihre Beziehungen zum Städtebau, in alter und neuer Zeit," *Städtebauliche Vorträge*, Band 6, Heft 5, 1913.

Paine, Robert Treat, and Alexander Soper. The Art and Architecture of Japan. Baltimore. 1955. The Pelican History of Art.

Pevsner, Nikolaus. "Three Oxford Colleges," *Architectural Review*. Vol. CVI, No. 632, 1949.

Piccinato, L. L'Urbanistica dall' Antichità ad Oggi. Florence, 1943.

Pirenne, Henri. Mediaeval Cities. Translated from the French by Frank D. Halsey. Princeton, 1948.

Pirenne, Henri, Gustave Cohen, and Henri Foçillon. Histoire du Moyen Age. Paris, 1933.

Rappaport, Phil. D. "Die Entwicklung des deutschen Marktplatzes," *Städtebauliche Vorträge*, Band 7, Heft 3, 1914.

Rauda, Wolfgang. Raumprobleme im europäischen Städtebau. Munich, 1957.

Sharp, Thomas. The Anatomy of the Village. Harmondsworth, Middlesex, 1946.

—— Town and Countryside. London, 1937.

Sickman, Laurence C., and Alexander Soper. The Art and Architecture of China. Baltimore, 1956. The Pelican History of Art.

Siren, Osvald. The Walls and Gates of Peking. London, 1924.
Smith, E. Baldwin. Architectural Symbolism of Imperial Rome and the Middle Ages. Princeton, 1956.
Smith, G. E. Kidder. Italy Builds. New York, 1955.
Soper, Alexander Coburn. The Evolution of Buddhist Architecture in Japan. Princeton, 1942.
Stewart, Cecil. A Prospect of Cities: Being Studies towards a History of Town Planning. London, 1952.
Stiehl, Otto Max Johannes. Das deutsche Rathaus im Mittelalter. Leipzig, 1905.
Stübben, Josef. "Vom französischen Städtebau," *Städtebauliche Vorträge*, Band 8, Heft 2, 1915.
Taut, Bruno. Grundlinien der Architektur Japans. Tokyo, Japan, 1936.
Tout, F. T. Mediaeval Town Planning in England. Manchester, 1934.
Wilpert, Joseph. Die Römischen Mosaiken und Malereien der Kirchenbauten vom IV. bis XIII. Jahrhundert. Freiburg im Breisgau, 1924.
Wischnitzer, Rachel. "Rembrandt, Callot, and Tobias Stimmer," *Art Bulletin*, Vol. XXXIX, No. 3, 1957.
Zucker, Paul. Entwicklung des Stadtbildes. Berlin and Munich, 1929.

CHAPTER IV. THE RENNAISSANCE TOWN AND SQUARE

1. GENERAL

Giedion, Sigfried. "Space and the Elements of the Renaissance," *Magazine of Art*, Vol. XLV, 1952.
Tunnard, Christopher. The City of Man. New York, 1953.
Wittkower, Rudolf. Architectural Principles in the Age of Humanism. London, 1949; rev. ed., 1952. Studies of the Warburg Institute XIX.

2. ITALY

Ackerman, James S. The Cortile del Belvedere. Vatican City, Bibliotheca Apostolica Vaticana, 1954.
Alberti, Leone Battista. De re aedificatoria. Libri decem (in Liber IV). Florence, 1485.
Andreae, Johann Valentin. Christianopolis: An Ideal State of the Seventeenth Century. Translated from the Latin by Felix Emil Held. New York, 1916.
Beloch, K. Julius. Bevölkerungsgeschichte Italiens. 2 vols. Berlin, 1937, 1940.
Blaeu, Joannes. Teatrum statum regiae celsitudinis Sabaudiae ducis. Amsterdam, 1682.
Blunt, Anthony. Artistic Theory in Italy, 1450–1600. Oxford, 1940.
Braunfels, Wolfgang. Italienische Stadtbaukunst. Berlin, 1950. Beiträge zur Kunstgeschichte des Mittelalters.

Brinckmann, A. E. Platz und Monument als künstlerisches Formproblem. Berlin, 1923.
Campanella, Tommaso. City of the Sun. Translated by Thomas W. Halliday. In Henry Morley, Ideal Commonwealths. London, 1885.
Cataneo, Pietro. L'Architettura Venice, 1554.
Chambers, Isabel. "Piazzas of Italy," *Town Planning Review*, Vol. XII, No. 1, 1926.
Chastel, André. "Cités idéales: Marqueteurs italiens du XVme siècle," *L'Oeil*, December, 1957.
Dami, Luigi. The Italian Garden. New York, 1927.
Ebhardt, Bodo. Die Zehn Bücher der Architektur des Vitruv und ihre Herausgeber. Berlin-Grunewald, 1919.
Filarete, Antonio Averlino. Tractat über die Baukunst nebst seinen Büchern von der Zeichenkunst und den Bauten der Medici. Ed. by Dr. Wolfgang von Oettingen. Vienna, 1890. Quellenschriften für Kunstgeschichte und Kunsttechnik, N. F. Band III.
Francesco di Giorgio Martini. Trattato di Architettura civile e militare [*ca.* 1500] . . . per la prima volta pubblicato per cura del cavaliere Cesare Saluzzo. Turin, 1841.
Franckenberg, Abraham Samuel von. Theatrum urbium . . . Wahrhaftige Contrafeyung. . . . Frankfurt, 1595.
Gengaro, M. L. Leone Battista Alberti. Milan, 1938.
Geymüller, Heinrich von. Les Du Cerceau. Paris and London, 1887.
Gibberd, Frederick. Town Design. New York, 1953.
Giedion, Sigfried. Space, Time, and Architecture. Cambridge, Mass., 1954.
Gotheim, Marie-Louise. A History of Garden Art. London, 1928.
Grothe, Hans. Leonardo da Vinci als Ingenieur und Philosoph. Berlin, 1874.
Guadet, Julien. Eléments et théorie de l'architecture. Paris, 1902.
Heidenreich, L. H. Leonardo. Berlin, 1943.
Kimball, Fiske. "Luciano Laurana," *Art Bulletin*, Vol. X, 1928.
Lang, S. "The Ideal City from Plato to Howard," *Architectural Review*, Vol. CXII, 1952.
Lehmann-Hartleben, Karl. "The Impact of Ancient Planning on European Architecture," *Journal of the Society of Architectural Historians*, Vol. III, No. 1–2, 1943.
Leonardo da Vinci. Il Codice Atlantico. Milan, 1894–1904. 35 fasc.
Maggi, Girolamo. Della fortificazione della città. Venice, 1584.
Marchi, Francesco di. Dell' architettura militare. Liber III. Brescia, 1599.
More, Sir Thomas. Utopia [translated by Ralph Robinson] and A Dialogue of Comfort. Introduction by John Warrington. Rev. ed. New York, 1955.
Münter, Georg. Idealstädte: Ihre Geschichte vom 15.–17. Jahrhundert. Berlin, 1957. Studien zur Architektur- und Kunstwissenschaft, Heft 1.

Palladio, Andrea. I Quattro Libri dell' Architettura. Venice, 1507.
Papini, Roberto. Francesco di Giorgio, architetto. 2 vols. Florence, 1946.
Pignatti, Ferisio. Piazza di San Marco. Novara, 1958.
Reps, John W. "Urban Redevelopment in the 19th Century: The Squaring of Circleville," *Journal of the Society of Architectural Historians*, Vol. XIV, No. 4, 1955.
Richter, Jean Paul. The Literary Works of Leonardo da Vinci. London, 1938.
Scamozzi, Vincenzo. L'Idea dell' Architettura Universale. Venice, *ca.* 1615.
Schiavo, Armando. Michelangelo Architetto. Rome, 1949.
Smith, G. E. Kidder. Italy Builds. New York, 1955.
Stein, Otto. Die Architekturtheoretiker der italienischen Renaissance. Karlsruhe, 1914.
Tunnard, Christopher. The City of Man. New York, 1953.
Vasari il Giovane. Citta ideal del Cavaliere Vasari . . . inventa designata l'anno 1598. MS. Uffici, Florence.
Vegetius. Military Institutions of Vegetius, in 5 Books. [Epitoma re militaris sive institutorum rei militaris. Libri quinque.] Translated from the original Latin. With a preface and notes by Lieutenant John Clarke. London, 1767.
Verga, Ettore. Bibliografia Vinciana, 1493–1930. Bologna, 1931.
Vitruvius. On Architecture. Edited from the Harleian MS 2767 and translated into English by Frank Granger. Cambridge, Mass., 1955–56.
Volkmann, Hans. Die künstlerische Verwertung des Wassers in der Stadtbaukunst. Berlin, 1928.
Willich, Hans, and Paul Zucker. Die Baukunst der Renaissance in Italien. Potsdam, 1927. Handbuch der Kunstwissenschaft.
Wittkower, Rudolf. Architectural Principles in the Age of Humanism. London, 1949; rev. ed., 1952. Studies of the Warburg Institute XIX.
Zucker, Paul. "Space Concept and Pattern Design in Radio-centric City Planning," *Art Quarterly*, No. 2, 1945.

3. FRANCE AND GERMANY

Bachmann, Friedrich. Die alten Städtebilder: Ein Verzeichnis der graphischen Ortsansichten von Schedel bis Merian. Leipzig, 1939.
Blaeu, Joannes. Novum et magnum theatrum Urbium Belgiae. Amsterdam, 1649.
Blumenfeld, Hans. "Russian City Planning of the 18th and Early 19th Century," *Journal of the Society of Architectural Historians*, Vol. IV, No. 1, 1944.
Blunt, Anthony. Art and Architecture in France, 1500–1700. Baltimore, 1953. The Pelican History of Art.
Boyceau de la Baraudière, Jacques. Traité du Jardinage. Paris, 1638.
Braun, George, Simon Novellanus, and Franz Hogenberg. Beschreibung und Kontrafactur der vornehmsten Staedte der Welt. Cologne, 1574.

Burke, Gerald L. The Making of Dutch Towns. London, 1956.
Dillich, Wilhelm. Peripologia oder Bericht . . . von Festungsgebewen. . . . Frankfurt, 1640.
Dögen, Mathias. Architectura militaris moderna. Amsterdam, 1647.
Du Cerceau, Jacques Androuet. Livre d'Architecture contenant les plans et dessaings. Paris, n.d.
Dürer, Albrecht. Ettliche underricht zur befestigung der Stadt, Schloss und Flecken (Opera das ist alle Bücher . . .). Arnheim, 1604?
Errard, I. La fortification. 4 vols. Paris, 1604.
Furttenbach, Joseph, the Elder. Architectura civilis. Ulm, 1628.
—— Architectura martialis. Ulm, 1630.
—— Architectura universalis. Ulm, 1635.
Furttenbach, Joseph, the Younger. Feriae architectonicae . . . der siebente Teil. N.p., 1662.
Goldmann, N. La nouvelle fortification. Leiden, 1645.
Gruber, Karl. Die Gestalt der deutschen Stadt: Ihr Wandel aus der geistigen Ordnung der Zeiten. Munich, 1952.
Hasemann, Hennig. Synopsis architectonicae. Oder Summarischer Begriff. . . . Frankfurt, 1626.
Hautecoeur, L. Histoire de l'Architecture classique en France. Paris, 1943.
Heer, Christoph. Speculum artis muniendae lucidissimum. Leipzig, 1694.
Palm, Erwin Walter. "Tenochtitlan y la Ciudad ideal de Dürer," *Journal de la Société des Américanistes*, N.S. 1951.
Perret de Chambery, Jacques. Des fortifications et artifices architecture et perspective. Paris, 1601.
Rasmussen, Steen Eiler. Towns and Buildings. Liverpool, 1951.
Rieger, Christian. Universae architecturae militaris elementa. Vienna, 1758.
Schille, H. von. Form und weis zu bauwesen . . . und auff zu richten . . . allerley wehrliche Vestung, Schlösser, Burgen und Stadt. Antwerp, 1573.
Speckle, Daniel. Architectura von Vestungen. Strasbourg, 1589.
Sturm, Leonhard Christoph. Architectura civili militaris. . . . Augsburg, 1719.
Waetzoldt, Wilhelm. Dürer's Befestigungslehre. Berlin, 1916.
Zeiller, Martin. Topographia Burgundiae. Frankfurt am Main, 1654.
Zucker, Paul. Entwicklung des Stadtbildes. Munich, 1929.

4. SPAIN AND THE NEW WORLD

Jürgens, Oscar. Spanische Städte: Ihre bauliche Entwicklung und Ausgestaltung. Hamburg, 1926. Abhandlungen aus dem Gebiet der Auslandskunde, Band 23.
Kelemen, Pál. Battlefield of the Gods. London, 1937.
—— Medieval American Art. New York, 1956.

Kubler, George. Mexican Architecture of the Sixteenth Century. New Haven, 1948.
McAndrew, John, and Manuel Toussaint. "Tecali, Zacatlán, and the Renacimiento in Mexico," *Art Bulletin,* Vol. XXIV, 1942.
Marquina, Ignacio. Architectura pre-hispanica. Mexico, 1951.
Martin, Paul S., George J. Quimby, and Donald Collier. Indians before Columbus. Chicago, 1947.
Moorehead, Warren King. Etowah Papers. New Haven, 1932.
Morley, Sylvanus G. The Ancient Maya. Stanford, 1947.
Palm, Erwin Walter. Los Origenes del Urbanismo Imperial en America. Mexico, Istituto Panamericano de Geografia e Historia. Comision de Historia, 1951.
—— "Tenochtitlan y la Ciudad ideal de Dürer," *Journal de la Société des Américanistes,* N.S. 1951.
Rivet, Paul. Cités maya. Paris, 1954.
Smith, Robert C. "Colonial Towns of Spanish and Portuguese America," *Journal of the Society of Architectural Historians,* Vol. XIV, No. 4, 1955.
Stanislawski, Dan. The Anatomy of Eleven Towns in Michoacán. Austin, Texas, 1950.
—— "Early Spanish Town Planning in the New World," *Geographical Review,* Vol. XXXVII, 1947.
Vaillant, George Clapp. Aztecs of Mexico. New York, 1941.

CHAPTER V. TOWN AND SQUARE FROM THE SEVENTEENTH TO THE NINETEENTH CENTURY

1. GENERAL

Boas, George. "Historical Periods," *Journal of Aesthetics and Art Criticism,* Vol. XI, No. 3, 1953.
Brinckmann, A. E. Die Baukunst des 17. und 18. Jahrhunderts in den romanischen Ländern. Berlin-Neubabelsberg, 1915. Handbuch der Kunstwissenschaft.
—— Plastik und Raum als Grundformen künstlerischer Gestaltung. Munich, 1924.
Frankl, Paul L. "Historical or Stylistic Periods," *Journal of Aesthetics and Art Criticism,* Vol. XIII, No. 4, 1955.
Gurlitt, Cornelius. Geschichte des Barockstiles und des Rococo in Deutschland. Stuttgart, 1889.
Logie, Gordon. The Urban Scene. London, 1954.
Martin, John Rupert. "The Baroque from the Point of View of the Art Historian," *Journal of Aesthetics and Art Criticism,* Vol. XIV, No. 2, 1955.
Neutra, Richard. Survival through Design. New York, 1953.
Ricci, Corrado. Baroque Architecture and Sculpture in Italy. New York, 1912.
Rose, Hans. Spätbarock. Munich, 1922.

Willich, Hans, and Paul Zucker. Die Baukunst der Renaissance in Italien. Potsdam, 1927. Handbuch der Kunstwissenschaft.

2. ITALY

Ashby, Thomas. "The Capitol, Rome: Its History and Development," *Town Planning Review*, Vol. XII, No. 3, 1927.

Ashby, Thomas, and S. Rowland Pierce. "The Piazza del Popolo: Its History and Development," *Town Planning Review*, Vol. XI, No. 2, 1924.

Bauer, Heinrich, and Rudolf Wittkower. Armando Schiavo: Piazza di San Pietro nel Pensiero e nell' opere del Bernini. *Emporium*, Anno XLVI, No. 6, Vol. XCL, No. 546, June, 1940.

—— Die Zeichnungen des Gian Lorenzo Bernini. Berlin, 1931.

Beloch, K. Julius. Bevölkerungsgeschichte Italiens. 2 vols. Berlin, 1937, 1940.

Blumenfeld, Hans. "Russian City Planning of the 18th and Early 19th Century," *Journal of the Society of Architectural Historians*, Vol. IV, No. 1, 1944.

Brinckmann, A. E. Stadtbaukunst. Berlin-Neubabelsberg, 1920. Handbuch der Kunstwissenschaft.

—— Theatrum novum Pedemontii. Düsseldorf, 1931.

Busiri-Vici, Andrea. La piazza di San Pietro in Vaticano. Rome, 1893.

Chierici, Giovanni. La reggia di Caserta. Rome, 1937.

Cooke, Hereward Lester, Jr. "The Documents Relating to the Fountain of Trevi," *Art Bulletin*, Vol. XXXVIII, No. 3, 1956.

De Tolnay, Charles. "Das Capitolinum," *Jahrbuch der Preussischen Kunstsammlungen*, Vol. LI (1930), Vol. LIII (1932).

Egger, Herrmann. Carlo Maderna's Projekt für den Vorplatz von San Pietro in Vaticano. Leipzig, 1928. Römische Forschungen. Band 6.

Falda, Giovanni Battista. Le Fontane di Roma. Rome, 1675.

—— Il Nuovo Teatro delle fabriche ed edifici in prospettiva di Roma moderna. . . . Rome, 1665.

Foerster, Otto Helmut. Bramante. Vienna and Munich, 1956.

Fokker, T. H. Roman Baroque Art. 2 vols. Oxford, 1938.

Fontana, Carlo. Il Tempio Vaticano e la sua origine. Rome, 1694.

Frascetti, Stanislao. Il Bernini, la sua vita. . . . Milan, 1900.

Geymüller, Heinrich von. Les projets primitifs pour la basilique de Saint-Pierre de Rome par Bramante, Raphael Sanzio, Fra-Giocondo, Les Sangello, etc. Paris, 1875–80.

Gotheim, Marie-Louise. A History of Garden Art. London, 1928.

Grassi, Luigi. Disegni del Bernini. Bergamo, 1944.

Hempel, Eberhard. Francesco Borromini. Vienna, 1924.

Letarouilly, Paul Marie. Le Vatican. Paris, 1882.

Matthiae, Guglielmo. Piazza del Popolo. Rome, n.d.

—— Piazza del Popolo, Attraverso i Documenti del primo ottocento. Rome, 1946.
Mayor, A. Hyatt. The Bibiena Family. New York, 1945.
—— Giovanni Battista Piranesi. New York, 1952.
Milizia, Francesco di. Memorie degli architetti antichi e moderni. Bassano, 1785.
—— Principi di Architettura civile. Bassano, 1785.
Niccolini, Luigi. La Reggia di Caserta. Bari, 1911.
Norton, Richard. Bernini and Other Studies in the History of Art. Boston, 1914.
Passanti, Mario. "La Palazzina di caccia di Stupinigi," *Architettura,* August, 1957.
Pecchiai, P. Il Campidoglio nel cinquecento. Rome, 1950.
Ricci, Corrado. La Scenografia Italiana. Milan, 1930.
Romano, Pietro, and P. Partini. Piazza di Spagna nella storia e nell' arte. Rome, n.d.
—— Piazza Novona nella storia e nell' arte. Rome [1945?].
Savoja, Umberto. "Turin, the Regular Town," *Town Planning Review,* Vol. XII, No. 3, 1927.
Schiavo, Armando. Michelangelo Architetto. Rome, 1949.
Sedlmayr, Hans. Die Architektur Borrominis. Berlin, 1930.
Siebenhüner, Herbert. Das Kapitol in Rom, Idee und Gestalt. Munich, 1954. Italienische Forschungen berausgegeben vom Kunsthistorischen Institut in Florenz. 3. Folge, Band I.
Telluccini, Augusto. L'arte dell' architetto Filippo Juvara in Piemonte. Turin, 1926.
Vanvitelli, Luigi. Dichiarazione dei disegni del Real Palazzo di Caserta. Naples, 1756.
Wittkower, Rudolf. Art and Architecture in Italy, 1600–1750. Baltimore, 1958. The Pelican History of Art.
—— Gian Lorenzo Bernini, the Sculptor of the Roman Baroque. London, 1955. With selected bibliography.
Zevi, Bruno. Architecture as Space. New York, 1957.
Zucker, Paul. Die Theaterdekoration des Barock. Berlin, 1925.

3. FRANCE

Bier, Erich. Fran Ludvig XIV's Paris. Pierre Bullets originalritningar . . . Exhibition Nationalmuseum. Stockholm, 1945.
Blomfield, Sir Reginald. Sébastien le Prestre de Vauban. London, 1938.
Blondel, Jean François. Cours d'Architecture. Paris, 1675–83.
Blumenfeld, Hans. "Russian City Planning of the 18th and Early 19th Century," *Journal of the Society of Architectural Historians,* Vol. IV, No. 1, 1944.
Blunt, Anthony. Art and Architecture in France, 1500–1700. Baltimore, 1953. The Pelican History of Art.
Bourget, Pierre. Jules Hardouin-Mansart et son œuvre. Paris, 1947. Institut Technique du Bâtiment et des travaux publics.

Brinckmann, A. E. Baukunst: Die künstlerischen Werte im Werk des Architekten. Tübingen, 1956.

Cain, Georges. La Place Vendôme. Paris, 1908.

Daviler, A. Ch. Cours d'Architecture. Paris, 1675–83.

Dezallier d'Argenville, Antoine Joseph. La théorie, et la pratique du jardinage. . . . 1st ed., Paris, 1709; La Haye, 1739.

Durand, J. N. L., Precis des leçons d'architecture. Paris, 1802–5.

Felibien, Fr. A. Description de Versailles. Paris, 1703. The literature on Versailles from contemporaneous works to modern publications is too numerous to be listed here.

Fels, Edmond, Comte de. Ange-Jacques Gabriel. Paris, 1912; 2d ed., 1924.

Fischer von Erlach, Johann Bernhard. Entwurff einer historischen Architektur. . . . Leipzig, 1725.

Gantner, Josef. Grundformen der europäischen Stadt. Vienna, 1928.

Gromont, Georges. Jacques-Ange Gabriel. Paris, 1933.

Hautecoeur, L. Historie de l'Architecture classique en France. Vol. I, part 1 and 2. Paris, 1943.

Héré de Corny, Emmanuel. Plans et elevations de la Place Royale de Nancy. 1753.

Kaufmann, Emil. "Three Revolutionary Architects, Boulée, Ledoux and Lequeu," *Translations of the American Philosophical Society*, Philadelphia, Oct., 1952.

—— Von Ledoux bis Le Corbusier. Vienna, 1943.

Kunoth, George. Die historische Architektur Fischers von Erlach. Düsseldorf, 1956.

Lang, S. "The Ideal City from Plato to Howard," *Architectural Review*, Vol. CXII, 1952.

Laugier, P. Essai sur l'Architecture. Paris, 1753.

Lavedan, Pierre. Histoire de l'Urbanisme, Vol. II. Paris, 1941.

Ledoux, Claude Nicholas. L'Architecture considerée sous le rapport de l'Art, des Moeurs, et de la Legislation. Paris, 1804.

Lavallet-Haug, Genevieve. Claude-Nicolas Ledoux, 1736–1806. Paris and Strasbourg, 1934.

Marot, Jean. Le magnifiqve chasteav de Richeliev. . . . en general et en particulier. . . . N.p., n.d. (16 . . ?)

Patte, Pierre. Mémoires sur les objets les plus importants de l'Architecture. Paris, 1769.

Perrault, Claude. Ordonnance du cinq especes de colonnes. Paris, 1683.

Raval, Marcel. Claude-Nicolas Ledoux, 1736–1806; Commentaires, Cartes et Croquis de J.-Ch. Moreaux. Paris, 1946.

Roland Le Virloys, Charles François. Dictionnaire d'Architecture. Paris, 1770.

Ruggieri, D. Catalogue des Livres rares et précieux composant la Bibliothèque de M. E. F. Paris, 1873.

Savot, Louis. L'Architecture française. 2d ed. Paris, 1685.

Sedlmayr, Hans. Johann Bernhard Fischer von Erlach. Vienna, 1956.
Speckter, Hans. Die raumkünstlerische Entwicklung der Stadt Paris seit dem 16. Jahrhundert. Hanover, 1946.
Stuart, James, and Nicholas Revett. The Antiquities of Athens Measured and Delineated. New edition by William Kinnard. London, 1825–30.
Tassin, Nicolas. Les Plans et Profiles des Toutes les principales Villes et Lieux. . . . Paris, 1636.
Vauban, Sebastien de. Manière de fortifier les places. Paris, 1683.
Zucker, Paul. Die Brücke. Berlin, 1921.

4. OTHER COUNTRIES

Adshead, S. D. Sir Christopher Wren and His Plan for London. Sir Christopher Wren Bicentenary Memorial Volume, published under the auspices of the Royal Institute of British Architects. London, 1923.
Bolton, Arthur Thomas. The Architecture of Robert and James Adam. London, 1922.
Briggs, Martin Shaw. Christopher Wren. London, 1951.
Campbell, Colin. Vitruvius Britannicus, or, The British Architect. London, 1715–71.
Carrier, Robert, and Oliver Lawson Dick. The Vanished City: A Study of London. London, 1957.
Chancellor, E. Beresford. The History of the Squares of London. London, 1907.
Cotton, M. Aylwin. Excavations at Silchester, 1938–39 (Archaeologia or Miscellaneous Tracts Relating to Antiquity Published by the Society of Antiquaries of London. Second Series, Vol. XLII). Oxford, 1947.
Cullen, Gordon. "A Square for Every Taste," *Architectural Review*, Vol. CII, No. 610, 1947.
Dobert, Johannes-Paul. Bauten und Baumeister in Ludwigslust. Magdeburg, 1920.
Eckhardt, Anton. Die Baukunst in Salzburg während des XVII. Jahrhunderts. Strasbourg, 1910.
Ehrenberg, K. Baugeschichte von Karlsruhe. Karlsruhe, 1909.
Fraenkel, Hugo. Das Mannheimer Stadtbild Einst und Jetzt. Mannheim, 1925.
Freeden, Max H. von. Balthasar Neumann als Stadtbaumeister. Berlin, 1937.
Frey, Dagobert. Johann Bernhard Fischer von Erlach. Vienna, 1923.
Giedion, Sigfried. Space, Time and Architecture. Cambridge, Mass., 1954.
Gotch, John Alfred. Inigo Jones. London, 1928.
Gotheim, Marie-Louise. A History of Garden Art. London, 1928.
Green, Mowbray Aston. The Eighteenth Century Architecture of Bath. Bath, 1904.
Gutkind, E. A. Our World from the Air. New York, 1952.
Hager, Werner. Die Bauten des deutschen Barocks, 1690–1770. Jena, 1942.

Haupt, Albrecht. Baukunst der Renaissance in Frankreich und Deutschland. Berlin-Neubabelsberg, 1916. Handbuch der Kunstwissenschaft.
Jenny, H. Kunstführer der Schweiz. 1934.
Joyant, E. Traité d'Urbanisme. Paris, 1923.
Jürgens, Oscar. Spanische Städte: Ihre bauliche Entwicklung und Ausgestaltung. Hamburg, 1926. Abhandlungen aus dem Gebiet der Auslandskunde, Band 23.
Kuntze, F. A. Das alte Berlin. Berlin, 1937.
Lees-Milne, James. The Age of Inigo Jones. London, 1953.
Lohmeyer, Karl. Die Baumeister des Rheinisch-Fränkischen Barocks. Vienna and Augsburg, 1931.
Mackowsky, Hans. "Die geschichtliche Entwicklung des Stadtplans," *Der Städtebau*, 1908, 5, Jahrgang.
Nicolai, F. Beschreibung der Königlichen Residenzstädte Berlin und Potsdam. 3. Auflage. Berlin, 1786.
Rasmussen, Steen Eiler. London: The Unique City. With an introduction by James Bone. London, 1937 (Danish ed., 1934).
—— Towns and Buildings. Liverpool, 1951.
Reddaway, R. T. The Rebuilding of London after the Great Fire. 2d ed. London, 1951.
Schmitz, Hermann. Berliner Baumeister des 18. Jahrhunderts. Berlin, 1925.
Sedlmaier, Richard, and Rudolf Pfister. Die fürstbischöfliche Residenz zu Würzburg. Munich, 1923.
Sedlmayr, Hans. Johann Bernhard Fischer von Erlach. Vienna and Munich, 1956.
Sekler, Eduard F. Wren and His Place in European Architecture. New York, 1956.
Smith, Robert C. "Colonial Towns of Spanish and Portuguese America," *Journal of the Society of Architectural Historians*, Vol. XIV, No. 4, 1955.
Summerson, John. Georgian London. New York, 1946.
—— John Nash, Architect to King George IV. London, 1935.
—— Sir Christopher Wren. London, 1953.
Thurah, Laurids Lauridsen de. Den Danske Vitruvius. Copenhagen, 1746.
Tietze, Hans. Wien, Kultur, Kunst und Geschichte. Vienna and Leipzig, 1931.
Tunnard, Christopher. The City of Man. New York, 1953.
Turnor, Reginald. Nineteenth Century Architecture in Britain. London, 1950.
Valdenaire, Arthur. Friedrich Weinbrenner. Karlsruhe, 1919.
Webb, Geoffrey. Sir Christopher Wren. London, 1951.
Wood, John. A Description of Bath. 2 vols. 2d ed. London, 1765.

CHAPTER VI. EARLY AMERICAN PUBLIC SQUARES

Barber, J. W. Historical Collections . . . of Every Town in Massachusetts, with Geographical Descriptions. Worcester, 1839.

—— Our Whole Country. Vol. II. Cincinnati, 1861.
Beck, John. Authentic History of Lancaster Country. N.p., n.d.
Brien, Stephen. Historical Sketches of Hudson. N.p., 1862.
Dwight, Timothy. Travels in New England and New York. N.p., 1821.
Garvan, Anthony N. B. Architecture and Town Planning in Colonial Connecticut. New Haven, 1951.
Howe, M. A. De Wolfe. Boston Landmarks. New York, 1946.
Payne, William. Cleveland Illustrated: A Pictorial Hand-book of the Forest City. Cleveland, 1876.
Reps, John W. "Planning in the Wilderness; Detroit, 1805–1830," *Town Planning Review*, January, 1955.
Stevenson, F. R., and Carl Feiss. The American Heritage of Planned Communities. Unpublished MS.
Terry, Robert M. The "Hudsonian": Old Times and New. Hudson, N.Y., 1894.
Tunnard, Christopher. "The American Planning Tradition," *Architectural Review*. Vol. XCVIII, No. 584, 587, 1945.
Whittlesey, Charles. Early History of Cleveland, Ohio. Cleveland, 1867.
—— A Sketch of the Settlement and Progress of the Township of Tallmadge. Cleveland, 1842.
WPA. American Guide Series. Maryland. New York, 1940.
—— Massachusetts. Boston, 1937.
—— New Orleans City Guide. Boston, 1938.
—— New York. New York, 1940.
—— New York City Guide. New York, 1939.
—— North Carolina. Chapel Hill, N.C., 1939.
—— Virginia. New York, 1940.
—— Washington, City and Capital. Washington, D.C., 1937.
WPA in the State of Ohio. Gallipolis [pamphlet]. 1940.
Zook, John G. Historical and Pictorial Lititz. Lititz, Pa., 1905.

INDEX